JOHN KEATS IN CONTEXT

John Keats (1795–1821) continues to delight and challenge readers both within and beyond the academic community through his poems and letters. This volume provides frameworks for enhanced analysis and appreciation of Keats and his work, with each chapter supplying a succinct, informed, and accessible account of a particular topic. Leading scholars examine the life and work of Keats against the backdrop of his influences, contemporaries, and reception, and explore the interaction of poet and world. The essays consider his enduring but ever-altering appeal, engage with critical discussion and debate, and offer revisionary close reading of the poems and letters. Students and specialists will find their knowledge of Keats's life and work enriched by chapters that survey subjects ranging from education, relationships, and religion to art, genre, and film.

MICHAEL O'NEILL is Professor of English at the University of Durham, and has published widely on Romantic, Victorian, and twentieth-century poetry. His works include *The Human Mind's Imaginings: Conflict and Achievement in Shelley's Poetry* (1989), *Romanticism and the Self-Conscious Poem* (1997), *The All-Sustaining Air* (2007), and, as editor, *The Cambridge History of English Poetry* (Cambridge, 2010). He is also the co-author (with Michael D. Hurley) of *Poetic Form* (Cambridge, 2012) and the co-editor (with Anthony Howe and with the assistance of Madeleine Callaghan) of *The Oxford Handbook of Percy Bysshe Shelley* (2013). His latest collection of poems is *Gangs of Shadow* (2014).

JOHN KEATS IN CONTEXT

EDITED BY

MICHAEL O'NEILL

University of Durham

CAMBRIDGE
UNIVERSITY PRESS

University Printing House, Cambridge CB2 8BS, United Kingdom

One Liberty Plaza, 20th Floor, New York, NY 10006, USA

477 Williamstown Road, Port Melbourne, VIC 3207, Australia

314-321, 3rd Floor, Plot 3, Splendor Forum, Jasola District Centre, New Delhi - 110025, India

79 Anson Road, #06-04/06, Singapore 079906

Cambridge University Press is part of the University of Cambridge.

It furthers the University's mission by disseminating knowledge in the pursuit of education, learning and research at the highest international levels of excellence.

www.cambridge.org
Information on this title: www.cambridge.org/9781107674370
DOI : 10.1017/9781107707474

First published 2017
First paperback edition 2019

A catalogue record for this publication is available from the British Library

Library of Congress Cataloging in Publication data
Names: O'Neill, Michael, 1953– editor.
Title: John Keats in context / Michael O'Neill, University of Durham [editor].
Description: Cambridge; New York, NY: Cambridge University Press, 2017. |
Includes bibliographical references and index.
Identifiers: LCCN 2016059500 | ISBN 9781107070554 (hard back)
Subjects: LCSH: Keats, John, 1795–1821 – Criticism and interpretation.
Classification: LCC PR4837.J58 2017 | DDC 821/.7–dc23
LC record available at https://lccn.loc.gov/2016059500

ISBN 978-1-107-07055-4 Hardback
ISBN 978-1-107-67437-0 Paperback

Contents

Notes on Contributors		*page* ix
Acknowledgements		xv
Note on Texts, Citations, and Abbreviations		xvii
	Introduction	1

PART I LIFE, LETTERS, TEXTS

1	Biographies and Film *Sarah Wootton*	9
2	Formative Years and Medical Training *Hrileena Ghosh and Nicholas Roe*	19
3	Surgery, Science and Suffering *Nicholas Roe*	28
4	Fanny Brawne and Other Women *Heidi Thomson*	38
5	Mortality *Shahidha Bari*	47
6	Travel *Jeffrey C. Robinson*	56
7	Letters *Madeleine Callaghan*	66
8	Manuscripts and Publishing History *John Barnard*	75

PART II CULTURAL CONTEXTS

9 The Hunt Circle and the Cockney School 89
Gregory Leadbetter

10 London 99
Timothy Webb

11 Politics 108
Richard Cronin

12 Sociability 117
Grant F. Scott

13 The Visual and Plastic Arts 126
Nancy Moore Goslee

14 Religion and Myth 136
Anthony John Harding

PART III IDEAS AND POETICS

15 The Enlightenment and History 149
Porscha Fermanis

16 Keats and Hazlitt 159
Duncan Wu

17 Imagination, Beauty and Truth 168
Charles W. Mahoney

18 The Poetical Character 178
Seamus Perry

19 The Senses and Sensation 188
Stacey McDowell

20 Prosody and Versification in the Odes 198
Michael O'Neill

PART IV POETIC CONTEXTS

21 Poetic Precursors (1): Dante and Shakespeare 209
Chris Murray

22 Poetic Precursors (2): Spenser, Milton, Dryden, Pope 220
Beth Lau

23 Contemporaries (1) (and Immediate Predecessors): Tighe, Radcliffe, Southey, Burns, Chatterton, Hunt, Wordsworth 229
Michael O'Neill

24 Contemporaries (2): Coleridge, Byron, Shelley 238
Jane Stabler

25 Ballad, Romance and Narrative 248
Andrew Bennett

26 Epic and Tragedy 258
Susan J. Wolfson

27 Lyrical Genres 269
Christopher R. Miller

PART V INFLUENCE

28 Tennyson to Wilde 281
Herbert F. Tucker

29 Hardy, Edward Thomas, Stevens, Bishop, Heaney 291
Michael O'Neill

30 American Writing 300
Mark Sandy

PART VI CRITICAL RECEPTION

31 Contemporary Reviews 313
Kelvin Everest

32 Critical Reception, 1821–1900 323
Francis O'Gorman

33 Keats Criticism, 1900–1963 331
Matthew Scott

34 Keats Criticism, Post-1963 340
Richard Marggraf Turley

Further Reading 351
Index 363

Contributors

SHAHIDHA BARI is Senior Lecturer in Romanticism at Queen Mary, University of London. She is the author of *Keats and Philosophy: The Life of Sensations* (2012).

JOHN BARNARD, Emeritus Professor of English, University of Leeds, has published widely on Keats, the second-generation Romantics, and seventeenth-century literature, drama, and book history. His many publications include *John Keats* (1987) and editions of Keats's poems (1973) and his letters (2014).

ANDREW BENNETT is Professor of English at the University of Bristol. He is the editor of *William Wordsworth in Context* (2015) and the author of *Wordsworth Writing* (2007), *Romantic Poets and the Culture of Posterity* (1999), and *Keats, Narrative and Audience* (1994). His other books are *Ignorance: Literature and Agnoiology* (2009), *The Author* (2005), *Katherine Mansfield* (2004), and, with Nicholas Royle, *This Thing Called Literature: Reading, Thinking, Writing* (2015), *An Introduction to Literature, Criticism and Theory* (5th edn, 2016), and *Elizabeth Bowen and the Dissolution of the Novel* (1995).

MADELEINE CALLAGHAN is Lecturer in Romantic Literature at the University of Sheffield. She has published various articles and chapters on Romantic and post-Romantic poetry. She is the co-editor of *Twentieth-Century British and Irish Poetry: Hardy to Mahon* (2011), the assistant editor of *The Oxford Handbook of Percy Bysshe Shelley* (2013), the author of *Shelley's Living Artistry: Letters, Poems, Plays* (2017) and the co-author of *The Romantic Poetry Handbook* (2018).

RICHARD CRONIN is Professor Emeritus at the University of Glasgow and Visiting Professor at Oxford Brookes. His most recent books are *Romantic Victorians* (2002), *Paper Pellets* (2010), and *Reading Victorian Poetry* (2012).

With Dorothy McMillan, he published an edition of Robert Browning in 2013.

KELVIN EVEREST is Bradley Professor of Modern Literature Emeritus at the University of Liverpool. He has published widely on English Romantic poetry, including *John Keats* (2002), and is the co-editor of the Longman Annotated English Poets edition of Shelley's complete poetry.

PORSCHA FERMANIS is Associate Professor of Romantic Literature at University College Dublin. She is the author of *John Keats and the Ideas of the Enlightenment* (2009) and, with Carmen Casaliggi, *Romanticism: A Literary and Cultural History* (2016). With John Regan, she is the co-editor of *Rethinking British Romantic History, 1770–1845* (2014). She is currently working on a monograph on narrative history in Britain and Ireland from 1770 to 1850, as well as acting as principal investigator of a European Research Council grant on white settler and indigenous writing in the British-controlled Southern Hemisphere from 1783 to 1870.

HRILEENA GHOSH received her PhD from the University of St Andrews, where she researched John Keats's medical notebook and his career at Guy's Hospital. She is currently working on her first book.

NANCY MOORE GOSLEE is Professor of English Emerita at the University of Tennessee, Knoxville, where she also held a Distinguished Humanities Professorship. She has published essays and monographs in two broad areas: visual and verbal relationships in Romantic poetry, including aspects of material textuality, and Scottish Romanticism. After publishing *Shelley's Visual Imagination* in 2011, she is now completing a study that traces aesthetic and ideological refigurings of the Scottish hero William Wallace in British Romantic writers.

ANTHONY JOHN HARDING is Emeritus Professor of English, University of Saskatchewan. He co-edited volume V of *The Notebooks of Samuel Taylor Coleridge* (2002) with the late Kathleen Coburn, and is the author of *The Reception of Myth in English Romanticism* (1995). His more recent publications include 'The *"I"* in *The Prelude*', in *The Oxford Handbook of William Wordsworth*, ed. Richard Gravil and Daniel Robinson (2015), and 'Shelley, Mythology, and the Classical Tradition', in *The Oxford Handbook of Percy Bysshe Shelley*, ed. Michael O'Neill and Anthony Howe (2012). He has also published articles in *The Wordsworth Circle*, *Keats-Shelley Journal*, *English Studies in Canada*, and *Proceedings of the German Association of University Teachers of English*.

BETH LAU is Professor of English Emerita at California State University, Long Beach. She is the author of *Keats's Reading of the Romantic Poets* (1991) and *Keats's 'Paradise Lost'* (1998), as well as of numerous articles on various Romantic writers. She also edited *Fellow Romantics: Male and Female British Writers, 1790–1835* (2009), Jane Austen's *Sense and Sensibility* (2002), and co-edited (with Diane Hoeveler) *Approaches to Teaching Brontë's 'Jane Eyre'* (1993). She is currently working on a volume featuring cognitive approaches to Jane Austen's novels.

GREGORY LEADBETTER is Reader in Literature and Creative Writing at Birmingham City University. His book *Coleridge and the Daemonic Imagination* (2011) won the University English Book Prize in 2012. As a poet, his works include *The Fetch* (2016) and the pamphlet *The Body in the Well* (2007).

CHARLES W. MAHONEY, Professor and Director of Graduate Studies in the Department of English at the University of Connecticut, has published widely on Romantic writing. He is the co-editor (with Michael O'Neill) of *Romantic Poetry: An Annotated Anthology* (2008), the editor of *A Companion to Romantic Poetry* (2011), and is currently completing work on *Coleridge on Shakespeare*.

STACEY MCDOWELL is a College Lecturer in English and Fellow of St John's College, Cambridge. She wrote her doctoral thesis on Keats and has published various essays on Romantic poetry. She is currently interested in the representation of reading in nineteenth-century literature.

CHRISTOPHER R. MILLER is Professor of English at the College of Staten Island, City University of New York. He is the author of *Surprise: The Poetics of the Unexpected from Milton to Austen* (2015) and *The Invention of Evening: Perception and Time in Romantic Poetry* (2006).

CHRIS MURRAY is Lecturer in Literary Studies at Monash University. He is the author of *Tragic Coleridge* (2013), which examines the tragic vision in Coleridge's poetical works, and various essays that explore British Romanticism's dialogues with Orientalism and classical reception.

FRANCIS O'GORMAN's most recent work has been an edition of Swinburne (2016) and *The Cambridge Companion to John Ruskin* (2015). He is Saintsbury Professor of English Literature at the University of Edinburgh.

MICHAEL O'NEILL is Professor of English at Durham University. His books include *Romanticism and the Self-Conscious Poem* (1997) and, as editor,

Keats: Bicentenary Readings (1997) and *The Cambridge History of English Poetry* (2010).

SEAMUS PERRY is Professor of English Literature at the University of Oxford and a Fellow of Balliol College. He has written books about Coleridge, Tennyson, and T. S. Eliot, and he is the editor of a selection from Coleridge's notebooks. He is editor, with Christopher Ricks, of the Oxford journal *Essays in Criticism.*

JEFFREY C. ROBINSON's recent work includes *Unfettering Poetry: The Fancy in British Romanticism* (2006), *Poems for the Millennium, Volume Three: The University of California Book of Romantic and Postromantic Poetry,* co-edited with Jerome Rothenberg (2009; winner of the American Book Award for the Before Columbus Foundation, 2010); *Untam'd Wing: Riffs on Romantic Poetry* [original poems] (2010); and *Active Romanticism: The Radical Impulse in Nineteenth-Century and Contemporary Poetic Practice,* co-edited with Julie Carr (2015). He is completing a monograph, *Fibres of These Thoughts: Poetic Innovation in Wordsworth: 1825–1833.* Professor Emeritus at the University of Colorado, Boulder, he is currently Honorary Senior Research Fellow at the University of Glasgow.

NICHOLAS ROE is Professor of English Literature at the University of St Andrews, Scotland. Having published *John Keats. A New Life* in 2012, he is continuing his research into John Keats and his circle.

MARK SANDY is Reader in English Studies at Durham University. His publications include *Poetics of Self and Form in Keats and Shelley* (2005) and *Romanticism, Memory, and Mourning* (2013). He has edited *Romantic Presences in the Twentieth Century* (2012) and recently co-edited a volume on *Decadent Romanticism 1780–1914* (2015). He is currently researching a monograph on the influence of British Romanticism on twentieth-century American literature.

GRANT F. SCOTT is Professor of English at Muhlenberg College in Allentown, PA. He is the author of *The Sculpted Word: Keats, Ekphrasis, and the Visual Arts* (1994) and the editor of *Selected Letters of John Keats* (2002), *Joseph Severn: Letters and Memoirs* (2005), *New Letters from Charles Brown to Joseph Severn* (2010), and most recently, *The Illustrated Letters of Richard Doyle to His Father, 1842–1843* (2016).

MATTHEW SCOTT teaches in the Department of English Literature at the University of Reading. He has published widely on the literature of Romanticism and has a particular interest in the history of criticism. He is an editor of the academic journal *Symbiosis* and the reviews editor of *The London Magazine*.

JANE STABLER teaches English literature at the University of St Andrews. Her books include *Byron, Poetics and History* (2002), which was awarded the Elma Dangerfield Prize and the British Academy's Crawshay Prize in 2003, and *The Artistry of Exile: Romantic and Victorian Writers in Italy* (2013). She currently holds a Major Leverhulme Fellowship to complete work on a new edition of *Don Juan* for the Longman Annotated English Poets Edition of Lord Byron's poetry.

HEIDI THOMSON is Associate Professor of English Literature at Victoria University of Wellington, New Zealand, and President of the Romantic Studies Association of Australasia. She is the author of *Coleridge and the Romantic Newspaper: The Morning Post and Advertising Dejection* (2016) and the editor of novels by Maria Edgeworth.

HERBERT F. TUCKER holds the John C. Coleman Chair in English at the University of Virginia, where he is also an associate editor for *New Literary History* and the Victorian series editor for the University of Virginia Press. He is at work on a study correlating the ineffability of charm with such nonsemantic dimensions of literary performance as prosody, for which his interactive teaching site *For Better for Verse* is freely available at prosody.lib.virginia.edu. His books include *Epic* (2nd edn, 2013), *Tennyson and the Doom of Romanticism* (1988), and *Browning's Beginnings* (1980), as well as several anthologies.

RICHARD MARGGRAF TURLEY is Professor of English Literature at Aberystwyth University. He is the author of several books on Romantic writers, including *Keats's Boyish Imagination* (2004) and *Bright Stars: John Keats, Barry Cornwall and Romantic Literary Culture* (2009). Most recently, he is the co-author, with Jayne Archer and Howard Thomas, of *Food and the Literary Imagination* (2014). His historical crime novel *The Cunning House* (2015) is set in 1810, and explores Romantic sexual subcultures.

TIMOTHY WEBB has written and lectured widely, especially on Romantic and Irish topics. He has published books on Percy Shelley (at least nine titles), English Romantic Hellenism, editions of Leigh Hunt and Yeats, and detailed essays on a wide range of authors, especially of the nineteenth and twentieth centuries. Work in progress includes a reader on stones, a book-length study of Ireland and the English Romantics, and an edition of Shelley's prose (with Michael O'Neill).

SUSAN J. WOLFSON is Professor of English at Princeton University, and the author, most recently, of *Reading John Keats* (2015). She is also the editor of (and contributor to) *The Cambridge Companion to John Keats,* and of *The Annotated Northanger Abbey* (2014) which includes a unique, freshly edited text of Austen's novel; and, with Ron Levao, she is the co-editor of *The Annotated Frankenstein* (2012).

SARAH WOOTTON is Senior Lecturer in English Studies at Durham University. She is the author of *Consuming Keats: Nineteenth-Century Representations in Art and Literature* (2006) and *Byronic Heroes in Nineteenth-Century Women's Writing and Screen Adaptation* (2016), and co-editor, with Michael O'Neill and Mark Sandy, of *Venice and the Cultural Imagination* (2012) and *The Persistence of Beauty: Victorians to Moderns* (2015).

DUNCAN WU is the Raymond Wagner Professor of Literary Studies at Georgetown University, Washington, DC. He is Vice Chairman of the Keats-Shelley Memorial Association and editor of *Romanticism: An Anthology,* now in its fourth edition.

Acknowledgements

The editor would like to thank Linda Bree for commissioning this volume and for all her patient, meticulous, and enabling guidance. He would also like to thank the readers of the original proposal for comments that were at once positive and perceptive. He is grateful to all the contributors for their fine essays and collegiality. For various forms of help and advice, he is particularly indebted to Andrew Bennett, Madeleine Callaghan, Oliver Clarkson, Nicholas Roe, Mark Sandy, Sharon Tai, and Sarah Wootton.

Note on Texts, Citations, and Abbreviations

Unless indicated otherwise, Keats's poetry is quoted from *P* and his letters from *L* (see the list of abbreviations at the end of this section). Keats's often idiosyncratic spellings are reproduced as given in *L*. Numbers provided after citations from Keats's poetry refer to line numbers, except in cases where Keats wrote in books (*Endymion*, *Hyperion*), cantos (*The Fall of Hyperion*), or parts (*Lamia*), in which case the book, canto, or part number comes first, followed by the line number. Citations from *Otho the Great* and *King Stephen* provide numbers for acts, scenes, and lines, in that order. Shakespeare is quoted from *The Norton Shakespeare*, ed. Stephen Greenblatt and others (New York: Norton, 1997).

The following abbreviations are used in the volume. (Sometimes individual chapters also use abbreviations after an initial full reference.)

CH *Keats: The Critical Heritage*, ed. G. M. Matthews. London: Routledge, 1971.

K *John Keats*. Longman Cultural Edition. Ed. Susan J. Wolfson. New York: Pearson Longman, 2007.

KC *The Keats Circle: Letters and Papers 1816–1878 and More Letters and Poems 1814–1879*, ed. Hyder Edward Rollins, 2nd edn 2 vols. Cambridge, MA: Harvard University Press, 1965.

L *The Letters of John Keats, 1814–1821*, ed. Hyder Edward Rollins. 2 vols. Cambridge, MA: Harvard University Press, 1958.

P *The Poems of John Keats*, ed. Jack Stillinger. Cambridge, MA: Harvard University Press, 1978.

Introduction

In *Adonais*, sometimes criticised for creating an image of Keats as weakly vulnerable, Shelley saluted his fellow poet, just a few months dead, as a living, dynamic presence in civilisation's great battle and as destined for poetic immortality:

> And he is gathered to the kings of thought
> Who waged contention with their time's decay,
> And of the past are all that cannot pass away.
>
> (430–2)[1]

Stirringly Keats/Adonais rises here from the ashes of Tory, patrician condescension and rejection, and assumes a truly regal identity, one among 'the kings of thought'.

We might want to remark that Keats was more a poet of 'Sensations' rather than of 'Thoughts' (*L* 1, 185), remembering his asserted preference for the former over the latter. Yet both feature prominently in his work and do so with a unique cast, and it is unsurprising that in the same letter the young poet contemplates the nature and, implicitly, the acquisition of 'a complex Mind' that 'would exist partly on sensation partly on thought', one, he goes on to say, 'to whom it is necessary that years should bring the philosophic Mind' (*L* 1, 186).

Keats's life and works are vibrant with tensions. The man is at once ablaze with passion and ambition, yet ready to embrace a near-passive openness to experience. Liberal in his political views he may have been, but he was not inclined to 'believe' in a vapidly optimistic 'sort of perfectibility'; 'the nature of the world will not admit of it' (*L* 2, 101), he adds, with the tough realism of a young man who knew, on his pulses, the brutal, sapping fact of mortality, having lost his father to a tragic accident, then nursed his mother and younger brother Tom through their final illnesses; having, moreover, treated sick people as an apprentice apothecary, and seen first-hand at Guy's Hospital the sufferings of those requiring surgical intervention in an age without effective anaesthetics. He was, as befits a medically trained poet, ardent that poetry should be 'a friend to man' (48), as his 'Ode on a Grecian Urn' would put it. At the same time, he relished poetry's capacity for recreating experience through acts of verbal expressiveness. And he was aware of and, indeed, drawn to poetry's possibly treacherous offer of imaginative escape and transcendence. Moneta, the stern muse-figure of *The Fall of Hyperion*, is ventriloquised as asking the poem's 'I', in a tone halfway between mockery and genuine enquiry, 'What benefit canst thou do, or all thy tribe, / To the great world? Thou art a dreaming thing; / A fever of thyself' (I. 167–9). In so doing, she decisively sets the terms for any authentic exploration of poetic value. Her question is one that Keats asks of the art he loves and brings to the fore as a central concern of modern poetry.

Keats registers such tensions and frames such questions with a generosity of spirit, and with qualities of courage, honesty, delighted attention, and verbal originality that have drawn generations of readers to his work as well as to the fascinating, tragic story of his brilliant short career. His letters, among the finest ever written by a poet, combine spontaneity and affection for his fortunate addressees with self-aware commitment to his development as a writer; they are required reading. And his poems have inspired many responses from later writers, including the sequence 'Voyages: A Homage to John Keats' by the American poet, Amy Clampitt. Referring to the correspondence buried with Keats's body, correspondence particularly from Fanny Brawne, the young woman with whom he had forged a deep intimacy, Clampitt concludes the sequence with the affecting phrase, 'Letters no one will ever open'.[2] The phrase allows Clampitt to suggest, beyond biographical fact, that there are aspects of Keats we shall never fathom, that he possesses the inexhaustibility of those few writers who are necessary.

It is clear from the sustained production of first-rate biographies, critical studies, and even cinematic work that Keats continues to enchant and challenge readers both within academe and beyond. The present volume responds to that enchantment and challenge, and seeks to understand them and provide frameworks for enhanced analysis and appreciation. Each essay supplies a succinct, informed, accessible, and incisive account of some particular context for the study of Keats's life and work. The essays display first-hand responsiveness while showing awareness of relevant critical discussion and debate. The volume's title is *John Keats in Context*, and its contents bear out the view that Keats and his texts matter as much as, are, indeed, part of, what it comprehends by 'context'.

One of the pleasures of shaping and assembling the collection has been observing the many-angled lights brought to bear on Keats's oeuvre by the contributors. Certainly now is an appropriate time for a full-scale reconsideration of Keats's achievement and its enabling contexts. Keatsian criticism will always be associated with the work of critics such as W. J. Bate (*John Keats*, 1963), Helen Vendler (*The Odes of John Keats*, 1983), Stuart M. Sperry (*Keats the Poet*, 1973; 1994 rev. edn), and others, critics who emphasised the poet's sympathy, artistry, and capacity for development. But challenges to or nuancing of these approaches arose from critics who drew energy from new historicism, feminism, and deconstruction: these critics include Jerome J. McGann ('Keats and the Historical Method in Literary Criticism', 1979), Marjorie Levinson (*Keats's Life of Allegory: The Origins of a Style*, 1988), and Anne K. Mellor (*Romanticism and Gender*, 1993). Andrew Bennett contributed a sophisticated study of Keats as a narrative poet in 1994: *Keats, Narrative and Audience: The Posthumous Life of Writing*. After the reassessments prompted by the poet's bicentenary in 1995, especially collections of essays edited by Nicholas Roe (*Keats and History*, 1995), Michael O'Neill (*Keats: Bicentenary Readings*, 1997), and Robert M. Ryan and Ronald A. Sharp (*The Persistence of Poetry: Bicentennial Essays on Keats*, 1998), there has been significant work in recent years exploring his thought and his intellectual and cultural situatedness: books such as Jeffrey N. Cox's *Poetry and Politics in the Cockney School* (1998), Porscha Fermanis's *John Keats and the Ideas of the Enlightenment* (2009), and Shahidha Bari's *Keats and Philosophy: The Life of Sensations* (2012). Susan J. Wolfson's 2001 Cambridge Companion to the poet provides a valuable resource, while her recent study of the poet, *Reading John Keats* (2015), responds creatively to the invitation implicitly extended by Stuart Sperry in 1994, who asked whether we could 'continue to prize as he deserves the poet who of all the great Romantics was the most pleasure-loving and pleasure-giving, the most generous and humane in his responses, and the most committed to the life of the imagination'.[3]

The present volume offers an exciting body of work that engages with Keats's biography, writing, and cultural meaning. The volume is aimed at undergraduate, postgraduate, and academic audiences as well as interested non-academic readers. Building on recent interest in Keats's world, on his life, times, and affiliations with others, it explores his letters, his poetic artistry and development, his relationship with previous poetry, myth, and religion, his influence on other writers, and his critical reception.

It consists of the following six parts: 'Life, Letters, Texts'; 'Cultural Contexts'; 'Ideas and Poetics'; 'Poetic Contexts'; 'Influence'; and 'Critical Reception'. 'Life, Letters, Texts' contains eight chapters discussing Keats in relation to biographies and film; his formative years, including his medical training; his involvement in the medicine and science of the time; his relationships with Fanny Brawne and other women; his understanding of mortality; his experience of travel; his achievement as a letter writer; and the complex history of his manuscripts and dealings with his publishers and editors. 'Cultural Contexts' contains six chapters and examines his participation in Leigh Hunt's circle and possible membership of a 'Cockney' school of poets; the London of the pre- and post-Waterloo period; the poet's attitude to political matters, especially as shown in and by his style; the importance he gave to friendship and sociability; the influence on him of painting and sculpture; and his thinking about religion and myth.

'Ideas and Poetics' contains six chapters, five of which explore the nature and the contexts of Keats's thinking, including his response to the Enlightenment, especially its ideas about history; and to Hazlitt and his notion of disinterestedness. It also considers his attitudes to beauty, truth, and imagination; his notion of the poetical character; and his dealings with the senses and sensations. The last chapter in this part considers the embodied sensuousness of Keats's verbal craft in the prosody and versification of his odes. The fourth part, 'Poetic Contexts', contains seven chapters: they explore Keats's relationship with previous and contemporary poets, including Dante and Shakespeare; Spenser, Milton, Dryden, and Pope; Tighe, Radcliffe, Southey, Burns, Chatterton, Hunt, and Wordsworth; and Coleridge, Byron, and Shelley. This part also examines the ways in which his poetry breathes new and individual life into various genres: ballad, romance, and narrative; epic and tragedy; and shorter lyrical forms.

The fifth part, 'Influence', consists of three chapters and inspects Keats's influence on British poets from Tennyson to Wilde (in one chapter) and on a group of poets writing in English from Hardy to Heaney in another. The second chapter in the fifth part includes reference to two American poets, Stevens and Bishop, and a subsequent chapter considers his influence on a range of American writers. The final part, 'Critical Reception', consists of four chapters which describe, in turn, the response of his contemporaries, especially in reviews; nineteenth-century criticism after his death; twentieth-century criticism up to the publication of W. J. Bate's biography in 1963; and criticism after Bate's book to the present.

'That which is creative must create itself' (*L* 1, 374), Keats wrote to his publisher with *Endymion* in mind. All good poetry asks to be experienced for what it is, in and on its own terms, but this is unusually the case with Keats, a writer who invites his readers to display an answerable capacity for 'sensation & watchfulness' (*L* 1, 374). Keatsian creativity prompts, too, our desire to know more about its shaping contexts and ability to go on shaping our own culture. The present volume, in its editor's view, offers a variegated, polyphonic approach to a poet whose 'knowledge of contrast, feeling for light and shade' (*L* 2, 360) continue to compel.

Notes

1 *Percy Bysshe Shelley: The Major Works*, ed. Zachary Leader and Michael O'Neill (Oxford: Oxford University Press, 2003).

2 Amy Clampitt, *What the Light Was Like* (London: Faber, 1985).

3 Stuart M. Sperry, *Keats the Poet* (1973; Princeton: Princeton University Press, 1994), p. 346. For further significant work by Susan J. Wolfson, see, among other publications, her chapter in *Formal Charges: The Shaping of Poetry in British Romanticism* (Stanford: Stanford University Press, 1997) and chapters on questions of Keats and gender in her *Borderlines: The Shiftings of Gender in British Romanticism* (Stanford: Stanford University Press, 2006).

PART I

Life, Letters, Texts

CHAPTER I

Biographies and Film

Sarah Wootton

This chapter is less a comprehensive account of individual biographies of John Keats, analysed in the final chapters of this volume, than a meditation on ways in which his career has been presented in the genres of biography and film. Biographies and films of Keats are more than the record of a Romantic writer's life and work. They are not solely concerned with *a* poet. Walter Jackson Bate begins his monumental literary biography of 1963 with the following statement: 'The life of Keats provides a unique opportunity for the study of literary greatness and of what permits or encourages its development.' What factors 'helped and what hindered', Bate asks, in the writing of poems and letters that remain among the most influential in the English language.[1] Even as biographers and critics have established a 'historical' Keats over the last few decades – considering his political leanings, the artistic coteries he worked within, his medical training and promising career as an Apothecary – Andrew Motion reiterated, at the close of the twentieth century, 'Readers have made him a byword for the poetic identity.'[2] The impetus for any biography of this subject – who was John Keats? – raises the related questions of what does John Keats represent and why?

To consider biographies of and films featuring Keats is to consider the cultural reconfigurations of an archetype. What is at stake in tracing the daily events and wider contexts of Keats's existence is nothing less than the figure of *the* poet and his enduring legacies. An inherited image of Keats as a 'perfect' poet is underpinned by the elevated status accorded to certain poems, with Motion expressing his admiration for 'Ode on a Grecian Urn' as 'a perfect example of a perfect type'.[3] The emblematic value of Keats's life and work extends to the lives of Keats, moreover. The publication of three major biographies in the 1960s, by Walter Jackson Bate, Aileen Ward and Robert Gittings, collectively represents a 'golden age' of Keats scholarship, a point made clear in Helen Vendler's review of Motion's biography: 'I must look at what he claims to add to the view of Keats's life and work that one possesses after reading Bate, Ward and Gittings, and ask how his writing compares with theirs as a way into Keats.'[4] Bate's biography, in particular, has become a touchstone for subsequent biographers of Keats as well as for readers of his poetry. For Bate, Keats's poetic ideal of '*Negative Capability*' (*L* 1, 193) is the governing characteristic of his existence. The poems are not adjuncts to or illustrations of the life, but part of a mode of being that embodies 'imaginative identification', a projection of sympathy that 'was not a mere escape hatch from the prison of egocentricity, but something thoroughgoing, something indigenous and inseparable from all activities of the mind'.[5]

The many lives and memoirs that have been written about Keats, with one published on average every six years since the 1920s, are not simply about their subject.[6] Scholarship on Keats has traditionally been at the forefront of debates about the significance of social status and politics for the creative life of a poet and the extent to which the imagination is invested in 'reality' or abstracted from it. If biographies of Keats have tended to present the life with an ideological inflection, or sideline the subject for a wider theoretical agenda, then surely the literary biopic brings him centre stage.

Keats has not featured in films as prominently as some other notable Romantic writers, such as Jane Austen and Lord Byron. That changed, in 2009, with the cinema release of *Bright Star*, written and directed by Jane Campion.[7] The film, which takes its name from a sonnet by Keats, does not purport to be a biopic in terms of bringing the life of this poet to the screen. The film's events cover the period from late 1818 to early 1821 and focus on Keats's relationship with Fanny Brawne – or, rather, on Fanny Brawne's experience of that relationship. That the main 'star' of Keats's story should be someone other than the poet sparked controversy among critics. Christopher Ricks questioned whether Campion had undermined Keats by generating literal pictures out of his 'graphic' imagination.[8] Ricks's comments on the displacement of Keats and his poetry are pertinent to *Bright Star* and to Keats's afterlives more generally, from Percy Bysshe Shelley's elegy *Adonais* (1821) onwards. What can this 'biopic', which takes as its subject the recipient of Keats's most heartfelt and anguished letters, tell us about the history of biographies of Keats as well as perceptions of the poet and his poetry in the twenty-first century? In what ways, and with what effect, does *Bright Star* place or displace Keats and his poetry?

Bright Star's Fanny Brawne is not exclusively 'an object intensely desireable', as Keats describes his fiancée in a distraught letter of July 1820 (*L* 1, 304). Brawne, as played by Abbie Cornish, is a spirited seamstress who is combative in her opposition to Keats's friend, Charles Armitage Brown, and what are portrayed on-screen as his coarse jealousies. Brawne is the '*Minx*' that Keats dubs her after their first meeting, and scenes stage their quarrels about the 'penchant she has for acting stylishly' (*L* 2, 13, original emphasis). Her 'still stedfast, still unchangeable' (9) passion for the poet, to borrow a line from 'Bright star, would I were stedfast as thou art', equals his intense appeals to her in letters: 'I cannot exist without you … You have absorb'd me … I have no limit now to my love' (*L* 2, 223). It is the tender agonies of a 'deep love' (*L* 2, 132), expressed in Keats's letters, that drew Campion to their story, with Fanny acting out his intoxicating words, 'I cannot breathe without you', in the rawness of her grief (*L* 2, 224).

In opting for a romantic storyline, with Keats enthralled by a talented and vivacious woman, *Bright Star* comes close to reprising the abiding image of a hypersensitive poet who was killed by a heedless world before he could realise his potential. A slim volume published by Penguin Classics to coincide with the film's release, *So Bright and Delicate: Love Letters and Poems of John Keats to Fanny Brawne*, reinforces an impression of the apolitical aesthete who self-mythologised the role with declarations like 'O for a Life of Sensations rather than of Thoughts!' (*L* 1, 185).[9] There is an otherworldly quality to Campion's Keats, played by Ben Whishaw, as he lies on the canopy of a tree to be closer to the nightingale of his ode, embodying the axiom, in his letter of 27 February 1818, 'That if Poetry comes not as naturally as the Leaves to a tree it had better not come at all' (*L* 1, 238–9). Yet if this Keats is passive, he is also, by turns, solicitous, expectant, tranquil and febrile, without foreknowledge of his death casting him as the 'dying kind of Lover' that he resists (*L* 2, 281). The predictable and yet poignant narrative of a 'dying' Keats is both brought into play and reworked by Campion (the poet's death takes place off-screen, for example). Pathos characterises *Bright Star*, with a pervading atmosphere of elegiac quietude, but this pathos has a purpose.

Whishaw's understated performance channels Keatsian aesthetics as he opens out a space on-screen for Cornish's Fanny Brawne. It is Keats's negation of self, what he defined as the 'camelion Poet' (*L* 1, 387), that refocuses attention on a neglected aspect of literary history. But this passive 'dissolving' is neither the languor nor the effeminacy that concerned contemporary supporters such as Leigh Hunt and offered up the poet posthumously to repeated acts of artistic and biographical appropriation. The selflessness that Keats relished, and Bate praised in his biography, is employed by Campion as a means of 're-discovering' the character of Fanny Brawne. In so doing, the film's revisionary feminism raises significant questions about commemorating past lives. 'Through Fanny', Hila Shachar argues, 'Campion compels her audience to consider the process of biographical reconstruction as a subjective, politicized, present-informed enterprise … like a piece of art.'[10]

Art, and the production and value of it, is an overriding concern of *Bright Star*. Campion's emphasis on Fanny's sewing revalues this feminine craft in relation to what is presented as the more masculine pastime of poetry. Although Fanny admits to an ignorance of poetry, she is frank in her appreciation of what speaks to her and eager to learn from Keats. *Bright Star* is engaged with poetry on a level that is uncommon for films about writers without ever managing to integrate the activity of composing this art form into the art of film. Lines recited from 'Bright Star' and 'Ode to a Nightingale' pay tribute to and trap Keats's poems in a mood of melancholy stasis that he sought to explore creatively and against which he struggled. It is the poignancy of the former poem that prevails when Fanny walks along Hampstead Heath, dressed as a widow, after Keats's death. The poetry that conspicuously permeates Campion's film is the opening of *Endymion*: 'A thing of beauty is a joy forever: / Its loveliness increases; it will never / Pass into nothingness' (I. 1–3). Yet the resonance of these lines belies their predictability. *Bright Star* creates a visual space, a cinematic 'palace of art', for Keats's practical and theoretical worship of beauty; it is inspired by the words ' "Beauty is truth, truth beauty" ' ('Ode on a Grecian Urn', 49). The film also accommodates viewpoints that are far from uncritical of this sentiment, framed as implied speech in the poem, as reflected in Mrs Brawne's reservations about the 'blissful' anguish of her eldest daughter.

Margarida Esteves Pereira comments on the cinematic 'interart' of *Bright Star*.[11] What Pereira identifies as Impressionism is closer stylistically to an art movement that is associated with Keats's visual afterlife. Scenes of bluebells carpeting a field and the butterfly farm in Fanny Brawne's bedroom borrow a Pre-Raphaelite palette of intense colouring and convey a sense of claustrophobia. Fanny's gaudily elaborate gowns imitate a Pre-Raphaelite fixation with the decorative female form, while her younger sister Margaret, nicknamed 'Toots', with tumbling ginger curls, might be a model from a painting by John Everett Millais. That *Bright Star* should luxuriate in such imagery is apt, given that the Pre-Raphaelites and their followers were instrumental in promoting Keats's posthumous reputation. Founding members of the Pre-Raphaelite Brotherhood first met in front of William Holman Hunt's painting *The Eve of St Agnes* (1848); Dante Gabriel Rossetti wrote that 'the next Keats must be a painter'; and his brother,

William Michael Rossetti, wrote a life of Keats for the *Great Writers Series* in 1887.[12] Presenting Keats on film as 'the forerunner of the Pre-Raphaelite School' breathes new life into the portrait of the Romantic aesthete that Oscar Wilde enshrined at the close of the nineteenth century.[13] The impression of Keats as a word painter prized for his sensuous ornamentation is translated into a filmic *tableau vivant*. Campion's intimate close-ups of needlework visualise what Marjorie Levinson dubbed 'the gorgeous tapestry school', with *Bright Star* as a cinematic rendering of the 'hedonistic arguments' about Keats's poetry that the critic objected to.[14] And yet the treatment of Keats's poetry as alluring surface, as weavings that are 'flat, stylized, and concretely allegorical', is necessarily fleshed out on film. The screen projects a moving picture rather than a static, and potentially limiting, set piece. Campion's film acts as a visual commentary on Keats's 'life of Allegory' as well as extending and animating his creative afterlife.[15]

The literary biopic is positioned precariously between artistic representation and the representation of an actual existence. But how can a biography encapsulate, rather than merely contribute to, the 'continual allegory' that Keats proposed as a way of understanding how a life could be modelled into literature (*L* 2, 67)? Andrew Motion's *Keats* (1997) is conscious of the past lives of its subject and positions this life as a reaction to and departure from previous ones. Drawing on a growing body of scholarship that sought to restore the poet to his social milieu, Motion gives us a re-historicised and 'radical' Keats. The first full biography, Richard Monckton Milnes's *Life, Letters, and Literary Remains of John Keats*, published in 1848, played down any political dimension in an attempt to establish the poet's literary credentials. Milnes worked hard to salvage Keats from imminent obscurity after the wrangling of friends and relatives hampered the progress of proposed memoirs. Having compiled materials from various sources, Milnes took the bold decision to let Keats speak for himself: 'I thus came to the conclusion, that it was best to act simply as the editor of the Life which was, as it were, already written.'[16] Milnes felt confident that an unobtrusive 'arrangement' of the poems and letters would convey the impression of a striving and subtle intelligence. The pains Milnes took to position Keats within the middle class – 'the upper rank of the middle-class' in a later memoir – is a concession to Victorian respectability, as William Michael Rossetti pointed out in his life of the poet, but it also worked towards securing Keats's fame.[17] Writing a century and a half later, Motion is more attuned to the precariousness of the poet's social standing: 'Keats was unsure whether he was climbing out of the working class, or likely to slip at any moment from the lower rungs of the middle class.'[18]

Motion is equally keen to dispel the enduring sense of Romantic alienation that clings about Keats. The image of a martyr to art, the victim who withdrew into his imagination as a refuge from reality, was propagated by the Victorians and passed on, as well as parodied, by writers in the first half of the twentieth century. For Motion, the biographies that appeared after Sidney Colvin's life of the poet was published in 1887 and before Hyder E. Rollins's invaluable editorial work emerged in the 1940s and 1950s are largely belletristic; they are wedded to Keats as 'a confectioner of verbal sweetmeats', a beloved boy who was born to die.[19] However, to so characterise studies from this period, which include Amy Lowell's *John Keats* (1925), Dorothy Hewlett's *Adonais: A Life of John Keats* (1938), Betty Askwith's *Keats* (1941) and Blanche Williams's *Forever Young: A Life of John Keats* (1943), is to perpetuate a trivialising attitude towards the women writers, artists and readers who were active in promoting Keats's reputation. Lowell's two-volume *John Keats* was the longest and most ambitious biography to be published by that date. It was, according to William Henry Marquess, a 'heroic labor', which, along with Colvin's serially reprinted *Keats*, 'establish[ed] the twentieth-century view of the poet'.[20] Lowell's Keats is memorable for many reasons. Of particular significance is her championing of Fanny Brawne following the public indignation at Keats's love letters, which appeared in Harry Buxton Forman's edition of 1878. Lowell's sympathetic reappraisal is sometimes at the expense of Keats's friends, however, forming a further parallel with Campion's *Bright Star*. The psychological acuity of this life-long Keats devotee is impressive, as is her extensive use of the Keatsiana she collected (Walter Jackson Bate and Robert Gittings likewise draw on Keatsiana for their respective biographies of 1963 and 1968). But Lowell's insistence on Keats as a modern man, valuing his contemporaneity, brings the biographer and her own ambitions and anxieties as a writer to the fore.

Motion seeks to recontextualise Keats. But he too inevitably reveals the stamp of the biographer and the cultural preoccupations of his time. That Motion is a poet, like Lowell before him, is evident in a reading of 'To Autumn', for instance, which is alert to the 'sympathetic poise in the tone of his [Keats's] writing', and traces the intensifying ambivalence of a poem that 'holds its balances so expertly'.[21] The topical pursuit of political allusions in this ode is somewhat more of a stretch. Motion also demonstrates an awareness of Keats's posthumous existence in ways that most biographers cannot or simply will not accommodate. Motion acknowledges, with regard to the 'story' of Keats, that 'Its fascination is endless; its power to move and inspire is inexhaustible.'[22] The 'myth', however, is brought into conflict with a historicist approach as Motion falteringly asserts: 'And yet, and yet … Keats's "posthumous existence" has blurred his "reality".' The use of inverted commas implies that the poet's legacy and the actual life are regarded as equally subjective. Yet Motion proceeds to criticise Milnes for failing to 'capture Keats whole'. Motion's *Keats*, which sensitively entwines the texture of the poet's personality with his verse, also begs the question of whether biography has the capacity for, or can reconcile itself to, the intrinsic plurality of Keats's life, his work and his afterlives. Doesn't Jack Stillinger's 'Multiple Keats', a poet of 'unresolved imaginative dividedness', run counter to more traditional forms of life writing?[23]

Nicholas Roe confronts and negotiates this 'dividedness' in the most recent biography, *John Keats: A New Life* (2012). It is a riposte to the portrait of an effete Keats spawned by reviewers such as John Gibson Lockhart and his snobbish dismissal of the poet as an 'uneducated and flimsy stripling' (*CH* 101). The 'myth' of Keats was already mushrooming through politically motivated attacks on the poet, counter-attacks, early memoirs and elegies by the time biographers came to his defence: Milnes's Keats was manly and courageous, Colvin's pugnacious and Bate's intelligent and robust. Roe's Keats is a fighter, whose writing 'was from first to last a means of resistance, a way to stand his ground'; he is also a restless man with an appetite for stimulants.[24] Personal experience and empathy, following Richard Holmes's 'footsteps' method, is key to this portrait of Keats. Roe visits the places Keats visited, retraces the paths he walked and researches every locality of the life, finding the most minor sights stored up as an image that reappears in the poems.

The section on the time Keats spent at Guy's Hospital – site of the first statue of the poet – conveys the sense of a rapidly changing existence. Place, for Roe, precipitates a Keats of creative contingencies, on the verge of London's inner city: 'the liminal suburban landscape – part city, part open fields – encouraged his imaginative stationings on darkling thresholds and elusive borderlines'.[25] This approach yields interpretative possibilities and leads to suppositions and hesitation. Speculative maybes have a precedent in Gittings's bold biography of the poet (1968) and in Ward's as well (1963). Ward's biography is rich in psychological insights and, like Roe's, places emphasis on Keats's parents and their early deaths. On occasion, Roe regards what is provisional as an asset for the biographer of Keats, weaving the poet's famed negative capability into the fabric of the life: 'Like Keats, I have at times left matters open to question.'[26]

Jonathan Bate begins his review article in the *TLS*, 'The real John Keats', by channelling the observations made by the other Bate that are quoted at the start of this chapter: 'What was he really like? When, and under the influence of what shaping forces, did he become a great poet? Any literary biographer who can answer those two questions will have achieved the holy grail of Life-writing.'[27] The answer to these questions comes within reach only in as much as a biographer of Keats acknowledges what Walter Jackson Bate identified some half a century ago, that 'the very essence of the appeal of the subject is its own amplitude and debatability, its diversity and richness of implication'.[28] The 'Holy Grail' of a 'real' John Keats 'is captured most clearly', Roe suggests, 'when least definitively'.[29]

Keats's 'life of Allegory' enters the twenty-first century as it began two centuries ago. Jane Campion's *Bright Star* (2009) and Nicholas Roe's *John Keats: A New Life* (2012) present opposing portraits of the poet. Campion's Keats is a lover of 'fine Phrases' (*L* 2, 139) and, most notably, the lover of Fanny Brawne. Roe's Keats wrestles with the erratic and tempering energies of experience. The biography and the biopic have more in common than initially appear to be the case, however. Both are rooted in, reflect on and reinvent the cultural reception of the poet. The most compelling parallel between the biography and the biopic relates to artistic agency and elusive states of being. Roe's Keats is animated and sustained by tentative or shadowy thresholds. Campion's Keats is portrayed as watching or being watched from windows and doorways, situated on the figurative threshold of the film. Where, for Roe, Keats's resonant incompletion enables a new life of the poet, for Campion, his self-effacing elasticity enables a new life for Fanny Brawne. The twenty-first-century Keats is, like the 'camelion Poet' he coined, 'every thing and nothing' (*L* 1, 387), an accumulation of past lives out of which indefinite renewals are possible.

Notes

1 Walter Jackson Bate, *John Keats* (1963; London: Hogarth, 1992), p. vii.
2 Andrew Motion, *Keats* (London: Faber, 1997), p. xix.
3 Motion, *Keats,* p. 391.
4 Helen Vendler, 'Inspiration, Accident, Genius', review of Andrew Motion, *Keats, London Review of Books*, 16 October 1997.
5 Bate, *John Keats*, pp. 27, 257, 514 (for 'imaginative identification'), 256.
6 The calculation is by Nicholas Roe. See 'Undefinitive Keats', in *Literature and Authenticity, 1780–1900: Essays in Honour of Vincent Newey*, ed. Ashley Chantler, Michael Davies and Philip Shaw (Farnham: Ashgate, 2011), pp. 39–50, p. 39.

7 *Bright Star*, dir. Jane Campion, starring Abbie Cornish and Ben Whishaw (Pathé, 2009).
8 See Christopher Ricks, 'Undermining Keats', *New York Review of Books*, 17 December 2009, 46–9.
9 John Keats, *So Bright and Delicate: Love Letters and Poems of John Keats to Fanny Brawne*, intro. Jane Campion (London: Penguin, 2009). See, also, *Bright Star: The Complete Poems and Selected Letters of John Keats*, intro. Jane Campion (London: Vintage, 2009).
10 Hila Shachar, 'Authorial Histories: The Historical Film and the Literary Biopic', in *A Companion to the Historical Film*, eds. Robert A. Rosenstone and Constantin Parvulescu (Chichester: Wiley-Blackwell, 2013), pp. 199–218, pp. 209–10. Grant F. Scott considers the treatment of Fanny Brawne in a review of the film. See '*Bright Star*', *Studies in Romanticism*, 49 (2010): 507–12.
11 Margarida Esteves Pereira, '*Bright Star*: Reinventing Romantic Poetry for the Screen', in *Relational Designs in Literature and the Arts: Page and Stage, Canvas and Screen*, ed. Rui Carvalho Homem (Amsterdam: Rodopi, 2012), pp. 153–65, p. 153.
12 Dante Gabriel Rossetti, quoted in *Memorials of Edward Burne-Jones*, ed. Georgiana Burne-Jones, 2 vols. (1904; London: Lund Humphries, 1993), vol. 1, p. 145.
13 Oscar Wilde, quoted in Robert Woof and Stephen Hebron, *John Keats* (Grasmere: Wordsworth Trust, 1995), p. 175.
14 Marjorie Levinson, *Keats's Life of Allegory: The Origins of a Style* (Oxford: Blackwell, 1988), pp. 101, 104.
15 Keats refers to Shakespeare's 'life of Allegory' in a letter dated 19 February 1819, adding 'his works are the comments on it' (*L* 2, 67).
16 *Life, Letters, and Literary Remains of John Keats*, ed. Richard Monckton Milnes, Cambridge Library Collection, 2 vols. (1848; Cambridge: Cambridge University Press, 2013), vol. 1, p. xix.
17 Milnes, *Life, Letters*, quoted in J. R. MacGillivray, *Keats: A Bibliography and Reference Guide with an Essay on Keats' Reputation* (Toronto: University of Toronto Press, 1949), p. liii.
18 Motion, *Keats*, p. xxiv.
19 MacGillivray, *Bibliography and Reference Guide*, p. xii.
20 William Henry Marquess, *Lives of the Poet: The First Century of Keats Biography* (University Park, PA, and London: Pennsylvania State University Press, 1984), pp. 95, 109.
21 Motion, *Keats*, p. 461.
22 Motion, *Keats*, p. xix.
23 Jack Stillinger, 'The "Story" of Keats', in *The Cambridge Companion to Keats*, ed. Susan J. Wolfson (Cambridge: Cambridge University Press, 2001), pp. 246–60, p. 253.
24 Nicholas Roe, *John Keats: A New Life* (New Haven: Yale University Press, 2012), p. xviii.

25 Roe, *John Keats*, p. xix.
26 Roe, *John Keats*, p. xx.
27 Jonathan Bate, 'The Real John Keats', *TLS*, 4 December 2012.
28 Bate, *John Keats*, p. ix.
29 Roe, 'Undefinitive Keats', p. 46.

CHAPTER 2

Formative Years and Medical Training

Hrileena Ghosh and Nicholas Roe

'This day is my Birth day', John Keats announced in October 1818, without making clear what day he was referring to (*L* 1, 405). The register in St. Boltoph's Bishopsgate, where he was baptised on 18 December 1795, gives his birth date as Saturday, 31 October 1795; other sources suggest it was the 29th. His father, Thomas Keates, worked at John Jennings's Swan and Hoop livery stables at Moorfields, London, and married Jennings's daughter Frances at St George's, Hanover Square, on 9 October 1794. John was the eldest of their children: he had three brothers – George, Tom, and Edward (who died as a baby) – and a sister, Frances (Fanny) Keats.

By 1798, the family had moved to Craven Street, a new development of London's northern suburbs. Located between a stinking vinegar factory and the open fields of Middlesex, Craven Street offered 'the knowledge of contrast, feeling for light and shade' that Keats would later believe was 'necessary for a poem' (*L* 2, 360). The few anecdotes of Keats as a child come from this time: a neighbour, Mrs. Grafty, recalled how instead of answering questions he would make a rhyme on the last word and laugh. He was apparently an emotional child: aged five he held his mother at sword point to prevent her going out and 'threatened her so furiously that she burst into tears'.[1] While Keats was close to his mother, as he grew up his physique resembled his father's short, sturdy frame – very unlike his tall, thin brother Tom.

In 1802, Thomas Keates took over the lease for the Swan and Hoop from his father-in-law. He renamed it Keates's Livery Stables, and the family moved back to Moorfields where his eldest son got used to hearing 'the clang / Of clattering hoofs' ('Calidore', 75–6). Opposite their home loomed the Royal Bethlem Hospital, or Bedlam, with Caius Cibber's massive statues of 'Raving Madness' and 'Melancholy Madness' on the gateposts. Years later, inter-twined with memories from the Guy's Hospital ward for 'incurables',[2] these early visions revived in the anguished figures of the Titans in *Hyperion*. A walk up the road to Finsbury Square led to

James Lackington's domed bookshop, the Temple of the Muses – perhaps re-imagined as Moneta's 'eternal domed monument' (1. 71) in *The Fall of Hyperion*. Keats's future publishers, John Taylor and James Hessey, met while working there in 1803–1804.

In August 1803, aged seven, Keats and his brother George were sent to Enfield School. Their uncle Lieutenant Midgley John Jennings, who served in the British Fleet at the Battle of Camperdown (October 1797), was a former pupil, and the boys aimed to keep up the family's reputation for courage. Founded in 1786 by the Baptist John Ryland, in Keats's time the school was run by Ryland's colleague John Clarke: it offered a progressive curriculum suitable for those who would have to earn their living, and open-mindedness was encouraged. Keats would learn reading, writing, and basic science – and that England owed its freedoms to the Dissenting tradition with John Milton at its head. Clarke, who had known liberal Dissenters such as the scientist Joseph Priestley and classicist George Dyer, believed in encouraging students by engaging their interest and imagination, and sought to inculcate self-discipline through the exercise of self-consciousness. Students were taught astronomy by having them form a 'living orrery', performing the movements of the planets in the schoolyard. Ryland – who knew the great astronomer William Herschel – held that this practical approach to education was more likely to be absorbed by pupils, and his view seems to be borne out by Keats, many years later, writing the awe-inspired lines: 'Then felt I like some watcher of the skies / When a new planet swims into his ken' ('On First Looking into Chapman's Homer', 9–10). At Enfield, Keats quickly established a reputation for spirit and determination: one of his school friends, Edward Holmes, later recalled that any one might have thought he would become great – but that it would be in a military capacity (*KC* 2, 164).

'Circumstances are like Clouds continually gathering and bursting – While we are laughing the seed of some trouble is put into the wide arable land of events – while we are laughing it sprouts [it] grows and suddenly bears a poison fruit which we must pluck' (*L* 2, 79). So Keats wrote in March 1819, aware that the story of the Keats family was largely one that had borne 'poison fruit'. It began with a visit from their father on Saturday, 14 April 1804; they passed some happy hours, and then Thomas Keates mounted his horse to ride back home. In the early hours of the next morning a night watchman at Bunhill Fields saw a riderless horse go past: as Robert Gittings drily observed, in an era when everyone could ride, this was a sign of trouble akin to 'a loose ice-axe slipping down a Swiss mountain'.[3] A watchman found Thomas Keates, insensible and bleeding from his head; he was carried home, and he died without regaining consciousness. The Keats boys, when they heard, must have been devastated. Perhaps the surest sign of the effect of this sudden loss is the extraordinary power with which the word 'gone' is imbued throughout Keats's poetry and prose.

Thomas Keates's death would prove a seed of trouble from which the family would never recover. His funeral was held on 23 April – St George's day, traditionally held to be Shakespeare's birthday. In later years Keats's veneration for Shakespeare would merge with memories of his father and the security his father's presence had imparted – a sense of stability that he never experienced again. In the spring of 1817, about to begin *Endymion*, he travelled alone on the anniversary night of Monday 14 April from London to Southampton. Arrived at Southampton, he wrote enigmatically to his brothers '*N.B. this tuesday Morn saw the Sun rise* – of which I shall say nothing' (*L* 1, 128), and in subsequent weeks became increasingly preoccupied with the idea of Shakespeare as his 'Presider' (*L* 1, 142). From now on Thomas Keates's death would be associated with the life of poetry so vividly available in Shakespeare's words.

Immediately after their father's funeral, the younger children (Tom and Fanny) went to live with their Jennings grandparents, while Elizabeth Keats – presumably related to Thomas – attended to the business. John and George returned to school, where they 'loved, jangled, and fought alternately' (*KC* 1, 284). Then, on 20 June 1804, John Jennings transferred the lease on Keates's Livery Stables to their mother – apparently without knowing of Frances Keats's future plans. On 27 June 1804, she married William Rawlings, a young bank clerk, once again at St George's Hanover Square. The speed of this re-marriage deeply affected her children, aroused the distrust and disapproval of her parents, and would have far-reaching consequences for them all. John Jennings, having seen a business he had built up over thirty years pass with this marriage into the hands of a stranger, attempted, when he made his will on 1 February 1805, to ensure that any offspring of Frances's second marriage would not benefit from his property. In doing so, he produced a document that was ambiguous in some of its details, but clearly left his daughter a far smaller share of his estate than either his wife, Alice, or his son Midgley John, both of whom were appointed executors. When John Jennings died on 8 March 1805, Frances was struggling with Keates's Livery Stables, which had been failing since Thomas's death. Eleven days after Jennings's funeral on 14 March, the lease on the Stables was due for renewal, and for those eleven days, the executors did nothing. To Frances, who was desperately trying to keep her business viable and hard-pressed for money, this must have seemed deliberately provocative.

It was only in early April that Frances learnt of her legacy – a £50 annuity payment each year. Dissatisfied with their relatively modest portion, Frances and Rawlings drew up a 'Bill of Complaint' alleging that the executors had concealed information; possessed stocks, funds and securities not mentioned in the will; and withheld Frances's annuity. Furthermore, they contended that they were entitled to a third share of the capital that produced Alice's annuity, a half share of Midgley John's capital after his death, and any undisposed funds. Now, they sought to place the will before 'a Court of Equity'. If they were hoping for a quick resolution, they were to be disappointed: Midgley John and Alice both responded promptly, presenting their views of the situation (which naturally differed from and challenged the Rawlings's bill), and the case dragged on in Chancery, with the first of many hearings held on 8 May 1805, and judgement being given only on 29 July 1806. In the interim, Frances's annuity was 'retained', and – with both her mother and brother opposed to her in court – she had no family support to fall back on either. As the case continued, with no end in sight, Frances and her husband gave up the lease on Keates's Livery Stables.[4]

When Chancery finally ruled, the judgement went against Frances. With her hopes dashed and her marriage in ruins, she disappeared. The result of the Chancery case was a complicated settlement that set the Keats children and their uncle's family at odds. Midgley John did not survive long to enjoy his victory: in late 1807, he received four months' sick leave from the navy: ominously, he was spitting blood, and died of consumption in November 1808. By the terms of the Chancery judgement in 1806, his inheritance was now returned to the estate and Alice Jennings duly received a share of it. When Chancery reported again in the following summer, £1000 in cash was allocated to the Keats children, to be held until they came of age.

In midsummer 1806, Alice moved to Edmonton, and her grandsons walked over from Enfield to spend the summer holidays. Keats would later recall for his sister his adventures exploring the fields and streams and 'how fond I used to be of Goldfinches, Tomtits, Minnows, Mice, Ticklebacks, Dace, Cock salmons and all the whole tribe of the Bushes and the Brooks' (*L* 2, 46) many of which he tried to keep in 'washing tubs' ignoring the protests of his 'Granny-good' (*L* 1, 314). Life for the Keats children appears to have continued steadily, even happily: Alice provided her grandchildren with a home, and the boys spent their terms in the nurturing atmosphere of Clarke's Academy. John and Isabella Clarke took a close interest in the Keats boys, and their son, Charles Cowden Clarke, an assistant master in the school, was a mentor to them – especially John. In time, this relationship would deepen and prove to be one of the most influential of Keats's life.

It was at this period of their lives in late 1808 to early 1809 that their mother reappeared. Where Frances Keats had gone to and what had happened to her are unknown; it is certain, though, that she returned ill with 'a rheumatism' (*KC* 1, 288). With nowhere to go, she was reconciled with her mother, and Alice Jennings took her in. Her return, in such a state, affected her eldest son deeply. Frances was in need of medical assistance, and the local apothecary-surgeon, Thomas Hammond, was summoned. As Frances's illness progressed and showed signs of taking a turn for the worst, Hammond remained in attendance.

From now on Keats proved to be a voracious, and committed, reader. Earlier no one had thought to describe him as a scholar; now there was always a book in front of him. He read as much as he could, whenever he could: at mealtimes there was a book open as his hand groped for the next morsel; he read in bed; he had to be chased out of the school room by masters to take exercise. Clarke remembered that he was an orderly scholar, and read a surprising amount. Much of his reading at this time would influence his later poetry, from Robertson's *History of America*, to Milton's works, copies of *The Examiner*, and three books that Clarke said he 'appeared to *learn*':[5] Lemprière's *Bibliotheca Classica*, Spence's *Polymetis*, and *The Pantheon*. All three were encyclopaedic compilations of classical learning. There is little doubt that the immediate cause of this sudden scholarly dedication was the return of his mother. He earned his first school prize at midsummer 1809: a copy of Kauffman's *Dictionary of Merchandize* – an unlikely source for poetic inspiration that Keats transmuted into poetic gold in works such as *The Eve of St. Agnes* and *Lamia*.

On their Christmas holiday from Enfield, the boys must have known that their mother was desperately ill and Keats, then fourteen, took over the duties of nursing her. He helped her with her food, administered medicines, read to her in her quiet moments, and slept in a chair by her bed. When he returned to school in January 1810, he clung desperately to the hope that she would recover – but in March she died. When Keats heard of his mother's death, he withdrew under the master's desk, hiding from the sympathy of his fellows. His conviction, expressed as an adult, that a malign star blasted the lives of the Keatses surely originated in these childhood experiences, when every experience of happiness or stability seemed to 'sprout' devastation and sorrow.

Aware that her grandchildren were now orphans, Alice acted to ensure that, should anything befall her, they would still be provided for: on 30 July 1810, she placed all of her capital (£8,500 stock plus some £270 cash) in a trust for her grandchildren, appointing two businessmen, Richard Abbey and John Nowland Sandell, as trustees. The Keats children now had two separate funds available to them: their grandmother's trust, as just described, and, separately, the funds in Chancery comprising the £1000 cash legacy allocated to them from their grandfather's estate, plus the stock that had supplied their mother's annuity (this amounted to some £800 for each child, plus interest, at age twenty-one).[6] This money in Chancery, rightfully theirs and preserved to secure their future, was seemingly unknown to the Keats children and never claimed by them: as an old woman in her eighties Fanny Keats was still trying to track down what had happened to it. Had Keats actually received this money from Chancery, his life might have played out very differently in the years that produced his last and greatest volume of poetry, *Lamia, Isabella, The Eve of St. Agnes, and Other Poems*. With his financial constraints eased there would have been less pressure to publish, and his book might never have appeared at all.

Keats most likely left Enfield school in the summer of 1810, and was apprenticed for five years to Thomas Hammond, the apothecary-surgeon at Edmonton. Living close to Enfield, Keats could walk there on holidays to meet Clarke and read poetry – thus, his medical and poetic apprenticeships overlapped right from the start. While Hammond instructed him in the basics of medical practice (setting broken bones, pulling teeth, dressing wounds, bloodletting, compounding medicines), Clarke discussed poetic metres and forms: 'all the sweets of song: / The grand, the sweet, the terse, the free, the fine' ('Epistle to Charles Cowden Clarke', 53–4). He encouraged Keats to complete a translation of Virgil's *Aeneid* and introduced him to Spenser and Shakespeare; meanwhile, a fellow apprentice at Hammond's recalled Keats as 'an idle loafing fellow, always writing poetry'.[7]

Clarke said later that this was the 'most placid period' of Keats's life, although he was not happy as Hammond's apprentice.[8] In September 1819, Keats recalled how 'seven years ago … this hand … clench'd itself against Hammond' (*L* 2, 208); Richard Abbey – Keats's guardian – told John Taylor that Hammond 'did not however conduct himself as … he ought to have done to his young Pupil' (*KC* 1, 307). There is thus good reason to suppose that Keats quit his apprenticeship before his full five years was completed, apparently with Hammond's agreement.[9] If that was so, by mid-1814 he may have made his way to London and the teaching hospitals there, apparently losing touch with Clarke as he did so.

He was certainly in London by the summer of 1815, when he met George Felton Mathew, a minor poet, and joined the circle around him. Registered as a Surgeon's Pupil at the united teaching hospitals of Guy's and St Thomas's on 1 October 1815, he enrolled for lecture courses on Chemistry, Practice of Medicine, Theory of Medicine and Materia Medica (medical materials). His attendance at Astley Cooper's and Henry Cline Junior's joint course on 'Anatomy, and the Principal Operations of Surgery' is recorded in his notebook (which survives at London Metropolitan Archives). He also bought a ticket with 'perpetual' validity to attend William Allen's lectures on Experimental Philosophy, and very likely attended Cooper's more specialised evening lecture course on Surgery. Within four weeks of enrolling he was informed that he would be appointed to a Dressership on 3 March 1816. Dressers had a senior role, assisting surgeons in the performance of operations and providing much of the pre- and post-operative patient care. During 'Duty' week, a Dresser lived full-time in the hospital and attended emergencies. Keats's swift promotion to a Dressership suggests that his skills were already well-known at Guy's, and may indicate that he had been present in London medical circles for some time. Certainly it speaks for a professional medical status and sense of responsibility in months when he had also been developing productively as a poet.[10] Between October 1815 and 25 July 1816, when he took his Licentiate Examination, Keats wrote ten and possibly as many as twelve poems, including his first to be published – 'To Solitude!' – in *The Examiner* on 5 May 1816.

At first Keats lodged with two senior medical students, George Cooper and Frederick Tyrell, then moved in with fellow students Henry Stephens and George Wilson Mackereth. Stephens recollected that he was 'quick & apt at learning', adding that 'Poetry was … the zenith of all his Aspirations' (*KC* 2, 210; 208). Keats's medical notebook shows him to have been an interested student, with an ear for Cooper's flamboyant details and well-turned phrases, who paid attention to lectures and took care to organise his notes. Apt at learning and competent in Latin, Keats passed his Licentiate Examination when both of his fellow-lodgers failed. Having thereby secured one means of gaining a living, in August 1816, he holidayed at Margate and started to contemplate a different kind of future. Hitherto, he had pursued his medical training, lodging close to the hospitals; at Margate, he was accompanied by his brother Tom, and the three poems he wrote there were addressed to figures beyond his circle at Guy's: his brother George and Charles Cowden Clarke. A new note also entered his poetry at this point: it became more introspective, ambitious and thought-provoking, looking to his past to open questions about his future – thinking 'on what will be, and what has been' (sonnet 'To My Brother George', 8). His 'Epistle to Charles Cowden Clarke' would be particularly significant to his development as a poet: by reconnecting him with his old mentor, the poem to Clarke would eventually lead to 'an Era in [his] existence' (*L* 1, 113) and his first meeting with Leigh Hunt on 19 October 1816. In Hunt and his acquaintances Benjamin Robert Haydon and John Hamilton Reynolds, Keats made contact with established writers and artists who thought highly of his poetic talents, and were acquainted with two of Keats's poetic heroes: Byron and Wordsworth.

The effect on his poetic output was immediate: while continuing as a Dresser at Guy's he wrote at least twenty-six poems during the eight months from late July 1816 to early March 1817. In terms of quality, too, there was a change: the first poem he wrote after meeting Hunt was 'On First Looking into Chapman's Homer', a sonnet that displays formal control as well as the extraordinary verbal concentration that would characterise much of his greatest poetry.

After the Margate summer of 1816, the attractions of life outside medical circles grew stronger. Keats was now living with his brothers in Dean Street, Southwark, from where they moved across the Thames to Cheapside. Despite his heavy workload at Guy's he frequently visited Haydon's studio and Hunt's home at the Vale of Health. In the autumn of 1816, he took the decision to publish his first collection of poems, and by December he was preparing it for the press.[11] Haydon's admiration, Clarke's support, Reynolds's friendship, and the adulation of his brothers all encouraged that decision, and Hunt's public enrolment of Keats alongside Shelley and Reynolds in his 'new school of poetry rising of late' set a seal upon it.[12] Stephens certainly recalled this moment as a turning point: it was now that Keats 'gave himself up more completely than before to Poetry' (*KC* 2, 211). Thus, December 1816 is likely to be when he resolved not to pursue a medical career when his Dressership at Guy's ended.

In taking this decision, Keats was not abandoning his medical training altogether, and the idea of returning to it would be repeatedly voiced in his letters. As late as June 1820, for instance, he suggested that he might try what he could 'do in the Apothecary line' (*L* 2, 298) – as if he was attempting to recover the productive 'busy time' of his life at Guy's (*L* 1, 113) when *Poems, by John Keats* was assembled during his free hours at home in Cheapside. He kept his medical books long after leaving the hospital, writing in May 1818 that he was 'glad at not having given [them] away' (*L* 1, 277) and believed that medicine and poetry shared the same purpose: to aid humanity by relieving suffering. That Keatsian ideal is perhaps best expressed in *The Fall of Hyperion*, where the poet is explicitly described as 'physician to all men' (1. 190). Among the details of human anatomy and physiology that Keats jotted down in his medical notebook are vignettes that were later reworked into poetry. Behind the fallen Titans in *Hyperion*, 'horribly convuls'd / With sanguine feverous boiling gurge of pulse' (2. 27–8) may lie the observation that feverish conditions of 'Heat readily increases the Pulse' and that arteries 'have power of expelling the Blood in the last Struggles of Life';[13] that Apollo dies into life 'with fierce convulse' may likewise be a recollection from Guy's (3. 129). *Poems, by John Keats*, with its dedication to Leigh Hunt declaring his literary and liberal sympathies, was published around 3 March 1817, at exactly the moment when his contracted year as a Dresser at Guy's ended. From now onwards, Keats told his guardian Richard Abbey, he would 'rely upon [his] Abilities as a Poet' to 'gain [his] Living' (*KC* 1, 307).

Notes

1 *The Diary of Benjamin Robert Haydon*, ed. W. B. Pope, 5 vols. (Cambridge, MA: Harvard University Press, 1960), vol. 2, p. 107.
2 H. C. Cameron, *Mr. Guy's Hospital 1726–1948* (London: Longmans, 1954), p. 40.
3 Robert Gittings, *John Keats* (London: Heinemann, 1968), p. 18.
4 For the complex Chancery case, see Robert Gittings, *The Keats Inheritance* (London: Heinemann, 1964).
5 Charles and Mary Cowden Clarke, *Recollections of Writers* (London: Sampson Low, Marston, Searle, and Rivington, 1878), p. 124.
6 These accounts are summarised in Nicholas Roe, *John Keats. A New Life* (London and New Haven: Yale University Press, 2012), pp. 41–2.
7 Sidney Colvin, *John Keats, His Life and Poetry His Friends Critics and After-Fame* (London: Macmillan, 1917), p. 17.
8 Clarke, *Recollections*, p. 125.
9 See Roe, *John Keats*, pp. 47–8; 55–7.
10 See 'Dressing for Art: Notes from Keats in the Emergency Ward', *Times Literary Supplement* (29 May 2015), pp. 14–15.
11 Roe, *John Keats*, pp. 133–8.
12 'Young Poets', *The Examiner* (1 December 1816), p. 761.
13 *John Keats's Anatomical and Physiological Note Book*, ed. Maurice Buxton Forman (Oxford: Oxford University Press, 1934), pp. 9, 10.

CHAPTER 3

Surgery, Science and Suffering

Nicholas Roe

> Feel, feel my pulse, how much in love I am;
> And if your science is not all a sham,
> Tell me some means to get the lady here.
> (400–2)

In John Keats's strange late poem 'The Jealousies', magician Hum's mastery of medicine and science is matched by his lyrical command of language. Keats, too, was an adept in 'magian' lore: at school he studied astronomy, botany, history, latin, mathematics, mechanics and optics, then left to write his poems while apprenticed to Thomas Hammond. When he registered at Guy's Hospital, he was already experienced, and was swiftly promoted to a Dressership – an Assistant Surgeon. On 25 July 1816, he qualified as an Apothecary and continued as a Dresser until he left Guy's. His first collection, *Poems, by John Keats*, appeared early in March 1817. Its publication has been understood to signal that Keats had abandoned medicine, although such single-mindedness is unlikely in a poet who confessed to being 'undecided', 'uncertain', 'all in a mist' (*P* 102–3; *L* 2, 167). For Keats the alternatives of medicine and poetry were never fully resolved. 'I have been ... turning it in my head whether I should ... study for a physician', he admitted in March 1819, just before he composed 'La Belle Dame sans Merci'. In May 1819 – the month of 'Ode to a Nightingale' – he thought of becoming a ship's surgeon. And in June 1820, seriously ill and with his *Lamia* volume forthcoming, he proposed to 'try ... the Apothecary line' (*L* 2, 70, 95, 114–5, 298). Throughout Keats's writing life, medicine and science continued to surface in his poetry. In his medical notebook he recorded that at the body's extremities, the colour of blood 'undergoes a change from its florid'. Five years later, as tuberculosis destroyed his lungs, 'This living hand' voiced a bitter rejoinder: 'thou would wish thine own heart dry of blood, / So in my veins red life might stream again' (5–6).[1]

His seventeen months at Guy's coincided with transitions in medicine.[2] He was among the first to take the new Licentiate Examination, introduced in summer 1816 to regulate the profession. While traditional medicines were losing favour (surgeon Astley Cooper warned against mercury), Edward Jenner's development of vaccination marked a leap forward in preventative treatment. Opium and plant extracts could induce 'drowsy numbness', and the more effective anaesthetic power of nitrous oxide, recently discovered, would soon be adopted. Herbs and other plants had been cures and poisons since classical times, and Keats's poems imagine the double nature of henbane, wolf's bane and nightshade. His sense that a sickroom 'must be poisonous to life' anticipates modern understanding of disease transmission, as does his awareness that air 'too confined' was harmful (*L* 1, 267, 369).

Keats studied courses on 'Anatomy and the Operations of Surgery' (taught by Astley Cooper and Henry Cline Jr.), the Practice of Medicine, Chemistry, the Theory of Medicine and Materia Medica.[3] At evening classes on 'Principles and Practice of Surgery', Cooper brought patients from the wards, showed specimens and conducted dissections. These evening lectures were necessary if Keats aimed to become a Surgeon, and all the indications are that this was what he planned.[4] His ticket for William Allen's lectures on 'Experimental Philosophy' gave him access to more esoteric knowledge. Allen was a Quaker scientist–philanthropist who experimented with anaesthetic gases and campaigned to abolish slavery and capital punishment; his lectures ranged through astronomy, gravity, electrical fluid, evaporation, organic forms, the speed of light, the spectrum and human senses.[5] Keats's idea that a poet's imagination 'alchymized' impressions to create an ideal 'essence' may well have grown from one of Allen's speculative forays (*L* 1, 218; *Endymion*, 1. 777–81).[6]

Keats's daily routine at Guy's was as follows: at 10 am on Mondays, Wednesdays and Fridays – lectures on the Practice of Medicine; at 10 am on Tuesdays, Thursdays and Saturdays – lectures on Chemistry. Afterwards he dashed off for hospital rounds or the operating theatre, and on Wednesdays and Thursdays helped admit and discharge patients. At 2 pm he was ready for Cooper's lecture at St Thomas's, and at 4 joined in dissecting corpses supplied by 'resurrection men'. As many as two hundred students dissected, and the stench of rotten flesh was overwhelming.[7] Cutting into a corpse was also hazardous: a slight wound to a finger could lead to infection and death.[8] The poet who wrote in *Isabella* of Lorenzo's 'soilèd glove' (369) and 'each eye's sepulchral cell' (404) knew what a resurrected body looked like.

Living at 28 St Thomas's Street, Southwark, Keats was close to the sites of Chaucer's Tabard Inn and Shakespeare's Globe; a little further away was

Surrey prison, where Leigh Hunt was held until February 1815. Confined in the inner city, Keats was drawn to imagined 'regions of his own' beyond the wards, and with Chaucer, Shakespeare and Hunt as inspiring neighbours, poetry was never out of mind – even while studying for his Licentiate examination. Cooper's lectures were lively prompts to poetic reflection. He was struck by Cooper's speculation about whether 'Blood possessed Vitality' and noted Cooper's anecdote about the Polish patriot Kosciusko: 'having had the Sciatic Nerve divided by a Pike wound [it] was a long while before his limb recovered its sensibility'. Oddities like 'the Behaviour of a Frog after having been guilloteened' caught his attention, as did Cooper's recommendation: 'Snuff to ye Nose, Purgatives to ye intestines'.[9] His medical notebook survives as an extraordinary document that can stand comparison with his poetry manuscripts. The impression throughout is of a diligent student arranging notes for clarity and accessibility; additional remarks were written along margins, or inserted later, creating structural patterns anticipating the great odes of 1819. Like his prize copies of Kauffman's *Dictionary of Merchandise* and Bonnycastle's *Introduction to Astronomy*, Keats's medical notebook became a quarry for poetry. Before Guy's his poems featured conventional figures of 'Despair' and 'Hope'. After Guy's, he could imagine the throbbing life of muscles, nerves, arteries, bone and blood – most powerfully perhaps in Lamia's convulsive change, as her feverish inflammation becomes a virulent eruption of 'volcanian' intensity (*Lamia*, I. 148–56).

One cue for poetry was William Babington lecturing on the philosophical merits of art and science. Whereas the artist is 'selfish [and] constantly labouring in his own interest … from imitation and without principle', a 'Phylosopher or man of Science is in search of truth … to make a general application … for the benefit of his fellow creatures'.[10] Babington challenged Keats with questions about poetic identity and how poetry could 'benefit' others, and we can hear his voice in *The Fall of Hyperion* when Moneta parleys with the poet-dreamer:

> What benefit canst thou do, or all thy tribe,
> To the great world? Thou art a dreaming thing;
> A fever of thyself – think of the earth …
> (*The Fall of Hyperion*, I. 167–9)

Like Babington's lectures, William Hazlitt's lecture 'On Poetry in General' captured poetry's crisis in an age of scientific advance: 'The province of the imagination is … visionary', Hazlitt claimed, whereas 'the understanding restores things to their natural boundaries, and strips them of … fanciful pretensions'.[11] Keats feared that his 'teeming brain' might not find its voice, that he would never fulfil his ambition, that 'cold philosophy' – science as a mere 'catalogue' of observations – had robbed the rainbow of its mystery.[12] For Keats – as Richard Dawkins's *Unweaving the Rainbow* omitted to notice – Newtonian science became a prompt to embrace poetry's warm knowledge of life. Like the great astronomer William Herschel, who discovered the 'new planet', poets were passionate 'watchers of the sky' too (see 'On First Looking into Chapman's Homer', 10, 9).

Early in 1816 Keats's fellow students Henry Stephens and George Mackereth enrolled in Guy's Physical Society, where medical discoveries were discussed (John Thelwall's pioneering lecture on 'Animal Vitality' was delivered here in January 1793). Keats's acquaintance John Spurgin also attended and spoke, but there is no record that Keats himself joined.[13] While he kept to the hospital's routines it was poetry, Stephens remembered, that claimed 'the zenith of … his Aspirations' (*KC* 2, 206–14).[14]

On 3 March 1816, he became a Dresser: every three weeks one of the senior surgeons took a week's duty, and for that week one of his Dressers would stay all day, every day, at the hospital.[15] The duty Dresser was 'called to the first management of serious accidents', treated outpatients, performed minor operations and took charge of patients before the surgeon attended.[16]

Surgical operations, scheduled for Friday afternoons, were conducted on a simple wooden table with students watching.[17] Half a century before Pasteur and Lister, there was little understanding of antisepsis and, apart from traditional sedatives, nothing to offset the agony of surgery. As a Dresser Keats would have restrained patients, applied tourniquets, bandaged wounds and disposed of amputated limbs. Richard Hengist Horne, former pupil at Enfield School, reported him saying that there was 'great pleasure in alleviating suffering, but it was a dreadful profession on account of having to witness so much'.[18]

Dressing and binding wounds was a responsibility in which Keats reportedly found 'great pleasure'; accordingly, the words 'dress', 'drest', 'bind' and 'band' acquired particular force, linking the gratification of healing with poetry's assuaging discipline. One of the few accounts of Keats at Guy's comes from Henry Stephens, who recalled that he had 'no desire to excel' in medicine – his 'absolute devotion' was to poetry (*KC* 2, 208, 210–11). Stephens seems to have held a grudge at having failed the qualifying examination when Keats's skill at latin ('the common language of medicine'[19]) enabled him to pass.[20] The 'Regulations of the Apothecaries' Society' required students to 'translate grammatically parts of the Pharmacopoeia

Londoniensis, and Physicians' Prescriptions', and warned: 'The Court are anxious to impress ... the necessity of a knowledge of ... Latin, because they have had the painful duty ... of rejecting several persons ... from their deficiency in this important pre-requisite of a Medical Education.[21] Stephens recalled that Keats's 'knowledge of the Classics helped him ... – He was a tolerable swimmer for I remember going with him once to the New River, to Bathe' (*KC* 2, 211). Stephens' deflection to a swimming jaunt takes us to the source of Keats's expertise at Latin. The New River flowed past the schoolhouse at Enfield, where Keats had translated *The Aeneid* and explored Lemprière's *Classical Dictionary*.

Now that the 'busy time has just gone by', Keats told Charles Cowden Clarke, he could anticipate meeting Leigh Hunt (*L* 1, 113). Evident here is Keats's endeavour to keep hospital commitments separate from poetry. What Keats feared most, Charles Brown remembered, were moments when his clinical poise might be lost, rendering him 'unfit to perform a surgical operation' (*KC* 2, 56). We have many records of Keats's tendency towards poetic abstraction, and just one account of him actually working at Guy's.

On Monday 25 March 1816, Jane Hull went to a public house in South London and called for a drink, whereupon a man walked up to her and fired a pistol. She collapsed, wounded in her head, and was hurried to Guy's Hospital. A pistol, powder and ball were found in the man's pockets along with letters 'informing him that his wife was false to him'.[22] Four weeks later Mrs. Hull was interviewed about the shooting, as were witnesses. Also present to give evidence was 'Mr. Keats, one of the Surgeons belonging to Guy's Hospital'.[23] Keats had begun his dressership just three weeks before Mrs. Hull was admitted, and his report to the inquest, printed by the *Morning Chronicle* on 23 April 1816, described her head wounds:

> Mr. Keats, one of the Surgeons belonging to Guy's Hospital, stated, that Mrs. Hull was brought into the hospital on the 25th of March. She had received a severe wound in the back part of her head with a pistol ball; the ball had pierced the lobe of her ear, taken a direction along the occiput, and lodged in the neck, from whence the witness extracted it. Mr. Keats produced the ball, which fitted the pistol found upon the prisoner.[24]

Keats's medical notebook locates the 'occiput' at the lower back of the skull: the 'Os Occipitis', Keats noted, 'is but rarely broken'.[25] Thus, the pistol ball had not penetrated the woman's skull, but glanced off the bone sideways 'along the occiput' to embed itself in her neck from where Keats had 'extracted it'. Evidently his role corresponded to what would now be called 'Accident and Emergency'.

For Keats this case had occurred at a significant moment. It shows that, as an experienced physician, he could have hoped to build a career at a London hospital. For the aspirant poet who had yet to see print, it may well have brought about his first publication. *The Morning Chronicle* reported 'Mr. Keats, one of the Surgeons' on 23 April, by coincidence a date of personal significance (his father had died 'of a mortal bruise … upon his head', and his funeral was on this day in 1804; 23 April was traditionally the birthday of Keats's 'presider' Shakespeare).[26] When *The Examiner* noticed the inquiry it did not mention 'Mr. Keats', although this issue for Sunday 28 April 1816 proved momentous nevertheless. In it Leigh Hunt mentioned Keats's poetry for the first time: 'J. K., and other Communications, next week'.[27] Seven days later Keats's sonnet 'To Solitude' appeared, introducing a new poet from that 'beastly place' surrounding Guy's Hospital:

O SOLITUDE! if I must with thee dwell,
   Let it not be among the jumbled heap
   Of murky buildings; – climb with me the steep,
Nature's Observatory – whence the dell,
Its flowery slopes – its river's crystal swell
   May seem a span: let me thy vigils keep
   'Mongst boughs pavilioned; where the Deer's swift leap
Startles the wild Bee from the Fox-glove bell.
Ah! fain would I frequent such scenes with thee;
   But the sweet converse of an innocent mind,
   Whose words are images of thoughts refin'd,
Is my soul's pleasure; and it sure must be
   Almost the highest bliss of human kind,
When to thy haunts two kindred spirits flee.

J. K.[28]

'To Solitude' marked Keats's intervention in a debate about Wordsworth's egotism and remoteness in Hazlitt's *Examiner* review of *The Excursion* and Shelley's *Alastor*. By responding to Wordsworth's seclusion with a sonnet of sympathetic 'converse', 'J.K.' aligned himself with Hazlitt and Hunt. South of the Thames, his sonnet voiced a more personal longing to escape his hospital vigils, while 'innocent converse' could reflect upon the Hull story of 'false intimacy' and 'criminal conversation'.

'[T]wo kindred spirits flee', Keats's sonnet concludes. Yet repeated wrenching transitions between bloody lancets and lyrical beauties brought home to him how inextricably his lives as physician and poet were connected. From his recognition that both roles sought to alleviate suffering sprang his ambition for 'a nobler life, / Where I may find the agonies, the strife / Of human hearts' ('Sleep and Poetry', 123–5). That 'nobler life' measured 'poetical purposes' against dreadful scenes at Guy's; thus, a self-imposed test in *Endymion* was to imagine the physiognomy of pain, in 'the trembling knee / And frantic gape of lonely Niobe' (1. 337–8) and Glaucus's 'convuls'd clenches' (3. 231). *Hyperion* surveys the Titans' 'hearts / Heaving in pain', and 'eyes at horrid working' (2. 24, 24–5, 26–7, 51–2), with the imaginative sympathy and calm detachment that had enabled Keats to conduct surgical operations. This complex act of identification and distancing, steadying him as a surgeon amid uncertainties and doubt of success, anticipates his self-effacing ideal of 'negative capability' – 'that is when a man is capable of being in uncertainties, Mysteries, doubts'. As a surgeon and poet Keats operated in 'half knowledge' – tentatively feeling his way into what he called the 'Penetralium', the innermost part.[29]

Jane Hull survived, and her story may resurface in Keats's later writing. Having quit the Isle of Wight for Margate, Keats anticipated resuming *Endymion*: 'I was not right in my head when I came [to Margate]', he told his publishers, '– At Cant^{y} I hope that the Remembrance of Chaucer will set me forward like a Billiard-Ball – I am gald to hear of M^{r} T's health' (*L* 1, 146–7). His letter moves from 'not right in my head' to a ball 'set forward', reversing the sequence of a ball 'set forward' to cause a head wound. That might seem far-fetched, yet Keats's word 'gald' for 'glad' makes it plausible in that the OED cites one sense of 'gald' as harassed or annoyed by gunshot.[30]

Hopes of being 'set forward like a Billiard-Ball' also foreshadowed his thoughts on 'poetical character' in a letter of 27 October 1818. Richard Woodhouse's 'Notes on a Letter from Keats' reports that '[Keats] affirmed that he can conceive of a billiard Ball that it may have a sense of delight from its own roundness, smoothness & very volubility & the rapidity of its own motion' (*KC* 1, 59). While a billiard ball is not a pistol ball, their roundness, smoothness and rapidity are shared – like their 'volubility', that is, their rolling, revolving motion and tendency to 'take a direction' – into a pocket, or 'along the occiput' to 'lodge in the neck'. Lurking behind these associations may be the fact that 'a fashionable pursuit with medical students' was a 'pernicious' recreation – '*billiards*'. Wasting time at billiards, 'Aesculapius' warned, was a 'prominent method of *murdering talent*' (italics in original).[31]

In his report to the Hull inquest we hear the Keats who might have made a career as a surgeon. That he would become a poet of Shakespearean imagination was less obvious when he 'produced the ball', although his explanation of Mrs. Hull's head wound held imaginative potential. The pistol ball took 'a direction along the occiput': that clinical expression may forestall any possibility that 'along the occiput' echoed Wordsworth's phrase 'felt along the heart' in 'Tintern Abbey'. Yet it is almost as if 'Mr. Keats' the surgeon changes places with 'J.K.' the poet for whom, two years later, 'Tintern Abbey' prompted speculation about the dark passages and chambers of human consciousness in his letter to John Hamilton Reynolds of May 1818. Opening with reflections on Reynolds's illness, Tom Keats's fever and his own 'uneasy state of Mind', this letter suggests how 'study [of] physic or rather Medicine' and 'medical Books' had led to 'widening speculation' that sharpens 'one's vision into the head and nature of Man' (*L* I, 275–81).

This letter to Reynolds survives in a transcript by Woodhouse's clerk, in which Woodhouse himself corrected 'head and nature' to read 'heart and nature'. On the face of it, Keats had originally written 'heart' which Woodhouse's clerk misread as 'head' – a simple mistranscription, caught and corrected by Woodhouse. As Rollins pointed out in his edition of Keats's letters, Woodhouse was 'a painstaking copyist whose transcripts are, in the main, reliable' – and, in this instance, Rollins bracketed the cancelled reading 'head' as 'of interest or significance' (*L* I, 16, 18). Possibly Woodhouse's correction of 'head' to 'heart' reproduced an identical alteration in Keats's manuscript, overlooked by the clerk; the cerebral tendency of surrounding phrases – 'thoughtless Chamber ... thinking principle ... Chamber of Maiden-Thought ... advance of intellect ... greatness of Mind' – suggest that 'vision into the head' could have been Keats's first thought (*L* I, 280–1). In this context of passages, chambers, 'Misery and Heartbreak, Pain, Sickness', the thought of 'vision into the head' might well have awoken memories of peering into the flesh that surrounded a human skull and brain.

The Hull story shows Keats as an accomplished young surgeon, at a time when lectures, dissections, surgery and scientific speculations were providing material for the imaginative and verbal world of his poetry. The little sketches of a human skull and flowering plants with which he decorated his medical notebook were much more than distractions from lectures. Together they prefigured Lorenzo's mouldering head and the sweet basil plant of *Isabella*. And in *The Fall of Hyperion*, perhaps it was his memory of a pistol ball's passage along a human occiput that came to him as he wrote of 'sad Moneta' – and of how he 'ached to see ... what high tragedy / In the dark secret chambers of her skull / Was acting' (I. 256, 276–8).

Notes

1 See *John Keats's Anatomical and Physiological Notebook*, ed. Maurice Buxton Forman (Oxford: Oxford University Press, 1934), pp. 4–5.

2 For the wider 'chaotic' context, see S. W. F. Holloway, 'The Apothecaries' Act, 1815: A Reinterpretation, Part I', *Medical History*, 10. 2 (1966): 107–29.

3 Guy's Hospital Papers at King's College London Archive: 'Anatomical Pupils 1814–21', TH/FP1/2; *Memorials of John Flint South*, 31; F. G. Parsons, *The History of St. Thomas's Hospital,* 3 vols. (London, 1932–6), vol. 3, p. 35.
4 See John Barnard, '"The Busy Time": Keats's Duties at Guy's Hospital from Autumn 1816 to March 1817', *Romanticism*, 13. 3 (2007): 201–3, and Donald C. Goellnicht, *The Poet-Physician. Keats and Medical Science* (Pittsburgh: University of Pittsburgh Press, 1984), pp. 23–4, 32.
5 William Allen, *Substance of an Address to the Students at Guy's Hospital* (London, 1823).
6 Stuart Sperry, *Keats the Poet* (Princeton: Princeton University Press, 1973), pp. 302–7 and my *John Keats and the Culture of Dissent* (Oxford: Oxford University Press, 1997), pp. 187–91.
7 Benjamin Golding, *An Historical Account of St Thomas's Hospital, Southwark* (London, 1819), p. 128; Bransby Blake Cooper, *The Life of Sir Astley Cooper, Bart,* 2 vols. (London, 1843), vol. 2, pp. 411–13.
8 See Druin Burch, *Digging Up the Dead. Uncovering the Life and Times of an Extraordinary Surgeon* (London: Chatto & Windus, 2007), pp. 198–9.
9 JKAP, pp. 5, 10, 55, 56, 64.
10 Introductory Lecture 'On Chemistry', in Goellnicht, *The Poet-Physician*, pp. 51–2.
11 *Lectures on the English Poets*; 'On Poetry in General', *The Complete Works of William* Hazlitt, ed. P. P. Howe, 21 vols. (London: Dent, 1930–4), vol. 5, p. 9.
12 See Keats's review 'Mr Kean', *The Champion* (21 December 1817), in *John Keats. The Complete Poems*, ed. John Barnard (Harmondsworth: Penguin, 1973), pp. 529–31 and compare *Lamia*, 2. 229–37.
13 'Physical Society Guy's Hospital 1813–20', KCL Archive, G/S4/M9.
14 William S. Pierpoint, *John Keats, Henry Stephens and George Wilson Mackereth: The Unparallel Lives of Three Medical Students* (London: The Stephens Collection, 2010), hereafter TMS.
15 See Barnard, '"The Busy Time"' and H. C. Cameron, *Mr. Guy's Hospital, 1726–1948* (London: Longmans, 1954), pp. 146–7, 151–2.
16 'Aesculapius', *The Hospital Pupil's Guide, Being Oracular Communications, Addressed to Students of the Medical Profession*, 2nd. edn (1818), p. 29, hereafter HPG. See also R. S. White, *John Keats. A Literary Life* (Houndmills: Palgrave Macmillan, 2010), pp. 15–40.
17 *Mr. Guy's Hospital*, p. 153.
18 'Keats at Edmonton', *Daily News* (8 April 1871), p. 5.
19 HPG, p. 23.
20 See TMS.
21 *The Medical Calendar: Or Students' Guide to the Medical Schools* (Edinburgh and London, 1828), p. 123.
22 See *Morning Chronicle* (27 March, 1816), p. 3.
23 For a full account of this episode, see my article 'Dressing for Art: Notes from Keats in the Emergency Ward', *TLS* (29 May 2015), pp. 14–15, and 'Mr Keats', *Essays in Criticism*, 65. 3 (July 2015): 274–88.

24 *Morning Chronicle* (23 April 1816), p. 3. HPG, 28, mentions 'being called to accidents, the first treatment of which devolves usually upon the dresser for the week'.
25 JKAP, p. 29.
26 'Inquisition Taken the 27th day of April 1804 on Thomas Keates', London Metropolitan Archive, CLA/041/1Q/02/017. For more on 23 April, Thomas Keates and Shakespeare, see my *John Keats: A New Life* (London and New Haven: Yale University Press, 2012).
27 *The Examiner* (28 April 1816), p. 264.
28 *The Examiner* (5 May 1816), p. 282 and *L* 1, 114.
29 *L* 1, 193–4. See also M. Faith McLellan, 'Literature and Medicine: Physician-Writers', *The Lancet* (22 February 1997), p. 564.
30 See OED: Gall, *v.* 1, sense 5, 'gaule them with shot' (1603).
31 HPG, pp. 49–50.

CHAPTER 4

Fanny Brawne and Other Women

Heidi Thomson

When John Keats died of tuberculosis in February 1821, he was not yet twenty-six and had been suffering intermittently from ill health for the last three years. Unlike Wordsworth, Coleridge and Blake, he was not married, and unlike Shelley and Byron, he did not have a richly documented track record of various relationships with women. Instead, Keats had much experience of nursing, an activity usually delegated to women. The awareness of his own vulnerability and mortality was exacerbated by the premature deaths of his mother and his brother Tom. Keats's youth, early death, his poetics of empathy and the sensuality of his early poetry all combined into a characterisation of delicacy and effeminacy which lasted throughout the nineteenth century: 'We see in him the youth, without the manhood of poetry.'[1] Some twentieth-century critics have read Keats's poetry in terms of his supposed misogyny.[2] Recent scholarship offers a more contextual approach, reading Keats as a great poet, as well as a mercurial young man in developmental throes.[3] At the moment of his death Keats was consumed by love for Fanny Brawne, but the full record of his life and work also points to many, more harmonious, reciprocal relationships with women of all ages. Keats's sympathetic interactions with, appreciation of and apprehensive anxiety about women inform his poetry throughout.

The first woman in Keats's life was Frances Jennings Keats who bore him a year after her marriage to Thomas Keats in 1794. Three more surviving siblings followed with whom Keats was to develop very close relationships, particularly in the wake of their father's death in April 1804 which was followed, only two months later, by their mother's re-marriage after which she mysteriously disappeared from the children's lives for a number of years. Frances' reputation as a lusty woman who re-married too soon was fuelled by Richard Abbey who alleged, as reported by John Taylor, that she 'must & would have a Husband; and her passions were so ardent, he said that it was dangerous to be alone with her' (*KC* 1, 303). By the end of 1809, her second marriage a failure, Frances was terminally ill and she died in March

1810 at the age of thirty-five, having been nursed by her fourteen-year-old son over the Christmas holidays. Back at school in Enfield by the time of her death, Keats was devastated, withdrawing 'into a nook under the master's desk'.[4] Her death, compounded by her earlier disappearance, affected Keats deeply. His loving care had failed to save her, and her premature loss would be tied up with thoughts about transience and the threat of cruelty or, as in 'La Belle Dame sans Merci', abandonment by women. He did not refer to his mother in his correspondence apart from in this postscript which also revealed his devotion to Fanny Brawne: 'My seal is mark'd like a family table cloth with my Mother's initial F for Fanny: put between my Father's initials. You will soon hear from me again. My respectful Compts to your Mother' (*L* 2, 133).

The principal woman during Keats's childhood and adolescence was Alice Jennings, the maternal grandmother with whom the Keats siblings lived during the decade between their father's death in 1804 and her own death in December 1814 at the age of seventy-eight. Keats commemorated this beacon in the children's lives in a Petrarchan sonnet written about five days after her death (*P* 4–5, 418). While this elegy consigns the dearly loved woman to 'realms above, / Regions of peace and everlasting love' (4–5), it also concludes on an early expression of the bittersweet quality of human experience: 'Wherefore does any grief our joy impair?' (14). Prompted by the loss of his beloved grandmother, Keats anticipated what became in the *Epistle to Reynolds* the 'flaw in happiness to see beyond our bourn' (82–3) and in 'Ode on Melancholy' the awareness that 'in the very temple of Delight / Veil'd Melancholy has her sovran shrine' (25–6). Keats's fond memories trickled into the graphic, largely sympathetic characterizations of old women as mediators for young people. In 'Isabella', the heroine's 'aged nurse' (343) wonders at the young woman's desperate digging but 'her heart felt pity to the core / At sight of such a dismal laboring, / And so she kneeled, with her locks all hoar, / And put her lean hands to the horrid thing' (378–81). Angela, Madeline's nurse in *The Eve of St. Agnes*, is described in her interaction with Porphyro who looked upon her face '[l]ike puzzled urchin on an aged crone / Who keepeth clos'd a wond'rous riddle book, / As spectacled she sits in chimney nook' (129–31). Without her, Porphyro would not have been able to fulfill his 'stratagem' (139). Despite her 'busy fear' (181) and worry that Porphyro 'must needs the lady wed' (179), Angela, herself on the threshold of death, promotes new life in the union of the young lovers.

The resilience of old women is also humorously celebrated in 'Old Meg she was a gipsey' with Meg 'brave as Margaret Queen / And tall as

Amazon: / An old red blanket cloak she wore; / A chip hat had she on' (25–8). Even Mrs Cameron, 'the fattest woman in all inverness shire' (*P* 450), is admired for her grit in 'Upon my life, Sir Nevis, I am piqu'd'. The letters of the Scottish Tour are full of observations of women of all ages, from the 'Duchess of Dunghill' to the 'two ragged tattered Girls' who carried her 'sadan' (*L* 1, 321). In July 1818, he admits to 'thinking better of Womankind than to suppose they care whether Mister John Keats five feet hight like them or not' (*L* 1, 342) and resolves to 'conquer my passions hereafter better than I have yet done' (*L* 1, 351).

Keats befriended the sisters and wives of his mostly older friends, the mother of his girlfriend Fanny Brawne, and, tellingly as an instance of familial loyalty, his brother's mother-in-law, Mrs James Wylie. In the wake of George and Georgiana's emigration to America, Keats wrote to Mrs Wylie: 'I should like to have remained near you, were it but for an atom of consolation, after parting with so dear a daughter. My brother George has ever been more than a brother to me, he has been my greatest friend, & I can never forget the sacrifice you have made for his happiness' (*L* 1, 358). And when Keats could no longer bring himself to write to Fanny Brawne herself, he still wrote to her mother and confided in her: 'I dare not fix my Mind upon Fanny. I have not dared to think of her' (*L* 2, 350).

Among Keats's relationships with younger women, the earliest and most important one was with his sister Fanny. Richard Abbey, under whose guardianship Fanny was placed after their grandmother's death, did not approve of visits between the siblings. Keats compensated for this by writing long, solicitous letters. On 10 September 1817, he urged Fanny to write frequently 'for we ought to become intimately acquainted, in order that I may not only, as you grow up love you[r] as my only Sister, but confide in you as my dearest friend' (*L* 1, 153). In that same letter he summarised the plot of *Endymion*, and explained how the Moon 'was growing mad in Love with [Endymion] – However so it was; and when he was asleep on the Grass, she used to come down from heaven and admire him excessively [for] a long time; and at last could not refrain from carrying him away in her arms to the top of that high Mountain Latmus while he was a dreaming' (*L* 1, 154). *Endymion* also featured the tempering presence of the sympathetic 'midnight spirit nurse' Peona, Endymion's 'sweet sister: of all those, / His friends, the dearest' (1. 413, 408–9). Peona was also inspired by Georgiana Wylie, his brother's future wife to whom, already in December 1816, he had written a dedicatory sonnet 'To G. A. W.' at the request of his brother. Shortly after the young couple's departure for America, in June 1818, he celebrated Georgiana in an acrostic, 'Give me your patience, sister, while

I frame', and also included the poem in a journal letter on 18 September 1819 because the original letter was returned (*L* 2, 195). To Benjamin Bailey he defined her as 'the most disinterrested woman I ever knew', and his letters to her are unfailingly witty and appreciative (*L* 1, 293).

Keats's platonic friendships with women he thought of as sisters were offset by unease and mistrust about women as lovers: 'I am certain I have not a right feeling towards Women … Is it because they fall so far beneath my Boyish imagination? … When I am among Women I have evil thoughts, malice spleen' (to Bailey, 18 July 1818, *L* 1, 341). Self-consciousness about his short stature played a part in these feelings, and when he first described Fanny Brawne to George and Georgiana in the journal letter of 16 December 1818, he started off by saying that she was 'about my height' (*L* 2, 13). But we certainly cannot attribute his unease to physical squeamishness. Keats was not yet fifteen when he was apprenticed to surgeon Thomas Hammond in August 1810, the beginning of a medical education which would extend for another six years, including training at Guy's Hospital, and which would expose him to women's bodies in various states of suffering. He would have assisted with delivering babies and alleviating the pain of ill and injured women of various ages, and this awareness transpired in his poetry. Isabella's madness as she plots to sing a 'latest lullaby' (340) to her dead lover Lorenzo is associated with maternal psychosis: when she finds Lorenzo's glove in a shallow grave she 'put it in her bosom, where it dries / And freezes utterly unto the bone / Those dainties made to still an infant's cries: / Then 'gan she work again; nor stay'd her care, / But to throw back at times her veiling hair' (372–6).

Keats infuses grief and suffering into impressions of female beauty, as in the roundelay 'O Sorrow' in Book 4 of *Endymion* (146–81). In *Hyperion*, Thea's sculptured, stoic strength is qualified by misery: 'But oh! how unlike marble was that face: / How beautiful, if sorrow had not made / Sorrow more beautiful than Beauty's self' (1. 34–6). The nightingale's song finds its way into 'the sad heart of Ruth' who 'stood in tears amid the alien corn' (67–8). La Belle Dame is 'full beautiful', but she also 'wept' and 'sigh'd full sore' (14, 30). Lamia's metamorphosis from snake to woman reverberates with searing 'scarlet pain' (1. 154), while her sad disaffection during the preparations for her doomed wedding to Lycius speaks from her movements in a 'pale contented sort of discontent' (2. 135). Moneta in *The Fall of Hyperion* symbolises eternal suffering, with her face 'bright blanch'd / By an immortal sickness which kills not; / It works a constant change, which happy death / Can put no end to; deathwards progressing / To no death was that visage' (1. 257–61). This poem also features another appearance of Thea who, compared to Moneta, is 'in her sorrow nearer woman's tears' (I. 338).

In August 1814, a few months short of nineteen, Keats wrote his first extant poem about the need for 'sweet relief' to erotic frustration. Triggered by the sight of a woman 'ungloving her hand' at Vauxhall Pleasure Gardens, 'Fill for me a brimming bowl' expresses the tension between the embarrassment and vulnerability of 'lewd desiring' and the rapturous passion for the 'melting softness of that face–/ The beaminess of those bright eyes–/ That breast, earth's only paradise' (14–16).[5] The same woman brought 'grief unto [the] darling joys' (14) of the speaker who was 'snared by the ungloving of thy hand' (4) in 'Time's sea hath been', and may also have been the 'fair creature of an hour' (9) who inspired the loss of 'unreflecting love' (12) in the 'When I have fears' sonnet. Various flirtatious, occasional poems between 1815 and 1817, are inspired by, and addressed to, sisters and cousins of friends: Caroline and Ann Mathew, cousins of close friend George Felton Mathew; Richard Woodhouse's cousin Mary Frogley; J. H. Reynolds' sisters Jane, Mariane, Eliza and Charlotte. In October 1818, the cousin of the Reynolds sisters, Jane Cox, impressed him with 'the Beauty of a Leopardess' (*L* I, 395).

In May 1817, Keats met Isabella Jones, 'clever, talented, sociable, witty and tantalizingly enigmatic', and her significance as a sexual mentor propelled his poetry into a more confident erotic dimension.[6] On 24 October 1818, he writes to George: 'I have met with that same Lady again,' and, 'I passed her and turrned back – she seemed glad of it; glad to see me and not offended at my passing her before' (*L* I, 402). He manages to turn a potentially self-indulgent account of the rejection of his renewed sexual advances into a generous tribute to a woman he placed alongside Georgiana in disinterested affection: 'As I had warmed with her before and kissed her – I though[t] it would be living backwards not to do so again – she had a better taste: she perceived how much a thing of course it was and shrunk from it – not in a prudish way but in as I say a good taste – She cont[r]ived to disappoint me in a way which made me feel more pleasure than a simple kiss could do' (*L* I, 403). As a result, he professes: 'I have no libidinous thought about her – she and your George [Georgiana] are the only women à peu près de mon age whom I would be content to know for their mind and friendship alone' (*L* I, 403). This warming with Isabella Jones inspired the passion of Endymion in Book One, while her free-spirited independence in 1818 may have inspired *Fancy*: 'Oh, sweet Fancy! let her loose; / Everything is spoilt by use: / Where's the cheek that doth not fade, / Too much gaz'd at?' (67–70). The conventional 'carpe diem' love lyrics of the summer of 1817, 'Unfelt, unheard, unseen', 'Hither, hither, love', and 'You say you love; but with a voice', may also reflect Keats's relationship with Isabella Jones. More specifically, the 1818 lyric 'Hush, hush, tread softly; hush, hush, my dear' stages a secret tryst and implores 'sweet Isabel' to be quiet because 'the jealous, the jealous old baldpate may hear' (3–4), while it also serves as an early instance of how much Keats himself was prone to sexual jealousy, '[f]or less than a nothing the jealous can hear' (8).

According to Richard Woodhouse, Isabella Jones suggested the topic of *The Eve of St. Agnes*, which became Keats's most sexually controversial poem (*P* 454). A shocked Woodhouse insisted that the poem would be 'unfit for ladies' unless the consummation of Madeline and Porphyro's love were made less explicit, to which Keats reportedly responded that he 'does not want ladies to read his poetry' (*P* 455). Keats wrote for men and women, not ladies and gentlemen, and he often attributes a strong sense of agency to women in his love poems. Already in a February 1818 letter to Reynolds he wondered 'who shall say between Man and Woman which is the most delighted' (*L* 1, 232), and the need for requited reciprocity permeates his mature poetry about sexual or erotic encounters. Keats categorised 'Love' in the letter of 13 March 1818 to Bailey, among things 'semireal', because they 'require a greeting of the Spirit to make them wholly exist' (*L* 1, 243), and this included mutual affection and effort: 'as the rose / Blendeth its odour with the violet, – / Solution sweet' (*The Eve of St. Agnes*, 320–1). Madeline's response to her lover's rendition of 'La belle dame sans mercy' is to implore him to 'Give me that voice again, my Porphyro' (312). Unlike the 'fairy's child' (14) who remains an indefinite spectre of the knight's imagination in 'La Belle Dame Sans Merci: A Ballad', Madeline and Porphyro flee together.

In *The Eve of St. Mark*, the unfinished companion piece to *The Eve of St. Agnes*, Bertha forgoes real life in favour of reading about the 'fervent martyrdom' of Saint Mark (116). Her frustrated status as a pent-up 'poor cheated soul' (69) is highlighted and gently satirised by the shadow of the parrot's cage and the fire screen picture of animal life, riotously evoked but arrested all the same like the figures on the Grecian Urn (76–82). In contrast, Keats's luxurious catalogue of the objects and creatures in Isabella Jones's 'tasty' sitting room, a possible inspiration for the description in *The Eve of St. Mark*, creates a scene for potential seduction with 'Books, Pictures a bronze statue of Buonaparte, Music, aeolian Harp; a Parrot a Linnet – A Case of choice Liquers &c &c' (*L* 1, 402). The memory of Isabella Jones's 'choice Liquers' and gifts of grouse and game, sensual pleasures, also emerges in the oriental 'delicates' which Porphyro 'heap'd with glowing hand / On golden dishes and in baskets bright / Of wreathed silver' in *The Eve of St. Agnes* (272–3).

Isabella Jones may, or may not, have been the 'widow of Lieutenant William Jones, killed on Nelson's *Victory* at Trafalgar on 21 October 1805'.[7] She would have been 'around thirty-eight years old when Keats met her, under the protection of the [Irish aristocratic] O'Callaghans as the widow of a war hero. For them, her liaison with a twenty-one-year-old poet who published in *The Examiner* would have been unthinkable.'[8] Jones's scathing response to Joseph Severn's sentimental account of Keats's final weeks gives us an incontrovertible sense of her loyalty to Keats's memory in this letter to John Taylor of 14 April 1821: 'Of all the cants, in this canting world the cant of sentiment is the most disgusting and I never saw better specimens than these letters afford – they are extremely well got up and will impose upon the most literate – but do let me flatter myself that, *we* carry a test in the true feeling of *our* hearts, that exposes all such hollow pretentions – *His* own letter to Mr. B. – with all its quaintness and harmless conceit is worth a wagon load of Mr. Egotist's productions' (italics in original).[9]

Fanny Brawne (1800–1865), whom Keats met and fell in love with in Hampstead at the end of 1818, combined the erotic attraction of a lover and the domestic familiarity of a sister. Keats first describes her in the journal letter to George and Georgiana of 16 December 1818 as 'beautiful and elegant, graceful, silly, fashionable and strange' (*L* 2, 8). She was, in some ways, a 'maiden most unmeek', not unlike the 'demon Poesy' in 'Ode on Indolence' (29, 30). Keats found it difficult to reconcile his desperate passion for her with his declining health and uncertain prospects, and already from mid-1819 his letters from the Isle of Wight and Winchester were marred by outbursts of jealous possessiveness and resentment at having his own freedom 'destroyed' (*L* 2, 123). Both *Otho the Great* and *The Jealousies* feature mismatched, jealous lovers, while Queen Maud in *King Stephen* is a powerful belle dame sans merci. Yet, he also believed in her love for him: 'I love you the more in that I believe you have liked me for my own sake and for nothing else' (*L* 2, 127). Keats's complete infatuation with her inspired the great, bittersweet poems of 1819, in which eros and thanatos are never far apart. Her frustratingly seductive proximity, quite literally next door during his illness in 1820, teased him out of thought. Many of the 1819 poems have a cruel streak of desperate suffering in them, with 'maidens loth' trying to escape bold lovers who cannot kiss them anyway, arrested as they are on the Grecian Urn (8). All ideal beauty transcends the pathology of human passion that 'leaves a heart high-sorrowful and cloy'd, / A burning forehead, and a parching tongue' (29–30). There is a somewhat sadistic delight in the 'rich anger' of the mistress when the speaker 'emprison[s] her soft hand, and let[s] her rave' ('Ode on Melancholy', 19–20). Similarly, Lycius' ensnaring cruelty to Lamia mirrors Keats's self-conscious mood swings in his letters to Fanny Brawne:

> Besides, for all his love, in self despite,
> Against his better self, he took delight
> Luxurious in her sorrows, soft and new.
> His passion, cruel grown, took on a hue
> Fierce and sanguineous as 'twas possible
> In one whose brow had no dark veins to swell.
> (2.73–7)

The agony of helpless frustration and remembrance is expressed in 'The day is gone, and all its sweets are gone', in 'I cry your mercy – pity – love! – aye, love' ('withhold no atom's atom or I die') (10), and in 'What can I do to drive away' (374–6). In 'To Fanny' he implores her to 'keep me free / From torturing jealousy' (47–8), but the dream he invokes through 'Physician Nature' has nightmarish qualities: 'Who now, with greedy looks, eats up my feast?' (17). 'How illness stands as a barrier betwixt me and you!' he writes to her in February 1820 (*L* 2, 263).

Keats transcribed 'Bright star, would I were stedfast as thou art' in a volume of Shakespeare 'when he was aboard ship on his way to Italy' where he would die four months later (*P* 460). He would never again have a chance to rest upon his 'fair love's ripening breast, / To feel for ever its soft swell and fall' (10–11). Her image haunted him throughout the excruciating journey to Rome: 'I cannot bear to leave her. Oh, God! God! God! Every thing I have in my trunks that reminds me of her goes through me like a spear. The silk lining she put in my travelling cap scalds my head. My imagination is horribly vivid about her – I see her – I hear her. There is nothing in the world of sufficient interest to divert me from her a moment' (*L* 2, 351). Fanny Brawne bore 'the signs of her widowhood' until 1827.[10]

On 18 September 1820, Fanny Brawne began a correspondence with Fanny Keats, because Keats had 'expressed a wish that I should occasionally write to you'.[11] She added: 'You see I have been quite intimate with you, most likely without you ever having heard of my name.'[12] Keats wrote to Brown on 30 September 1820 about these two young women: 'The one seems to absorb the other to a degree incredible' (*L* 2, 345). By setting up their correspondence, Keats brought the women he loved most, his lover and his sister, together in the 'richer entanglement' of friendship's 'steady splendour' (*Endymion* 1. 798, 805).

Notes

1 William Hazlitt, 'On Effeminacy of Character', in *Table Talk*, ed. Catherine Macdonald Maclean (London: Dent, 1959[1822]), p. 255.
2 See, for instance, Karen Swann, 'Harassing the Muse', in *Romanticism and Feminism*, ed. Anne K. Mellor (Indiana: Indiana University Press, 1988), pp. 81–92.
3 See, for instance, Nicholas Roe's *John Keats: A New Life* (New Haven: Yale University Press, 2012).
4 Roe, *John Keats: A New Life,* p. 40.
5 Roe, *John Keats: A New Life,* p. 60.
6 Roe, *John Keats: A New Life*, p. 169.
7 Roe, *John Keats: A New Life*, p. 171.
8 Roe, *John Keats: A New Life*, p. 172.
9 Robert Gittings, *John Keats: The Living Year* (London: Heinemann, 1954), p. 232.
10 Joanna Richardson, *Fanny Brawne: A Biography* (London: Thames and Hudson, 1952), p. 112.
11 *Letters of Fanny Brawne to Fanny Keats*, ed. Fred Edgcumbe (London: Oxford University Press, 1936), p. 1.
12 *Letters of Fanny Brawne to Fanny Keats*, pp. 1–2.

CHAPTER 5

Mortality

Shahidha Bari

Keats arrived in Rome with the artist Joseph Severn in November 1820, dangerously ill and bleak-hearted. Funded by donations from his friends and advances from his publisher, the trip was undertaken in the last hope that a warm climate might offer respite from the pulmonary tuberculosis that had so fiercely gripped him for much of the last year. He died only a few months later, in the February of 1821, in a room on the second floor of a four-storey house positioned at the base of the Spanish Steps and east of the Piazza di Spagna. The building, now beloved as the Keats–Shelley Memorial house, sits beneath the church of the Santissima Trinità dei Monti and faces out to Gian Lorenzo Bernini's boat-shaped Fontana della Barcaccia. With its aprico-coloured façade, baroque pediments and cornices, the house absorbs the warmth of its continental aspect and exudes the romance of its Roman history. Not all of this was lost on Keats who arrived in Rome wasted in body and broken in spirit but nonetheless conscious of the vivid world at his window and the injustice of his exclusion from it. Lying on his deathbed, gazing at the pale blue rosettes dotted between the ceiling rafters of his small room, the beautiful melancholia so characteristic of his work in life seemed available to him still even as he faced death, although deepened, now, into a grimly mordant certainty: 'O! I can feel', he exclaimed to Severn, 'the cold earth upon me – the daisies growing over me – this quiet – it will be my first' (*L* 2, 378).

Declaring himself 'half in love with easeful Death' (52) in the 'Ode to a Nightingale', Keats thought of death as fanciful, romantic, almost a seduction, and yet it was for him also anchored in the reality of personal knowledge and a profound awareness of bodily frailty – the former gathered from the terrible accumulation of family deaths (father, mother, grandmother and brother) over a period of fourteen years, and the latter learned from his early training as an apothecary and then work as a dresser at Guy's Hospital between 1815 and 1817. If the absentminded scribbles recorded in his anatomical notebooks suggested a certain disengagement from his academic studies, there can be no doubt that, aside from the theory, Keats knew in practice and felt keenly the vulnerability of human life. His father, Thomas Keates, had died in April 1804, falling from his horse after visiting his sons at their school in Enfield. In his recent biography, Nicholas Roe narrates how this death dramatically disrupted the Keatses's peaceable domesticity, fragmenting the family and plunging them into the financial and emotional tumult that would overshadow the rest of their lives. 'How this took hold of Keats's imagination emerged only gradually', Roe observes, suggesting that 'the numerous valedictions, farewells and adieus in his poems and letters may touch upon their last parting'.[1] Richard Monckton Milnes in his reverential early biography similarly notes Keats's distress at the death of his mother in 1810.[2] These early experiences of domestic tragedy seemed to forge the melancholic pathways that would be re-trod in the poetry in later life. In both cases, the biographers speculate about the impact of such catastrophes on the formation of a young poetic mind. The overwhelming devastation of Tom Keats's death, though, succumbing to tuberculosis in 1818 after several months in Keats's care, is incontrovertible. Its effect on Keats was noted by many of his friends, including the painter, Benjamin Robert Haydon, who wrote with a palpable pity that Tom's death had 'wounded him [Keats] deeply'.[3] The effect on Keats was visible and profound. Keats himself reflected bitterly, 'I have never known any unalloy'd Happiness for many days together: the death or sickness of some one has always spoilt my hours' (*L* 2, 123).

Keats understood the fact of mortality in complex ways: personally in life, professionally as a medic and poetically as a fantasy that must inevitably turn real beauty become the ultimate truth. Yet private and professional experiences did not simply inform his work. Rather, Keats understood how poetry could function variously as a mirror, a testing ground and a sounding board. In poetry, he carved out a space for his deepening reflections on the brevity of a life always shaded by death, thinking through the fact of mortality, variously taunting it, toying with it, romanticising it and railing against it. Debilitating grief and desperate agitation at the inevitable coming of death all feature in his work, painfully considered and expressed. Yet death surfaces in his poetry not simply as a theme or a motif, but as the utterly absorbing subject of his investigation, equal to, if not surpassing, his concerns for love and beauty. It is perhaps in the letters that this relay between life and work was made explicit. Writing in September 1818, after a particularly gruelling time nursing his brother, Keats concedes the profound consequences of the experience on his poetic practice:

> I wish I could say Tom was any better. His identity presses upon me so all day that I am obliged to go out – and although I intended to have given some time to study alone, I am obliged to write and plunge into abstract images to ease myself of his countenance, his voice, and feebleness – so that I live now in a continual fever. It must be poisonous to life, although I feel well. Imagine 'the hateful siege of contraries'– if I think of fame, of poetry, it seems a crime to me, and yet I must do so or suffer. I am sorry to give you pain – I am almost resolved to burn this – but I really have not self–possession and magnanimity enough to manage the thing otherwise.
>
> (L 1, 368–9)

In such intimate proximity to death, Keats writes for relief, almost to keep death at bay, but writing then also asserts one's survival, becoming an activity freighted with guilt so unbearable that it almost compels its own destruction. The fragment poem 'This Living Hand', dated 1819, seems to articulate that commingled horror and guilt when it imagines the chilling grasp extended by a figure from the grave and the fraught conscience of those that survive the dead. In the poem, the dead are a presence on the border of life, coolly menacing, but the living are plagued both by the guilt of their survival and the imperative to write, as though writing were a talisman, warding off death. For Keats, the living hand is a scribe, 'warm and capable' (2) of attesting to a rude bodily presence in defiance of death.[4]

Death and writing are then deeply imbricated practices, as oppositional as they are coextensive for Keats. Stuart Sperry argues that this ambivalence is visible in the entire body of poetic work: 'One senses that, if Apollo represents an emotional and poetic ideal Keats was struggling to achieve, Hyperion conveys the nervous intensity and distraction to which the poet was actually a prey. [...] He had returned from the walking tour in ill-health to find Tom desperately unwell.'[5] Sperry consequently reads the opening lines of the third part of *Hyperion* as a kind of threnody, not for fallen gods, but expressive of a more singular grief, like that felt by the poet for his dead brother.

> O leave them, Muse! O leave them to their woes;
> For thou art weak to sing such tumults dire:
> A solitary sorrow best befits
> Thy lips, and antheming a lonely grief.
>
> (*Hyperion*, 2. 3–6)

The muse that the narrating poet-dreamer addresses is better fitted, Keats oddly notes, for the expression of a 'solitary sorrow', a lonelier grief than that of the many gods. Writing to George and Georgiana Keats on December 18 1819, he informs them despondently, 'I went on a little with [Hyperion] last night – but it will take some time to get into the vein again' (*L* 2, 12), conceding both the difficulty of writing after Tom's death, but also that he is writing. Indeed, the fact of Tom's death makes itself felt in *Hyperion*. When Apollo gazes into the eyes of Mnemosyne, he convulses and Keats describes it with the precision of a witness, not as flight of fancy:

> Soon wild commotions shook him, and made flush
> All the immortal fairness of his limbs;
> Most like the struggle at the gate of death;
> Or liker still to one who should take leave
> Of pale immortal death, and with a pang
> As hot as death's is chill, with fierce convulse
> Die into life: so young Apollo anguish'd;
> (*Hyperion*, 3. 124–30)

Keats's work centres around this question of what it might mean to 'die into life', a curiously upended and yet suggestive formulation. This dying life is an evocative construction that echoes the similarly seductive 'embalmed darkness' (43) of the 'Ode to a Nightingale'. The phrase, Stuart Ende thinks, suggests 'both death and a rich distilled perfume of his own making', an idea of a life shot through with death like a fragrance permeating air.[6] For Keats, death is not stumbled upon as an event in life or even an awakening; rather, it takes the form of an apprehension of the constant presence of death, a recognition that death has been there all along, the ever present companion to all his experiences.

This apprehension is as apparent in the odes as it is in the apocalyptic final poems. Helen Vendler reads the 'Ode to a Nightingale' as a 'tryst' with death, observing how Keats's language is studded with the suicidal seductions of Hamlet's soliloquy: 'To die, to sleep'. She notes

> Hamlet's wish that his flesh might 'melt/ Thaw, and resolve itself into a dew' reappears in Keats's wish to 'fade far away, dissolve, and quite forget'; as the Ghost in Hamlet 'fades', so Keats wishes to 'fade away' and so the nightingale's anthem 'fades'; and we hear the Ghosts's 'Adieu! Adieu!'[7]

Despite its soaring beauty, the birdsong is weighed down by Keats's pain since that which the nightingale abandons him to is the 'weariness, the fever, and the fret' (23) of human life. The nightingale flees a world where 'youth grows pale, and spectre-thin, and dies' (26), an image impossible not to attach to the memory of Tom Keats. And yet, it is not death itself that causes pain to Keats here, since 'to think is to be full of sorrow' (27).

Consciousness, not death per se, is the cause of grief, and this allows Keats to establish the ode's astonishing contradiction, or what Vendler summarises as the choice between an 'unhappy consciousness and the unconsciousness of death'.[8] For Vendler, the ode turns on this false choice, and the choice itself is posed as though it could deny their necessary conjunction – the sorrow of life *and* the inevitability of death.

It is, however, birdsong, and by association, poetry itself, that seems able to provide some sort of redemption in the ode. Vendler attends to how pleasingly 'the murmurousness of the flies modulates into Keats's own murmur to Death' when he calls death 'soft names in many a mused rhyme' (53).[9] Keats imagines a language capable of coaxing and taming death that could be turned object of seduction, not terror. Ende writes that 'As the bird continues to sing, the poet's listening regard begins to assume a deathly quietude', but it is from such quietude that the poem itself springs.[10] The nightingale's song is immortalised by the poem, imagined like the unfading lovers on a Grecian urn who are permanently poised on the cusp of gratification and never yet gratified.

Yet the ode itself is perhaps more ambiguous than the birdsong upon which it reflects. If, in the poem's movement, the bird that is 'not born for death' (61) alerts Keats to his opposite status as a man who lives to die, its song provides succour, permitting Keats to imagine a beautiful oblivion, removed from the realities of physical infirmity or disease. When this alertness to life itself turns painful, the poem poses a dilemma between death that is figured in the unfeeling non-existence of 'sod' or dirt, and a life characterised by fever and fret, and redeemed only by the nightingale song it might contain too. By the process of Keats's meditation, though, the fact of death becomes eclipsed by the possibility of death instead, transformed so that to think upon one's death is to immerse oneself in a luxurious melancholia: 'Now more than ever seems it rich to die' (55), he muses.

This notion of a transfigured, luxurious, triumphant death emerges in the sonnets too. At the close of 'Why did I laugh tonight? No voice will tell', Keats declares 'Verse, fame, and beauty are intense indeed / But death intenser – death is life's high meed' (13–14). The closing couplet allots to death the summit of life and seems to end with a disavowal of art in favour of a transcendental mortality. Yet death here does not discharge the service of art; rather, art dedicates itself to death and it, in turn, compels the poet's creation. John Jones notes that the couplet 'rings hard, sententious, uncomfortable because it is not quite true'.[11] Perhaps Keats does deploy the drama of death for the sense of an ending, and our discomfort with the theatricality of the gesture betrays the seduction of mortality, to which both Keats and his readers are subject. Yet death for Keats here is also complex: not an absolute end, death is 'life's high meed' and so the possibility that realises life most profoundly. Death is almost alive, as Keats figures it in this and other sonnets. The voluptuous death at the close of 'Bright star' is even sexualised in the narrator who longs to lie 'Pillow'd upon my fair love's ripening breast' (10) and there 'live ever – or else swoon to death' (14). Jones notes that to Keats's mind 'life and death weigh equal; two comparably intense alternatives are being asserted'.[12] Death has a theatrical sensuality here, oddly equal to the body of the imagined lover, and either outcome, the pillowed breast or the swooning death, seems satisfactory. Writing to Fanny Brawne in 1819, Keats acknowledged this curious coupling of sex and death: 'I have two luxuries to brood over in my walks, your Loveliness and the hour of my death. O that I could have possession of them both in the same minute' (*L* 2, 133).

The Keats of the 'Ode to a Nightingale' is in love with death, but death is a powerful component of the poet's depictions of love too. Desire and death are certainly entwined in the letters to Fanny Brawne: 'You cannot conceive how I ache to be with you: how I would die for one hour' (*L* 2, 132). These real life romantic professions possess a dark richness that is already apparent in the poetry. In 'La Belle Dame sans Merci', the sexual tension kindled between knight and belle dame ultimately fizzles out. The curiously etiolated and yet desirous knight exists in a hinterland where 'no birds sing' (4), bound to a woman who stanza by stanza depletes him even as she seduces him. In *Isabella*, too, Lorenzo, is diminished by love, not only in his decapitation, but also in the pared down, disembodied voice to which he is reduced in the poem. Isabella tends to the severed head as though it were a relic, her love ironically flowering alongside the rites she performs in memory of her dead lover. Deborah Lutz cites Keats as a poet for whom the body itself becomes a relic: his own death imagined and refigured in his poetry, the poems becoming 'monuments to the enlivening principle of death: little objects themselves that spark an endlessness'.[13]

Certainly, the 'Ode on a Grecian Urn' and the sonnets to the Elgin Marbles indicate the funereal weight with which Keats could imbue objects. Mortality 'weighs heavily' (2) in the Elgin Marbles, as though the burden of coming death were equal to the vast load and magnitude of the object itself – indeed, the object is transfigured under Keats's gaze and understanding so as to bear such a thing.[14] Relics like the marbles and the urn are emblems of mortality that are, in turn, immortalised in Keats's poems. The poems are the remains too, in some form, of the poet from whom they come. This idea spirals vertiginously in the case of the urn, since it is itself an object intended to contain remains, amplifying the death-defying impulse of the ode devoted to it. In this way, it is not unlike Keats's own paradoxical epitaph, 'Here lies one whose name was writ in water', whose very ephemerality is reversed by its permanent inscription. The immortalising impulse of this aestheticisation is itself only a conjuring trick and one of which Keats is only too aware. The urn that represents eternity is resolutely inhuman. There is, writes Martin Aske, a 'tone of rebuke' that is betrayed in the declaration 'Cold Pastoral!' (45), and so paltry comfort to be drawn from Keats's claim that

> When old age shall this generation waste,
>   Thou shalt remain, in midst of other woe
> Than ours, a friend to man, to whom thou say'st
> 'Beauty is truth, truth beauty', – that is all
>   Ye know on earth, and all ye need to know.
> (46–50)[15]

T. S. Eliot famously damned the poem's closing apothegm as 'a serious blemish on a beautiful poem'.[16] But Aske redeems this, arguing that this very sententiousness exposes the urn's betrayal: 'No matter how ornate and embellished the urn appears, it cannot defraud the reality of death.'[17] Sperry endorses this with his meditation that '[I]t is the expression of our desire to invest the intimations art affords with the permanence of certainty. It is as if the poet, frustrated by the silence of the urn in the face of his human questioning, had forced it to speak beyond the power of its means.'[18]

Perhaps what distinguishes Keats in this immortalising aesthetic impulse is the self-conscious casting of his entire body of work as a kind of future riposte to his death. For Andrew Bennett, the impulse to survive in his writing makes Keats eminently Romantic insofar as one of the key motivations of the literary 'is the possibility of the future, posthumous recognition or canonization'.[19] The idea of posterity as 'the necessary ground of artistic production' could not have been alien to a poet who wrote quietly to his brother in 1818, 'I think I shall be among the English Poets after my death' (*L* 1, 394).[20] The important sentiment here is not the confidence of future greatness, but the understanding that such a thing could come only at the expense of life.

Writing 'lives on' after the death of the author, a posthumous supplement. For Bennett, Keats fends off death in a poetics of posterity that promises for itself an afterlife of repetition. That very word, 'posthumous', seems to haunt him at the end. In the final, eerie letter to his friend, Charles

Armitage Brown, he concedes to 'an habitual feeling of my real life having past, and that I am leading a posthumous existence. God knows how it would have been – but it appears to me –' (*L* 2, 359), trailing off. Severn, too, notes how at the last, 'Each day he would look up in the doctor's face to discover how long he should live – he would say – "how long will this posthumous life of mine last" – that look was more than we could ever bear – the extreme brightness of his eyes – with his poor pallid face – were not earthly…' (*KC* 1, 224).

Nearly 200 years later, that face is itself immortalised in a plaster mask that was cast in Rome just days after Keats's death, 'very possibly', Gittings notes, 'by Ghiradi, the mask-master to Canova'.[21] Encased in a glass box, the face is enigmatic, with eyes so heavy-lidded that the print of downcast lashes are faintly discernible; the lips are pressed shut, the deathly body as taciturn as the 'masque-like figures on the dreary urn' that Keats himself once interrogated ('Ode to Indolence', 61). Thomas McFarland compares the death mask to the life mask which had been cast by Haydon four years earlier in December 1816, noting that dying so young, Keats 'had a life mask and a death mask that constitute virtually a Janus head of simultaneity'.[22] They are, for McFarland, inseparable and indicative of something peculiar to Keats: 'Keats and death, death and Keats: the two cannot be separated.'[23]

The mask, alongside a lock of auburn hair, is now on permanent display at the Keats–Shelley Memorial House, not far from Keats's grave in the English Cemetery. McFarland reads the mask as a 'reminder that in the midst of life we are in death'. That understanding of a commingled life and death was for Keats both a seductive fantasy and a sobering truth. The romance of an 'easeful death' was countered by the reality of mortality. His brief writing career was dogged by the anxiety of dying before a pen could glean the substance of his 'rich teaming brain' ('When I have fears that I may cease to be', 2). Death snaps at the heels of the poet dreamer climbing the immortal stairs in *Hyperion*, but it is an impossible foe for Keats to outrun too. Severn, at his bedside in Rome, wrote to Keats's publisher, James Taylor, bewildered by the desperate circumstances unfolding before him: 'Keats is desiring his death with dreadful earnestness – the idea of death seems his only comfort – the only prospect of ease – he talks of it with delight – it sooths his present torture – The strangeness of his mind every day surprises us' (*KC* 1, 205). Severn's harrowing record of Keats's final days closes the story of his mortal life, but it also begins an extraordinary poetic afterlife. In his 1821 elegy to Keats, *Adonais*, Shelley insists that 'He lives, he wakes – 'tis Death is dead, not he;/ Mourn not for

Adonais' (361–2). In a curious way the extended memorialisation of Keats has itself now become a crucial aspect of our understanding of the poet, an acknowledgement both of his tragic death and the profound ways in which his meditations on mortality shaped his work.

Notes

1 Nicholas Roe, *John Keats* (New Haven: Yale University Press, 2012), p. 24.
2 Richard Monckton Milnes, *Life and Letters of John Keats* (London: Oxford University Press, 1951), p. 3.
3 *The Diary of Benjamin Robert Haydon,* ed. Willard Bissell Pope, 5 vols. (Cambridge, MA: Harvard University Press, 1960–3), vol. 2, p. 317.
4 Shahidha Bari, *Keats and Philosophy* (London: Routledge, 2012), pp. 6–9.
5 Stuart Sperry, *Keats the Poet* (Princeton: Princeton University Press, 1973), p. 189.
6 Stuart Ende, *Keats and the Sublime* (New Haven: Yale University Press, 1976), p. 137.
7 Helen Vendler, *The Odes of John Keats* (Boston: Harvard University Press, 1983), p. 85.
8 Vendler, *Odes*, p. 88.
9 Vendler, *Odes*, pp. 92–3.
10 Ende, *Keats and the Sublime*, p. 139.
11 John Jones, *John Keats's Dream of Truth* (London: Chatto & Windus, 1969), pp. 202–3.
12 Jones, *Keats's Dream of Truth*, p. 203.
13 Deborah Lutz, *Relics of Death in Victorian Literature and Culture* (Cambridge: Cambridge University Press, 2015), p. 26.
14 Bari, *Keats and Philosophy*, pp. 12–21.
15 Martin Aske, *Keats and Hellenism* (Cambridge: Cambridge University Press, 1985), p. 126.
16 T. S. Eliot, *Selected Essays* (New York: Harcourt, 1950), p. 231.
17 Aske, *Keats and Hellenism*, p. 127.
18 Sperry, *Keats the Poet*, p. 276.
19 Andrew Bennett, *Romantic Poets and the Culture of Posterity* (Cambridge: Cambridge University Press, 1999), p. 200.
20 Andrew Bennett, *Keats, Narrative and Audience* (Cambridge: Cambridge University Press, 1994), p. 9.
21 Robert Gittings, *The Mask of Keats* (London: Heinemann, 1956), p. 1.
22 Thomas McFarland, *The Masks of Keats* (Oxford: Oxford University Press, 2000), p. 59.
23 McFarland, *Masks of Keats*, p. 64.

CHAPTER 6

Travel

Jeffrey C. Robinson

In visual portraits Keats is never seen standing or walking but sitting, indoors or out of doors. A room at the Hampstead house where he lived with Charles Brown in 1819 copies an 1821 portrait of a Keats imagined by Joseph Severn; it features two chairs, one for Keats sitting and the other, at right angles to the first, for placing his elbow so that arm and hand can support his head while reading a book resting on his knee. In such an image, Keats comes to us with his body at rest; he thus appears to differ from many other, mostly male, Romantics whose peripatetic movements, and indeed whose travels to other lands as indicative of a cosmopolitan reach, are part and parcel of Romantic vision itself.

This chapter attempts to shift the emphasis to Keats as a poet for whom travel, defined broadly, figures centrally in his life and his poetic practice. Biographies of Keats – particularly those by Aileen Ward, Robert Gittings, and most recently Nicholas Roe – have noted this deep connection. As seen in his poems and letters, Keats's mind is a 'thoroughfare'; it 'wanders', 'travels', 'journeys', and 'surpasses'; journeying and walking occupy the domain of thought and sensation which often merge: 'There was wide wand'ring for the greediest eye' ('I stood tiptoe upon a little hill', 15). I propose that he learns to translate this travelling mind into poetry itself by taking on travel with its constant sense of change and renewal as a formal feature and driving force. By reviewing the trips he took, I can show how these metaphors perfuse experiments in his writing as pervasively as actual travel moulds his life.

Keats's travels are of two types: there are journeys taken away from the London area to English holiday villages and small urban centres south of the metropolis and on or near the sea. In these cases, although with friends or visiting others, he travels in order to write. He makes a new, temporary home, setting up part of a house deemed compatible with nurturing and furthering his own composition. As he wrote to Leigh Hunt: 'I went to the Isle of Wight – thought so much about Poetry so long together that I could not get to sleep at night' (*L* 1, 138). Significantly, he wrote most of his long poems in one or more of these 'southern' spaces. Second, there is the tour to the genuinely foreign place of Scotland for six weeks in summer 1818; the difference of the land and the people along with the threadbare physical condition of their journey contributes to an unsettled quality of the poetry, its appearance, its content, and its playfully critical attitude. His final journey to Italy in a desperate attempt to recover from tuberculosis and during which a few letters and no poetry were written has the unique character of, as he says, a 'posthumous existence'; responses to his Roman environment are vitiated by intense absorption in the ravages to his body and mind.

As with everything else in Keats's life, the journeys occurred over only three years, 1817–1819, or four years with the journey to Rome.[1] In this hyper-shortened life, travel either seems just completed, is anticipated as imminent, or is happening at the moment. After having moved to Hampstead in the north of London in March 1817, Keats went to the Isle of Wight (Shanklin and then Carisbrooke) and then, moving east, to Canterbury and Margate, all between mid-April and mid-May. Here he wrote much of *Endymion.* In September he finished *Endymion* in Oxford ('the finest City in the world') and then went south to Burford Bridge. In March and April of 1818, he travelled to Teignmouth in the southwest with Tom, where he wrote *Isabella* and the ambitious verse *Epistle to J. H. Reynolds* ('Dear Reynolds, as last night I lay in bed'). During these months he planned his Scottish Tour carried out with Charles Brown from late June to mid-August. Letters home from the Lakes and Scotland are rich in detail and speculation, at times having the density of poetry in the medium of prose. The poems written on the Tour are all short experiments in form and self-exploration. A month after the death of Tom in December 1818, he went south again to Chichester and Bedhampton where he composed *The Eve of St. Agnes*. He stayed in Hampstead during the winter and spring of 1819 writing his magnificent journal letter to George and Georgiana Keats in America (February–May) and the Odes ('Psyche', 'Nightingale', 'Grecian Urn', 'Melancholy', and 'Indolence', all full of movement and 'travel' imagery), but then travelled from July through September: in July and August, again, to Shanklin, and in September to Winchester ('the pleasantest Town I ever was in' – *L* 2, 147). During these months he wrote *Lamia*, *Otho the Great*, *King Stephen*, *The Fall of Hyperion* and 'To Autumn'. Diagnosed with tuberculosis in February 1820 and 'housebound' for weeks, he did not go away from the greater London area until leaving for Rome in September. During his last year he wrote passionate letters to Fanny Brawne.

In his travels to the south of England, the arrival and not the journey matters. He writes to J. H. Reynolds in Carisbrooke on the Isle of Wight: 'at this moment I am about to become settled. for I have unpacked my books, put them into a snug corner – pinned up Haydon – Mary Queen [of] Scotts, and Milton with his daughters in a row. In the passage I found a head of Shakespeare … this head I have hung over my Books, just above the three in a row, having first discarded a french Ambassador – Now this alone is a good morning's work –' (*L* I, 130). Keats doesn't so much enter as construct a home, in this case placing himself, in anticipation, 'among the English poets'. It's obviously done seriously, the way a child methodically sets up house. Yet with a politically critical playfulness anticipating much of his writing, he can 'discard' the bust of a representative of corrupt government with ease, while establishing his personal pantheon of poetic genius and politically adversarial temperaments.

Constructing a proper home demands of Keats a proper landscape, rural or urban or both; letters show how sensitive he is to acceptable surroundings. In 1817 the sea off Shanklin is beautiful, but inland Carisbrooke allows him greater access to walking the island, and also he is within eyeshot of a castle. He is constructing not an eighteenth-century 'pleasing prospect' with its implications of middle-class acquisition and possession, but rather a field of vision in which he can 'peer about' ('I stood tiptoe', 16) and then walk through the landscapes, rural and urban – journeys within the journey.

Perhaps his penchant for homes away from home has a genetic source: the early deaths of his father and mother along with the general instability of his London living conditions. He makes homes over which he has perfect control. There is a conservative element here; the home becomes an act of reconstitution and self-preservation. At the same time, the writing suggests something much more expansive, or as he says, 'elastic'. The temporary, make-shift character of his dwellings can also transform them into a nomadic vision of mobility of body and mind in which a situation never overwhelms and narrows the view of the subject. This 'nomad poetics' (following Pierre Joris[2]) is consonant with one of Negative Capability, a capacity to live in 'uncertainties, Mysteries, doubts, without any irritable reaching after fact & reason' (*L* I, 193). As his negatively capable mind emerges from the constructed 'homes' of his journeys, it 'wanders' and marks everything that his sensibility encounters; but this instinctively means for him that while he is drawn to the power of natural scenes, he remains compelled by a human presence and social meaning in what he sees. 'Scenery is fine–but human nature is finer' (*L* I, 242).

On the Scottish Tour he cultivates a tension between often overwhelming sights in nature and the people he encounters, with an acute sense of their social standing, in some cases of poverty, and of regional dialects. In all of his journeys he satirises the middle classes for their acquisitive relationship to 'nature', those who 'come hunting after the picturesque like beagles' (*L* 2, 130) and the accompanying aesthetics of the sublime and the picturesque. He riffs on Ann Radcliffe's tour language: 'I'll cavern you, and grotto you, and waterfall you, and wood you, and water you, and immense-rock you, and tremendous sound you, and solitude you' (*L* 1, 245) and later comments on this Huntian, 'Cockney' critique of tour aesthetics: 'I may call myself an old Stager in the picturesque' (*L* 2, 135).

Underneath this riffing and staging of the popular middle-class aesthetics of the tour in which Keats desacralises the rigid coordinates of the sublime lies his rethinking of the mental faculties of art prized most highly in the late eighteenth and early nineteenth century, 'reason' and 'imagination'. Supported by Huntian and Cockney literary politics, Keats reveals an urban or sub-urban scepticism about the isolating, absorptive, and transcendental powers of the mind claimed by the Lake Poets and their advocates in response to the beauty of the natural world. For him the sublime, even though it privileges 'reason' and 'imagination' (Wordsworth: imagination is 'reason in its most exalted mood'[3]), in fact brings all thinking, by which he means critical thinking, to a halt. On the Scottish Tour he develops his own peculiar term of privilege, the 'intellect', that doesn't so much sublimely transcend reality as *continue to think in its presence.* A letter to Benjamin Bailey concludes with a vision of mental activity, of 'intellect', that rationalises his repeated journey from nature to mind by relying on travel and geographical metaphors: '[I]t is an old maxim of mine and of course must be well known that evey [*sic*] point of thought is the centre of an intellectual world – the two uppermost thoughts in a Man's mind are the two poles of his World he revolves on them and every thing is southward or northward to him through their means – We take but three steps from feathers to iron' (*L* 1, 243).

In a letter from the Scottish Tour to Tom Keats, Keats analyses his response to waterfalls and mountains in a way that revises a dominant Wordsworthian poetics of the sublime, the epiphany, and recollection:

> What astonishes me more than any thing is the tone, the coloring, the slate, the stone, the moss, the rock-weed; or, if I may so say, the intellect, the countenance of such places. The space, the magnitude of mountains and waterfalls are well imagined before one sees them; but this countenance or intellectual tone must surpass every imagination and defy any remembrance.

> I shall learn poetry here … I cannot think with Hazlitt that these scenes make man appear little. I never forgot my stature so completely – I live in the eye; and my imagination, surpassed, is at rest – .
>
> (*L* 1, 301)

In the remark that his imagination has been surpassed, 'imagination' may refer to the image-making power that he brings to an object before he actually sees it, but more likely it resonates to two recent monumental publications, Wordsworth's Preface to his Collected Poems of 1815 and Coleridge's *Biographia Literaria* of 1817 where 'imagination' synthesises and 'reconciles' 'opposite and discordant qualities'. Critical of their accounts of poetic faculties, Keats turns to the 'intellect' as part of the 'grand march' of human and social progress. Reason is the triumphant faculty of sublime experience, transcending a reality seen as powerful and frighteningly absorptive. The intellect, however, stays independently active in an encounter with anything overwhelming. More surprising and anticipating an ecological imagination, it is able to imagine and acknowledge alterity, another's subjectivity, the 'intellect' of the waterfalls themselves.[4]

A brief sketch of the Scottish Tour reveals its fruitful though costly unpredictability for both Keats's mind and body. After accompanying his newly wed brother George and his wife Georgiana in Liverpool where they departed for the United States, Keats continued north with his tour companion Charles Brown to Lancaster. There they began their walk, stopping first at the Lakes. Continuing into southwest Scotland, they took a brief tour in Ireland where he was stunned by the poverty he saw. Returning to Scotland they visited Burns Country (Dumfries and Alloway) and then went north to Glasgow, Loch Lomond, the Isle of Mull, the ancient religious community of Iona and the strange, magical rock formations of the island of Staffa. Keats acknowledged that while on Mull he caught a bad cold in the throat that compromised and eventually put a premature end to his tour, but not before he climbed Britain's highest mountain, Ben Nevis. Greatly weakened physically, he returned to London, not on foot and two months later as planned, but by boat.

He intuited that the Scottish Tour would 'give me more experience, rub off more Prejudice, use [me] to more hardship, identify finer scenes load me with grander Mountains, and strengthen more my reach in Poetry, than would stopping at home among Books even though I should reach Homer –' (*L* 1, 342). The effects, in other words, would seem to be quantitative: more experience and 'reach', but his actual experiences suggest a qualitative change in poetry and poetics. In the above sentence 'Homer' contains 'home', the 'familiar', a place you don't 'travel' to: staring at the

Pacific of reading Chapman's Homer in Keats's early sonnet may in fact not be travelling but 'stopping at home'. In the letters he discovers that the overwhelming sights of lakes, mountains, vistas, and other natural phenomena in the sublime mode challenged his imagination but no more and, in fact, less than what he saw of Scottish persons and their social institutions: the 'Kirkmen' of Scotland who seek to banish puns and kissing, the extreme poverty of 'the Duchess of Dunghill' he encounters in Ireland, and, positively, a scene of Scottish dancing. '[T]here was as fine a row of boys & girls as you ever saw, some beautiful faces, & one exquisite mouth', this last a sight that made him feel 'the glory of making by any means a country happier' *(L* 1, 307). An exuberant if critical social consciousness, or 'intellect', is released in Scotland alongside and at times supplanting his response to 'the sublime'. Given his predispositions, how does he respond in poetry to this mix of unfamiliar information?

At certain characteristic moments Keats felt that the journey, his absorption in the compelling foreignness of situations and the beating his body took – six hundred miles of walking and hiking often in bad weather – led to a dangerously precarious state of self where he might 'forget his mortal way'. But the foreignness and the extent of the trip also led away from the 'homes' of traditional verse to experiments in writing, both the prose of his letters and the unpredictable, experimental poems. Robin Jarvis calls the most characteristic writing of the tour the 'intrusion' of 'Cockney Carnivalesque' into eighteenth-century travel discourse, including quotation, ironic ventriloquism, juxtaposition of picturesque and quotidian urban speech, dialect, and play with signifiers.[5] As Jarvis puts it: 'Keats's travel writing might be taken to depict an urbanizing excursion into the wilder parts of the country, an ironic counterpart to the "ruralizing imagination" at work in much literature of the city.'[6]

Jarvis' superb reading of the Scottish Tour writing, however, does not fully register the paradigm shift in poetics that Keats underwent during these weeks, reinforced unintentionally by his disappointment with two literary pilgrimages: the first a visit to Wordsworth at Rydal Mount whose campaigning for local Tory candidates made him absent when Keats showed up and the second to a visit to Burns's cottage at Alloway where the guide was a drunken purveyor of clichés about the 'ploughman poet'. The poems and letters written on the Tour seem therefore released from any 'anxiety of influence' particularly of Wordsworthian (Tory) sublimity and consequently open to play with local dialect and popular poetic materials. They are 'open form' experiments; indeed, the true 'poetry' of the Scottish Tour ought to be seen as the fast-moving, associative, carnivalesque letters mixed with verse. The poems themselves range from acrostics to quatrains to octosyllabic couplets to fourteener couplets to sonnets to ballads. He ventriloquises popular ballad materials and Scots dialect. In subject matter he moves from Westmoreland politics to climbing Ben Nevis to the home and death of a great poet Burns to a poetry of child's play.

The jingling rhymes and skinny lines sent from the Tour to his sister epitomise the 'open', vulnerable intentions of this travel poetry, beginning: 'There was a naughty boy / A naughty boy was he / He would not stop at home / He could not quiet be– / He took / In his knapsack / A book / Full of vowels / And a shirt / With some towels–' (1–10). The poet is 'naughty' because among other things he links mere non-signifying vowels next to material objects, towels (as his contemporary Byron might do) in his backpack 'And follow'd his nose / To the north' (24–5). This playful throw-away poem (as Keats says, 'scribbled') actually develops a transgressive (naughty) poetics, in which language is stripped of signification and is heralded for its sounds. His mental guide is not reason or 'vision' but the more primitive sense organ of smell, and all of this may be the poetics for the largest transgression, his journey to a 'foreign' country, where to 'wonder' ('He stood in his / Shoes and he wonder'd–' [116–17]) signals the proper nomadic state of mind for exploring the other: wandering or moving, as Charles Olson said, 'from perception to perception'.[7] Hinting towards a poetics of democracy with the levelling of all objects for acknowledgement and apprehension, Keats later said, 'The great beauty of Poetry is, that it makes every thing every place interesting–' *(L* 2, 201).

This nomadic Keats rethinks a crucial issue in Romantic poetry, the representation of the self in the poetry of experience. Indeed, through the poetry of the Scottish Tour we may come to a clear understanding of his famous phrase, directed critically towards Wordsworth's poetry, the 'egotistical sublime'. 'Imagination' guides the Lake Poet's Simplon Pass and Mt. Snowden moments of sublime transcendence as well as the lyric epiphanies of 'I wandered lonely as a cloud' and 'The solitary reaper', the ego liberated into some register of visionary clarity and thus celebrated. By contrast, on the Scottish Tour, Keats hammers out accounts of the strenuous, unrelenting burden of the ego in the presence of sublime scenery, caught up by the power of Burns, frightened of 'forget[ting] his mortal way' while 'footing slow across a silent plain' ('There is a joy in footing slow across a silent plain', 32, 1), and when looking into the chasms and shrouds vaporous on the top of Ben Nevis stunned by mist and Crag with no sublime clarity emerging. And yet these are not poems of failed sublime experience but rather precise bodily apprehension. They radiate a gritty buoyancy of spirit that, in the Ben Nevis sonnet, for example, comes from a negatively capable acceptance of the full import of Wordsworth's phrase, 'the burden of the mystery' as more honest than a so-called triumph of 'reason':

> Here are the craggy stones beneath my feet;
> Thus much I know, that, a poor witless elf,
> I tread on them; that all my eye doth meet
> Is mist and crag – not only on this height,
> But in the world of thought and mental might.
> ('Read me a lesson, Muse', 10–14)

The speaker is not a 'self' of ordinary consciousness but an 'elf' of livelier, more unpredictable mind. This poetry encounters the world through the feet, as he later says, 'a pair of patient sublunary legs' (*L* 2, 128). Yet in walking, the legs as conduits of bodily perception lead to the triumph of the 'intellect' (thought and mental might).

Encumbered Nomad

'O what an account I could give you of the Bay of Naples if I could once more feel myself a Citizen of this world – I feel a Spirit in my Brain would lay it forth pleasantly – O what a misery it is to have an intellect in splints!' (*L* 2, 350). Written in Naples just before traveling to Rome and to the apartment on the Piazza di Spagna, this sentence is poised on the edge of a final debility; the poet envisions a condition of mind, or intellect, as it was on the Scottish Tour or earlier in Shanklin, still imagined in its health as pedestrian movement. Disease, however, has attacked the intellect, figured as a leg broken and in need of a splint which, of course, also constrains the leg and weighs it down. 'Citizen of this world' recalls Oliver Goldsmith's eighteenth-century suite of essays (*Citizen of the World*) in which a Chinese traveller to England comments on the strangeness of foreign places.

Even though poetry stops, the language of travel applied to the mind continues to Rome.[8] In fact, this journey can seem more than biographical, a journey into poetry itself crossing to domains of myth, apparition, and metaphor. The storms in the English Channel battering the ship *Maria Crowther* and its human cargo make setting out uncomfortable and precarious and are followed by the long quarantine in Naples, the slow trip over land to Rome, and Keats's final months at the Piazza di Spagna. But leaving England smacks of the Homeric or Virgilian archetype, as he passes by the signs of an earlier life, the 'homes' of Margate and the Isle of Wight, stopping briefly at nearby Bedhampton, all sites of the writing of poems, sites that Keats's companion Joseph Severn said 'were the means of transporting Keats once more into the regions of poetry'.[9]

He is shifting from this world to another one: 'I have an habitual feeling of my real life having past, and that I am leading a posthumous existence' (*L* 2, 359). At the same time, further skewing his relationship to the real, passion for Fanny Brawne absorbs him wholly, increasing with the increasing certainty of his death away from her. He speaks as if he is on an Orphic journey to the underworld: 'I eternally see her figure eternally vanishing' (*L* 2, 345).[10] A life of travel intertwined with the writing of poems, a life where 'a longer stay / Would bar return and make a man forget his mortal way', has become poetry itself.

Death and Wit

The early death of Keats is surely tragic and his life has often been cast in heroic-elegiac terms. This does not mean that we need to interpret his poetry primarily as elegy; better to mark the travelling, the continual awakening, of his mind, its increasingly passionate motions and his poems as formal journeys of 'intellect' and critical consciousness. His travels to the south of England, to Scotland, and even to Italy permeate the rhythms and linguistic freedom of his poetry. It is no accident that this Cockney poet, chained before death to Rome, his most 'southern' of homes, 'summoned up more puns, in a sort of desperation, in one week than in any year of my life' (*L* 2, 360).

Notes

1 He went on holiday to the seaside town of Margate in 1816.

2 Pierre Joris, *A Nomad Poetics* (Middletown, CT: Wesleyan University Press, 2003).

3 William Wordsworth, *The Prelude* (1805), Bk. 13, line 170.

4 An early version of an object-oriented ontology. See also Timothy Morton, *Ecology without Nature* (Cambridge, MA: Harvard University Press, 2007).

5 See Robin Jarvis, *Romantic Writing and Pedestrian Travel* (Basingstoke: Macmillan, 1997), p. 203. For example, 'the mountaintop changes its weather more often than a lady her head-dress' (p. 201).

6 Jarvis, *Romantic Writing and Pedestrian Travel*, p. 206.

7 See Charles Olson's essay 'Projective Verse', in *Selected Writings of Charles Olson* (New York: New Directions, 1966), p. 15.

8 Keats did write down and possibly revise his sonnet 'Bright Star' off the Dorset coast.

9 Quoted in Nicholas Roe, *John Keats: A New Life* (New Haven: Yale University Prss, 2012), p. 380. Roe also notes that Keats coming to Rome passed by signs of classical art and civilisation, frescoes of Apollo and 'fragments of columns, friezes and pediments, blocks of granite and marble' (p. 388).

10 Roe, *John Keats*, p. 381.

CHAPTER 7

Letters

Madeleine Callaghan

Keats's letters reveal his conception of the letter writer as a protean being as he plays with and makes use of the flexible conventions of the epistolary mode through his focus on the imagination. Keats's letters are attentive to audience, openly adapting themselves to their addressee even as the poet's life is reported, lamented, or celebrated; this life, as Timothy Webb shows, is the 'recurrent theme which gives them unity and purpose'.[1] Keats negotiates between poetic reflections and delineating the details of his daily life, often within the confines of a single letter. From the earliest letters, Keats's poetic ambition makes itself felt. Invoking Chatterton, Shakespeare, Milton, and Spenser in a poem enclosed in a letter in 1815, Keats's aspirant sense of the 'bright golden wing / Of genius' (*L* I, 102) shows how he weaves poetry into his letters. Likewise, the letters show Keats refusing to exclude poetic imagination from personal fact, where, to quote from Shelley's *Epipsychidion*, both spheres 'Touch, mingle, are transfigured' (578) within the letter itself.[2] 'Keats's epistolary self-consciousness', writes Webb, 'alerted him to the possibility that he might construct his style and the persona of his correspondence according to a fictional model'.[3] The dramatic or poetic tones in his letters show Keats performing the self,[4] and imaginative role-playing becomes the vital element of Keats's letters. Keats creates a mutable self that alludes to, borrows from, and inhabits other voices to fashion a multi-faceted self that remains alert to his addressee.

Mixing modes of thought becomes a hallmark of Keats's letters, where his mobility bids him move from domestic and social concerns to larger meditations on the nature of the mind and imagination. Writing to Benjamin Bailey in a letter intended, in part, to soothe the breach between Bailey and Haydon, Keats displays the powers of imaginative flight and grounded attention to his addressee that distinguish his epistolary style. Enjoining Bailey not to 'think of this unpleasant affair' where Haydon had written Bailey an intemperate letter, Keats delineates the difference between Men of Genius and Men of Power (*L* I, 184) before expounding some of his central imaginative ideas. The letter sparkles with intellectual gems, as when Keats claims: 'I am certain of nothing but of the holiness of the Heart's affections and the truth of Imagination – What the imagination seizes as Beauty must be truth – whether it existed before or not –' (*L* I, 184). Such an affirmation of the power and the truth of the imagination foreshadows the 'Ode on a Grecian Urn'.

Bailey remained an important correspondent for Keats, and following two apparently despairing letters to which Bailey had replied expressing his concern, Keats writes:

> And here, Bailey, I will say a few words written in a sane and sober Mind, a very scarce thing with me, for they may her[eaf]ter save you a great deal of trouble about me, which you do not deserve, and for which I ought to be ba[s]tinadoed. I carry all matters to an extreme – so that when I have any little vexation it grows in five minutes into a theme for Sophocles – then and in that temper if I write to any friend I have so little selfpossession that I give him matter for grieving at the very time perhaps when I am laughing at a Pun. Your last letter made me blush for the pain I had given you – I know my own disposition so well that I am certain of writing many times hereafter in the same strain to you – now you know how far to believe in them – you must allow for imagination – I know I shall not be able to help it.
>
> (*L* I, 340–1)

Warming to his theme with a self-mocking allowance for his rarely stable moods and apology for wounding Bailey, Keats immediately leaps to an excessive punishment, almost teasing with the severity and exoticism of 'bastinadoed'. Though there is, as Thomson notes, a 'delicate apology' and an instruction for how Bailey must respond to Keats's letters,[5] there is also a note of irritation at being taken literally. Yet Keats connects himself as letter writer and the self he was when the letter was written through language. Laughing at a pun seems different from mournfully writing a letter by degree rather than type; language remains the binding force in Keats's imagination. Referring to petty vexations as being magnified in the poet's mind into 'a theme for Sophocles', Keats poeticises himself, reminding Bailey that he is an artist and that the appropriate response to the artist is to 'allow for imagination'. Keats is the poet-hero, prompting Lionel Trilling to suggest that in the letters we trace 'Keats's conscious desire to live life in the heroic mode'.[6] Imaginative mobility allows him to write himself into the role of the hero, but such role-playing should not be literalised as the expression of his 'true' self. The life recreated in language requires from his reader a response attuned to the poet in the letter-writer, rather than the man. Paradoxically, as Keats's imaginative mobility will not alter, it is Bailey who must.

Moving from this semi-apologetic assertion of the poet-hero within the man, Keats begins to explain his absence from the Reynolds' house owing to his 'Vexation' (*L* 1, 341) with women that they were better not to experience. Rather than seeking to place blame on the specific women or women in general, Keats begins to diagnose his failure to 'be just to them, but I cannot':

> Is it because they fall so far beneath my Boyish imagination? When I was a Schoolboy I though[t] a fair woman a pure Goddess, my mind was a soft nest in which some one of them slept though she knew it not – I have no right to expect more than their reality. I thought them etherial above Men – I find then perhaps equal – great by comparison is very small.
>
> (*L* 1, 341)

Keats pinpoints the source of his difficulty with women; it derives from his early image of them as goddesses even as he admits the injustice of such idealising. Having placed them above men, their reality as equals renders them disappointing. Once more, this becomes a facet of the poet's imagination. The Spenserian themes on which Keats's imagination had fed enable beauty but deny truth.[7] The painfully idealistic quality of Keats's previous apprehension of women is not hidden, but seems to foreshadow his later poetry. But rather than sinking into a tragic posture, Keats provides a self-mocking aside that 'I do think better of Womankind than to suppose they care whether Mister John Keats five feet hight likes them or not' (*L* 1, 342) and passes to a description of his travels, landscape and people that should 'strengthen more my reach in Poetry' (*L* 1, 342).

Experiences, from letter writing to travels in Scotland, prove grist to the poetic mill. Describing a country dancing school's performance, Keats's description enters into the dynamic experience, attempting to deliver the physicality of the dance in his charged language:

> No they kickit & jumpit with mettle extraordinary, & whiskit, & fleckkit, & toe'd it, & go'd it, & twirld it, & wheel'd it, & stampt it, & sweated it, tattooing the floor like mad; The differenc[e] between our country dances & these scotch figures, is about the same as leisurely stirring a cup o' Tea & heating [*for* beating] up a batter pudding.
>
> (*L* 1, 307)

The energy of the words responds to that of the dance; staccato syllables tattoo the page as the dancers' feet did the floor. Choosing a domestic comparison, Keats delivers an analogy that can speak directly to his experience with the appropriate tang of excitement. Such sense of the possibilities of language drives him as a letter writer and as a poet: as he writes to Bailey, 'I look upon fine Phrases like a Lover' (*L* 2, 139), embracing the attendant connotations of possession and delight. When Keats writes as a lover he distinguishes his letters from 'proper down-right love-letters' (*L* 2, 136–7) even as possession and delight create passionate and despairing poses. Keats emphasises the physical, claiming that beauty prompts love, mocking the overly literary quality of some attractions when he observes that 'I have met <wht> with women whom I really think would like to be married to a Poem and to be given away by a Novel' (*L* 2, 127). But language becomes a means of being 'present and absent at once',[8] using words to give flesh and blood to absence. Sidney Colvin refers to Keats's letters to Fanny Brawne as 'constrained and painful',[9] but it is the intensity of emotion that comes to the fore, in a manner reminiscent of Keats's earlier remark that 'the excellence of every Art is its intensity' (*L* 1, 192). Imagination allows the poet to inhabit the role of the lover as a means of expressing the personal self even as it is voiced in part through other literary lovers.

> Ask yourself my love whether you are not very cruel to have so entrammelled me, so destroyed my freedom. Will you confess this in the Letter you must write immediately, and do all you can to console me in it – make it rich as a draught of poppies to intoxicate me – write the softest words and kiss them that I may at least touch my lips where yours have been. For myself I know not how to express my devotion to so fair a form: I want a brighter word than bright, a fairer word than fair. I almost wish we were butterflies and liv'd but three summer days – three such days with you I could fill with more delight than fifty common years could ever contain.
>
> (*L* 2, 123)

Though Matthew Arnold, among a host of others, has registered the embarrassment induced by passages such as this, here, Keats's touch is sure as he orchestrates the response he desires. Ordering the letter that he longs to receive, desiring intoxication and a simulacra of presence, Keats both commands and is commanded by the power of his love. The allusion to Shakespeare's *Love's Labour's Lost* noted by Rollins is far from innocent. Asking for 'a fairer word than fair', we are returned to Don Armando's love letter to Jaquenetta, where he calls her: 'More fairer than fair, beautiful than beauteous, truer than truth itself, have commiseration on thy heroical vassal' (*Love's Labour's Lost*, 4. 1. 62–3). A love letter within a love letter, Keats uses Don Armando, a representative of male desire to strengthen his claim on Fanny Brawne and protect him from seeming a prisoner of his love. Keats is, like Don Armando, a 'heroical vassal' but he is also, like Shakespeare, a poet with power over language. Paul D. Sheats shows in relation to *The Fall of Hyperion* that '[Keats's] vulnerability is his strength',[10] and here, the apparent vulnerability expressed disguises the strength of his subtle Shakespearean invocation. This rapturous passage seems carried away by the beauty and energy of his words, where three intense days can outweigh 'fifty common years'. Imagination invigorates Keats's letters, mingling with personal experience to deepen and enrich the writing.

Dramatising the self allows the poet to entertain himself and his interlocutor with his quicksilver moods and his weaving together of the personal and the poetic. Keats's letters to his friends, particularly to J. H. Reynolds, Richard Woodhouse, Benjamin Bailey, and Charles Brown, reveal the esteem and intimacy that bound together his circle of friends. His letters to his sister, Fanny Keats, and to his invalid brother, Tom Keats, continue as long as they live, creating closeness with the former, despite the difficulty of having a relationship with her owing to Richard Abbey, Fanny's guardian, who discouraged their communication, and his letters to Tom offered him the chance 'to taste a little of our pleasure' (*L* 1, 301) by virtue of Keats's descriptive and energetic letters when Tom was bedbound with tuberculosis and unable to join Keats when he travelled. Yet it is in his letters to George and Georgiana Keats, who had resettled in Louisville, Kentucky, that Keats reaches the pinnacle of his epistolary style. The letter to George and Georgiana of 14 February–3 May 1819 is, as Trilling states, a 'dazzling letter' and 'one of the most remarkable documents of the culture of the century'.[11] Its power comes from the variety of tones that Keats packs into the single letter. Adding accretions every few days or weeks, the letter, from its beginning, makes a virtue of its scope where Keats ranges from an angry aside on the painful slight to his status by Lewis with 'You see what it is to be under six foot and not a lord' (*L* 2, 61) to sensual descriptions of the 'gushing freshness' (*L* 2, 64) of claret, from Keats's despair at his failure to achieve plaudits as a poet, to an amusing application to St Luke's, a hospital for the mentally ill, based on his devotion to 'the art & mystery of poetry' (*L* 2, 69). Attempting to transcend distance, Keats seeks to 'please myself in the fancy of speaking a prayer and a blessing over you and your lives – God bless you – I whisper good night in your ears and you will dream of me – ' (*L* 2, 74) but Keats is not content to conjure himself as a physical presence. Quoting Hazlitt's letter to William Gifford at length, Keats has his addresses share in the power of Hazlitt's writing, subtly asking them to join with him in saluting the 'style of genius' (*L* 2, 76) he detects in the work. Leaping from delivering his news to broader mediations on life, Keats's blends his personal with his poetic development. Continuing from his slight misquotation of Wordsworth's line from 'The Old Cumberland Beggar', 'we have all of us one human heart',[12] Keats muses deeply on the idea through his experience as a poet:

> Even here though I myself am pursueing the same instinctive course as the veriest human animal you can think of – I am however young writing at random – straining at particles of light in the midst of a great darkness – without knowing the bearing of any one assertion of any one opinion. Yet may I not in this be free from sin? May there not be superior beings amused with any graceful, though instinctive attitude my mind my fall into, as I am entertained with the alertness of a Stoat or the anxiety of a Deer? Though a quarrel in the streets is a thing to be hated, the energies displayed in it are fine; the commonest Man shows a grace in his quarrel – .
>
> (*L* 2, 80)

Self-consciously tracing his development as revealing a similar arc to that of the human animal, Keats claims to be 'writing at random' even as the metaphor chosen seems gorgeously apt as it promotes his poetry to the status of the philosophy which he claims is superior to his own imaginative art.[13] The lack of poetic creed moves from ignorance to an enabling freedom as the 'energies' of Keats's poetry speak to energies that can be expressed through fighting. The mind can 'call into' attitudes that entertain unspecified 'superior beings', but Keats does not allow this potential endorsement of his poetic experimentation to lapse into content. Quoting Milton and then writing out his sonnet 'Why did I laugh tonight?' Keats reveals the 'Agony' of ignorance (*L* 2, 81) even while reassuring his brother and sister-in-law that his torment was not so profound as to disturb him completely: 'Sane I went to bed and sane I arose' (*L* 2, 82). Looping back to his life, Keats even threatens to abandon poetry (*L* 2, 84) before once again returning to poetry, writing an extempore piece for their pleasure until 'I am tired of rhyming' (*L* 2, 88).

Dancing from a pastiche of Spenser to a sonnet prompted by a dream of Dante's Paulo and Francesca, Keats directly addresses Georgiana, asking question after question of her, even offering tongue-in-cheek advice on her breakfasting habits (*L* 2, 92–3). The letter begins its ascent after this piece of domestic intimacy, and Keats crowds the letter with poetry, from 'La belle dame sans merci – ' to 'The Ode to Psyche' and 'If by dull rhymes our English must be chained', amongst others, and with his famous account of the world as the 'vale of Soul-making' (*L* 2, 102) where the poet outlines his personal response to the problem of evil: 'Do you not see how necessary a World of Pains and troubles is to school an Intelligence and make it a soul?' (*L* 2, 102) Returning to his earlier formulation in the letter that only experience can make an idea a reality (*L* 2, 81), Keats shows man as 'formed by circumstances – and what are circumstances? – but touchstones of his heart – ? And what are touch stones? – but proovings of his hearrt?' (*L* 2, 103). This letter reveals the intensity, range, and power of his creative imagination, where letters become, like poetry itself, 'proovings of his hearrt'.

Keats's final letter, addressed to Charles Brown from his deathbed in Rome on 30 November 1820, is deeply affecting. It reveals Keats's bravery without concealing his pain-fraught struggle with the spectre of impending death. After admitting his physical infirmity though claiming an improvement, Keats passes to his psychological torment: 'I have an habitual feeling of my real life having passed, and that I am leading a posthumous existence. God knows how it would have been – but it appears to me – however, I will not speak of that subject' (*L* 2, 359). The almost abrupt entry of existential meditation follows hard on the heels of Keats avoiding 'the proing and conning of any thing interesting to me in England' (*L* 2, 359) and has the air of breaking into the letter against Keats's gritted teeth and determination to remain stoic in the face of death. Starting to imagine a life that might have been, Keats stops himself before he starts, with the 'I will not speak of that subject' witnessing both the strength of his resolve but also the nearly overwhelming temptation to speculate about what he almost had. Passing on to how he and Brown did not manage to meet on their last visits in England despite their proximity, Keats manages to achieve a lightness of tone that quickly darkens again when he admits that he cannot face seeing the handwriting of his friends. Touching in its refusal to state baldly that this is owing to his rapidly worsening health, Keats confesses the most devastating element of his decline:

> There is one thought enough to kill me – I have been well, healthy, alert, &c, walking with her – and now – the knowledge of contrast, feeling for light and shade, all that information (primitive sense) necessary for a poem are great enemies to the recovery of the stomach. There, you rogue, I put you to the torture, – but you must bring your philosophy to bear – as I do mine, really – or how should I be able to live?
>
> (*L* 2, 359)

The gulf between what had been and what is comes to haunt the dying poet. Listing the former species of his vitality, 'walking with her' comes to form the heart of what has been lost. The nuances of perception that had fired his art are lost to him as they detract from his health, but Keats recovers himself, sympathetically attuned to Brown's own 'torture' as he reads of the poet's. Demanding that Brown applies a philosophic eye to suffering as Keats does to his, Keats's rhetorical 'or how should I be able to live' both heroically and pitifully delineates how he mentally survives his physical collapse. Running through the list of friends that he will contact and when he will do so, Keats makes a will of sorts, remembering himself to them and asking that Brown write to his siblings. Closing his letter with, 'I can scarcely bid you good bye, even in a letter. I always made an awkward bow', the touching self-deprecation coupled with his devastation offer a deep emotional charge, not only to Brown, but also to his readers reading the final words of his 'posthumous existence' (*L* 2, 358). Taking all the heart for speech, Keats's last letter reveals his gift for intimacy, wit, and friendship even in the midst of intense turmoil.

The imaginative power and variety of Keats's letters capture their reader in part, owing to the brevity of his life. The letters to Keats's friends reveal his witty intimacy with his chosen acquaintances, where Keats's poetic theories and musings jostle with gossip, where snatches from his poetry mingle with witty segues and philosophical problems. Uniting experience with artifice, Keats's remark 'for axioms in philosophy are not axioms until they are proved upon our pulses … now I shall relish Hamlet more than I have ever done' (*L* 1, 279) is suggestive of how he uses allusion in his letters. Keats's imaginative mobility dramatises his voice and allows him to inhabit other roles in order to express himself. The letters do not merely provide a supplement for the poetry. They show Keats's radical inventiveness where the sheer volume of ideas, tones, and moods shows the imagination to be the guiding force that transforms the self from stable entity to shifting and dynamic force.

Notes

1 Timothy Webb, '"Cutting Figures": Rhetorical Strategies in Keats's *Letters*', *Keats: Bicentenary Readings*, ed. Michael O'Neill (Edinburgh: Edinburgh University Press, 1997), pp. 144–69 (146).
2 Qtd. from *Percy Bysshe Shelley: The Major Works*, ed. Zachary Leader and Michael O'Neill (Oxford: Oxford University Press, 2003).
3 Webb, '"Cutting Figures"', p. 145.
4 Susan Wolfson defines the letters as 'deftly performative' in Susan J. Wolfson, 'Keats the Letter-Writer: Epistolary Poetics', *Romanticism Past and Present* 6.2 (1982): 43–61 (44).
5 Heidi Thomson, 'Keats's Letters: "A Wilful and Dramatic Exercise of Our Minds Towards Each Other"', *Keats-Shelley Review* 25.2 (2011): 160–74, 166.
6 Lionel Trilling, *The Opposing Self: Nine Essays in Criticism* (1950; New York: Viking Press, 1968), p. 4.

7 For Keats's intellectual and poetic engagement with Spenser's *Faerie Queene*, see Greg Kucich, *Keats, Shelley, and Romantic Spenserianism* (University Park, PA: Pennsylvania State University Press, 1991).

8 C. A. Plasa, 'Lost in the Post-Miltonic: Reading Keats's letters', *Prose Studies* 15.1 (1992): 30–48 (30).

9 Sir Sidney Colvin, 'Preface', *Letters of John Keats to His Family and Friends* (1891; London: Macmillan, 1925), p. vi.

10 Paul D. Sheats, 'Stylistic Discipline in *The Fall of Hyperion*', *Keats–Shelley Journal* 17 (1968): 88.

11 Trilling, *Opposing Self*, p. 42.

12 William Wordsworth and Samuel Taylor Coleridge, 'The Old Cumberland Beggar', *Lyrical Ballads, 1798 and 1802*, ed. Fiona Stafford (Oxford: Oxford University Press, 2013), l.146. Keats remembers the line as 'we have all one human heart', *L* 2, 80.

13 See *L* 2, 81.

CHAPTER 8

Manuscripts and Publishing History

John Barnard

1817–1821

When Keats died in Rome on 23 February 1821, he had published three volumes containing forty poems. A further eight had been published in periodicals or in Leigh Hunt's *Literary Pocket-Book* for 1819. The publishing history of these forty-eight poems reflects Keats ambivalent attitude to contemporary readers and 'the poisonous suffrage of a public' (*L* 2, 146). *Poems* (1817), which Keats put together in late 1816 and early 1817 while still a dresser at Guy's Hospital, was published at his own expense by Charles and James Ollier, newly set up in business. Keats was therefore responsible for the choice of poems, their ordering into four sections, and the head of Shakespeare on the title page. The last minute inclusion of the dedicatory sonnet to Leigh Hunt ensured the Tory reviewers' identification of its author as 'Hunt's elevé', as Keats swiftly came to fear. *Endymion* (1818) was published by John Taylor and James Hessey, an established firm building up their poetry list. Keats's anxieties about the reception of his 'Poetic Romance' lie behind the unstable mixture of self-deprecatory modesty, pride, and distrust of the reading public which marks both the original draft of his Preface, rejected by his friends and publishers, and the published version. Taylor took considerable care over the poem's text, undertaking much of the proofreading (*P* 574–5, *L* 1, 270–3).

The role played by Taylor and his lawyer and literary adviser, Richard Woodhouse, in the final form of *Lamia, Isabella, The Eve of St. Agnes, and Other Poems* (1820) was altogether more substantial. Despite Keats's intentions, *Lamia*, and not *The Eve of St. Agnes*, opened the volume (*L* 2 276), and, according to Taylor's prefatory note, the epic fragment of *Hyperion*, which at one point Keats had thought of publishing in a joint volume with Hunt (*KC* 2, 234),[1] was printed only at the publishers' 'particular request' 'contrary to the wish of the author'.[2] Further, Taylor refused to print Keats's more sexually explicit revisions to *The Eve of St. Agnes*. As Woodhouse reported, Keats left it 'to his Publishers to adopt which [readings] they pleased, & to revise the Whole'[3] and Woodhouse and Taylor suggested many changes to *Isabella*.[4] This gives some credence to Keats's claim to Shelley that the volume 'would never have been publish'd but from a hope of gain' (*L* 2, 323). Keats's distrust of the literary marketplace is evident from the pseudonym 'Caviare' he adopted for the periodical publication of 'La Belle Dame Sans Merci' shortly before the *Lamia* volume appeared.

Keats's three volumes found relatively few contemporary readers, though his final volume received positive reviews. Ironically, the substantial passages from Keats's poems quoted in periodical reviews, most of them antagonistic, were the most widely circulated examples of his poetry during his lifetime. Where the editions of his books numbered from 500 to, at most, 1,000, the newly founded *Blackwood's* had a circulation of around 4,000 and the *Quarterly Review* around 12,000.

But Keats had another readership. During his lifetime as many as two-thirds of his poems circulated only in manuscript. Many of these are short or *jeux d'esprits*, but they include over half of Keats's sixty-one sonnets, some his best known: the 'Ode on Indolence', 'The Eve of St Mark', the visionary fragment, *The Fall of Hyperion*, his tragedy, *Otho the Great*, co-authored with Charles Brown, and his late unsettled and unsettling poems to Fanny Brawne. Also in manuscript were the very substantial number of letters preserved by family and friends, many containing drafts or copies of published and unpublished poems. Although this body of material was scattered, from very early on members of Keats's circle, including his brothers, Joseph Severn, Charles Cowden Clarke and John Hamilton Reynolds, made copies of his poems or held on to the autograph manuscripts freely given away by Keats as keepsakes. The most systematic was Richard Woodhouse, who from 1818 made extensive copies of Keats's autographs of poems and letters (including many now lost), and annotated his copies of Keats's first two volumes, recording textual variations and adding other notes. Woodhouse's collection of 'Keatsiana' makes him Keats's first editor. Charles Brown made copies of his poems while the two men were walking in Scotland, a practice he continued with Keats's agreement when, following Tom's death on 1 December 1818, the two men began lodging together at Wentworth Place. Brown eventually had 'four MS books in my hand writing'.[5] In addition, his publisher, John Taylor, also possessed a significant number of Keats's letters and documents.

It is not surprising therefore that, shortly after Keats's death, Taylor advertised in the *New Times* on 29 March 1821, 'Speedily will be Published, with Portrait, Memoirs and Remains of John Keats'. Taylor had swiftly set about asking Woodhouse, Brown, Severn, Reynolds and others for their help in gathering together materials for his memoir. Keats's admirers fell out with one another. Brown, like Severn, thought Taylor's was a mere bookseller's venture, and that he, Brown, should write the biography. Cowden Clarke also had thoughts of doing so. In consequence, none of them did. Nevertheless, these abortive attempts ensured that this considerable body of material was preserved. On Woodhouse's death his 'Keatsiana' passed into Taylor's hands, and eventually this, together with Brown's collections, provided the nucleus of the extant manuscript archive from which Keats's unpublished poems and letters gradually found their way into print and upon which our understanding of the textual transmission of Keats's poetry and his habits of composition depend.

1821–1883

Although Keats remained a figure of interest in the periodicals, his poems had to wait until 1829 before they were eventually published in Paris by A. and W. Galignani in *Poetical Works of Coleridge, Shelley, and Keats.* This circulated mainly on the continent and included all the poems from Keats's three volumes and four short poems added from elsewhere. The frequent reprints of this edition in the United States, beginning in 1831, meant that Keats's poems were more easily available to American than English readers.[6] But if Keats was being read in Harvard, he was also being read in Cambridge by Tennyson, whose *Poems, Chiefly Lyrical* (1830) were immediately likened to those of Keats. It was not until 1840 that Keats's *Poetical Works* were published in London as part of William Smith's Standard Library for 2s. Five years later, John Taylor sold his copyright to Keats's poems and letters to Edward Moxon (*KC* 2, 128–9), the publisher and supporter of Wordsworth, Tennyson, and the Brownings. Moxon's publication of Keats's *Poetical Works* (1846) and its frequent reprints mark the point at which his poetry entered the Victorian poetic canon.

It was also Moxon who shortly after published Richard Monckton Milnes's two-volume *Life, Letters, and Literary Remains, of John Keats* (1848). Milnes, a minor poet and Cambridge friend of Tennyson, drew on the manuscript collections earlier assembled by Taylor, Woodhouse, and Brown and sought out Keats's acquaintances for information, notably Joseph Severn, C. W. Dilke, Bailey, and Reynolds. He got further help from George Keats's widow in America. This was the first time a substantial body of Keats's letters reached the public. One letter had been printed in 1828 by Leigh Hunt, and in summer 1836, two more were published, the second incompletely, in the Kentucky *Western Messenger* (*L* I, 298–301, 346ff.). Milnes described his *Life* as a 'compilation' not a biography, saying he was simply an 'editor of the Life which was, as it were, already written', connecting 'the letters freely supplied by kinsmen and friends'. In all Milnes printed some eighty letters in whole or part (*L* I, 3), and included sixty-six poems and parts of two others of which forty (including *Otho the Great* and *King Stephen*) and the first four lines of 'Over the hill' were hitherto unpublished (*Texts* 75). In the following decade Milnes printed *The Fall of Hyperion* in the *Miscellanies of the Philobiblon Society* (1856–7) describing it merely as 'Another Version of Keats's "Hyperion"'.

By the mid-century Keats was sufficiently well known for *Endymion*'s 'A thing of beauty is a joy for ever' to be inscribed over the entrance to Manchester's great Art Treasures Exhibition of 1857 (and in 1870 Trollope was able to drop the line, without quotation marks, into *The Vicar of Bullhampton*[7]). But it was another two decades before his collected works appeared, edited by H. Buxton Forman who had recently completed his major four-volume edition of Shelley (1876–7). He proved indefatigable in searching out new manuscript material. As early as 1876, he obtained Fanny Brawne's collection of Keats's love letters from her son, Herbert Lindon. These had previously been in the hands of Sir Charles W. Dilke who not only attempted to prevent their publication, but held back two letters and may have destroyed others. Despite Dilke's strenuous objections, Forman's *Letters of John Keats to Fanny Brawne*, containing thirty-seven letters, was published in 1878 and promptly reprinted in New York. It was immediately condemned as shockingly unmanly by, among others, Swinburne. Forman subsequently persuaded Keats's sister, Fanny, who had carefully preserved her brother's letters, that they were worth publishing. These, together with much new manuscript material, and extensive notes, textual and explanatory, were gathered into the four volumes of Forman's great 'library edition', *The Poetical Works and Other Writings of John Keats, now First Brought Together, including Poems and Numerous Letters not before published. Edited with Notes and Appendices* (1883). This added another 8 minor poems[8] and contains 196 letters (*L* I, 5). Keats's letters to Fanny Brawne are presented together as a separate group and add two further letters, originally held back by Dilke, bringing the number up to thirty-nine. Ten of these are now known only through Forman's transcripts. Forman continued to add new material as it became available, notably in the five-volume *Complete Works* of 1901 which brought the number of letters or parts of letters up to 217. Since 1883 only fifteen short poems have been added to the canon, the most recent in 1939. Forman's 1901 edition, revised and expanded by his son, M. B. Forman, for the handsome eight-volume Hampstead edition (New York, 1938–9) remains the only complete edition of Keats's poetry, letters, reviews, and marginalia, and is still useful. Forman's arrangement of Keats's poems, starting with the three volumes published in his lifetime and followed by 'Posthumous and Fugitive Poems', directly reflecting their publishing history, is that followed by subsequent editions of the complete poems in the nineteenth century and most of the twentieth.

If Forman's publication in 1883 marks a high point of Keats scholarship and his unquestionable canonical status, the 1880s were, partly due to Forman's researches, an important decade in the uncovering and stabilisation of Keats's manuscript archive. The two main bodies of manuscript material in England were by then owned by Monckton Milnes, Sir Charles Wentworth Dilke, who had inherited and added to his grandfather's collection of Keatsiana, and Frederick Locker-Lampson. In the United States, George Keats's descendants owned an important body of Keats's letters and poetry manuscripts, and American collectors had already obtained Keats fragments from Joseph Severn in Rome. Following Severn's death in 1879, the large majority of Keats manuscripts still in his possession were sold through Henry Sotheran in 1881, but not before Forman was allowed access. In March 1882, Fanny Brawne's letters were auctioned off and dispersed. However, Fanny Keats (Llanos) kept her brother's letters in the family. The fascinating history of the provenance and current location of Keats's manuscripts is well told in Stephen Hebron's *John Keats: A Poet and His Manuscripts* (2009). In brief, Sir Charles Dilke gave his collection to Hampstead Public Library in 1911, the start of the Keats House collection, and Fanny Keats's family gifted her brother's letters to the British Museum (now the British Library). In America Amy Lowell bequeathed her considerable Keats collection, much of which came from Locker-Lampson's library, to Harvard in 1925. The subsequent gift by Arthur A. Houghton, Jr., who in the 1940s had purchased Monckton Milnes's enlarged collection from his son, the Marquess of Crewe, accounts for the outstanding fullness of the Harvard Keats Collection. Other important holdings are in the Morgan Library and Princeton University Library.

1883–2015

The standard text of Keats's poetry from 1883 until well into the second half of the twentieth century was that of Forman, who died in 1917. His edition of the poems for the Oxford Standard Authors (OSA), first published in 1908, went through many editions, and was revised in 1956 with only minor revisions. Ernest de Selincourt published a valuable annotated edition in 1905 (5th edn 1926) and in 1915 Sidney Colvin's two-volume edition, arranged chronologically, appeared (reprinted New York 1920). In 1939, H. W. Garrod's *Keats's Poetical Works* in the Oxford English Texts series, based on a fresh examination of the manuscripts available to him in England, replaced Forman's as the scholarly edition. Garrod provided an extensive textual apparatus but no commentary, and there was a second edition in 1958. Miriam Allott's Longman edition of the *Poems* (1970) modernises the texts, is arranged chronologically following Colvin's example and the series policy, and its full annotation remains useful.

However, Jack Stillinger's systematic re-examination of all the manuscripts, and his analysis of their relationship to one another and the printed texts, in *The Texts of Keats's Poems* (1974) revealed the inaccuracies, misdating, and inconsistencies of Milnes, Forman, Garrod, and Allott. He concluded: '[T]he modern editing of Keats is a patchwork affair resting on rather shaky foundations.' His subsequent edition of the *Poems*, published by Harvard in 1978, is now the standard text. The poems are, like Allott, arranged chronologically, with extensive textual notes, a record of the emendations of all substantives and accidentals, historical collations, the order of poems in Keats's first and last volumes, a summary account of the manuscripts, and a section on questionable attributions. The only substantial change from the conclusions of his earlier book is the decision to use the published version of *The Eve of St. Agnes* rather than Keats's more explicit revised version.

Until the mid-twentieth century, the fullest edition of Keats's letters was M. B. Forman's Oxford edition of 1931, based on his father's *Complete Works* (1901). By its fourth edition in 1952, it included a total of 244 letters (one a forgery). This was replaced in 1958 by H. E. Rollins's magisterial *Letters of John Keats 1814–1821*. Based on a fresh collation of the known manuscripts and transcripts, this two-volume edition contains 320 letters and documents, adding 7 items by Keats and new texts of 7 letters. It includes the relatively small extant number of incoming letters to Keats, and his friends' letters to and from Italy recording the painful progress of his final illness. Rollins's annotation contains a wealth of information. Since then the final leaf of Keats's journal letter to George and Georgiana Keats of 14 February–5 May 1819[9] and two new letters, those to his brothers of 30 January 1818 and that to William Haslam of 2 November 1819, have been discovered.

Rollins had previously edited *The Keats Circle: Letters and Papers 1816–1878* (1948) drawn entirely from the Harvard Keats Collection, supplemented in 1955 by *More Letters and Poems of the Keats Circle* (issued together in 1965). Rollins's editions of the letters and of the manuscripts in the *Keats Circle* are, together with Stillinger's edition of the poems and his work on their texts, the essential printed sources for the study of Keats.

Transcriptions of Keats's marginalia, together with his reviews, were included in Forman's collected editions from 1883 onwards, and some are given as appendices in selections of Keats's works. Caroline Spurgeon's *Keats's Shakespeare* (1928, rpt. 1966) provides a descriptive account of the extensive annotations in his seven-volume edition of Shakespeare. A full analysis and transcription of Keats's marginalia in his copy of Milton at Keats House is given in Beth Lau's invaluable *Keats's 'Paradise Lost'* (1998). Digital images of Keats's four annotated books at Harvard can now be consulted online.

Although Stillinger's and Rollins's editions of the poems and letters are the standard reference works, a wide range of dependable editions are generally available. There are three selections of Keats's letters. Robert Gittings's selection, first published in 1970, was revised in 2002 for Oxford World's Classics by Jon Mee, adding an incisive introduction and substantial annotation. Grant F. Scott's *Selected Letters* (Harvard, 2002), 'based on the texts of Hyder Edward Rollins', modernises both Keats's spelling and his punctuation sacrificing immediacy for accessibility. Unlike Gittings's selection, it includes a substantial number of letters by Severn and others describing Keats's last months in addition to the new letters and part of a letter discovered since Rollins's edition. John Barnard's Penguin Classics edition (2014), like that of Gittings and Mee, follows Keats's spelling and punctuation. By interspersing the letters Keats wrote over several days, or in some cases months, with those written to others in the meantime, and adding brief biographical links, it allows the reader to follow Keats's life through his letters.

The choice among editions of Keats's poetry is much wider. There are two ways of ordering the poems, both with a powerful logic – that dictated by the publishing history or that based on their date of composition. The former (the three volumes published in Keats's lifetime followed by 'Posthumous and Fugitive Verse') is the dominant arrangement from Forman in 1883 to Garrod in 1958, though it is confusing and obscures Keats's poetic development. The chronological ordering adopted by Allott in 1970 is followed by John Barnard's *Complete Poems* (Penguin), first published in 1973 but revised in the light of Stillinger's 1974 textual findings for the second edition (1977). This has substantial annotation, a dictionary of classical names based on Keats's reading in Lempriere and others, and appendices including his Milton marginalia and the review of Kean's acting. Jack Stillinger's 'reading edition' of the *Complete Poems* (1982) follows the chronological order of his earlier scholarly edition, omitting the textual apparatus in favour of a compact commentary. The Oxford Authors *John Keats* (1990), edited by Elizabeth Cook, reissued from 2001 as his *Major Works*, gives a generous selection of the poetry and letters, with appendices drawing on his prose and printing Keats's preferred version of *The Eve of St. Agnes*. Unlike other editions which normalise, and hence homogenise, the poems which circulated in manuscript, Cook retains the spelling and punctuation of the originals. The Everyman *Poems* (revised version, 1999) has a brief introduction by David Bromwich, compact notes by Nicholas Roe, and begins with the three volumes published by Keats, followed by the subsequently printed poems divided between shorter and longer posthumous poems.

Two later editions reflect the historicist move initiated by Jerome McGann's *Romantic Ideology* (1983) which reads Keats in his literary, political and social worlds, bringing together Keats's poetry and prose in its immediate publishing context within an overall chronological structure. Susan Wolfson's Longman Cultural edition (2007), 'an experiment in editorial form', describes itself as the 'first edition organized to give a sense of the poet's thinking by interspersing letters, poems, and publications of reviews and contemporary works'. Keats's autograph letters are set in italic to indicate their differing textual status and Keats's three volumes represented by selections. Jeffrey N. Cox's Norton Critical Edition, *Keats's Poetry and Prose* (2009), takes this approach further, and is an editorial embodiment of his reading of Keats in *Poetry and Politics in the Cockney School* (1998). The three volumes published by Keats are given in full, framed by the periodical reviews and a selection of his letters so that 'readers can see how his poetry entered into public life', and there is detailed annotation throughout. A final section brings together substantial selections from influential studies of Keats between 1966 and 2002 which include Paul de Man, Nicholas Roe, Stuart Sperry, Grant F. Scott, and Cox himself among others.

Manuscript Facsimiles

Keats's rich manuscript archive is an essential resource for establishing the texts of his poems, and for studying his habits of composition. For most of the twentieth century the expense of reproductions meant that very few were available and often of poor quality. Exceptions are Ernest de Selincourt's 1905 facsimile of the British Library's autograph of *Hyperion*, and George Williamson's fifty-nine collotype facsimiles of the Keats manuscripts included in Sir Charles W. Dilke's 1911 bequest to what is now Keats House.[10] Robert Gitting's *The Odes of John Keats* (1970) has good black and white reproductions of the major odes excluding 'Indolence', with transcriptions and notes. The major breakthrough for Keats scholars came in the 1980s when a very substantial number of Keats's poetry manuscripts and transcripts were made available in high-quality print facsimile editions in Garland's *The Manuscripts of the Younger Romantics* (*MYR*). Jack Stillinger's seven volumes in the series (1985–8, *MYR: John Keats*, vols. 1–7), all with introductions and valuable explanatory notes, contain Woodhouse's marked up copies of *Poems* (1817) and *Endymion* in the Huntington and Morgan Libraries respectively, the poetry manuscripts in the Berg Collection and the British Library, and Woodhouse's and Brown's transcripts at Harvard. These together with the facsimile edition, also by Stillinger, of the poetry manuscripts at Harvard (1990)[11] cover the majority of the extant manuscripts of Keats's poems. However, all of these are library editions.

Stephen Hebron's *John Keats: A Poet and His Manuscripts* (2009) with its high-quality colour reproductions of twenty-one poems and letters, and historical introduction and commentary, provides an excellent starting point for the study of the manuscripts. But the major twenty-first-century advance is the digitisation of Harvard's Keats manuscripts under the direction of Leslie Morris. Since 2010 digital facsimiles of these have been freely available online.[12] Included are the drafts, fair copies, and transcripts of Keats's poems, the originals and transcripts of his letters, and examples of his marginalia, notably the seven-volume Shakespeare which Keats acquired in 1817, but also those in his copies of books by Hazlitt, Spenser, and Francisco de Moraes. As the Harvard Keats Collection contains three quarters of his extant poetry autographs, the Woodhouse and Brown transcripts, and a third (86) of his known letters, facsimiles of a very substantial part of Keats's manuscript archive are now generally available for the first time.

Facsimiles cannot replace the study of the original but they allow the viewer to see for themselves what lies behind the printed text. Richard Woodhouse reported that Keats 'never sits down to write unless he is full of ideas – and then thoughts come about him in troops, as tho' soliciting to be acc^{d} & he selects – one of his Maxims is that if P[oetry] does not come naturally, it had better not come at all' (*KC* I, 128). Keats's manuscripts bear this out. The draft of 'Ode to a Nightingale' has very few revisions (Gittings, *Odes*, 36–43), and the British Museum's draft of *Hyperion* (*MYR: John Keats*, 5) was, according to Woodhouse, 'composed & written down at once as it now stands'. In both cases, these drafts are remarkably close to Keats's published texts. On the other hand, although the draft of *The Eve of St. Agnes* shows the extraordinary fluency with which Keats composed, it is also one of his most heavily worked-over drafts (see, for instance, his two deleted attempts at stanza 25, 'A casement high and triple-arch'd there was', Harvard Keats MS 2.21, sequence 13–14). The manuscripts of his letters, with their use of dashes, and abrupt changes of tone and direction, reflect Keats's mental and emotional agility while the very few corrections show Keats writing to the minute. An acquaintance with Keats's manuscripts is a forcible reminder of the extent to which the circulation of his poems and letters among his family and close friends gave him the liberty and space to experiment poetically and follow through his 'speculations' on art and life, free from the inhibitions and anxieties stemming from his distrust of the reading public.

Notes

1 J. H. Reynolds's 'remonstrance' against 'printing … Hyperion with a work of Leigh Hunt' is corroborated by Hunt's possession of Keats's holograph (Jack Stillinger, *The Texts of Keats Poems* [Cambridge, MA: Harvard University Press, 1974], p. 230; hereafter *Texts*). This explains why Woodhouse's transcript was used as copy for the published text.

2 Woodhouse's draft is essentially the same (*KC* I, 115–16).

3 *Texts*, p. 219.

4 See Jack Stillinger, 'Keats and His Helpers: The Multiple Authorship of *Isabella*', *Multiple Authorship and the Myth of Solitary Genius* (New York: Oxford University Press, 1991), pp. 25–49.

5 *Texts*, p. 51.

6 See J. R. MacGillivray, *Keats: A Bibliography and Reference Guide with an Essay on Keats' Reputation* (Toronto: University of Toronto Press, 1949), pp. 2–9, and H. E. Rollins, *Keats's Reputation in America to 1848* (Cambridge, MA: Harvard University Press, 1946).

7 Anthony Trollope, *The Vicar of Bullhampton*, ed. David Skilton (Oxford: Oxford University Press, 1988), p. 8.

8 *Texts*, pp. 80–1.

9 Keats misdates the last part of his letter 'Wednesday May 4' (*John Keats: Selected Letters*, ed. John Barnard [London: Penguin, 2014], pp. 366–7).

10 *Keats Letters, Papers and Other Relics, Forming the Dilke Bequest in the Hampstead Public Library* (London: John Lane, The Bodley Head, 1914).

11 *John Keats: Poetry Manuscripts at Harvard: A Facsimile Edition*, ed. Jack Stillinger (Cambridge, MA: Harvard University Press, 1990).

12 http://hcl.harvard.edu/libraries/houghton/collections/modern/keats.cfm. Subsequent references are to the Harvard catalogue number and digital sequence.

PART II

Cultural Contexts

CHAPTER 9

The Hunt Circle and the Cockney School

Gregory Leadbetter

The 'Hunt circle' and the 'Cockney School' are in a sense rival terms: two ways of characterising the same loose grouping – among them the Shelleys, William Hazlitt, Charles Lamb, Benjamin Haydon, Charles Cowden Clarke, and John Hamilton Reynolds – associated with the liberal reformist, poet and journalist, Leigh Hunt, especially in those post-war years of acute political crisis and extraordinary literary abundance, 1815–1822. For Keats, who sought out and, through Cowden Clarke, first met Hunt in October 1816, the social, intellectual and artistic support network he entered was of lasting importance to his career – but also cast a critical shadow across his work, both during and after his life. This chapter examines this creative and cultural nexus, and its dynamic presence in Keats's life as a poet.

In October 1817, *Blackwood's Edinburgh Magazine* ran the first of a series of articles by their anonymous reviewer – 'Z' – 'On the Cockney School of Poetry', whose 'chief Doctor and Professor', the article declared, 'is Mr Leigh Hunt': 'a man certainly of some talents, of extravagant pretensions both in wit, poetry, and politics, and withal of exquisitely bad taste, and extremely vulgar modes of thinking and manners in all respects. He is a man of little education'.[1] 'Z' was in fact the Scottish critic John Gibson Lockhart, and here he gave currency to the charges of bad taste, vulgarity and poor education with which he aimed to discredit Hunt and his associates. The motivation was unashamedly political: by 1817, Hunt had long been an outspoken opponent of the social, political and economic *status quo*, having served two years in prison – albeit in surprisingly lenient conditions – for libelling the Prince Regent. For Keats at that time, Hunt was an authentic champion of liberty – half-mythologised as 'Libertas' in his poems – with whom he was proud to be publicly connected. Lockhart spoke for a Tory establishment emphatically opposed to the threat Hunt and his ilk were thought to present. It was, as Hunt would later call it,

'Literary Warfare'.[2] The principles of poetry were the battleground for a contest of ideas with far-reaching social ramifications.

Keats was struck by Z's 'flaming attack upon Hunt' (*L* I, 179). 'I never read any thing so virulent', he wrote, and guessed that it would be his turn soon: 'I have no doubt that the second Number was intended for me' (*L* I, 180). In the event, Keats had to wait until the fourth of Lockhart's articles on the 'Cockney School', in August 1818, which took on the *Poems* of 1817 and *Endymion*. It is a striking representative of the cultural cross-fire into which Keats's verse emerged. 'Of all the manias of this mad age', Lockhart began, 'the most incurable, as well as the most common, seems to be no other than the *Metromanie*'. Keats had succumbed to the 'mania' for poetry – a diseased and inexcusable 'phrenzy' in the face of civilised conventions – which had now settled into 'drivelling idiocy' (*CH* 98). Lockhart concedes that Keats has 'talents of an excellent, perhaps even of a superior order' – though these have been utterly perverted under the influence of Hunt, 'the most worthless and affected of all the versifiers of our time', 'the meanest, the filthiest, and the most vulgar of Cockney poetasters' (*CH* 98, 99). As a result of associating with Hunt's 'uneducated' gang of 'fanciful dreaming tea-drinkers', 'Mr Keats has adopted the loose, nerveless versification, and Cockney rhymes of the poet of *Rimini*' (*CH* 101, 104). In a final flourish, Lockhart unveils the political animus of his attack: 'Keats belongs to the Cockney School of Politics, as well as the Cockney School of Poetry', he remarks, and – casting a cold eye on the opening lines of *Endymion* Book III, which mock those 'who lord it o'er their fellow-men' (l.1) – quipped that 'their bantling has already learned to lisp sedition' (*CH* 109).

'Z' left his mark: the 'Cockney' moniker stuck. Only a month after Lockhart's hatchet job, John Wilson Croker (likewise anonymously) entered the fray in the *Quarterly Review*: Keats was 'unhappily a disciple of the new school of what has been somewhere called Cockney poetry; which may be defined to consist of the most incongruous ideas in the most uncouth language' (*CH* 111). Like Lockhart, Croker affects an attitude of benevolence towards a sadly misguided youth: Keats has 'powers of language, rays of fancy, and gleams of genius', but 'he is of an age and temper which imperiously require mental discipline' (*CH* 111, 112) – lacking which, and 'being bitten by Mr Leigh Hunt's insane criticism', Keats 'more than rivals the insanity of his poetry' (*CH* 111).

Such were the terms upon which the idea of a 'Cockney School' was founded. In their eagerness to assume the role of sober cultural guardianship, Lockhart and Croker seem oblivious to the extremity of their own prose. While purporting to act in the name of poetic principle, in practice reviews in the style of the 'Cockney School' essays appealed to a crude form of sensationalism. They played to their crowd: it was a mode akin to baiting, dressed up as civilised discourse.

Moreover, this form of 'literary warfare' was not based upon a generational divide: in donning the mantle of 'correct' taste, Lockhart was something of a young fogey, only a year older than Keats himself. Nor even does it characterise one political stance rather than another – a fact not often noticed in criticism. In September 1816, Hazlitt had published a spiteful mock-review of Coleridge's *Statesman's Manual* in Hunt's *Examiner* before it had even been published, and did not hold back elsewhere either: unlike Lockhart, however, as Marilyn Butler notes, 'Hazlitt has on the whole got away with his trivializing and his nastiness'.[3] At the time Keats came to public notice, poetry reviews could very rarely claim to be disinterested enquiries into principle, but, as Coleridge complained feelingly in *Biographia Literaria* – published in 1817 into that same heated atmosphere – showed 'the too manifest and too frequent interference of NATIONAL PARTY, and even PERSONAL predilection or aversion'.[4] The stakes could be high. In December 1818 – with the 'Cockney School' essays still in the air – the editor of Baldwin's *London Magazine*, John Scott, called *Blackwood's* to account, as a publication in which 'the violation of decency was to render it *piquant*, and the affectation of piety to render it persuasive, and servility to power render it profitable' (*CH* 22). As a result of this attack, Scott would fight a duel with Lockhart's friend John Christie in February 1821: Scott – who had publicly defended Keats (*CH* 115–16, 219–27) – was fatally wounded, and died the same month as the poet.

Keats's mauling (along with Hunt) in the journals gave him something in common with the older generation of poets whose emergence had been equally contentious. If, by 1817, Wordsworth had achieved a certain eminence – he was a favourite of Lockhart's, ironically – he had done so despite the notices which had often greeted his work: Francis Jeffrey's attack on the 'Lake School' in 1802 resembled the charges levelled at Keats, and he later dismissed Wordsworth's *Poems, in Two Volumes* (1807) as 'namby-pamby' verse.[5] Coleridge's return to publication with the *Christabel* volume (1816) and *Sibylline Leaves* (1817) coincided with Keats's first appearance – and was similarly abused in the press. The parallels are telling, and should make readers wary of reducing a complex set of intellectual, political and literary relationships to simplistic or conveniently dichotomous history. Hunt and Wordsworth are presented in Butler's misleading taxonomy as sheer opposites, 'radical'/'liberal' versus 'Tory'/'conservative' respectively[6] – but the facts are far more involved than such blunt categories allow. As Hunt's own remarks makes clear, 'Cockney' and 'Laker' – the two 'new schools' of poetry – were closer than critical convention has tended to read them in the context of post-1815 literary-political controversy.

The subtleties of such connections were not so apparent in the combative atmosphere of the time, however, and the 'Cockney School' tag persisted as a derisive term, often blending its stream with the burgeoning discourse of manliness and moral character that would characterise a good deal of the century's subsequent paranoia. When Keats died in 1821, the story quickly spread that the attacks he had suffered in the *Quarterly* and *Blackwood's* had effectively killed the poet. Both Hunt and Shelley made remarks of this kind (see *CH* 17), and Shelley's *Adonais* turned 'Keats' into a myth. The once-popular image of Keats's death – that he was 'snuffed out by an article', as Byron put it (*Don Juan*, canto 11, stanza 60) – fostered the notion that Keats was a feeble youth, who, in Thomas Carlyle's words, 'wanted a world of treacle'.[7]

While Keats was understandably unsettled by the reviews he received, he was very far from being snuffed out in 1818. Although he could not have predicted the furore that followed, Keats had walked into the politicised literary drama of the day with his eyes open. Keats had been jostled and stamped as one of the 'Cockneys' – but he had also entered the cultural and political life of the times.

Keats's debut collection laid open his sympathies. 'To Charles Cowden Clarke', published in *Poems* (1817), celebrates his friend as the one who 'first taught me all the sweets of song', together with 'the patriot's stern duty' (53, 69). Keats identifies his liberal politics with his poetic cause: 'Spenserian vowels that elope with ease' line up with 'the might of Alfred, and the shaft of Tell; / The hand of Brutus, that so grandly fell / Upon a tyrant's head' (56, 70–2). Those 'eloping' vowels hint at the willing transgressions of verse with 'little fit to please a classic ear', which nonetheless scoops up 'sparkling Helicon' and 'Apollo's glories' (24, 27, 45) – along with Tasso, Milton and Mozart – into its range of reference. The loose and chatty couplets – 'as my hand was warm, I thought I'd better / Trust to my feelings, and write you a letter' (103–4) – parody formality, trailing 'the true voice of feeling' (*L* 2, 167) over Augustan manners. The poem, like the poet's hand, is warm with its social impulse.

Cowden Clarke passed a copy of the poem to Hunt, ahead of Keats's meeting with him, and if 'Keats had known Hunt personally', Nicholas Roe observes, he could not have combined form and content in a way 'better calculated to win his approval'.[8] Hunt was suitably impressed.

The Examiner gave Keats his first publication as a poet ('O Solitude!'), and Keats's *Poems* of 1817 affirmed their new connection. Its dedicatory sonnet, 'To Leigh Hunt, Esq.', captures their common feeling for 'a free, / A leafy luxury' in a time when 'Pan is no longer sought' (12–13), just as its epigraph from Spenser hailed Hunt's cherished ethos of 'delight with liberty'. Praising Hunt 'for showing truth to flattered state' ('Written on the Day That Mr. Leigh Hunt Left Prison', 1), Keats was writing himself into Hunt's programme of social and poetical reform.

Hunt had already welcomed Keats to the cause. Writing in *The Examiner* in December 1816, he named Keats – along with Shelley and Reynolds – as 'Young Poets' whose work promised to advance 'a new school of poetry rising of late', characterised by its 'love of Nature, and of *thinking* instead of mere *talking*' (*CH* 41–2). In the summer of 1817, Hunt extended his notice of Keats with a review of *Poems*, expanding upon the 'new school of poetry' by way of contrast to the formerly dominant 'school of wit and ethics in verse', which he associated with Dryden and Pope (*CH* 55). For Hunt, this was not so much an innovation as a return to authenticity: 'something which was not poetry has made way for the return of something which is' (*CH* 55). Hunt developed the point in his Preface to *The Story of Rimini* (1816), in which he accused 'Pope and the French school' of having 'mistaken mere smoothness for harmony'.[9] In its place, Hunt had endeavoured to achieve 'a freer spirit of versification', and 'a free and idiomatic cast of language': for 'the proper language of poetry', he continued, 'is in fact nothing different from that of real life'.[10] Hunt consciously echoed Wordsworth's 1800/1802 Prefaces to *Lyrical Ballads*. In his 1817 review of Keats, Hunt wrote that the 'Lake Poets' were 'the first to revive a true taste for nature' (*CH* 56); in *Foliage* (1818), he identified Wordsworth as the 'most prominent ornament' of the 'new school of poetry', and Coleridge its 'inner priest'.[11] Hunt's 'Cockney' manifesto took in Keats by way of the 'Lake School'.

The virtues that Hunt admires in Keats are expressions of his own poetics. He praises Keats for 'giving himself up to his own impressions', and for exercising 'a fancy and imagination at will, and an intense feeling of external beauty in it's most natural and least expressible simplicity' (*CH* 57, 59). Bringing the review to a close under the title '*Happy Poetry Preferred*' (*CH* 62) – as Wu remarks, 'a headline so recognizably Huntian that it could be a Cockney-School slogan'[12] – Hunt quotes with approval 'Sleep and Poetry', on 'the great end / Of poesy': 'it should be a friend / To soothe the cares, and lift the thoughts of man' (245–7).

Here Keats had given voice to one of Hunt's key principles. For Shelley, Hunt was 'one of those happy souls / Which are the salt of the Earth, and without whom / This world would smell like what it is – a tomb' ('Letter to Maria Gisborne', 209–11). In 1817, Keats also valued the 'social smile' ('Addressed to [Haydon]', 6) as characteristic of Hunt's literary and political identity. Hunt wrote expressly 'in the cause of cheerfulness': 'One of the especial parts of our vocation is to draw sweet out of bitter'.[13] When he joined the Hunt circle, Keats entered this determinedly uplifting – if sometimes cloying – atmosphere. Writing to Hunt in August 1820, Keats was grateful: 'I feel really attach'd to you for your many sympathies with me, and patience at my lunes' (*L* 2, 316).

In *Politics and Poetics – The Desperate Situation of a Journalist Unhappily Smitten with the Love of Rhyme* (1811), Hunt playfully isolated the tension, so evident in his own career, between a poetics of ease and pleasure and a socially reformist politics. Hunt found a way of justifying and reconciling these appetites in terms that he could live with – largely by keeping them discrete, as Rodney Stenning Edgecombe puts it, in 'reluctant symbiosis': the 'moments of escape replenish an exhausted soul and fire a jaded imagination'.[14] In the early days of their relationship, Keats could enter into the spirit of this – not least, of course, because the poetics he shared with Hunt *were* political, and publicly contested. With Spenser as its touchstone, Hunt's 'new school' was, in John Kandl's words, to be 'a renaissance of the Renaissance',[15] in which, as Roe discerns, the Spenserian bower was to be the 'counterpart' rather than the 'alternative' to practical social improvement.[16]

For both Hunt and Keats, the mental space figured in that bower drew chiefly upon the 'beautiful Tales which have come down from the ancient times of that beautiful Greece' (*L* 1, 154). Greek mythology not only represented a shared ideal of beauty, but also a realm of warmth and freedom from the refrigerating effects of contemporary religious mores. Keats hailed Hunt's use of *The Examiner* as a 'Battering Ram against Christianity' (*L* 1, 137), and Hunt expressed elsewhere the genial hope that someday 'a voice will be heard along the water saying "The great God Pan is alive again – upon which the villagers will leave off starving, and singing profane hymns, and fall to dancing again" '.[17] Keats's sonnet 'Written in Disgust of Vulgar Superstition' looks forward to the hold of the Church 'dying like an outburnt lamp', in the confidence that 'fresh flowers will grow' in its place (11, 13): he would have sympathised with Hunt's sense that the 'best piety is that which is most alive to the beauty of the creation, and would see all enjoy it alike'.[18]

The implicit commonwealth in that social reflex was fundamental to Hunt's vision, and its nostalgia for an idealised ancient Greece was matched by a nostalgia for a lost Merry England, which yet might rise again. This other England found its poetic embodiment in the 'Pre-Drydenism' (*CH* 370) of Hunt's 'new school', with which Keats aligned himself in 'Sleep and Poetry', railing against Restoration 'foppery and barbarism' and a poetry 'wed / To musty laws lined out with wretched rule / And compass vile' (182, 194–6). William Keach has highlighted the political implications of the looser, enjambed couplets typical of the Hunt circle, in contrast to the closed Augustan mode favoured by his fiercest critics:[19] Croker complained of *Endymion* that there is 'hardly a complete couplet inclosing a complete idea in the whole book' (*CH* 112). Likewise, Keats was pilloried, along with Hunt, for their poetic neologisms (*CH* 114): another characteristic, for the *Quarterly*, of 'Cockney' vulgarity.

The contest of ideas in which, as Richard Cronin remarks, 'a poet's most effective political act is the forging of a new language', was (and is) ongoing.[20] For Keats's role in that tradition, meeting Hunt was indeed 'an Era in [his] existence' (*L* 1, 113). Cronin has described Keats's verse as a poetry of 'encroachment' upon literary forms and themes patrolled by self-appointed guardians of the cultural establishment – and in this, Hunt was a principal ally.[21] Moreover, and contrary to the long-held view that after *Endymion* Keats distanced himself from his 'Cockney' influences, critics now tend to see in his mature style features that still link him to Hunt – that 'poet laureate of luxurious foliage', in Susan J. Wolfson's phrase.[22]

Their affinities, though, should not mask their differences. While Edgecombe can satisfyingly compare Hunt's poetry to 'the playful and lighthearted mode of the rococo',[23] Keats's own achievement is of another order. Keats had sought Hunt out in the name of shared ideals, but never lost his own spirited independence – and his unease within Hunt's honeyed fellowship became manifest soon after their acquaintance. Hunt's disavowal, in 1818, of writing 'for the sake of a moral',[24] might at first sight resonate with Keats's earnest rejection, in February that year, of 'poetry that has a palpable design upon us' – but in fact, Hunt is one of the writers Keats has in mind, whose poetry obtrudes upon the reader as such: only eighteen months after they met, Keats says he 'will have no more' of Hunt (*L* 1, 224). In May 1817, Keats had already written of Hunt's 'self delusions' about his own abilities as a poet, and in October, 'quite disgusted with literary Men', complained of having 'the Reputation of Hunt's elevé' (*L* 1, 143, 169, 170). By December 1818 he was 'complete[ly] tired' of Hunt's 'sickening stuff' (*L* 2, 7). On the face of it, these are surprising – but Keats's inward faith in his own devotion to poetry was self-reliant. He dismissed the attacks in *Blackwood's* and the *Quarterly* as 'a mere matter of the moment – I think I shall be among the English Poets after my death' (*L* 1, 394). His confidence came from his integrity as 'a severe critic on his own Works'; 'I will write independantly', he declared: 'That which is creative must create itself' (*L* 1, 374).

Keats could never entirely adapt to Hunt's determined 'cheerfulness'. He knew his own 'love of gloom' too well, and wished to explore in his poetry the 'dark passages' of the mind (*L* 2, 43, *L* 1, 281). Keats was troubled by his own psychic experience – 'It is a flaw / In happiness, to see beyond our bourn – / It forces us in summer skies to mourn' ('Dear Reynolds…' 82–4) – but he did not wish it away. Rather, it held him fascinated. The hymn to Pan in *Endymion* invokes the metaphysical desire of that fascination:

> be still the leaven,
> That spreading in this dull and clodded earth
> Gives it a touch ethereal – a new birth:
> Be still a symbol of immensity;
> A firmament reflected in a sea;
> An element filling the space between;
> An unknown –
>
> (1. 296–302)

The 'unknown' floods the 'space between' with its active presence. This is the voice not of escape from the actual, but an exhilarating pursuit of its fullness and complexity. Keats desynonymises the poet and the dreamer in *The Fall of Hyperion* to purge mere illusion from the poet's task as 'humanist, physician to all men' (1. 190) – fusing the mysterious work of the imagination with an authentic devotion to worldly well-being. Keats had found his own way to a poetry that, in R. P. Blackmur's words, 'adds to the stock of available reality'.[25]

The freshness and urgency of discovery in the evolution of Keats's poetics may have taken him beyond Hunt's own, but they had common roots. The development of Keats's 'Axioms' (*L* 1, 238) over time not only records his self-education in poetry, but also reveals an unboundaried Huntian exuberance: in 'the holiness of the Heart's affections and the truth of Imagination', in 'a Life of Sensations rather than of Thoughts', in the undogmatic open-endedness of '*Negative Capability*', and in 'a fine excess' (*L* 1, 184, 185, 193, 238). Keats's 'camelion Poet' – even in his 'relish of the dark side of things' (*L* 1, 387) – can be traced to their mutual admiration for Shakespeare and 'his astonishing sympathy with everything'.[26]

These qualities and appetites connect Keats not just to Hunt, but also to Coleridge and Wordsworth – the affiliation of the 'Cockney School' to the 'Lake School', upon which Hunt was vocal, even in the 'Literary Warfare' of 1815 to 1822. The Hunt circle's 'Cockney' Hellenism opened onto the same liberal ethos that quickened the Gothic, vatic poetry with which it is so often contrasted. Their shared impulse was to reimagine and renew humankind and its habitat – and in this lies the greater tradition to which Keats belongs, among the English poets.

Notes

1 'On the Cockney School of Poetry No. I', *Blackwood's Edinburgh Magazine* 2 (October 1817): p. 38.
2 Leigh Hunt, *Autobiography*, 3 vols. (London, 1850), vol. 2, pp. 83–113.
3 Marilyn Butler, *Romantics, Rebels and Reactionaries: English Literature and Its Background 1760–1830* (Oxford: Oxford University Press, 1981), p. 145.
4 S. T. Coleridge, *Biographia Literaria*, ed. James Engell and W. Jackson Bate, 2 vols. (Princeton: Princeton University Press, 1983), vol. 2, p. 111.
5 *William Wordsworth: The Critical Heritage, 1793–1820*, ed. Robert Woof (London: Routledge, 2001), p. 191.
6 Butler, *Romantics, Rebels and Reactionaries*, p. 144 passim.
7 In 1871, recorded in *William Allingham's Diary* (1907): cited *CH* 35.
8 Nicholas Roe, *John Keats* (New Haven: Yale University Press, 2012), p. 100.
9 Leigh Hunt, *The Story of Rimini* (London, 1816), pp. xiii–xiv.
10 Hunt, *The Story of Rimini*, p. xv.
11 Leigh Hunt, *Foliage* (London, 1818), p. 10.
12 Duncan Wu, 'Keats and the "Cockney School"', in *The Cambridge Companion to John Keats*, ed. Susan J. Wolfson (Cambridge: Cambridge University Press, 2001), pp. 37–52, 43.
13 Hunt, *Foliage*, pp. 30–1; Leigh Hunt, *A Jar of Honey from Mount Hybla* (London: John Murray, 1897), p. 2.
14 Rodney Stenning Edgecombe, *Leigh Hunt and the Poetry of Fancy* (London and Toronto: Associated University Presses, 1994), p. 144.
15 John Kandl, 'The Politics of Keats's Early Poetry: "Delight" with "Liberty"', *Cambridge Companion*, pp. 1–19, 7.
16 Nicholas Roe, *John Keats and the Culture of Dissent* (Oxford: Clarendon Press, 1997), p. 92.
17 *The Athenians*, ed. Walter Sidney Scott (London: Golden Cockerel Press, 1943), pp. 43–4.
18 *The Examiner* (16 February 1817), p. 98.
19 William Keach, 'Cockney Couplets: Keats and the Politics of Style', *Studies in Romanticism* 25 (1986): 182–96.
20 Richard Cronin, *The Politics of Romantic Poetry: In Search of the Pure Commonwealth* (Basingstoke: Macmillan, 2000), p. 13.
21 Ibid., pp. 181–99.
22 Susan J. Wolfson, *Reading John Keats* (Cambridge: Cambridge University Press, 2015), p. 67.

23 Edgecombe, *Leigh Hunt and the Poetry of Fancy*, p. 10 passim.
24 Hunt, *Foliage*, p. 18.
25 R. P. Blackmur, *Form and Value in Modern Poetry* (New York: Doubleday, 1952), p. 349.
26 Hunt, *Autobiography*, vol. 2, p. 282.

CHAPTER 10

London

Timothy Webb

Most books on London during the early years of the nineteenth century, even those with a literary dimension, have little or nothing to say about John Keats. Like his mentor Leigh Hunt, Keats was much mocked for his 'Cockney' aspirations, a cruel and snobbish way of rejecting his poetic originalities and imaginative excursions as risible and inappropriate in one from so demonstrably humble and uneducated a background. Yet, in a curious way, this definition succeeds in making an identification which nowadays is often forgotten by readers and admirers: by most definitions, Keats was truly a Londoner who lived in or near that city until he left for Italy near the end of his life. He made a number of expeditions, most of which left an immeasurably significant impression on his imagination and on his writing, both in poetry and in letters: to the Lake District and thence at length to Scotland, to the Isle of Wight, to Devon and especially Teignmouth, to Oxford, to Margate, to Winchester and to Chichester. Yet, in spite of these engagements with a variety of locations and in spite of the imaginative nourishment which they provided, Keats was recurrently, and it seems inescapably, a writer who was centred on London and environs, to which he inevitably returned.

His letters advance a rather different narrative from most surveys and from almost all of his poetry; even a cursory reading supplies a collection of addresses, street names and city activities which at first glance may appear oddly inappropriate to the nature of his poetic achievement. Although the catalogue of London place-names is large, it is far from Homeric, not least because such a concentration is not celebratory and was never intended by Keats himself; but it does show that throughout his working and writing life Keats pursued his everyday affairs within the bounds of a clearly defined urban topography. Like Dickens himself and many of his characters and like Charles Lamb and Keats's own mentor Leigh Hunt, he was familiar with the streets of London and with many of the city's activities. Sometimes his naming of specific streets is reminiscent of Defoe, though

Keats's vivacity and his metaphoric curiosity mark him out as distinctively different from Moll Flanders, or Colonel Jack, or the narrator of *Journal of the Plague Year*. Like many of his less affluent contemporaries, not least his fellow writers, he was in the habit of walking to many of his destinations and observing his surroundings. So, for example, he records that when he accompanied guests to tea at Mrs Millar's, the company 'were particularly struck with the light and shade through the Gate way at the Horse Guards' (*L* 1, 392). On a later occasion, he notes: 'When I left Mr Abbey on monday evening I walk'd up Cheapside but returned to put some letters in the Post and met him again in Bucklersbury: we walk'd together through the Poultry as far as the hatter's shop he has some concern in' (*L* 2, 192). In the most fundamental way, Keats was an urban being and, precisely because of its paradoxical otherness, his poetic concern with the natural world may be understood as a product of this very different context. Even when it seems so exotically liberated from urban details, Keats's poetry is often rooted in circumstances derived from experience in or of the city; he negotiates this difficult conjunction by alchemising urban particulars into a poetic texture which appears to transcend its origins.

Keats was a regular walker both in the country and the city (the concordance to his letters includes 134 entries for 'Walk', 'Walked' and related words). Walking the streets and navigating the unpredictable city sometimes provided unexpected encounters and even, on occasion, adventures. In January 1818 he was an hour too late for Hazlitt's lecture and was 'pounced upon' by various members of the audience as they came out (*L* 1, 214). In October of the same year he encountered Mrs Isabella Jones whom he had seen at Hastings: 'It was in a street which goes from Bedford Row to Lamb's Conduit Street – I passed her and turned back' (*L* 1, 402). Again, on 14 February 1819 he experienced a crowded agenda after an absence from direct contact with the city: 'Yesterday I went to town for the first time for these three weeks – I met people from all parts and of all sets' (*L* 2, 59). Keats does not specify the details of any of these meetings but continues: 'Mr Woodhouse was looking up at a Book-window in newgate street and being short-sighted twisted his Muscles into such a stupe that I stood by in doubt, if it was him or his brother, if he has one'. Calling at Taylor's [his publisher lived in Fleet Street], he discovered that Taylor and William Hilton [an artist who lived in Percy Street, Rathbone Place] 'had set out to dine with me: so I followed them immediately back – I walk'd with them townwards again as far as Cambden Town and smoak'd home a Segar' (*L* 2, 77–8). The end of this sentence provides a memorable detail and also presumably a phonetic rendering; Keats was not a Wallace Stevens but his smoking of a cigar suggests both contentment and a hedonistic tendency which is confirmed in other letters.

On another occasion, he passed the window of Colnaghi's print-shop and saw a profile portrait of the murderer of Kotzebue (*L* 2, 194). With Leigh Hunt he went to an exhibition at Sir John Leicester's Gallery; with Severn he made a 'turn round' the British Museum ('There is a Sphinx there of a giant size, & most voluptuous Egyptian expression', *L* 2, 68), where he also visited the Elgin Marbles with Haydon, and he reported on exhibitions in the British Gallery (*L* 1, 235–6) and 'of the old english portraits by Vandyck and Holbein, Sir Peter Lely and the great Sir Godfrey' (*L* 2, 299): the subjects were English but, at least by origin, the painters were not. His London excursions also brought him into contact with political events: for example, he witnessed the 'triumphal entry into London' of Henry Hunt: 'I[t] would take me a whole day and a quire of paper to give you any thing like detail – I will merely mention that it is calculated that 30,000 people were in the streets waiting for him – The whole distance from the Angel Islington to the Crown and anchor was lined with Multitudes' (*L* 2, 194). This experience made its impression since, not long afterwards, Keats declared to Haydon (*L* 2, 219): 'I have no doubt that if I had written Othello I should have been cheered by as good a Mob as Hunt' (compare Hugh MacDiarmid on the Ibrox crowds in 'Glasgow, 1960').

Life in London could be repetitive and even monotonous so it was certainly enhanced by the variations of his frequent expeditions; yet the letters demonstrate that, being a young man and belonging to some lively circles, Keats was often invited to dinner and attended a number of social events such as card-parties, 'routs', a Saturday 'Club' of which he was a member, a 'claret-feast', dances and a 'piano forte hop at Dilke's'; he also frequented the British Museum and Guy's Hospital where he was, famously, a medical student and a surgeon's dresser. On 14 February 1818, he records (*L* 1, 227) that Marianne Hunt had informed him he was to be invited to a party at Ollier's to keep Shakespeare's birthday; Leigh Hunt later wrote an essay on the importance of such occasions but initially Keats was a little startled by the invitation ('Shakespeare would stare to see me there'). Once Woodhouse took him to his coffee house and ordered a bottle of claret (*L* 2, 64), an event which inspired an excursus on the virtues of that kind of wine and on Keats's own compelling taste for it. On another occasion, Keats records that 'in the evening [Joseph] Severn [who had come to dinner] went home to paint & we other three went to the play to see Sheild's [*actually*, Sheil's] new tragedy ycleped Evadné – In the morning

Severn & I took a turn round the [British Museum]' (*L* 2, 68). The sudden modulation into archaic mode ('ycleped') may remind us of the student Stephen Dedalus, but is typical of his own poetic manoeuvres; it combines verbal high spirits and self-consciousness with a tone which may be less certain. In this brief account, too, city experiences transmute into each other with that metamorphic ease which also characterises the structure both of some poems and a number of letters.

These references, which could be multiplied, suggest something of the social life Keats followed during his London years, including the period of his greatest poetic creativity. His letters present Keats in the context of a city which is often diverting and sometimes exciting, but which, as he apologetically admits, can also be uninteresting and mundane. For example, we observe him standing in the Bank 'for an hour or two – to me worse than any thing in Dante' (*L* 2, 32). He tells Haydon: 'I went the other day into an ironmonger's shop, without any change in my sensations – men and tin kettles are much the same in these days' (*L* 2, 43). At least once he unconsciously places himself in a familiar London setting while making a complaint resembling that of Pope in *The Dunciad*: 'All I can say is that standing at Charing cross and looking east west north and south I can see nothing but dullness' (*L* 2, 244). More frequently, though, he is quiveringly alert to the possibilities of life in the city. He even seems to have regarded his responsibilities as a writer of letters to George and Georgiana in America as those of an urban impresario. So he presents them with a list of city topics and invites them to make a choice:

> Whether the affairs of Europe are more or less interesting to you – whether you would like to hear of the Theatre's – of the bear Garden – of the Boxers – the Painters – The Lecturers – the Dress – The Progress of Dandyism – The Progress of Courtship – or the fate of Mary Millar.
>
> (*L* 2, 29)

The concluding reference is to one of Georgiana's relatives but Keats is also allowing himself fun at the expense of dramatic titles. The other topics accord, closely enough, not only with the diverse attractions of city life but with his own interests. For instance, 'the brothers [that is, George and John] also enjoyed bachelor recreations such as billiards, boxing and bear-baiting'.[1] He contributed one or two passages to Leigh Hunt's *Indicator* essay 'A Now, Descriptive of a Hot Day'. Other city topics feature frequently. Through his report (*L* 2, 66), we hear Mrs Brawne complaining about the watchman's voice (watchmen provide the topic for another Hunt essay). Through his eyes, we encounter the velocipede (*L* 2, 69–70), a rich subject for city caricaturists. A visit to the Panorama delighted him: 'I have been very much pleased with the Panorama of the ships at the north Pole – with the icebergs, the Mountains, the Bears the Walrus – the seals the Penguins – and a large whale floating back above water – it is impossible to describe the place' (*L* 2, 95).

Keats's letters show that he had a particular interest in theatre. After copying out for the benefit of the George Keatses a long and rhetorically extravagant passage from *The Anatomy of Melancholy*, he comments: 'I would give my favou[r]ite leg to have written this as a speech in a Play: with what effect could Mathews [Charles Mathews, popular comic actor and impressionist, friend of Hunt and of Dickens] pop-gun it at the pit!' (*L* 2, 191–2). Sometimes this strong interest is revealed by seemingly insignificant details: for example, he remarks, from experience it seems, 'Our stage is loaded with mimics' (*L* 2, 190). Another letter records, 'The pantomime was excellent, I had seen it before & enjoyed it again (*L* 2, 68); on yet another occasion, Keats went at half-price to Covent Garden 'before I tumbled into bed' (*L* 2, 192). In a letter of 23, 24 January 1818, he reports: 'I saw from a Box the 1st Act of John Bull, then I went to Drury & did not return till it was over; when by Wells' interest we got behind the scenes' (*L* 1, 216). This is followed by a detailed description, not unlike those in Dickens, of the comical and grotesque realities of theatrical life. In one letter Keats writes (*L* 2, 214) 'I wish one could get change for a pun in silver currency. I would give three and a half any night to get into Drury-pit' (*L* 2, 214). Much like Dickens, Keats seems to have been particularly fascinated by bad actors and unsuccessful performances. Briefly, he even turned his hand to theatrical criticism though, unfortunately, he published only several reviews.

Indications of Keats's strong theatrical interest are evident in the unfinished, and by general critical agreement unsuccessful, *Otho the Great* which Keats wrote, together with Charles Brown, as a vehicle for Edmund Kean. This play indicates the importance in the imagination of Keats (and of Brown) in general of the drama and in particular of Edmund Kean. Obviously, Keats was a great admirer of Kean: he went with Brown (*L* 2, 8) to see his theatrical hero in *Brutus* ('the play was very bad' but Kean was 'excellent') while, on a later occasion, London was too stifling 'to remain there though I wanted to see Kean in Hotspur' (*L* 2, 71). At this time, Keats enjoyed Shakespearean intimations so his correspondence constantly recurs to his dramatic aspirations and specifically to the centrality of Kean: 'If he smokes the hotblooded character of Ludolph – and he is the only actor that can do it – He will add to his own fame, and improve my fortune' (*L* 2, 217). Keats's relatively brief review of Kean in *Riches: or the Wife and Brother* was printed in the *Champion* for 21 December 1817 and constitutes an acute analysis of several Shakespearean performances by an actor whose greatness is vital for imaginative survival in 'these cold and enfeebling times'.[2] Taking perhaps a cue from Hazlitt, Keats notes that 'There is an indescribable gusto in his voice, by which we feel that the utterer is thinking of the past and future, while speaking of the instant'. After describing Kean's 'intense power of anatomizing the passion of every syllable', Keats comments suggestively: 'Other actors are continually thinking of their sum-total effect throughout a play. Kean delivers himself up to the instant feeling, without the shadow of a thought about any thing else. He feels his being as deeply as Wordsworth, or any of our intellectual monopolists.' The example of Kean also encouraged him to aim for a verbal distinction which would 'signal the beginning of a new literary epoch as decisively as Kean had marked the end of "the Kemble religion" and the initiation of a style which was imaginatively new and compelling: "One of my Ambitions is to make as great a revolution in modern dramatic writing as Kean has done in acting." '[3]

Nearly all of these city interests must be extracted from his prose rather than directly from his poetical works. Close friends included not only Brown (whose *Narensky* had been produced at Covent Garden) but Hazlitt, Hunt and Reynolds, who in their different ways were pioneering in their literary treatment of city topics. Keats was also acquainted with Charles Lamb; but, in spite of these examples, he seems not have been much tempted by the literary possibilities of London. Like most of his contemporaries, and like most English poets before the second half of the nineteenth century or even later (impressive exceptions in Keats's period can be found in Wordsworth, Shelley, and Byron), Keats avoided the subject of London as unsuitable for serious verse. When he does address the matter, he usually translates it into a verse-form which distances the awkward urban facts. So, for instance, in the three stanzas on the character of Charles Brown his approach is rendered amusingly acceptable by the use of Spenserian diction and the Spenserian stanza. Behind these lines one can hear the 'slang of cities' which, as the poem claims, Brown did not know but which Keats himself knew well, even though it is generally avoided in his poetry – 'Tipping the wink', 'heathen Greek', old Tom and blue ruin (both references to gin) – but the potential contagion of the vernacular is held in place by the larger Spenserian framework. For a moment, Keats is exercising his linguistic prowess and his knowledge of urban speech in a manner not dissimilar to that of Byron in *Don Juan*, canto 11, stanza 19 when he laments the deceased footpad in a bravura stanza of knowingly flash language. The watchman's voice we have encountered before, more stridently, in one of the letters. Here it is tamed, as is the fact of prostitution which, in some views, had made London the prostitution capital of the world, or which was at least an urgent social problem (see 'the Harlots curse' and the 'Marriage hearse' in Blake's 'London'); in these stanzas we encounter the more harmonious and less disturbing presences of 'many a damsel hoarse and rouge of cheek' and 'curled Jewesses with ancles neat,/ Who as they walk abroad make tinkling with their feet' (5–6).

Keats's poetic anxiety in handling London subjects can be traced in other poems: 'Fragment of Castle-Builder' with its uncomfortable couplets and its description of Covent Garden as 'a monstrous beast' with an insatiable appetite; the patronising iambics of 'And what is Love?', with its references to 'Number Seven' and 'Brunswick Square' and its ponderously concessive conclusion 'That ye may love in spite of beaver hats'; the heavily comic couplets of 'Pensive they sit, and roll their languid eyes' with its awkward mention of unfashionable docklands Wapping (casually and effectively introduced in Shelley's *Peter Bell the Third*). Hunt's embarrassment is perhaps at its most extreme in *The Jealousies* (also known as *The Cap and Bells*), probably written during November and December 1819, which suddenly comes to an end in its eighty-ninth stanza. Although this poem (pointedly, not claimed as his own but attributed to a fictional 'Lucy Vaughan Lloyd of China Walk, Lambeth') seems to have been written close to his great year of poetic achievement, its main interest lies in its inability to animate its subjects (even the displacement on to an invented authoress hardly justifies or fully explains this poetic failure). One example of the poem's relative weakness is the four stanzas and four lines devoted to the subject of coaches and inserted without identification into Leigh Hunt's *Indicator* for 23 August 1820 at the end of a Hunt essay 'On Coaches'. Even the unusual precision of this passage seems pallid by comparison with the essay with which Hunt prefaces these verses, the account of the coach and the coachman (also by Hunt) in the following number, and Keats's own evocation in a letter of 'the Hercules Methodist' of a coachman nibbling a bit of bread, whistling and bowing to the girls on the road with 'a nameless graceful slang action' (*L* 2, 169–170).

It comes as a surprise, then, to find that Keats is represented in Mark Ford's recent *London: A History in Verse*[4] by three poems – the sonnets 'To one who has been long in city pent' and 'On Seeing the Elgin Marbles' and the jovial 'Lines on the Mermaid Tavern', which also features in Paul Bailey's *The Oxford Book of London* (1995). The first sonnet, composed in

June 1816, has an obviously Miltonic connection, by way of Coleridge's 'To the Nightingale', in its opening line and transforms the nightingale into 'Philomel', who also features in Coleridge's conversation poem; it is driven by an escapist argument which prefers 'the fair/ And open face of heaven' to claustrophobic city realities. The Elgin Marbles sonnet, which was written at the beginning of March 1817 can be connected to a British Museum visit with Haydon (to whom another sonnet on the same subject is specifically addressed), though the text of the poem provides no clue as to its London origins. The third poem represents a different kind of Keats and is essentially trivial, if symptomatic. Undeniably, all three can be classified as 'London poems' yet, compared to the animated specificities of the letters, the two sonnets in particular lack a clearly defined city dimension, even if they are grounded in experiences which took place in London. Strictly speaking, of course, it could be argued that much of Keats's poetry, including a significant proportion of his odes, is 'London' poetry, not least when it focuses on visions beyond the 'miasma' and the 'scuffle'. For example, 'On First Looking Into Chapman's Homer' arose out of Keats's invitation to Charles Cowden Clarke 'to visit him at Dean Street, giving him his directions through the narrow winding Borough streets after he had "run the Gauntlet over London Bridge" into the wilds of Southwark'.[5] In the event, the joint-reading took place not in Dean Street but at Clerkenwell, yet 'the Realms of Gold' and visions of Greece, 'the Skies' and South America are perhaps given greater intensity when imagined from the constraints of a London perspective. 'Ode to a Nightingale' is as much a city poem as 'To one who has been long in city pent' or Yeats's 'The Lake Isle of Innisfree' since, although it does not mention 'the roadway' or 'the pavements grey', it was written near a building-site in Hampstead and its longings to escape, like those of Yeats's short poem, were generated by trivial or unpleasant realities.

In Ford's anthology Keats is immediately preceded by his close friend John Hamilton Reynolds, who is represented by a sonnet called 'On Hearing St Martin's Bells on My Way Home from a Sparring Match at the Fives-Court' (this court was, it may be remembered, Hazlitt's probable destination for a game of rackets when Keats met him in the street). The urgencies of the sparring-match, supplemented by the cries of spectators, are, like the title of the poem, harmoniously absorbed into the larger texture of the sonnet which ends with 'peasants' pipes, at peace time in a valley'.[6] By yet another suggestive conjunction, Keats is immediately followed by Thomas Hood, who is represented by four poems[7] including an evocative 'Sonnet to Vauxhall', a pleasure-garden and concert venue which Keats attended with his brother George. Even though they shared a predilection for the pun, and sometimes for the merely facetious, and an amused and voracious eye for metropolitan particulars, Keats could never have been limited to the thinner poetics of Hood or to his narrow and pragmatic ambitions. Yet in some ways Hood, who was only four years younger and must have shared many of his city experiences, gives voice to a London which is recognisably close not to Keats's poetry but to the shrewdly observed world of his letters. That Keats took such care to omit these details, that he did not follow the course of Hood or of Reynolds, gives clear testimony to his grander ambitions for his own poetry and the carefully calculated cost at which it was written. The 'Cockney' poet may have composed many of his poems when he was living in London or carrying the city in his head but, with only a few exceptions, the objectives to which he turns his poetic attention are strikingly different.

Notes

1 Letters follow the dating in *Letters of John Keats*, ed. Robert Gittings (Oxford University Press; corrected edition, 1987); text and references follow the Rollins version. Denise Gigante, *The Keats Brothers: The Life of John and George* (Cambridge, MA: Harvard University Press, 2011), pp. 30–1.

2 Text from *John Keats*, ed. Elizabeth Cook (Oxford: Oxford University Press, 1990), pp. 345–7.

3 Timothy Webb, 'The Romantic Poet and the Stage: A Short, Sad History', in *The Romantic Theatre: An International Symposium*, ed. Richard Allen Cave (Gerrards Cross: Colin Smythe/Barnes and Noble, 1986), p. 24; *L* 2, 139.

4 Mark Ford (ed.), *London: A History in Verse* (Cambridge, MA: Harvard University Press, 2012), pp. 363–5.

5 Robert Gittings, *John Keats* (London: 1968; Penguin Books, 1985), p. 127.

6 Ford, *London*, p. 362.

7 Ford, *London*, pp. 366–73.

CHAPTER 11

Politics

Richard Cronin

Keats is unique amongst the major poets of his era in that critical debate has not focused on the character of his politics so much as on the question of whether he is appropriately regarded as a political poet at all. For T. S. Eliot, Keats was remarkable for his not having taken 'any absorbing interest in public affairs', offering in this 'an astonishing contrast' to the less attractive Shelley.[1] Eliot's position was persuasively challenged by Jerome McGann, who argued that in the *Poems* of 1817 and *Endymion* Keats had displayed so evident an interest in public affairs that it had provoked extreme critical hostility. It was this that prompted Keats, when he prepared his final volume of 1820, self-consciously to turn away from politics, which is itself, for McGann, a political stratagem. The poems of 1820 are a 'great and (politically) reactionary book'. The argument culminates in a reading of 'To Autumn', which understands the poem as arguing 'for the power of a specific type of imaginative art, that is, for an art that can imagine the sufficiency of the imagination'. In doing so the poem decisively removes itself from the England of 1819, from 'the Terror, King Ludd, Peterloo, the Six Acts, and the recurrent financial crises of the Regency'.[2]

McGann was himself challenged by a number of critics. William Keach, followed by Nicholas Roe, suggests that Keats's ode should be read against Leigh Hunt's 'Calendar of Nature' in *The Examiner* for 6 September 1819, in which autumn is presented as a season that offers a 'lesson on justice' that was particularly pertinent in the immediate aftermath of Peterloo. Tom Paulin finds in the ode's final stanza 'a coded elegy' for the Manchester dead. Andrew Motion agrees, and locates, like Keach, a political resonance too in Keats's bees: 'They are a reminder of the miserable facts of labour that Keats had condemned during his walking tour of Scotland.'[3] In a testy review of Motion's biography, Helen Vendler was flabbergasted by the suggestion: 'The bees? Swooning, glutted, in their happy delusion that "warm days will never cease," with their honeycombs "o'erbrimmed" with the nectar from the "more, and still more later flowers" provided by the generosity of Autumn? We are to take them as "a reminder of the miserable facts of labour"? Surely not.'[4] It remains a vexed issue whether the Keats of the 1820 volume was still actively engaged with the radical politics so evident in the earlier work, but rather than take one side or the other it might be better to recognise that Keats's feelings on this as on most other matters were conflicted.

In the *Poems* of 1817 Keats could scarcely have been more emphatic in associating himself with Leigh Hunt. The volume begins with a dedicatory sonnet addressed to Hunt, an epigraph from *The Story of Rimini* introduces the first poem, 'I stood tip-toe upon a little hill', Hunt, 'he of … [t]he social smile, the chain for Freedom's sake', underwrites, together with Wordsworth and Haydon, Keats's claim that 'Great spirits now on earth are sojourning', and another of the sonnets is 'Written on the day that Mr. Leigh Hunt left prison'. Hunt acknowledged the association when he printed in *The Examiner* Keats's sonnet 'On the Grasshopper and the Cricket' together with the sonnet that he had written himself in competition with it.[5] In Keats's *Poems* it is followed immediately by 'To Kosciusko', a sonnet evidently written in friendly competition with the sonnet that Hunt had published in *The Examiner* under the same title two years before.[6] Since the publication of Jeffrey Cox's study of Cockney poetry it has become conventional to describe Hunt's politics and his poetics as all of a piece.[7] The 'social smile', the intimacy that the Cockney poets most fully achieve stylistically, by developing a manner that refuses to maintain a formal distance from the reader, by forging the 'unchariest' style (*Endymion*, 2. 532) that had yet been deployed by a group of English poets, has been presented as continuous with the radical politics for which Hunt was condemned to two years imprisonment in the Surrey Gaol. Keats himself suggests in the 1817 volume how closely poetics and politics are linked by offering paired lists of his political and poetic heroes. Charles Cowden Clarke is thanked for awakening him to the beauties of Tasso, Spenser and Milton, and also for 'pointing out the patriot's stern duty; / The might of Alfred, and the shaft of Tell' ('To Charles Cowden Clarke', 69–70). Leigh Hunt, '[t]he wronged Libertas', who also tells tales of 'troops chivalrous prancing through a city / And tearful ladies made for love and pity' (44–7) belongs to both groups. But literature and politics were not always easily reconciled even by Hunt himself. In 1820 he launched *The Indicator* as a journal that would complement *The Examiner* because he felt the need, as Nicholas Roe puts it, for 'a private space' in which he could publish writings 'carefully insulated from the dangerous England of the Six Acts'.[8]

Cockney poets are characteristically torn between a need to enlist 'on the liberal side of the question' (*L* 2, 195)[9] and a contrasting need to situate their poems in a space removed from the hurly-burly of the political arena.

Keats sometimes writes as if a dedication to poetry and the 'cause of freedom' were indivisible. In 'To Charles Cowden Clarke' he imagines how his writings might direct 'the shaft of Tell; / The hand of Brutus, that so grandly fell / Upon a tyrant's head' (70–2), and in 'To My Brother George' he dreams of how the 'patriot' will one day 'in the senate thunder out my numbers / To startle princes from their easy slumbers' (73–5). These are youthful daydreams but they persisted. On September 13, 1819, Keats witnessed Henry Hunt's triumphal entry into London after Peterloo, 30,000 lining the streets the 'whole distance from the Angel Islington to the Crown and anchor', and the thought that came to him was what it would be like to write a poem that could inspire as much enthusiasm: 'if [he] had written Othello', he feels sure, he 'should have been cheered by as good as Mob as Hunt' (*L* 2, 194, 219). But even oftener he finds in the indifference of the reading public the more reliable indication of a poet's merit. It is the common fate of the 'finest writers' to be 'trampled aside into the bye paths of life' (*L* 2, 115), rather than applauded by thousands, and for such writers the making of the poem must be an end in itself rather than subservient to some lofty public purpose.

Keats's first attempts at poems of some length – 'I stood tip-toe', 'Sleep and Poetry', the epistles – never seem quite sure what they are about, until they stumble on the possibility that they might be about how Keats came to write them, that is, they might be poems about the process of their own composition. The capacity for in-feeling for which Keats has always and rightly been celebrated is as much a product of Keats's ability to feel his way into the verse lines and the stanzas that he chooses as it is into the objects that the verse addresses. He admires in Spenser not just the freedom with which his knights move across the landscape, 'pricking on the plaine', but the free movement of the lines, the 'Spenserian vowels that elope with ease' ('To Charles Cowden Clarke', 56). Jeremy Prynne has commented on the struggle of the figures on Keats's urn 'to escape from the frigid reduction of warm life into cold art',[10] but in these early poems life and art are not always easily distinguished. In 'To My Brother George', Keats lies on the grass, on one side of him the field of oats variegated with poppies, and on the other (Keats is writing from Margate) is 'Ocean's blue mantle streak'd with purple and green' on which sails 'a canvass'd ship' (132–3). The ship is canvassed, no doubt, because it is under sail, but the epithet suggests too how closely it resembles a ship that has been painted. In 'I stood tip-toe' it may be impossible to tell whether a line describes a tree or whether the tree acts as a metaphor for the stately movement of the line:

> In the calm grandeur of a sober line,
> We see the waving of the mountain pine.
> (127–8)

The *Poems* of 1817 clearly established Keats as the pert young radical whose association with Leigh Hunt made him so proper an object of attack to the *Quarterly* and *Blackwood's* reviewers. But it does not follow that the chief objection even of these reviewers was to Keats's politics. Lockhart, it is true, ends his account of *Endymion* by quoting the passage that opens Book 3, beginning 'There are who lord it o'er their fellow-men / With most prevailing tinsel' (1–2) in confirmation that Keats 'belongs to the Cockney School of Politics as well as the Cockney School of Poetry'. That the charge is offered as an afterthought only masks, it may be, the plain truth that it is the hostility to Keats's politics that provokes the whole attack. But it may equally be the case that Lockhart's principal objection is, as Lockhart indicates, not to Keats's principles but to his 'loose, nerveless versification, and Cockney rhymes', and that the baneful influence he regrets is that of 'the poet of Rimini' rather than the editor of *The Examiner*.[11] William Keach observes that Hunt's 'effort to reform the heroic couplet is an exact image of his reformist politics'. In *The Story of Rimini* he refuses the closed couplets of the Popean school as an expression of his opposition to a closed society. But Keach, unlike many of those who have followed him, treats sceptically all claims, including his own, for neat correspondence between the formal properties of the verse and its political import.

By 1818, when *Endymion* was published, it was clear that Keats's poems showed two contrary tendencies. There was an impulse to define the world of the poem by its distance from the world outside it: the realm of Flora and old Pan ('Sleep and Poetry', 101–2) is secured by its separation from the realm of everyday life. The poems find their subject matter in poetry itself. But there was always and from the first an antithetical tendency in which the ambition is to write a poetry the success of which is measured by its impact on the non-poetic world. In the couplets in which the longer poems are written the conflict between the two impulses is acted out. The couplets call attention to themselves (sometimes by the use of obtrusive cockney rhymes), and yet they are repeatedly assailed by a syntax that moves between couplets as if the poem were written in blank verse. The couplets act as a frame that, as in a Howard Hodgkin painting, becomes itself a part of the picture because it repeatedly fails to contain the thought that it seems intended to enclose. The *Poems* of 1817 and *Endymion* alternate between rather emphatic expressions of Keats's political sympathies and an equally emphatic impulse to deny that poetry has reference to any world other than itself. The poems of 1820 are, as McGann acknowledges, far less willing to admit any partisan politics, but they accommodate very similar hesitations.

The poems of 1820 seem at times to invite a disinterested gaze, the kind of gaze that in *Hyperion* the poem itself directs at Saturn and Thea. The reader is encouraged to view them as if they were a sculptural group. Contrast that with Hyperion snuffing up the incense burnt in his honour, and disconcerted to find that '[i]nstead of sweets, his ample palate took / Savour of poisonous brass and metal sick' (I. 188–9). The appeal here is not to the eyes, but, far more intimately, to the tongue, to the sickening penny-in-the-mouth taste from which Hyperion flinches. The poems in the 1820 volume repeatedly chart these movements in which the poem's objects are held at arm's length, and then realised with a disconcerting intimacy. The cockney refusal to maintain distinctions between different registers, producing effects that then and now have struck many as dismayingly bathetic, is far rarer than in the earlier volumes, but it has not disappeared. The poems in the 1820 volume never remain at a stable distance as one reads them: they repeatedly recede into the distance and then approach so close that the effect is almost uncomfortable, as if Keats's breath was warm on the ear. The story that Keats recounts in *Isabella* is seen from afar, removed from the reader by a lapse of years – 'And they are gone: ay, ages long ago', as Keats was to put it in *The Eve of St. Agnes* (370) – and refracted through the prose of Boccaccio in which Keats had found his story. But the poem is both a tribute to Boccaccio (see 158) and an assault on him, a 'mad assail / To make old prose in modern rhyme more sweet' (155–6). The thought strikes Keats as he parts company with Boccaccio's text to deliver a stinging rebuke to the brothers, less in their capacity as Florentine traders than as City of London merchants in disguise, 'ledger-men' (136) and, in the first use of the expression to describe a person recorded in *OED*, 'money-bags' (142). Nicholas Roe has cunningly traced the origin of Keats's fascination with Boccaccio's grisly tale to the 'little sketches of a human skull and flowering plants with which the inattentive student had decorated his medical notebook',[12] as if in illustration of the dilemma that he was living through, whether to continue to follow the medical profession or whether to abandon it and dedicate himself to the 'leafy luxury' of poetry ('To Leigh Hunt, Esq,' 13). The skull and the basil plant are brought together in a grim conjunction that seems to figure Keats's pained fascination with the problematic relationship between poetry and the inescapable reality of the skull beneath the skin to which, as Roe points out, Keats's medical training would have alerted him so forcibly (Roe's article brings to light Keats's testimony as a medical expert on the condition of the skull of a woman who had fortunately survived being shot in the head). The power of the basil's scent to mask the reek from the 'fast mouldering head' (430) is perhaps Keats's ghastliest representation of the consolation that poetry offers for the world's intolerable ills.

Keats had once measured the 'excellence of every Art' by its power 'of making all disagreeables evaporate' (*L* 1, 192), but in the poems of 1820 he seems more interested in testing that power to its breaking point. In 'Ode on a Grecian Urn', as in almost every poem of the volume, he works by inviting the reader to inspect the poem and the urn it describes from a distance, to view it from the outside, attentive, for example, to the border of acanthus leaves that frames the scenes inscribed on it: it is a 'leaf-fring'd legend' (5). But the poem, like the urn, is also urgent in the invitation it extends to ignore the frame and participate in the scenes depicted with an excitement only possible if the scenes are imagined to be real. As Prynne puts it, the poem's reader is 'positioned so as to gaze *at* the urn, and to gaze *into* the urn's apparently interior world'.[13]

Even in the poem's opening stanza those rival invitations carry with them unsettling political implications. The scene depicted in the first stanza, with its 'maidens loth', its 'mad pursuit', and its 'struggle to escape' is evidently a scene of rape. In Poussin's painting of the Rape of the Sabine Women, now in the Louvre, the topic seems chosen for the range of formal possibilities it allows: the intertwined and yet strongly contrasting male and female bodies; the excited human figures positioned within a formal architectural space; the range of emotions on display as the figures beseech, resist, panic, or surrender to desire; the play of rich colours allowed by their clothing; the strong diagonals that bring order to a scene of excited confusion. But even this painting, so much less visceral in its appeal than Rubens's treatment of the topic, on some level issues an invitation to the viewer to luxuriate in its display of masculine aggression. Keats certainly suggests as much when the detached questions of the first stanza – 'What men or gods are these?' (8) – give way to the exclamations of a viewer excitedly engaged with the events depicted, 'What wild ecstasy?' (10).

The poems of 1820 repeatedly engage with what one might loosely call the politics of sex. Keats can sometimes seem innocently un-misgiving of his own less comfortable proclivities, as when he recommends in response to a woman's display of anger that one '[e]mprison her soft hand, and let her rave, / And feed deep, deep upon her peerless eyes' ('Ode on Melancholy', 19–20). But the bluster with which he responded to John Taylor's objections to *The Eve of St. Agnes* suggests a more troubled poet. He insists, Richard Woodhouse reports to John Taylor, that he 'does not want ladies to read his poetry: that he writes for men'. He would despise a man who would 'be such an eunuch in sentiment as to leave a maid with that character about her', should he inveigle his way into her bedchamber and discover her asleep.[14] The protest seems strained, as if it issued from some deep internal conflict, but it is a conflict that energises the poem by prompting those shifts between cool detachment and hot proximity that characterise the whole volume. By secreting himself in Madeline's bedchamber Porphyro converts Madeline's innocent preparations for bed into a strip-tease the more seductive precisely because it is wholly unselfconscious. Porphyro watches as she undresses, and the verse maps the fluctuations of his feelings (226–31). When she frees her hair of 'all its wreathed pearls', her action seems graceful, almost formal in its charm, but then she '[u]nclasps her warmed jewels' (228), and the epithet betrays how intimately Porphyro has imagined the pressure of the gemstones on her skin.[15] Throughout the passage the verse is as attentive to Porphyro's responses as it is to Madeline's body. Keats seems more simply disapproving when Lycius is 'stung / Perverse' by Lamia's tears to take 'delight / Luxurious in her sorrows' (2. 69–74). But there is a sad self-knowledge implicit in the presentation of Porphyro, too, the self-knowledge that had prompted Keats just the year before to admit to Benjamin Bailey, 'I am certain I have not a right feeling towards Women'. 'I must absolutely get over this', he adds, '– but how?' He knows that 'an obstinate Prejudice can seldom be produced but from a gordian complication of feelings' (*L* 1, 341–2). But in the poems if not in the life that 'gordian complication' served Keats well.

It could be argued that Keats remains a political poet in his last volume if his political interests are more broadly defined, if they are allowed, for example, to accommodate sexual politics. But that is not the argument I want to advance here. I want rather to focus on the movement evident in so many of the poems, in which Keats assumes a formal distance from the objects of poems only to abandon it. Yeats likes to think of Keats, he tells us, as 'a schoolboy', 'With face and nose pressed to a sweet-shop window'. It is the pane that separates the boy from the confectionery and the nose flattened against the glass that gives the image its point, and it is, as Yeats goes on to make clear, a broadly political point. Keats's 'Luxuriant song' has its origin in a social predicament: 'being poor, ailing and ignorant, / Shut out from all the luxury of the world, / The coarse-bred son of a livery-stable keeper' ('Ego Dominus Tuus', 59–67). Helen Vendler might be right to claim that Keats's genius is to be found in his 'sensual imagination' rather than his interest in social reform, and that Peterloo and the social conditions of Scottish gleaners are less telling contexts for 'To Autumn' than the description he offered Charles Dilke, just three days after writing the poem, of what it felt like to swallow a nectarine: 'It went down soft pulpy, slushy, oozy – all its delicious embonpoint melted down my throat like a large beatified Strawberry' (*L* 2, 179). But the sensual imagination, as Yeats recognised, works its magic in social contexts. Would Keats have tasted the nectarine quite like that if he had been someone for whom conservatories and south-facing walled gardens were common appurtenances and nectarines a familiar fruit?

In the *Poems* of 1817 Keats includes a number of poems that directly address political issues within a sequence of poems most of which seem more intent on exploring the nature of poetry itself. Keats seems to entertain rival ambitions to write poems that might 'startle princes form their easy slumbers', and to fashion a poetry the beauty of which was sufficient to itself. For McGann the problem is resolved in the poems of 1820 when Keats makes the decision to turn away from politics. But it may be that the distinctive character of the poems of 1820 is achieved because Keats has found a way to pursue at once his two contradictory ambitions, to write poems that achieve a formal perfection that releases them from the contingent, and yet poems that also contrive to speak to the contingent world in which we all of us live our lives. It is not political poetry exactly, but it is a poetry that worries more searchingly than most about how far political poetry is possible.

Notes

1 T. S. Eliot, *The Use of Poetry and the Use of Criticism* (London: Faber, 1933), pp. 102 and 89.

2 Jerome McGann, 'Keats and Historical Method', in *The Beauty of Inflections: Literary Investigations in Historical Method and Theory* (Oxford: Clarendon Press, 1985), pp. 18–65.

3 Andrew Motion, *Keats* (London. Faber, 1997), pp. 461–2.

4 See William Keach, 'Cockney Couplets: Keats and the Politics of Style,' *Studies in Romanticism*, 25 (Summer, 1986): 182–96, and Nicholas Roe, 'Keats's Commonwealth', in *Keats and History*, ed. Nicholas Roe (Cambridge: Cambridge University Press, 1995), pp. 194–211, and Nicholas Roe, *John Keats* (New Haven: Yale University Press, 2012), pp. 354–6, Andrew Motion, *Keats* (London: Faber, 1997), pp. 461–2, Tom Paulin, *The Day-Star of Liberty: William*

Hazlitt's Radical Style (London: Faber, 1998), p. 48, Helen Vendler, 'Inspiration, Accident Genius,' Inspiration, Accident Genius,' *London Review of Books*, 19, no. 20 (October 1997): 9–11.

5 *The Examiner*, 508 (September 21, 1827): 599.

6 *The Examiner*, 412 (November 19, 1815): 746.

7 Jeffrey N. Cox, *Poetry and Politics in the Cockney School: Keats, Shelley, Hunt and their Circle* (Cambridge: Cambridge University Press, 1998).

8 Nicholas Roe, *Fiery Heart: The First Life of Leigh Hunt* (London: Pimlico, 2005), p. 324.

9 Keats was writing to Charles Brown three days after transcribing 'To Autumn' in a letter to Woodhouse.

10 See J. H. Prynne, '"Ode on a Grecian Urn": Study Notes', *Epsians*, 4 (2014): 49–86.

11 *Blackwood's Edinburgh Magazine*, 3 (August, 1818): 519–24.

12 'Dressing for Art: Notes from Keats in the Emergency Ward,' *Times Literary Supplement*, 582 (May 29, 2015): 14–15.

13 Prynne, 'Ode', 76.

14 *KC* I 92, as reported to Taylor by Richard Woodhouse.

15 Compare Christopher Ricks, *Keats and Embarrassment* (Oxford: Clarendon Press, 1974), p. 93.

CHAPTER 12

Sociability

Grant F. Scott

Much has been written in recent years about the reform politics and gregarious poetics of Leigh Hunt and his circle. Two new biographies along with a spate of critical studies have fueled a vibrant recovery of Hunt's work and a resurgence of interest in 'communal modes of cultural fashioning' and a form of 'Cockney coterie dynamics'.[1] Hunt created an aesthetics of conversation, community and cheerfulness in his writing. Literature provided him a 'sense of textual sociability' and 'was a site of conviviality between author and reader, a place where personality persisted'.[2] Jeffrey Cox focuses on Hunt's 'socialized scene of writing,' his genius for geniality and social power. He emphasises Hunt's reformist and utopian politics, the fact that 'the Hunt circle clearly believed not only that politics shape poetics but that poetry can alter ideology'. Cox amasses enough evidence to convince us of Hunt's profound importance as ideological centre for the second generation of Romantic writers. His revisionist study illuminates Keats's own sociability, arguing that poems in the 1817 volume 'demand to be read' as part of the Hunt circle's cultural and political project rather than as weak early drafts for the Great Odes.[3]

While Cockney School advocates make a persuasive case for understanding Keats's early career as a coterie writer who embraced Hunt's practices, their eagerness to enlist Keats as a partisan member of the Hunt team may need to be tempered. Take, for example, a letter to Bailey he wrote a few short months after the publication of the 1817 *Poems*, in which he grumbles that Hunt and Shelley's advice about his writing of *Endymion*, 'was of no avail – I refused to visit Shelley, that I might have my own unfettered scope – and after all I shall have the Reputation of Hunt's elevé – His corrections and amputations will by the knowing ones be trased in the Poem – This is to be sure the vexation of a day' (*L* 1, 170). Keats bristles at the idea of sociable and shared poetic experience. He's worried not only about Hunt's influence on his writing but also about his own reputation as the older poet's underling. And he expressly desires his independence, his 'own unfettered scope'. Three months later he bridles at Hunt and Shelley's further objections to *Endymion*: 'the fact is he & Shelley are hurt & perhaps justly, at my not having showed them the affair officiously & from several hints I have had they appear much disposed to dissect & anatomize, any trip or slip I may have made' (*L* I, 214). This smacks more of common rivalry and jealousy than the idyllic coterie culture described in recent studies of the Hunt circle.

In light of early ambivalence like this over Hunt's poetic guidance, we might wonder about the extent to which Keats becomes disillusioned with the Cockney School ideology he initially endorsed. Does he evolve a new understanding of literary friendship once the influence of the Hunt circle wanes? I want to focus here on the idea of sociability in the biographical context of Keats's letters, using them to test the ideal of Cockney geniality and the coterie dynamic. A more comprehensive view of his career reveals a figure who resists easy assimilation to this ideal. This Keats enjoyed shade as well as sun and took 'as much delight in conceiving an Iago as an Imogen' (*L* I, 387). He also, we must remember, confessed to 'a horrid Morbidity of Temperament' (*L* I, 142) and assured Bailey he sometimes felt not 'the influence of a Passion or Affection during a whole week' (*L* I, 186). This Keats of 'the feel of not to feel it' who 'saw / Too far into the sea … too distinct into the core / Of an eternal fierce destruction' ('In Drear-Nighted December,' 21; 'Dear Reynolds,' 93–97), has as strong a claim on our imagination as the genial spirit championed by recent critics, or the man unembarrassed of his magnanimity by Christopher Ricks.

There can be no doubt, however, that understood in the context of his early letters, Keats is preeminently the social poet. Here we glimpse the Keats who revels in his friendships with older mentors like Charles Cowden Clarke, Benjamin Robert Haydon and Benjamin Bailey, in addition to Leigh Hunt, and delights in the company of his two younger brothers. As early as the second line of his first known verse epistle to George Felton Matthew he announces his passion for friendship – 'Sweet are the pleasures that to verse belong / And doubly sweet a brotherhood in song' (*L* I, 100). A letter to J. H. Reynolds promises that in their next meeting they 'will read [their] verses in a delightful place I have set my heart upon' (*L* I, 134) and he and Bailey do just that a few months later at Oxford renting a boat and intoning Wordsworth in 'a Bed of rushes' (*L* I, 162). The poetry-writing competitions with Hunt and Shelley are justly famous, underscoring the social inspiration for verse and its very inception in friendly poetic rivalry, as do the sonnets that result from Keats's gatherings with poets and artists ('Great Spirits') and reading Homer with Clarke ('Chapman's Homer').

The letters to his brothers from November 1817 to February 1818 document the almost manic sociability he experienced during this time. He was dining out nearly every night, dancing at 'routs,' going to see plays and pantomimes, attending parties, art galleries and public lectures. He was also drinking – a lot – and boasting about it (*L* 1, 198). So genial was Keats during this period that the very idea of fellowship finds its way into one of his most creative letters, to J. H. Reynolds on the idea of 'delicious diligent Indolence' (*L* 1, 231). After imagining a 'voyage of conception' and offering a whimsical defence of 'passive existence,' Keats posits a creative utopia, a set of 'diverse Journeys' where fellowship would emerge out of contrary minds headed in different directions. At last they would 'greet each other at the Journeys end'. As he writes, 'Man should not dispute or assert but whisper results to his neighbour, and thus by every germ of Spirit sucking the Sap from mould ethereal every human might become great, and Humanity instead of being a wide heath of Furse and Briars with here and there a remote Oak or Pine, would become a grand democracy of Forest Trees' (*L* 1, 232). Keats democratises the process of creative discovery, proposing a world of minds, like a spider, in 'beautiful circuiting', spinning idea-webs that touch each other at various points and producing 'a tapestry empyrean'. All these minds interact at the end of their voyages in 'common taste and fellowship,' whispering their conclusions to their neighbours rather than disputing or asserting.

It can be no accident that Keats invented this allegory soon after reporting quarrels between his friends Hunt, Haydon and Reynolds, quarrels that sank him into 'great Perplexity' with their 'retorting and recriminating' (*L* 1, 210). Keats wished he could play the peace-maker and 'bring them together,' but he knew he had not yet won their esteem fully enough to do so. In the brilliant improvisation of his letter to Reynolds, however, he performs just such a fanciful reconciliation with imaginative gusto. It is to Reynolds also that he later admits, 'I could not live without the love of my friends' (*L* 1, 267) and to Reynolds again, in the famous letter comparing human life to a 'Mansion of Many Apartments,' that he describes the third chamber as 'stored with the wine of love – and the Bread of Friendship' (*L* 1, 283). That this holy friendship is woven not only into his personal credo but into the basic fabric of his aesthetic philosophy seems clear from his statement to his brother Tom that he wishes 'to add a mite to that mass of beauty which is harvested from these grand materials, by the finest spirits, and put into etherial existence for the relish of one's fellows'

(*L* 1, 301). The root essence of friendship is apparent in Keats's belief in the specifically '*gregarious* advance of intellect' (*L* 1, 281; my italics) and in his conviction that both Milton and the Grecian Urn shall eternally remain 'friends of man'. The consolation of art, then, its ability to mend antagonisms and soothe the sufferings of humanity elevates the idea of the social for Keats beyond the drawing-room and beyond the political exigencies of the Cockney School. As he later writes to George and Georgiana in responding to Dilke's obsession with Godwin's *Political Justice*: 'Now the first political duty a Man ought to have a Mind to is the happiness of his friends' (*L* 2, 213). All politics for Keats was social.

More revealing for our purposes than the 'Holiness of the heart's affections,' the homosocial alliances with the Hunt circle or even the philosophical speculations that wed imaginative allegory to fraternal feeling is Keats's use of language in his private correspondence. Keats's words aspire to the phonetic immediacy of conversation, aiming to simulate (and stimulate) spoken discourse. They attempt to narrow the divide between writer and reader and thereby eliminate the semantic and spatial distance between friends. In this way the letters find vivid life in the mistake, the slip, the solecism, the pun. Far from blemishes on canonical documents, these misspellings and neologisms body forth the letter-pages, infusing them with the red blood of the living hand and the timbre of Keats's voice. The rich colloquial and phonetic texture of the letters can be heard in the many words that Keats spells as he sounded them – 'atchieve' *(L* 1, 265), 'coppying' (*L* 1, 317), 'affraid' (*L* 2, 20), 'poeems' (*L* 2, 21), 'ramance' (*L* 1, 253; *L* 2, 28), 'Saciety' (*L* 2, 246), 'Librarry' (*L* 2, 147) and 'all the infernal imaginarry thunderstorms' (*L* 2, 173). He doubles letters at the syllable break and is not above a Cockneyism now and again: his studies 'ave been greatly interrupted lately' (*L* 2, 5). He also captures the exact moment of writing in sensuous details so frank they almost make one blush. Here is a gustatory digression in a letter to Dilke: 'Talking of Pleasure, this moment I was writing with one hand, and with the other holding to my Mouth a Nectarine – good god how fine – It went down soft pulpy, slushy, oozy – all its delicious embonpoint melted down my throat like a large beatified Strawberry. I shall certainly breed' (*L* 2, 179). Keats the decadent connoisseur, Keats the performance artist, Keats the divine sensualist, but above all Keats the friend bent on bringing Dilke *close*.

A similar gesture of dynamic verbal mimeticism appears in an excerpt from one of his Scots Walking Tour letters to his brother Tom: 'we walked to Ireby … Where we were greatly amused by a country dancing school, … they kickit & jumpit with mettle extraordinary, & whiskit, & fleckit, & toe'd it, & go'd it, & twirld it, & wheel'd it, & stampt it, & sweated it, tattooing the floor like mad; The difference between our country dances & these scotch figures, is about the same as leisurely stirring a cup o' Tea & beating up a batter pudding' (*L* 1, 307). The pace and free play of the language mirrors the wild dance itself as well as erasing the distance between Tom and the event described, a collapsing of time and space subtly telegraphed in the shift of tenses from 'kickit & jumpit' to 'toe'd it, & go'd it'. Keats simultaneously places his brother alongside him watching the dancers and at home reading the account as part of his brother's travelogue. The culinary domestic metaphor with which Keats ends the description wittily brings home cultural difference without alienating or discomfiting Tom or belittling the Scotch.

It would not be difficult to multiply instances where Keats embraces the idiomatic expression to transcend the implicit distance in written language and the temporal delay of a letter. But there is another tendency in Keats, a counter-movement that weighs the vital sociability demonstrated here against solitude and isolation, an impulse to get 'out of Town' (*L* 1, 125) and avoid the 'microscope of a Coterie' (*L* 2, 293). A crucial failing of the kind of Cockney sociability endorsed by Leigh Hunt is that it tends to overwhelm the self of the negatively capable poet, whose ambition is to cultivate, paradoxically and enablingly, 'no Identity' so that he can be 'in for – and filling some other Body' (*L* 1, 387). The danger of Huntian affability is that it risks suffocation, or worse disappearance. As Keats confesses to Woodhouse, 'When I am in a room with People if I ever am free from speculating on creations of my own brain, then not myself goes home to myself: but the identity of every one in the room begins to press upon me that, I am in a very little time anhilated – not only among Men; it would be the same in a Nursery of children' (*L* 1, 387). No doubt his brothers suspected this acute sensitivity to drawing-room life and thus, early on, urged him to 'go by [him]self into the country' in order that he should 'be alone to improve [him]self' (*L* 1, 25). Often, then, the letters are at pains to balance the temptations of friendship and society with the powerful inclination to write, and to write alone in locations distant from London like Margate, the Isle of Wight and Winchester.

Nearly everything in Keats's career as a poet is radically foreshortened and the narrative of his disillusionment with sociability proves no exception. Accelerated in part by the death of his brother Tom on 1 December 1818 and his own gradually worsening physical condition, Keats's antisocial behaviour rapidly intensifies. As early as New Year's Day 1819 he is already complaining to his brother and sister-in-law about the tedium of social dinners 'where all the evening's amusement consists in saying your good health' *your* good health, and YOUR good health – and (o I beg you pardon) your's Miss –' (*L* 2, 20). A note of cynicism and of weary misogyny, moreover, begins to creep into the letter as he laments the lack of handsome ladies at these affairs: 'let my eyes be fed or I'll never go out to dinner any where'. Barely a month later he writes that he sees 'very little now, and very few Persons – being almost tired of Men and things' (*L* 2, 59) and on the next leaf includes a list of all the friends he has 'not seen'. Seven months on things have deteriorated alarmingly. 'In the midst of the world,' he pronounces to his brother from Winchester, 'I live like a Hermit' (*L* 2, 186). He forces himself to go to London 'and it was a whole day before I could feel among Men – I had another strange sensation there was not one house I felt any pleasure to call at' (*L* 2, 187).

It is true that he continues to write extensive, detailed and gossipy letters to George and Georgiana in America, but his own life at home in England is increasingly circumscribed and asocial. As communication with his friends palls, interest in his books increases and they begin gradually to replace human companionship: 'Books are becoming more interesting and valuable to me,' he reveals to Haydon, 'I may say I could not live without them' (*L* 2, 220), an assertion that echoes and edits his earlier claim that he could not live without the love of his friends. So essential are his books, in fact, that he is made anxious when away from home, regretting the 'absence from my Books' and dreams 'over my Books, or rather other peoples Books' rather than other people (*L* 2, 239). When his brother and sister-in-law invite him to America, he retorts, 'What could I do there? How could I employ myself? Out of the reach of Libraries' (*L* 2, 210). And he is not joking.

By January 1820 Keats's anti-social feelings are sliding toward misanthropy. 'A Man is like a Magnet,' he explains to his brother in excusing his failure to meet the new Mrs Haslam, 'he must have a repelling end' (*L* 2, 240). And two days later: 'Upon the whole I dislike Mankind: whatever people on the other side of the question may advance they cannot deny that they are always surprised at hearing of a good action and never of a bad one' (*L* 2, 243). This bitterness and disaffection soon boils over in a Keats-like rodomontade in which he lists a few of his old friends – Haydon, Hunt, Dilke, the Miss Reynolds – and then systematically rehearses their stupifying dullness and predictability: 'If I go to Hunt's I run my head into many-times heard puns and music' (*L* 2, 244). Such is the magnitude of his disaffection that in the presence of these people he too is infected with vapidity; he is afraid to speak 'for fear of some sickly reiteration of Phrase or Sentiment'. Negative Capability sheds its paradoxical aura of achievement, of empathy and in-feeling, and here assumes its mundane literal meaning, the reverse of aptitude, a parroting of conventional platitudes. It's an extraordinary confession coming from the poet who only two short years before had idolised some of these same friends in verse and letters. Here instead Keats writes an epistle to dullness that mutes the high octane buzz of the odes, the excited identification with new modes of sensation and thought. 'All I can say,' he concludes wearily, 'is that standing at Charing cross and looking east west north and south I can see nothing but dullness' (*L* 2, 244).

The progression of his tuberculosis with its alternating states of haemorrhage and fever, lassitude and agitation combined with his medically prescribed 'confinement' at Wentworth Place (*L* 2, 269) contributes to his isolation, nervous anxiety, cynicism and despair. A restricted diet, 'living upon pseudo victuals,' as he says, certainly does nothing to alleviate his torments (*L* 2, 271). Nor does his deepening relationship with Fanny Brawne, of whom his friends disapprove and make the target of their 'tattle'. Keats's immobility and increasing dependency on others as an invalid reduces him to watching society through a window from his 'Sopha bed … in the front Parlour' (*L* 2, 253). Hardly the keen 'watcher of the skies' (9) in the sonnet on 'Chapman's Homer,' Keats settles into the role as passive observer of people's daily rounds, a social outsider. Gradually Fanny Brawne becomes his only friend – 'I am more and more concentrated in you,' he admits desperately (*L* 2, 311) – and reminds him ironically of his former self, continually 'going to Town' (*L* 2, 257), dancing and racing through 'a thousand activities' (*L* 2, 304). In Keats's mind the complex sociability and coterie culture of the Hunt circle has been whittled down to Fanny's flirtations and the overwhelming question, 'who have you smil'd with?' (*L* 2, 304). He blurts out that he is 'sickened at the brute world … I hate men and women more' (*L* 2, 312) and renounces his closest allies: 'I will indulge myself by never seeing any more Dilke or Brown or any of their Friends' (*L* 2, 313). Friendship is now pretence and poison.

As critics have shown, Leigh Hunt's sociability extended to readers. In prefaces and poems he tried to cultivate their sympathy and friendship, addressing them as 'kindred spirits'. In several poems he overtly eroticises this relationship, reaching out to the reader 'with a pleasurable moment of almost palpable human contact'.[4] One of Keats's final poetic fragments, 'This Living Hand,' does precisely the opposite. Instead of the warmth and geniality Hunt extends to the reader, Keats offers an 'icy' hand that threatens to 'chill thy dreaming nights'. Not a welcome but a warning and not erotic union but lethal quid pro quo. To vanquish this eerily Gothic floating body part, the reader must 'wish [his/her] own heart dry of blood, / So in my veins red life might stream again' (5–6). The psychic pay-off is relief, to feel 'conscience-calm'd' (7), though with a 'heart dry of blood'. It's a bad bargain, requiring the sacrifice of the reader's life in order for the poet's hand to continue living and writing: 'See, here it is – / I hold it towards you' (7–8). The reader has no choice. Hunt's genial handshake has become the deadly clasp of a wraith.

Fortunately for us, and for Keats's legacy, this is where the artist Joseph Severn enters the picture. He called many of Keats's friends his own, especially Haslam and the Novellos, and painted their portraits. His letters to friends and family are characterised by enthusiasm and expansiveness. Full of frantic dashes and misspellings, they read like records of Severn himself talking. They are convivial, full of bluff good cheer, and in this sense figure forth a man that Keats must have stared at in ironical bemusement. But it was this Severn, the man whose nerves were 'too strong to be hurt by other peoples illnesses' (*L* 2, 349), who kept rescuing Keats from his 'posthumous life' in Italy. He introduced him to other artists, walked with him on the Pincio, played Haydn to him in their rooms, read aloud to him from books that he trekked all over Rome to procure and endlessly conversed with and consoled him. Equally important, of course, he became the lifeline of information to Keats's friends, sending off detailed missives whenever he could. In ministering to Keats, he was also desperately trying to re-socialise him.

Small wonder that in the last days Severn pulled Keats back from the abyss of abjection and self-pity and inspired in him a new sociability – not the coterie cheer of the Hunt circle or the man-about-town bluster of the early letters – but a wiser, more sober sense of brotherhood and sympathy. At the approach of death, the poet lingered on his *friend's* agonies rather than his own: 'Severn – S – lift me up for I am dying – I shall die easy – don't be frightened – thank God it has come.'[5] At the thought of his final end, as Severn reports, 'he was calm and firm … to a most astonishing degree – he told [me] not to tremble for he did not think that he should be convulsed – he said – 'did you ever see any one die' – no – 'well then I pity you poor Severn – what trouble and danger you have got into for me – now you must be firm for it will not last long'.[6] Here Keats abandons his role as consumptive patient for a new profession, that of physician to men. The Keats who was earlier 'dissolving' (*L* 2, 223) now became 'firm' as he advised Severn how to respond to his death. And firm now was his bond of friendship with Severn. He must have realised that the painter, himself a physician of sorts, had all along been repairing his damaged humanity.

Notes

1 Greg Kucich, '"The Wit in the Dungeon': Leigh Hunt and the Insolent Politics of Cockney Coteries,' *Romanticism on the Net* 14 (May 1999): 1. See, for example, Nicholas Roe, *Fiery Heart: The First Life of Leigh Hunt* (London: Vintage, 2005); Nicholas Roe, ed., *Leigh Hunt: Life, Poetics, Politics* (London and New York: Routledge, 2003); Anthony Holden, *The Wit in the Dungeon: Leigh Hunt and His Circle* (London and New York: Little, Brown, 2005); and Michael Eberle-Sinatra, *Leigh Hunt and the London Literary Scene* (London and New York: Routledge, 2005).

2 Michael Tomko, 'Leigh Hunt's Cockney Canon: Sociability and Subversion from Homer to *Hyperion*,' in *A Companion to Romantic Poetry*, ed. Charles Mahoney (Malden, MA: Wiley-Blackwell, 2011), p. 288.

3 Jeffrey N. Cox, *Poetry and Politics in the Cockney School: Keats, Shelley, Hunt and their Circle* (Cambridge: Cambridge University Press, 1998), pp. 7, 61, 85.

4 Jane Stabler, 'Leigh Hunt's Aesthetics of Intimacy,' in *Leigh Hunt: Life, Poetics, Politics*, ed. Nicholas Roe (London: Routledge, 2003), p. 102.

5 *Joseph Severn: Letters and Memoirs*, ed. Grant F. Scott (Burlington, VT: Ashgate, 2005), p. 136.

6 *Joseph Severn*, p. 138.

CHAPTER 13

The Visual and Plastic Arts

Nancy Moore Goslee

When Keats visited the exhibit of Benjamin West's painting 'Death on a pale horse' in December 1817, his critical response led to wide-ranging 'speculations' about both visual and verbal art that later inform his own poetry. West's painting, he wrote his brothers,

> is a wonderful picture, when West's age is considered; But there is nothing to be intense upon; no women one feels mad to kiss; no face swelling into reality. the excellence of every Art is its intensity, capable of making all disagreeables evaporate, from their being in close relationship with Beauty & Truth.
>
> (*L* I, 192)

In contrast to *King Lear,* West's painting offers 'unpleasantness without any momentous depth of speculation excited, in which to bury its repulsiveness'. Returning to his letter a few days later, he reported that his own 'speculation[s]' 'dovetailed' to develop his theory of '*Negative Capability*, … when man is capable of being in uncertainties, Mysteries, doubts, without any irritable reaching after fact & reason' (*L* I, 193).

Moving from painting to poetic drama, Keats's discussion of 'intensity' suggests that either art may distill 'disagreeables' into a more profound and beautiful 'Truth'. Similarly, although his criterion of 'Negative Capability' defines 'a Man of Achievement especially in Literature', its sceptical viewpoint is also wide-ranging. As Keats developed both intensity and negative capability in his own poetry, he created a descriptive immediacy through visual and sculptural images to question what he saw, as in his 'Ode to Psyche': 'Surely I dreamt to-day, or did I see / The winged Psyche …?' (5–6). This capability of 'remaining content with half-knowledge' (*L* I, 194) also operates through his densely figurative exploration of tensions among these arts – not only between visual and verbal arts, but also between the visual and the sculptural.

Keats's objections to West's painting may also arise out of its subject. 'Death on a pale horse' illustrates an already highly pictorial verbal text,

Revelation, chapter 6, which personifies death. West's blurred, emaciated, yet still semi-fleshly human form entered an ongoing debate beginning with *Paradise Lost.* Milton's controversial description of Death as a 'shape that shape had none' (bk 2, line 668) later led Edmund Burke to praise this allegorical non-figure as exemplifying sublime obscurity. His influential opposition between the sublime and the beautiful differentiated them by gender and medium, the former defined as masculine, terrifyingly powerful, and most effectively represented by verbal means and the latter as feminine, gentle, and best represented through the visual arts.[1] This opposition then influenced G. E. Lessing's *Laocoon,* familiar to British artists and theorists through Henry Fuseli's Royal Academy lectures. Arguing that the visual is an art of space and the verbal, especially narrative, is an art of time, Lessing like Burke privileged the verbal, claiming that it occupies a 'wider sphere' through the 'infinite range of our imagination and the intangibility of its images'.[2] While W. J. T. Mitchell argues trenchantly that these spatial/temporal differences are superficial, he also argues that Lessing's iconophobia, his fear of the visual, springs from Burke's association of the beautiful with the visual arts and with the feminine.

Although Keats's letter focuses upon similarities among the arts, his critique is marked by a subtle distinction between two- and three-dimensional visual arts, even introducing an erotic sense of touch: 'no women one feels mad to kiss; no face swelling into reality'. Earlier in the letter he had celebrated the recent verdicts exonerating two radical publishers from libel charges as restoring 'Liberty's Emblazoning'. These plastic and visual images reflect Keats's active participation in the group of poets, critics, and artists associated with Leigh Hunt and sharing his political and social liberalism. Further, though the American-born West considered himself a champion of liberty, his presidency of the Royal Academy as well as the widespread advertising of this exhibit as ' "under the immediate patronage of His Royal Highness the Prince Regent" ' may well have conveyed a sense of governmental oppression and aesthetic conservatism – a death of sorts – for Keats.[3]

Keats critics had long ignored these ideological pressures. Our current historicist turn has remedied this omission – and has also prompted rethinking about the relationships between the ideological and the aesthetic.[4] This essay first surveys the many kinds of art, high and low, that Keats and his friends encountered in London. It then turns to a specific, formalist investigation of the figurative language through which the visual and plastic arts enter Keats's poetry. Finally, it considers how Victorian painters, notably the Pre-Raphaelites, re-appropriate his verbal art.

Visual and Plastic Arts in Keats's London

Although Keats's letter did not say whether he visited the West exhibit alone or in company, several friends had connections with the exhibit. Leigh Hunt, West's nephew, had acquired a deep knowledge of the arts, as well as training in drawing, from visiting West's studio with its paintings, plaster casts of Greek sculptures, prints, and books. Abandoning art for poetry and reviewing, he nevertheless recreated the atmosphere of that studio in his own Hampstead house (see Keats's 'Sleep and Poetry', 350–405). William Hazlitt, a painter also turned essayist and lecturer whose ideas profoundly interested Keats, had reviewed West's exhibit in *The Edinburgh Magazine* for December 1817, shaping Keats's response – but Hazlitt's critical metaphor is far less erotic.[5]

Keats and his friends benefitted, as Ian Jack points out, from Britain's growing and patriotic enthusiasm for the visual arts building upon the establishment of the Royal Academy in 1769. As an after-effect of the French Revolution, many old masters from French collections came to Britain. During the Peace of Amiens and after Waterloo, British artists travelled to Paris to see Napoleon's booty from Italy, reporting back with sketches and prints. With his friends, Keats attended exhibits of contemporary painters and sculptors at the RA; the paintings ranged hierarchically from history painting in the grand style that corresponded to epic, through landscapes, portraits, and genre paintings such as those of his friend David Wilkie. Many private collectors allowed the public to see their Renaissance and seventeenth-century collections – including Titians – as well as classical sculptures and vases. He saw Egyptian sculpture at the British Museum and a number of Raphael's Cartoons, exhibited at the British Institute from 1816 to 1818.[6]

His friend the history painter Benjamin Robert Haydon, who had arranged that exhibit, also introduced him to the sublime grandeur of the Elgin marbles and to the cultural and political debates prompted by their arrival in London. Writing in the politically liberal *Annals of the Fine Arts,* Haydon argued that these Parthenon marbles with their naturalistic representation of muscles and tendons under stress should replace the dominant models for classical Greek sculpture, models such as the Apollo Belvedere. The smooth, fluid contours and serene expressions of these figures, so fiercely defended by aristocratic collectors and connoisseurs as golden-age 'Praxitelean', were instead, as we now know, Hellenistic. As Grant Scott observes, Keats's two sonnets on the Elgin marbles avoid describing them directly, instead turning to images of sublime and fragmented landscape – alluding to the marbles' damaged state and showing his own anxiety about achieving some equivalent grandeur.[7]

In addition to London's wealth of art that Keats had seen directly, he also participated in a lively culture of mediated images, more affordable to the middle class – though seldom to Keats himself. Many of the original Renaissance paintings as well as prints owned and shared by his friends illustrated scenes from Greek mythology, deepening the knowledge that he like Hunt had gained from the handbooks of Greek mythology so criticised by *Blackwood's*: Joseph Lemprière's *Bibliotheca Classica*, Andrew Tooke's *Pantheon*, and Joseph Spence's *Polymetis*.[8] Keats also visited the studios which made plaster casts of classical sculptures like those Hunt and Shelley had bought. Looking through the stock of print shops and his friends' portfolios of prints, he saw engravings of the frescoes at the Campo Santo in Pisa as well as of Titian's, Claude's, and Poussin's paintings. He could afford several 'Tassie gems', miniature glass-paste bas-reliefs of classical subjects.[9]

In contrast to this high art, directly seen or mediated, were theatrical pantomimes with their silent bodies communicating through gesture, and the prints of Hogarth, long-standing favourites even before he encountered Charles Brown's series at Wentworth Place. Hogarth's subjects point the way to other visual entertainments appealing to all classes, 'shows of London' like those Wordsworth deplored in Book 7 of *The Prelude* but also including technical innovations such as panoramas and phantasmagorias, complicated light shows.[10]

Poetic Figures for the Arts

As Keats converted the visual and plastic arts into his poetry, he employed two broad categories of figuration. The first is *ekphrasis*, a rhetorical figure which at its most basic is mimetic: the verbal description of a visual scene or object. In its narrower but justifiably more celebrated form *ekphrasis* is the literary description of a visual or sculptural work of art. Developing from Homer's poetic description of Achilles' shield, this more aesthetic version of *ekphrasis* tests the poet's power to animate a still object while claiming that the artist has created this effect. James Heffernan describes the process as one of friction within an initial identification of visual with verbal art. Extending this analysis, W. J. T. Mitchell distinguishes three potential responses by poet or audience to the visual or sculptural object: ekphrastic indifference, ekphrastic hope, and ekphrastic fear.[11] However vexed, this relationship between perceiving subject, poet or reader, and an 'other' seldom distinguishes whether that other is a painting or a sculpture.

My second category for Keats's figuration analyses this distinction. Seventeenth-century history painters such as Claude and Poussin often included figures in the foreground mediating between viewer and more distant castle or altar in the landscape. Keats's verse letter to John Hamilton Reynolds, 25 March 1818, described and then supplemented such a composition in Claude's *Enchanted Castle* (lines 241–4). Educated eighteenth-century tourists looked at their own British landscapes by viewing them through a brown 'Claude glass', framing and tinting them to match the darkened varnish; guidebooks also instructed viewers where to 'station' themselves for the most 'picturesque' perspective, as if they owned the landscape. Although Keats mocked this habit in himself and others, he brought it to his reading of *Paradise Lost.* Pointing to Milton's '*stationing or statuary*', he wrote in the book's margins, the earlier poet 'is not content with simple description, he must station, – ... So we see Adam "*Fair indeed and tall – under a plantan*" and we see Satan "*disfigured –on the Assyrian Mount*"'.[12] In context, these examples show the reader a central figure's momentary stasis, the surrounding landscape, and an interested observer. Although Keats used 'stationing' and 'statuary' here as if they are synonyms, his own poetry often shifts its focus from figure within its setting to the figure itself, developing a tension between the two. In doing so, he also introduced larger historical patterns, testing ideas of temporal and historical process based upon analogues between sculpture and painting. He explored these distinctions most fully in his Miltonic epic fragment *Hyperion*; I will also look briefly at distinctions between painting and sculpture in *The Eve of St. Agnes* and the 'Ode on a Grecian Urn'.

At the beginning of *Hyperion,* Keats stations the fallen Titan Saturn 'Deep in the shady sadness of a vale' (1. 1), but his similes compare the Titans to massive sculpture. Reflecting their lapsarian inertia, this characterisation sets up Keats's apparent narrative plan, a revision of the archaic Greek Hesiod's *Theogony,* describing conflicts between successive generations of deities, into an allegory of natural evolution from one stage of sculpture to another. Even though the Titans are 'first-born of all shap'd and palpable Gods' (2. 154), 'in form and shape compact and beautiful, / In will, in action free, companionship' (2. 209–10), Egyptian or archaic Greek statue-like deities capable of motion and social action, the Olympians will surpass them in beauty and hence in power (2. 229) – and will in turn be surpassed. In these terms, an animate version of J. J. Winckelmann's *History of Ancient Art,* objective aesthetic form signals a capacity for moral truth and, implicitly, liberty – in classical Greece and also, given such an open-ended progression, in Keats's own time. At least two problems emerge from this new model of history, however: doubt that moderns can surpass ancient Greece's unified culture of art and liberty, and questions about the subjective agency of these beautiful objects. This recognition develops as Keats describes his Apollo, a subjective poet-musician who sees in Mnemosyne's face 'Names, deeds, gray legends, dire events, rebellions… [that] /Pour into the wide hollows of my brain, / And deify me' (3. 114, 116–8). Working from Friedrich Schiller and A. W. Schlegel, the latter translated into English in 1815 and familiar to Coleridge, Haydon, and Hazlitt, Keats's new pattern contrasts ancient and modern, classical and 'romantic' cultures through an analogy between the 'sculpturesque' and the 'picturesque'. The earlier culture is objective and the modern is subjective, looking back and embracing the classical from its modern, sentimental, and historically conscious perspective. If this pattern enables progress for the moderns over the enviable grandeur and political liberty of the ancient Greeks, however, its binary opposition obscures the way to further progress.

When the Beadsman at the opening of *The Eve of St. Agnes* returns 'wan' through the chapel, his 'weak spirit fails / To think' how the 'sculptur'd dead' 'may ache' with the cold (14, 17–18). Keats's witty Cockney ambiguities in these lines blur several boundaries between life and death, representation and actuality. These sculptural ambiguities re-enter the poem during the encounter between Madeline and Porphyro, growing out of but interrupting the 'warm gules' and 'Rose-bloom' emanating from the 'casement … triple-arch'd' (208, 218, 220). As this two-dimensional heraldic record of a cultural past is transformed, enwrapping but releasing Madeline, it recalls Keats's complaint that West's painting offered no 'women one feels mad to kiss', no 'face swelling into reality'. When she half-wakes to Porphyro's voice and lute, however, a more ominous sculptural image intrudes upon her dream: kneeling beside her bed, 'pallid, chill, and drear' (311), Porphyro seems all too close to those chapel effigies or to the bodies beneath. Although he soon proves his vitality, we are again left with questions: does Madeline's recognition of Porphyro's mortality lead to her consent or does she retreat to her own erotic stratagem of dreaming?

Keats's odes of 1819 link stationing and statuary to apostrophe and personification, figures of speech that address some object or concept and bring it to imaginary life. Although Keats appears to describe an actual urn in his most ekphrastic of odes, he nevertheless creates the work of art he describes. More than simply a composite of details from classical urns he had seen displayed in London or reproduced in prints, this imagined urn introduces through its material and its surface ornamentation thematic concerns central to relationships among arts – and to the relationship of artefacts, particularly classical Greek artefacts, to modern human life. The urn Keats addresses is doubly three-dimensional – or, more precisely, while the rounded shape of the urn itself inspires the poet's personification of it as 'still unravish'd bride', the 'leaf-fring'd legend' (1, 5) of visual scenes that encircle it are bas-relief, carved from the marble so that each stands out slightly from the larger curved surface of the urn. Although the lyric speaker does not clarify whether he or she walks around the urn to see the different scenes or whether he sees separate bands from one viewpoint, that potential freedom to move draws our attention to the paradox of the represented figures. For within these scenes, Keats employs a different form of stationing and statuary than he has earlier. Instead of figures precariously balanced on tip-toe for a moment, loitering, stunned by a fall, or sleeping, here his 'leaf-fring'd' framing surrounds figures described as if in motion, at first frantically and then gradually slowing as we move from scene to scene, from the 'mad pursuit' and 'wild ecstasy' of the first stanza to the 'Bold lover' who pursues a single female figure (9, 10, 17), to the religious procession of stanza 4. Almost part of the framing in stanzas two and three, the piping youth mediates between the central erotic figures and the lyric poet's gaze and speech. He resembles a Miltonic '*spectator ab extra*', a phrase Geoffrey Hartman borrows from Coleridge to describe Miltonic stationing. Yet he too is marble.

If the earlier 'ecstasy' and 'mad pursuit' recall Keats's ekphrastic allusion to Titian's 'Bacchus and Ariadne', the scene in stanza 4 of the ode is also ekphrastic, recalling the Pan-Athenian procession on the Elgin marbles, also a marble bas-relief – but with a sacrificial bull instead of Keats's 'unravish'd' heifer.[13] When the speaker asks the priest 'what green altar' is their goal (32), we realise that 'green' is the only specific image of colour in the poem, and that neither altar nor 'little town' (35) appears on the marble urn. With that recognition, the slow-moving procession stops, suddenly caught in the still world of its plastic yet stony art. Through this simultaneously visual and sculptural moment, Keats represents the people and the cultures that the urn's enduring marble has outlived; yet the cleverness mediating this pathos resembles the representational slippage that the beadsman falls into in *The Eve of St. Agnes*.

As if responding to the temporal and spatial distances so evoked, the lyric speaker backs up to apostrophise the urn itself, that 'Attic shape' and 'fair attitude' (41). From this phrase, Jeffrey Cox argues that Keats alludes wittily to the classical poses made popular by Emma Hamilton. Her temporarily frozen but doubtless panting stances as famous Greek statues, widely satirised in cartoons, point back to the urn as 'bride', to the lovers in stanzas 1–3,[14] and to Keats's criticism of West's painting – 'no face swelling into reality'. Yet Keats turns away from this sensual plasticity and momentary stationing to confront the Urn's material fixity. A Medusa-like agent, the urn as medium has turned the bas-relief scenes to stone and has also teased the speaker out of thought. Yet she too, of course, is stone. This marble both preserves the urn's beauty and marks, by contrast, the human history that has elapsed since its creation. Its simultaneous personification and resistant materiality offer an escape from the binary opposition of visual and verbal, feminine and masculine, into a sort of shared sympathy between urn and poet-speaker, a sympathy that points toward the shared burden of poet and Moneta in *The Fall of Hyperion*.

Victorian Artists' Responses to Keats

Although Haydon offered to paint a subject from *Endymion,* Keats urged him to wait for his more 'naked and grecian' (*L* 1, 207) epic *Hyperion*. Haydon never took up this alternative. In the late 1840s, however, as a new wave of revolutions began across Europe, a group of painters and writers resembling the Hunt circle in their liberal politics and aesthetic experimentation formed themselves around their discovery of the still largely-unknown poetry of Keats. Calling themselves the Pre-Raphaelites, this group took their style from pre-Renaissance Italian art, abjuring Raphael's classically inspired figures and Renaissance orthogonal perspective. Instead, they imitated the effect of medieval and early Renaissance frescoes. Identifying with Keats as victim of a philistine culture, they were fascinated by his medieval romances, especially *Isabella, The Eve of St. Agnes,* and 'La Belle Dame'. Aside from illustrated editions of Keats's poetry, editions that reveal the popularity of that long classical romance *Endymion* among readers and artists, the only non-romance representation by this group seems to be Dante Gabriel Rossetti's late painting *Mnemosyne,* dated 1881 and like its source *Hyperion* left unfinished.[15]

While this almost exclusive focus upon Keats's medieval-revival romances contributed to the poet's nineteenth- and early twentieth-century reputation as an apparent escapist from the political and social world into an aestheticised past, the Pre-Raphaelites and even their academic, more conservative successors saw and then represented in their own terms Keats's uses of historically distant romance to show contemporary conflicts between public and private spheres, social constraint and erotic desire. Recent analyses of these paintings, sketches, and prints examine specifically the shifting gender politics of the poet, the painters, and their rapidly changing social contexts, as the 'woman question' dominated much social and political debate. Thus the power dynamics between the two lovers, or between the couple and their blocking figures continue to change through the nineteenth century and on into the early twentieth. Because the primary medium here is visual, the viewer of the art work must recall the verbal text, interpret it, recognise how the artist interprets it, and then consider his or her own interpretation. In this complex mediation, the *paragone* or competition between arts as an expression of gender politics is still present but attenuated.

Notes

1 See Edmund Burke, *A Philosophical Enquiry into the Origin of Our Ideas of the Sublime and the Beautiful* (1757), ed., intro. James T. Boulton, 1958 (rpt. Oxford: Blackwell, 1967).

2 Qtd by W. J. T. Mitchell in *Iconology: Image, Text, Ideology* (Chicago: University of Chicago Press, 1986), p. 107.

3 Ian Jack, *Keats and the Mirror of Art* (Oxford: Clarendon Press, 1967), pp. 3–4; *L* I 192 n.

4 For an early example of this turn, see Nicholas Roe, ed., *Keats and History* (Cambridge: Cambridge University Press, 1995); yet in 'Keats, Ekphrasis, and History', pp. 212–37 in Roe's collection, Theresa Kelley links formalism to a flexible historicism.

5 See *L* 1, 192n9, and Morton. D. Paley, *The Apocalyptic Sublime* (New Haven: Yale University Press, 1986), ch. 2 and esp. p. 28; Benjamin Robert Haydon may also have reviewed the painting; see Jack, *Keats and the Mirror of Art*, p. 96 and n. 15, p. 260.

6 See *L* 2, 19; Jack, *Keats and the Mirror of Art*, pp. 96–8.

7 See Stephen A. Larrabee, *English Bards and Grecian Marbles: The Relationship Between Sculpture and Poetry Especially in the Romantic Period* (New York: Columbia University Press, 1943); Grant F. Scott, *The Sculpted Word: Keats, Ekphrasis, and the Visual Arts* (Hanover and London: University Press of New England, 1994), ch. 2; and Gillen D'Arcy Wood, *The Shock of the Real: Romanticism and Visual Culture 1760–1860* (New York: Palgrave, 2001), pp. 130–51, which also discusses the *Hyperion* poems.

8 See Jack, *Keats and the Mirror of Art*, pp. 2, 249n. 3.

9 See his poem 'On a Leander …', *P* 94 and a letter to his sister Fanny, *L* 2, 45; see also Mary Wollstonecraft Shelley, *Letters*, ed. Betty. T. Bennett, 3 vols. (Baltimore: Johns Hopkins University Press, 1980), vol. 1, p. 38n.

10 See Richard Altick, *The Shows of London* (Cambridge, MA: Belknap Press of Harvard University, 1978; William H. Galperin, *The Return of the Visible in British Romanticism* (Baltimore: Johns Hopkins University Press, 1993), ch. 2;

Gillen d'Arcy Wood, *The Shock of the Real,* ch. 3; Orrin Wang, 'Coming Attractions: "Lamia" and Cinematic Sensation', *Studies in Romanticism* 42 (2003): 461–500.

11 See James A. W. Heffernan, *Museum of Words: The Poetics of Ekphrasis from Homer to Ashbery* (Chicago: University of Chicago Press, 1993), p. 37; W. J. T. Mitchell, *Picture Theory: Essays on Visual and Verbal Representation* (Chicago: University of Chicago Press, 1994), pp. 152–4; and Theresa Kelley, 'Keats and "Ekphrasis"', in *The Cambridge Companion to Keats,* ed. Susan J. Wolfson (Cambridge: Cambridge University Press, 2001), pp. 170–5.

12 See Beth Lau, *Keats's 'Paradise Lost'* (Gainesville, FL: University Press of Florida, 1998), pp. 142–3.

13 Jack, *Keats and the Mirror of Art*, pp. 219–20.

14 See Jeffrey N. Cox, *Poetry and Politics in the Cockney School: Keats, Shelley, Hunt, and their Circle* (Cambridge: Cambridge University Press, 1998), pp. 169–86.

15 Helen E. Haworth, '"A Thing of Beauty Is a Joy Forever?" Early Illustrated Editions of Keats's Poetry', *Harvard Library Bulletin* 21 (1973): 88–103; Sarah Wootton, *Consuming Keats: Nineteenth-Century Representations in Art and Literature* (Basingstoke: Palgrave Macmillan, 2006); Grant F. Scott, 'Language Strange: A Visual History of Keats's "La Belle Dame sans Merci"', *Studies in Romanticism* 38 (1999): 503–35; and Julie F. Codell, 'Painting Keats: Pre-Raphaelite Artists Between Social Transgressions and Painterly Conventions', *Victorian Poetry* 33: 3–4 (1995): 341–70.

CHAPTER 14

Religion and Myth

Anthony John Harding

Beginnings

On 31 October 1820, after a long and exhausting voyage from England, John Keats and Joseph Severn stepped on to Italian soil at Naples. They spent the next eight days there, to recover from the voyage and see something of the city before travelling on to Rome. Severn records that his friend was strongly impressed by the magnificent Teatro San Carlo, particularly by the painting that covers the ceiling of the theatre. The painting, by Giuseppe Cammarano, depicts 'Apollo Introducing the Greatest Poets to the Goddess Minerva'.[1]

Whatever his anxieties about the rigours of the journey and the worsening symptoms of his disease, Keats must have felt that here, at least, he was in the right place. Since his schooldays at Clarke's Academy, he had been familiar with the classical pantheon. As a young medical student writing verse epistles to his friends, he had often invoked Apollo as presiding spirit of their coterie. In his more ambitious early poetry (such as 'Ode to Apollo', written February 1815), these apostrophes to the god were already more than just conventional classicising: they were a way of developing his concept of poetry as a *vocation*.[2]

Modern readers, struck by the repeated expressions of diffidence and self-doubt in the 'Preface' to *Endymion*, may tend to overemphasise Keats's sense of being an outsider to the culture of classical Greece and Rome, ignoring (for instance) the fact that he knew enough Latin to translate the whole of Virgil's *Aeneid* into English prose. Some, too, may be automatically distrustful of 'mythological' content, taking Keats's choice of such subject matter as evidence of a wish to put aside the social and political conflicts of his own time. Such a separation of classical learning from political engagement would have been wholly foreign to those in Keats's circle, and to the teachers at the school he attended: Clarke's Academy, a leading Dissenting centre of learning first established in Warwick in 1750 by the Baptist John Colet Ryland.

In 1803, when Keats enrolled at the school, Dissenters were still struggling to achieve the political and civil rights enjoyed by members of the Church of England, but it does not appear that Clarke's Academy imposed Calvinist doctrines on its pupils. It welcomed boys from many different backgrounds, and its Headmaster, John Clarke, allowed expression of a range of religious opinions.[3] At such a school, free-ranging enquiry, and conversations about constitutional reform and freedom of religious belief, would have been an integral part of the study of history and rhetoric. In his school years, Keats met boys of various religious backgrounds, and heard discussion of different creeds and forms of worship.

In 1809, Keats eagerly began reading the school library's books on classical literature and mythology, particularly John Lemprière's *Bibliotheca classica*, Joseph Spence's *Polymetis*, and Andrew Tooke's *Pantheon*.[4] He was encouraged in this course of study by Charles Cowden Clarke, the Headmaster's son and a teacher at the school, who became his friend and mentor. From such early poems as 'To George Felton Mathew' and the sonnet 'Many the wonders I this day have seen', it is clear that Keats approached Greek myth eagerly and with a keen imaginative curiosity. Even the rather formal and imitative 'Ode to Apollo', with its parade of great poets in the manner of Dryden or Gray, strongly evokes the sense of poetic possibility and reawakening of a long tradition: if Spenser, Milton and Tasso could move the reader by invoking classical myth, why not a modern poet?

Fifty years after the death of Alexander Pope, many critics considered classical mythology to be wholly used up, irretrievably drained of any poetic power it may once have had. This critical view did not disappear in the early 1800s – it informs J. G. Lockhart's contemptuous review of *Endymion* for *Blackwood's* – but at the same time there was a renewal of interest in the ancient world and its religious beliefs, driven partly by new archaeological discoveries and partly by late-Enlightenment speculation about the origins of religious belief in the responses of early human societies to the natural world. The work of philologists such as Christian Gottlob Heyne and Georg Friedrich Creuzer suggested that myths might be, as Wordsworth's Solitary expressed it, 'Fictions in form, but in their substance truths, / Tremendous truths!'[5] Knowledge of such developments in classical scholarship would certainly have been current among the teachers at Clarke's Academy.

For Keats, however, the more important objective was to explore the poetic possibilities of myth as imaginative response to the living nature he saw around him. It was in the poetry of Spenser that Keats found the richest possibilities. Spenser's 'Epithalamion' – which Cowden Clarke read to

Keats in 1812 – seamlessly blends mythological allusions ('The Rosy Morne long since left Tithones bed') with the sights and sounds of the countryside: 'The merry Larke hir mattins sings aloft.'[6] Keats's poetical tribute to Cowden Clarke, written in September 1816, is also a tribute to the poetry of Tasso, Spenser, and Milton, and to a contemporary from whom Keats was already learning: Clarke's friend Leigh Hunt.

The naming of Hunt as a champion of liberty, and the allusion to his *Feast of the Poets* ('The wrong'd Libertas, – who has told you stories / Of laurel chaplets, and Apollo's glories', 44–5), neatly communicate the political sympathies both of the writer and of his addressee. Not accidentally, it also indicates their shared attitude of religious tolerance – Hunt was a Deist, rejecting all Christian forms of worship. The passing reference to Apollo, in a poem that also mentions Helicon, Clio, and Cynthia, hints at Keats's hope of being accepted into the *Examiner* coterie. For these poets, the poetry of Greece and Rome was not a dried-up source, but a fertile territory to be reclaimed in the name of religious and political freedom.

This device, by which poetry is imagined as a territory to be claimed and explored, becomes the enabling metaphor of 'Sleep and Poetry', the poem in which Keats most explicitly represents himself as embarking on a journey into the poetic 'realm' that is at the same time an assertion of his own liberty: 'there ever rolls / A vast idea before me, and I glean / Therefrom my liberty' (290–2). 'On First Looking Into Chapman's Homer' likewise begins with thrilling imagery of Apollo's 'realms of gold', but then – as the unknown 'demesne' of Homer is revealed through the mediating voice of Chapman – we are confronted with a new order of distance: 'Then felt I like some watcher of the skies…' (9). As Martin Aske points out, 'The imagery of "watcher" and "planet" signifies an irrevocable distance separating the viewer and his object'[7] and yet the sense of new possibility, of Homer as a still-accessible source of new beginnings, remains.

Endymion

From his experience of translating the *Aeneid*, and his knowledge of Spenser and Milton, Keats would have become familiar with the idea that the creation of a long narrative was the true test of a poet's vocation. The choice of the Endymion myth was dictated by a number of circumstances. 'I stood tip-toe upon a little hill' (193–208) had already praised this erotic story of a goddess's love for a mortal, interpreted by Renaissance poets as an allegory of man's quest for transcendent knowledge. Keats may have known of Michael Drayton's neoPlatonic version,

Endimion and Phoebe (1595), though there is no conclusive evidence that he read it. The general outline of the myth would have been available in Lemprière, Tooke's *Pantheon*, and other encyclopaedic treatments of classical mythology. A more specific source, identified by Ernest de Selincourt, is the translation of Ovid's *Metamorphoses* by the early seventeenth-century poet George Sandys (1578–1644). In four quatrains of his own that claim to give the 'argument' of *Metamorphoses*, Sandys describes how Love unites the four elements, fire, air, earth, and water; and how, influenced by Athene, the human mind 'aspires / To Fame and Glorie'. De Selincourt's 1926 edition of Keats suggests that – as Keats certainly knew this version of Ovid – it is a probable source for the interpretation of the myth conveyed in Keats's poem, with its emphasis on the young hero's quest for both love and knowledge:

> Fire, Aire, Earth, Water, all the Opposites
> That strove in *Chaos*, powrefull LOVE unites;
> And from their Discord drew this Harmonie,
> Which smiles in *Nature* ...[8]

A passage in Book 2 of *Endymion* points to a further reason for Keats's choice: 'Although the sun of poetry is set, / These lovers did embrace...' (729–30). By telling the story of Endymion's seemingly impossible love for a celestial goddess, Keats shows that even at this time, when 'the sun of poetry is set', poetry can reaffirm the power of Love to unite the mortal lover with his immortal beloved.

One way in which Keats refreshes the familiar myth is through lavish description of nature, some scenes being depicted directly from places Keats visited during the eight months he spent writing the poem: for instance, the 'wooded cleft' through which Endymion wanders, glimpsing 'the blue / Of ocean' in the distance (2. 75–6), suggests Shanklin Chine, on the Isle of Wight. The idea that myths originally grew out of the ancients' responses to the natural world had been given new currency in Wordsworth's *Excursion* (4. 843–83); and Endymion, as a shepherd-prince, could combine the attributes of a mythic hero with the 'local' associations of a Wordsworthian shepherd.

The descent to the underworld in Book 2, and the confrontation with the witch Circe in Book 3, derive from ancient mythological motifs. Virgil's Aeneas descended to an underworld portrayed as the realm of the dead. Endymion's descent brings him not to a realm of death, however, but to a 'chamber, myrtle wall'd', where he finds a beautiful youth sleeping (2. 389). One of the attendant Cupids tells him the story of the love of

Venus, 'sea-born goddess', for the youth, Adonis (2. 458). (The scene is indebted to the 'bower of Adonis' in Spenser's *Faerie Queene* (Book 3, canto 6, stanzas 46–71), Shakespeare's *Venus and Adonis*, and Sandys's Ovid.) The story of how Adonis is brought back to life every year by the strength of Venus's love initiates Endymion into the knowledge of desire (Sandys's 'powrefull Love') as universal generative force.

The second and more perilous journey to the underwater realm alludes to Milton's *Comus* as well as Sandys's Ovid. Glaucus, once a 'child of nature', is kept trapped by the witch Circe's spells. Joining with Glaucus as 'twin brothers in this destiny' (3. 713), Endymion succeeds in freeing the thousands that Circe has held in thrall: a recognition that curing the ills of the world is a mark of the Apollonian hero. The episode is marked by Renaissance neoPlatonism. Yet Keats can also convey a startling sense of physical realities, as in the description of Venus as 'ooze-born' (3. 893).

Hyperion: A Fragment

Though *Endymion* aims to rejuvenate mythology by reconnecting it with sensuous imagery drawn from the natural world, this does not mean that Keats idealised nature, or thought that poetry should always do so. As he says in the verse epistle to John Hamilton Reynolds, written from Devon on 25 March 1818, 'though to-day / I've gathered young spring-leaves, and flowers gay / Of periwinkle and wild strawberry, / Still do I that most fierce destruction see, / The shark at savage prey' (99–103).

A few weeks later (3 May), Keats again wrote to Reynolds, using the image of the 'Chamber of Maiden Thought' as a way of conveying his sense of a 'sharpening' of his 'vision into the ~~head~~heart and nature of Man'. This probing of the mystery brings awareness of growing complexity: 'many doors are set open – but all dark … We see not the ballance of good and evil' (*L* 1, 281).[9] Keats's sense of darkening prospects had many causes that can be traced to his own situation – among them, anxiety about his brother Tom's illness. But this letter to Reynolds also reveals, philosophically, a turn away from the optimistic 'natural religion' associated with Enlightenment Deism towards a more complex outlook, in which nature is not straightforwardly benevolent, and human beings exist in a precarious 'ballance' between good and evil. Keats's subsequent remarks about how by Milton's time the Reformed churches had *reinforced* the 'remaining Dogmas and superstitions' of Protestantism reveal that he is not only aware of the intellectual stagnation the church had succumbed to over the previous two centuries, but anticipating how a post-Christian, more 'philosophical' religion such as Deism would fare in the nineteenth-century 'grand march of intellect' (*L* I, 282).

Keats's most ambitious attempt to think through these concerns, *Hyperion: A Fragment*, had its beginnings in the autumn of 1817, when he was still working on *Endymion* (see *L* I, 168). In January 1818, he wrote to Haydon: 'the Hero of the written tale [*Endymion*] being mortal is led on, like Buonaparte, by circumstance; whereas the Apollo in Hyperion being a fore-seeing God will shape his actions like one' (*L* I, 207). This remark shows how Keats was now conceiving of myth as a vehicle for serious reflection on his own times. For Keats, Apollo had become the embodiment of all that was creative and forward-looking. (Shelley's Prometheus is a comparable figure – though *Prometheus Unbound* was not to appear until August 1820.) Unlike Endymion, or Bonaparte, Apollo 'will shape his actions' like a fore-seeing God. The reference to Bonaparte as another mortal hero is not accidental. The poem would speak to the eternal hope that the old, exhausted order of things could be replaced, not through force of arms (the way of a conqueror like Bonaparte), but by the power of imagination and love creating a better world. This is the prediction of Oceanus: 'So on our heels a fresh perfection treads, / A power more strong in beauty' (2. 212–13). Keats's hope in narrating the triumph of Apollo over Hyperion was to claim a leading role for poetry in bringing a new age to birth.

However, the myth itself presented considerable difficulties. The stillness and silence of the opening scene has often been noted, and Andrew Bennett has pointed out that this emphasis on silence enacts a negation of 'the possibility of audience'.[10] In modern verse epic, the narrative voice speaks at several removes from the audience. The static imagery of this scene makes this remoteness only too apparent.

The transformation of Apollo into a god posed a further problem. Deification brings with it a god's all-encompassing knowledge, the knowledge (unbearable to ordinary human minds) of the dire panorama of history: 'Names, deeds, gray legends … / Creations and destroyings' (3. 114, 116).[11] Such essentially tragic knowledge is at odds with a plot that is to celebrate progress, the dawn of a new age. It also conflicts with the idea Keats had outlined in his letter to Haydon: that Apollo, as a fore-seeing god, would 'shape his actions like one'. It would be difficult to reconcile Apollo's newly acquired knowledge of 'Creations and destroyings' with an optimistic narrative about a brighter regime replacing an old, doomed one. Keats clearly did not feel that the poem, as he left it in the spring of 1819, was publishable (it subsequently appeared in the 1820 volume, but without Keats's approval).

Keats's thinking about human history, and particularly the problem of suffering, had significantly deepened by the spring of 1819. His conversations with Haydon, a fervent believer, would have turned on what kind of consolation the Christian faith could offer for those forced to endure pain and suffering. It is evident from his letters that he was re-reading the New Testament closely, and studying the history of the early church, not with any conscious intention of re-adopting the Christian faith, but rather to learn more about what Hazlitt called the 'sublime humanity' of Jesus, and how Jesus' teachings had become distorted by theological dogma and church politics.[12]

The Odes

The five major Odes, written between late April and the end of May, 1819, display a richness and inventiveness in the use of mythological materials that is unprecedented in Keats's work, and has few parallels anywhere in English poetry. Most critics agree that this extraordinary upsurge of creativity resulted from Keats's sustained attempt, in writing the first *Hyperion*, to reconcile a poet's consciousness of mutability, the transience of all things, with the desire to create something that would be beautiful and lasting. When Apollo's mind, imaged as a great chamber, is suddenly filled with knowledge of the broad sweep of human history (3. 117), the reader witnesses, as Helen Vendler says, a 'great widening of vision'.[13] In each of the great Odes, as if recalling this 'widening of vision' and trying different ways of realising it poetically, Keats creates a mental space that does not exclude the consciousness of transience and death (which is present even in 'Ode to Psyche'), but that holds within it something that appears to overcome the lapse of time: the goddess Psyche; the nightingale's song; the urn; the figure of Melancholy; the figures of Love, Ambition, Poesy (in 'Ode on Indolence'). Through this historically aware technique, in which the poet's situatedness in time is brought to the reader's attention simultaneously with the mythopoeic figure the poet perceives and addresses, the dialogue between the mind of the speaker and mythological tradition is placed on a new footing. The poet is aware that he half-creates the figure to which he attaches so much value.

This is most clearly apparent in 'Ode to Psyche'. As Keats explained in a letter to George and Georgiana Keats, 'Psyche was not embodied as a goddess before the time of Apulieus [*sic*] the Platonist … consequently … never worshipped or sacrificed to with any of the ancient fervour' (*L* 2, 106). The poem, then, embraces remembering as a form of worship. Its second line, adapting a phrase from the first stanza of Mary Tighe's *Psyche* (1811), reveals this intention: 'remembrance dear'. Such 'remembrance' is necessary precisely because of the pastness of mythology. When Psyche came into being, the worship of the Greek deities was dwindling; so, as the 'latest born' of goddesses, Psyche came 'too late for the fond believing lyre' (24, 37). Also lost with the disappearance of the old forms of worship was the sense of nature's spaces as 'holy' ('holy were the haunted forest boughs' [38] – a thought that Keats owed, in part, to *The Excursion*). Psyche's very lateness, however, brings her closer to our own time. The problem of the modern poet's belatedness is deftly solved here. The poet can himself be Psyche's 'priest', and 'build a fane / In some untrodden region' of his mind (50–1). Imagining the mind as a tract of land large enough to have an 'untrodden' region enables Keats to create his own forest of 'dark-cluster'd trees' (54), where Psyche's sanctuary will be protectively concealed.

With considerable subtlety, Keats also glances at one of the issues he had been discussing with Reynolds and Haydon: the future of religious belief. The allusions to Milton's 'On the Morning of Christ's Nativity' raise questions about the sustainability of belief in a more sceptical age. Milton's ode explicitly refers to the disappearance of pagan forms of worship at the dawn of the Christian era: 'No nightly trance, or breathed spell, / Inspires the pale-ey'd Priest from the prophetic cell'.[14] If worship of the pagan gods could be displaced by the coming of Christianity (Keats's allusions imply), could Christianity itself be entering its last phase ('dying like an outburnt lamp' (11), as his 1816 sonnet 'Written in Disgust of Vulgar Superstition' had claimed)? Perhaps, in the nineteenth century, belief was becoming more dependent on the mythopoeic imagination. ('To Autumn', written in September 1819 after Keats had stopped work on the second *Hyperion*, illustrates how the mythopoeic imagination can add reverence and wonder to apprehensions of the natural world.)

The imagined space within which classical myth can give shape to the poet's thinking about desire, beauty, and mortality is also there in 'Ode to a Nightingale' and 'Ode on a Grecian Urn', though in notably different ways. The nightingale's song 'fades' until it is 'buried deep / In the next valley-glades' (75, 77–8), echoing 'Psyche' and its expression of regret for the fading of the Olympian hierarchy; yet the possibility of a return is held out in the thought that, though the bird itself is a mortal creature, its song is timeless, 'heard / In ancient days by emperor and clown' (63–4). The Urn, offering a more material connection to antiquity, creates its own space, with scenes of 'marble men and maidens' (42) and a procession of worshippers going to a sacrifice. The scenes are static, and seem permanent: unlike the nightingale's song, the maiden depicted on the urn cannot 'fade'. But the scenes which have come to life for the poet's imagination are not real, but *represented* in carved stone, and as the poet asks his questions, and the scenes become animated for him, he cannot help but be intermittently aware of the static medium. The unique feature of this Ode, however, is the success with which it maintains both perceptions.

The Fall of Hyperion: A Dream

Myth as remembered truth in fictional form, the problem of the poet's belatedness, the difficulty of representing in language the vast conceptions of the imagination: all are crucial aspects of *The Fall of Hyperion*, written July–September 1819. The story of the overthrow of the Titans by the Olympian gods is now placed within a frame narrative, modelled on Dante's *Divine Comedy*. As in Dante, the poet falls into a dream, and within the dream is guided towards the vision of truth by a mediating figure. In Keats's poem, the guide and preceptor is Moneta; her name, meaning 'giver of counsel', comes from one of the attributes of the Roman goddess Juno, though the poet addresses her as 'Shade of Memory!' (1. 282), and she is also referred to by the Greek name Mnemosyne (2. 50). Her replies to the poet-dreamer's questions establish both the seriousness of the quest he has embarked upon (since he is seeking a knowledge that must give pain to the seeker) and the fact that he has been granted this privilege almost inadvertently, since he is not (or not *yet*) a true poet, merely a 'dreamer'. Yet, by grace of the goddess, he will be allowed to witness the scenes that she still remembers so vividly; and to witness them 'Free from all pain, if wonder pain thee not' (I. 248).

The Fall of Hyperion, often considered a significant advance in Keats's maturity, invites the reader to witness the maturing of the poet himself, as he proceeds to narrate the foundational myth of western poetry: the tragic end of Saturn's peaceful but moribund reign, and the dawn of the reign of the Olympians, with all that implies for the future of the world.

Notes

1 Nicholas Roe, *John Keats: A New Life* (New Haven: Yale University Press, 2012), p. 386.

2 Walter H. Evert's chapter 'Imitatio Apollinis' explores Keats's reasons for choosing Apollo as the figure that defined his hopes for poetry: *Aesthetic and Myth in the Poetry of Keats* (Princeton: Princeton University Press, 1965), pp. 23–87.

3 On Clarke's Academy, see Robert M. Ryan, *Keats: The Religious Sense* (Princeton: Princeton University Press, 1976), pp. 33–4; Roe, *New Life*, pp. 20–1.
4 Nicholas Roe, 'Keats's Commonwealth', *Keats and History*, ed. Nicholas Roe (Cambridge: Cambridge University Press, 1995), pp. 207–8.
5 *The Excursion* (1814), 6. 560–1.
6 'Epithalamion', lines 75, 80: *Yale Edition of the Shorter Poems of Edmund Spenser*, ed. William A. Oram, Einar Bjorvand, Ronald Bond, Thomas H. Cain, Alexander Dunlop, and Richard Schell. (New Haven: Yale University Press, 1989), p. 665.
7 *Keats and Hellenism: An Essay* (Cambridge: Cambridge University Press, 1985), 45.
8 George Sandys, *Ovid's Metamorphosis Englished*, ed. Karl K. Hulley and Stanley K. Vandersall (Lincoln: University of Nebraska Press, 1970), p. 2.
9 Reynolds was still, at this time, an Anglican, but later became a Unitarian.
10 *Keats, Narrative and Audience: The Posthumous Life of Writing* (Cambridge: Cambridge University Press, 1994), p. 144.
11 This moment may be compared to the scene in *Paradise Lost* in which the Archangel Michael reveals what the next few thousand years will bring (*Paradise Lost* Book 11, lines 423–901, Book 12, lines 1–465).
12 Ryan, *Keats*, pp. 184–5.
13 Helen Vendler, *The Odes of John Keats* (Cambridge, MA: Harvard University Press, 1983), p. 197.
14 'On the Morning of Christ's Nativity', lines 179–80; *Complete Poems and Major Prose*, ed. Merritt Y. Hughes (New York: Macmillan, 1957), p. 48. Keats's 'moan / Upon the midnight hours' (44–5) echoes line 191 of Milton's poem.

PART III

Ideas and Poetics

CHAPTER 15

The Enlightenment and History

Porscha Fermanis

'Well – I compare human life to a large Mansion of Many Apartments', writes Keats in one of the best-known passages in his letters.

> The first we step into we call the infant or thoughtless Chamber, in which we remain as long as we do not think … we no sooner get into the second Chamber, which I shall call the Chamber of Maiden-Thought, than we become intoxicated with the light and the atmosphere … However among the effects this breathing is father of is that tremendous one of sharpening one's vision into the heart and nature of Man – of convincing ones nerves that the World is full of Misery and Heartbreak, Pain, Sickness and oppression – whereby This Chamber … becomes gradually darken'd.
>
> (*L* 1, 280–1)

This letter of 3 May 1818 is frequently read as an allegory of individual or personal growth, but Keats's argument in the same letter that Wordsworth has progressed further (and deeper) than Milton in thinking 'into the human heart' (*L* 1, 282) suggests that his 'Mansion of Many Apartments' also marks stages in the development of poetic genius and, hence, stages in the evolution of the human mind or consciousness. Unlike Samuel Johnson and Walter Scott, both of whom privilege the rise of 'some highly-gifted individual…whose talents influence the taste of a whole nation',[1] Keats's 'evolutionary-aesthetics' represent the superiority of Wordsworth's poetry as the result of historical progress rather than individual greatness or achievement:[2] 'Here I must think Wordsworth is deeper than Milton – though I think it has depended more upon the general and gregarious advance of intellect, than individual greatness of Mind' (*L* 1, 281).

In framing the improvement of the individual with narratives of more general historical and cultural progress, Keats's 'Mansion of Life' echoes both the developmental logic and the methodological individualism of eighteenth-century historians, philosophers, and social theorists from Scottish Enlightenment stadial theorists, to French Enlightenment anthropological thinkers, to natural philosophers and theorists of biological evolution.[3] The Scottish historian William Robertson notes in Keats's beloved school prize *The History of America* (1777), for example, that '[a]s the individual advances from the ignorance and imbecility of the infant state, to vigour and maturity of understanding, something similar to this may be advanced in the progress of the species'.[4] In *La Philosophie de l'histoire* (1765), which was appended to Keats's copy of *Essai sur les mœurs et l'esprit des nations* (1756),[5] Voltaire, too, argues that primitive and civilised societies are distinguished by their modes of understanding or consciousness in a way suggestive of the reflective and unreflective 'Chambers' of Keats's 'Mansion', just as Lamarck, Buffon, and other natural philosophers link the notion of 'appetence' (or the biological impulse to evolve) with wider questions surrounding social formations and the advancement of the human mind.[6]

As I have discussed elsewhere, the developmental approach favoured by Robertson, Voltaire, and many other Enlightenment thinkers underscores much of Keats's own poetic endeavour, from his use of 'explicitly evolutionary setting[s]'[7] – see, for example, the first two lines of *Lamia* – to his speculative histories of the poet-figure in *Endymion*, *Hyperion,* and *The Fall of Hyperion: A Dream*: as society advances from primitive disorder to modern civility, so too does the poet grow from a stance of immature and selfish interiority to a more mature, humanist, and civic understanding of poetry as a socially significant act.[8] Keats's reflections on the poet in these poems present poetic imagination in philosophical, anthropological, and psychological terms; that is, as a 'distinctively human faculty', which not only involves the capacity to project oneself into the minds and feelings of others in the sense that Adam Smith describes in his *Theory of Moral Sentiments* (1759), but also draws on Enlightenment hypothetical or conjectural methodologies, which attempted to explain (and, crucially, to imagine) what the first human beings and their cultural productions were like, how infant cultures progressed through various stages of development, and whether ancient primitive cultures were comparable to contemporary ones.[9]

Keats's repeated use of developmental, conjectural, and comparative frameworks in his poems and letters points to his interest in what Maureen McLane has called a kind of 'literary anthropology', which specifically sought to link the development of the human species with the movements of literary history, and to consider the historical process of society's transition from rudeness to refinement.[10] Greg Kucich has demonstrated, for example, the extent to which Keats uses his extensive range of historical reading – including the work of Xenophon, Livy, Raleigh, Holinshed,

Vertot, Voltaire, Robertson, Gibbon, Burnet, and Mavor – in order to contextualise the personal and political challenges of his own life and times within a longer historical perspective, from his youthful understanding of British politics in 'Lines Written in 29 May', to his representation of political tyranny in Book 3 of *Endymion*, to the depiction of violent revolution in the *Hyperion* poems, to his late historical dramas, *Otho the Great* and *King Stephen*.[11] As Kucich points out, each of these works meditates on the ideas raised in Keats's letter to his brothers dated 17–27 September 1819, where he follows the model of Western European intellectual development set out in Enlightenment histories such as Robertson's *History of the Reign of the Emperor Charles V* (1769) and Voltaire's *Essai sur les mœurs* by adopting a 'model of general progress disrupted by temporary periods of decline':[12] 'All civiled [*sic*] countries become gradually more enlighten'd and there should be a continual change for the better … Three great changes have been in progress – First for the better, next for the worse, and a third time for the better once more' (*L* 2, 193).

Although his view of progress is hesitant ('there *should* be a continual change for the better'), Keats follows Robertson and Voltaire in arguing for the improvements or gradual enlightenment that occurred after the darkness of the eleventh century 'when kings found it their interest to conciliate the common people, elevate them and be just to them' (*L* 2, 193). The second change concerning the subsequent 'long struggle of kings to destroy all popular privileges' was a historical circumstance illuminated by Keats's reading of Voltaire's *Essai sur les mœurs* and *Le Siècle de Louis XIV* (1751): 'the french were abject slaves under Lewis 14th' (*L* 2, 193). Keats goes on to argue that 'the "unlucky termination" of the French revolution has had the temporary effect of returning Europe to an age of "horrid superstition"' (*L* 2, 193),[13] astutely recognising that the Revolution was as much a political crisis of the Enlightenment as a popular rejection of social or material conditions. Like Voltaire, he represents the development of human history as a constant struggle against religious and other forms of bigotry, but he is convinced that the 'third change, the change for the better' is 'in progress again', citing as evidence the reduction of factionalism or 'party spirit now in England' (*L* 2, 194).

If Keats's letter is broadly optimistic and fits into a Whig tradition of progress inherited from his days in the liberal environment of Enfield school, his representation of human history nonetheless alternates between a secular confidence in enlightened progress and an awareness of the extent to which the recurrence of political and cultural violence problematises such progressive optimism: 'But in truth', he concludes in his 'Soul-making' letter to his brothers of April 1819, 'I do not at all believe in this sort of perfectibility – the nature of the world will not admit of it' (*L* 2, 101). Stuart Sperry has rightly argued that Keats's scepticism towards the perfectibility theories of William Godwin, Joseph Priestley, Condorcet, and others in this letter must undermine our thinking of him as a 'Romantic idealist', pointing not only to Keats's anti-clericalism but also to the 'naturalism' that runs through his work:[14] 'The whole appears to resolve into this – that Man is originally "a poor forked creature" subject to the same mischances as the beasts of the forest … The point at which Man may arrive is as far as the paralel [*sic*] state in inanimate nature and no further' (*L* 2, 101). Drawing on natural history and catastrophist models derived from his reading of Buffon and Cuvier, Keats argues here that man's potential for improvement is limited by the dynamic imperfectibility that is an inherent part of the natural world.[15]

Far from being a naive optimist or idealist, Keats draws on a wide variety of historical models in his poems and letters: the aggressive imperialism of his 'Chapman's Homer' sonnet; the revisionary history of female suffering in the opening of Book 2 of *Endymion*; representations of feudal stagnation in *The Eve of St. Agnes*; neo-classical models of luxury, corruption, and civic decline in *Isabella* and *Lamia*; scientific models of biological evolution and violent revolution in *Hyperion* and *The Fall*; the natural revolutions of seasonal change in 'To Autumn' where 'barred clouds bloom the soft-dying day' (25). Each of these nuanced poems considers questions relating to historical progress and decline or, more often, a complex oscillation between the two states. Propelled both by the historical crises of revolution and war, and by his own humanist awareness of the world's perennial 'Heartbreak, Pain, Sickness and oppression' (*L* 1, 281), the question of whether mankind, society, and the arts were historically progressing or declining was one that occupied Keats for much of his poetic career, reaching a critical point in 1818–19 with his failure to finish his epic *Hyperion* project.

Given the increasing critical awareness of the complexity and sophistication of Keats's intellectual life, it is unsurprising that traditional readings of *Hyperion* as a progress poem – 'for 'tis the eternal law/ That first in beauty should be first in might' (2. 228–9) – have been undermined by revisionist accounts that emphasise the ambiguity between the poem's theories of progress, and the sorrow and suffering of the vanquished Titans: 'How beautiful, if sorrow had not made/ Sorrow more beautiful than Beauty's self' (I. 35–6). *Hyperion* has therefore increasingly been read as an allegory of the inevitable violence of historical change rather than as a poem that promotes or sanctions the idea of 'process-as-progress'.[16] For some critics,

Keats's identification with the Titans and his subversion of Oceanus's 'rationalizing stance' represents an uneasy rejection of Enlightenment progress and his more general 'ambiguity toward Enlightenment ideals',[17] but like many of Keats's other poems, *Hyperion* also points to a certain immersion in Enlightenment anthropological and developmental discourses. As the collective work of a number of scholars has shown us, Keats combines in the image of the Titans, various examples of primitive societies from the ancient Egyptians and Celts to the infant Native Americans in a way suggestive of the comparative methodology of Scottish Enlightenment thinkers such as Adam Ferguson and Hugh Blair, who argued that modern day 'savages' were best explicated by comparing them to their historical counterparts.[18]

Reading *Hyperion* as an ethnographic encounter between the 'primitive' Titans and the 'modern' Olympians directly situates it within Enlightenment debates regarding the 'science of man' or mankind's historical and biological development, but there is little doubt that the poem's intense sympathy for the Titans undermines the effect of Keats's apparent acceptance of 'fresh perfection' (2. 212) or 'organic self-evolution'.[19] While Apollo's vitality distinguishes him both from the sepulchral nature of Saturn's lifelessness, and from Hyperion's self-centred and misguided 'effigies of pain' (1. 228), the poem nonetheless interrogates Apollo's power and immortality, emphasising his intense sensitivity or sympathy towards the pain of the old gods rather than his triumph – 'He listen'd, and he wept, and his bright tears/ Went trickling down the golden bow he held' (3. 42–3) – and breaking off at a liminal moment at the cusp of his deity. Keats's ambivalence towards Apollo, and the disjunction in the poem between the simultaneously stadial and sympathetic representation of the Titans, echoes a similar disjunction in Robertson's *History of America* and Voltaire's *Essai sur les mœurs*, both of which emphasise Europe's repeated lapses into barbarity in the New World.[20]

While it is certainly true that Keats's thinking about history in *Hyperion* is increasingly able to accommodate the kind of radical tension between progress and decline outlined by Robertson and Voltaire,[21] Apollo's final shriek (3. 134-5) – and the poem's dual status as 'dream' vision and unfinished fragment – also points to a more specifically literary-humanist problem: the idea that literary cultivation, particularly of the old, 'artful' Miltonic variety (*L* 2, 167), may fail to humanise the dreamer-poet and instead leave him in a deluded state of aesthetic self-absorption. '[T]hink of the earth' (1. 169), Moneta admonishes the dreamer in *The Fall*, suggesting that the gap or 'gulf between Apollo and the human poet',[22] who requires Moneta to 'humanize my sayings to thine ear' (2. 2), has yet to be overcome, just as poets past – and the poet-figures of Keats's own previous works – have yet to demonstrate sufficient 'anxiety for Humanity' *(L* 1, 278). Once again, Keats seems to reject perfectibility theories by representing his poet as flawed, human, and groping towards a sense of self-identity that can abandon the selfish narcissism of his past endeavours.[23] Rejecting 'all mock lyricists, large self worshipers,/ And careless hectorers in proud bad verse' (1. 207–8), the poet of *The Fall* must not only act as witness to the Titans' suffering in the way that Apollo does in *Hyperion* but must also risk and even embrace self-loss by feeling the Titans' pain on his pulses in a moment of complete sensory immersion: 'a palsied chill / Struck from the paved level up my limbs, / And was ascending quick to put cold grasp / Upon those streams that pulse beside the throat' (1. 122–5).

Many critics have noted that Apollo's lesson in pain and suffering in *Hyperion* is resumed as the poet's lesson in *The Fall*, but few have emphasised the poem's repeated association of human and poetic development, or pointed to Keats's keen interest in the relationship between the poetic and the biological subject.[24] The poem asserts that poetry *can* have a communicative and transformative power – 'sure, not all / Those melodies sung into the world's ear / Are useless' (1. 187–8) – but only if the dreamer is able to ascend to a more mature or evolved level of human understanding represented by the empathetic humanist poet. The poem's continued anxiety over the role of the poet – 'Whether the dream now purposed to rehearse / Be poet's or fanatic's will be known / When this warm scribe my hand is in the grave' (1. 16–18) – therefore relates less to Keats's concerns about his own standing in the pantheon of the great poets and more to the ambiguous (and unresolved) utility of his chosen vocation, as well as to his more general concerns about commercialism, selfishness, and the decline of civic society.[25]

The Fall is by no means Keats's only attempt to define the status of the 'true' and 'false' poet.[26] Apollonius in *Lamia* can be read as a 'false' poet-figure, just as Glaucus in book 3 of *Endymion* is a certain poetic type, entrapped in the stasis of solipsism and egotism.[27] Certainly, *Lamia*, like *Endymion*, dramatises the tension between an idealised or glorified reality, and an acceptance of mortality and ordinary human circumstance. Lamia's power lies in her illusory appeal to the senses while Apollonius's power is that of 'cold philosophy' (2. 230) that would 'clip an Angel's wings' (2. 234). However, Apollonius's attempt to destroy the subversions of sensual gratification is ultimately as devastating as Lamia's own excesses: 'Do not all charms fly/ At the mere touch of cold philosophy?' (2. 229–30). While the poem can be read as an attack on Enlightenment rationalisation and systemisation, *Lamia* in fact confronts two kinds of illusion or deception: the first is sensual illusion, as represented by Lamia; the second, the deceptions exposed by the kind of rigid philosophical system proposed by Apollonius.[28]

Drawing on, but simultaneously subverting, the Enlightenment's emphasis on the 'true' discourses of empirical science, Keats's ambivalence towards the first kind of deception outlined in *Lamia* – the power of sensual illusion – is clearly apparent in other poems, such as *Endymion*, 'La Bella Dame sans Merci', *The Eve of St. Agnes* (where Madeline can be read as a hoodwinked dreamer), 'Ode to Psyche', 'Ode on a Grecian Urn', and 'Ode to a Nightingale', where the 'deceiving elf' (74) of an idealised illusory state gives way to a rationalised reality, albeit one sceptical of objective truth claims: 'Fled is that music: – Do I wake or sleep?' ('Nightingale', 80). In 'Psyche', the poet is also unsure of the status of his dream vision and asserts an empirical need to 'see, and sing, by my own eyes inspired' (43), while in 'Grecian Urn' an ongoing 'trope of puzzlement' contributes to the poem's almost Kantian insistence on the unrepresentability of the noumenal world.[29] To some extent, Keats follows Locke here in grounding his conceptions of poetry and the mind in sense experience, and many of his poems adopt the kind of associationalist logic for which *The Eve* is well known, but Keats is by no means a naive empiricist, just as Locke himself is best described as a sceptical rather than mechanistic empiricist.[30]

Keats's own scepticism towards ideas not grounded in sensation is most often explained by his experience in medical school, but his insistence that 'Axioms in philosophy are not axioms until they are proved on our pulses' (*L* 1, 279) can also be seen as part of a philosophical scepticism inherited from Locke and Voltaire. Like Voltaire in *Dictionnaire philosophique* (1764), which Keats read and owned, Keats is sceptical of speculation, superstition, *a priori* knowledge, theory, and the sort of Apollonian systematic philosophical accounts that attempt to overcome doubt by appealing to coherent explanations – 'Can it be that even the greatest Philosopher ever arrived at his goal without putting aside numerous objections' (*L* 1, 185) – instead maintaining that one should be content with uncertainty and 'half knowledge' (*L* 1, 194).[31]

In his sceptical idea of '*Negative Capability*' and his desire for 'a Life of Sensations rather than of Thoughts' (*L* 1, 193, 185), Keats also draws on the serious consideration given to the idea of 'sensation' by English and Scottish philosophers such as Francis Hutcheson, who Keats discovered in his friend Benjamin Bailey's 'An Essay on the Moral Principle' (1817).[32] As

Robert Ryan has noted, in his *Inquiry into the Original of our Ideas of Beauty and Virtue* (1725), Hutcheson argues that both moral distinctions and aesthetic appreciation are based on feelings or sensations and are therefore 'senses'. In his *Short Introduction to Moral Philosophy* (1747), Hutcheson goes on to maintain that beauty is an internal sense analogous to man's moral conscience, illuminating Keats's comment that '[w]hat the imagination seizes as Beauty must be truth' (*L* 1, 184) by suggesting an understanding of beauty that is directly linked to a capacity for moral benevolence. When Keats argues for a 'Life of Sensations rather than of Thoughts' he is therefore drawing on a strand of Enlightenment philosophy that sees the 'sensations' as integral to moral and aesthetic improvement rather than on the kind of sensual illusion he rejects in *Lamia* and other poems.

Keats's related musings on passivity, poetic purpose, and the poetical character also draw on Enlightenment moral philosophy and theories of the mind, particularly the Lockean idea of the passive or associative processes of the human mind in his *Essay Concerning Human Understanding* (1689–90), which finds its way into Keats's idea that 'Men of Genius' are more passive than 'Men of Power' – they 'have not any individuality, any determined Character' (*L* 1, 184) – as well as informing his recommendation that we 'open our leaves like a flower and be passive and receptive' (*L* 1, 232). For Keats, like Wordsworth before him, passive receptivity often displaces book-learning, which he sees as a symbol of purposive inquiry and unreflecting custom (see *L* 1, 231). Although he later retracts his opinion on 'serious books' in a letter to his brothers – 'I am reading Voltaire and Gibbon, although I wrote to Reynolds the other day to prove reading of no use' (*L* 1, 237) – Keats's observations on passive understanding and imaginative thinking are far from frivolous and form part of a serious reflection on the importance of 'non-purposive' or 'non-active' thought.[33]

Yet if Keats offers a kind of 'counter-Enlightenment' anti-rationalist argument here in the Wordsworthian mode, he nonetheless repeatedly echoes empiricist accounts of the importance of first-hand knowledge or experience, as well as drawing on Enlightenment developmental frameworks in his poems and letters. Even his growing scepticism towards perfectibility models and historical progress can be seen as emanating from the self-critique of progressive agendas within late Enlightenment thinking by Voltaire, Robertson, and others. Following studies by Robert Ryan, Alan Grob, and Greg Kucich on Enlightenment deism, moral philosophy, and historiography, respectively, as well as studies on evolution, anthropology, and species discourses by Stuart Sperry, Hermione de Almeida, and Maureen McLane, Keats's representation of his own development as a 'very gradual ripening of the intellectual powers' (*L* 1, 214) now seems to operate in tandem with a larger Enlightenment developmental logic in his work, which not only draws on a new, enlightened understanding of human agency and the developmental subject, but also on a new type of historiographical mode that situated temporality (or the ability to change over time) at the heart of its analysis. It is likely that for Keats, as for Kant, 'Enlightenment' was not a period in the history of ideas or a chronologically specific event but rather an ongoing process that was far from over in 1818–19. Any sense of 'Enlightenment' and 'Romanticism' as two opposing or successive time periods is therefore sorely tested by Keats's own sense of enlightenment as an incomplete and open-ended process of spiritual, ethical, political, social, cultural, and personal maturity: 'I compare human life to a large Mansion of Many Apartments, two of which I can only describe, the doors of the rest being as yet shut upon me' (*L* 1, 280).

Notes

1 Walter Scott, *Minstrelsy of the Scottish Border*, ed. T. F. Henderson, 4 vols. (1802–3; repr. Detroit: Singing Tree Press, 1968), vol. 1, p. 6.
2 Hermione de Almeida, *Romantic Medicine and John Keats* (New York: Oxford University Press, 1991), p. 260.
3 See De Almeida, *Romantic Medicine*, esp. p. 231.
4 William Robertson, *The History of America*, 2 vols. (London, 1777), vol. 1, p. 308.
5 Keats owned the French 1804–5 edition. See *KC* 1, 259.
6 De Almeida, *Romantic Medicine*, p. 11.
7 Nicola Trott, 'Keats and the Prison House of History', in *Keats and History*, ed. Nicholas Roe (Cambridge: Cambridge University Press, 1995), p. 272.
8 For a more detailed discussion of these and some of the other ideas in this chapter, see Porscha Fermanis, *John Keats and the Ideas of the Enlightenment* (Edinburgh: Edinburgh University Press, 2009).
9 Maureen McLane, *Romanticism and the Human Species: Poetry, Population, and the Discourse of the Species* (Cambridge: Cambridge University Press, 2000), pp. 30, 33.
10 McLane, *Romanticism*, pp. 10, 33. See also De Almeida, *Romantic Medicine*, p. 232.
11 Greg Kucich, 'Keats's Literary Tradition and the Politics of Historiographical Invention', in Roe, *Keats and History*, pp. 238–9.
12 Fermanis, *John Keats*, p. 25. Kucich, 'Keats's Literary Tradition', p. 239.
13 Fermanis, *John Keats*, pp. 25–6.
14 Stuart M. Sperry, 'Keats's Skepticism and Voltaire', *Keats-Shelley Journal* 12 (1965): 75, 81.
15 De Almeida, *Romantic Medicine*, p. 231. For Keats's knowledge of Buffon and Cuvier, see p. 242.

16 See, e.g., McLane, *Romanticism*, p. 202.
17 Vincent Newey, 'Keats, History, and the Poets', in Roe, *Keats and History*, p. 181. Mark Sandy, *Poetics of Self and Form in Keats and Shelley: Nietzschean Subjectivity and Genre* (Aldershot: Ashgate, 2005), p. 117.
18 For the poem's Egyptian imagery, see Alan Bewell, 'The Political Implications of Keats's Classicist Aesthetics', *Studies in Romanticism* 25 (1986): 220–9. On representations of Native American Indians, see Fermanis, *John Keats*, pp. 65–96. For Celts, see Fiona Stafford, 'Macpherson, Milton and Romantic Titanism', in *From Gaelic to Romanticic Ossianic Translations*, ed. Fiona Stafford and Howard Gaskill (Amsterdam: Rodopi, 1998), pp. 164–82.
19 De Almeida, *Romantic Medicine*, p. 246.
20 Fermanis, *John Keats*, pp. 94–6.
21 On this point, see Michael O'Neill, '"When This Warm Scribe My Hand": Writing and History in *Hyperion* and *The Fall of Hyperion*', in Roe, *Keats and History*, p. 145.
22 McLane, *Romanticism*, p. 208.
23 On immortality and perfectibility, see McLane, *Romanticism*, pp. 168–75.
24 See Fermanis, *John Keats*, pp. 121–50.
25 Fermanis, *John Keats*, pp. 97–9.
26 On the true and false poet, see De Almeida, *Romantic Medicine*, pp. 34–42.
27 Newey, 'Keats, History, and the Poets', p. 174.
28 Newey, 'Keats, History, and the Poets' p. 53.
29 See Susan J. Wolfson, *The Questioning Presence: Wordsworth, Keats and the Interrogative Mode in Romantic Poetry* (Ithaca: Cornell University Press, 1986); and Alan Grob, 'Noumenal Inferences: Keats as Metaphysician', in *Critical Essays on John Keats*, ed. Hermione de Almeida (Boston: G. K. Hall, 1990), p. 292.
30 Grob, 'Noumenal Inferences', pp. 295–6.
31 Keats owned a copy of *Dictionnaire philosophique*. *KC* 1, 258–9.
32 Robert Ryan, *Keats: The Religious Sense* (Princeton: Princeton University Press, 1976), p. 125. See also Fermanis, *John Keats*, pp. 123–4.
33 McLane, *Romanticism*, p. 68. See also Fermanis, *John Keats*, pp. 128–32.

CHAPTER 16

Keats and Hazlitt

Duncan Wu

Negative capability could not have been formulated without Hazlitt. It is as simple as that. Keats had a good education given the time and place in which he lived, but was largely self-taught in the field of aesthetic theory. That was not true of Hazlitt, who had been home-schooled by an intellectually ambitious father who had studied at the feet of Adam Smith and the finest minds of Enlightenment Scotland. It is hardly surprising that, of those by whom Keats was surrounded, Hazlitt had the most impact on his thought, leading him to describe the 'poetical Character' in correspondence with Richard Woodhouse on 27 October 1818:

> (I mean that sort of which, if I am any thing, I am a Member; that sort distinguished from the wordsworthian and egotistical sublime; which is a thing per se and stands alone) it is not itself – it has no self – it is every thing and nothing – It has no character – it enjoys light and shade; it lives in gusto, be it foul or fair, high or low, rich or poor, mean or elevated. It has as much delight in conceiving an Iago as an Imogen. What shocks the virtuous philosop[h]er, delights the camelion Poet.
>
> (*L* 1, 386–7)

Keats's analysis was shaped by Hazlitt. This chapter considers the extent and precise nature of the influence.

Keats was reading Hazlitt and Leigh Hunt's collection of essays, *The Round Table*, in September 1817,[1] when he visited Benjamin Bailey in Oxford, and wrote to John Hamilton Reynolds, 'How is Hazlitt? We were reading his Table last night – I know he thinks himself not estimated by ten People in the world – I wishe he knew he is' (*L* 1, 166). Among its contents, Keats probably read Hazlitt's 'On Posthumous Fame', first published on 22 May 1814 in *The Examiner*, and reprinted in the new book. Meditating the elusiveness of Shakespeare the writer, Hazlitt was drawn to observe, among other things, that the dramatist

> seemed scarcely to have an individual existence of his own, but to borrow that of others at will, and to pass successively through 'every variety of

> untried being', – to be now *Hamlet*, now *Othello*, now *Lear*, now *Falstaff*, now *Ariel*. In the mingled interests and feelings belonging to this wide range of imaginary reality, in the tumult and rapid transitions of this waking dream, the author could not easily find time to think of himself, nor wish to embody that personal identity in idle reputation after death, of which he was so little tenacious while living.[2]

This is proffered with its author's usual off-handed brilliance, as if it were obvious to all, but the attentive reader is unlikely to miss its boldness. It is easy to imagine Keats marking it emphatically in the margin, as he did when reading the chapter on *King Lear* in Hazlitt's *Characters of Shakespear's Plays* (1818).[3] (Lest there be any doubting the impact of Hazlitt's words, readers might recall that the phrase, 'waking dream', occurs also in the penultimate line of 'Ode to a Nightingale'.)

It would be an oversimplification to brandish this as an example of one writer saying something and being echoed by another. Because Hazlitt and Keats are not saying the same thing: Hazlitt is trying to explain, in a public forum, how Shakespeare formulated a 'wide range of imaginary reality', while in the more intimate confines of a letter Keats reveals why he is not like Wordsworth, whose genius was an 'egotistical sublime'. These are different tasks with divergent implications, yet Keats has adopted Hazlitt's critical architecture. Immediately following the passage just quoted from 'On Posthumous Fame', Hazlitt continued:

> To feel a strong desire that others should think highly of us, it is, in general, necessary that we should think highly of ourselves. There is something of egotism, and even pedantry, in this sentiment; and there is no author who was so little tinctured with these as Shakspeare.[4]

The principle by which Keats separates himself from Wordsworth (a poet he admired) owes everything to Hazlitt's division of writers into egotists and those 'little tinctured' by egotism, such as Shakespeare. Modesty inclined him to side with the latter party, and in April 1818 prompted him to declare, in a letter to Reynolds, 'I never wrote one single Line of Poetry with the least Shadow of public thought … I would jump down Ætna for any great Public good – but I hate a mawkish Popularity' (*L* 1, 267). Keats's desire to distance himself from Wordsworth, whose *Excursion* had, months before, been one of 'three things to rejoice at in this Age' (*L* 1, 203), was motivated also by personal acquaintance with the older writer, who he met at Haydon's 'immortal dinner'[5] in December 1817, and whose canvassing for the Tory peer Lord Lonsdale would preclude their meeting during Keats's walking tour in June 1818. ('Sad – sad – sad', *L* 1, 299 was Keats's judgement on Wordsworth's political infidelity.)

As he continued with *The Round Table* in September 1817, Keats would have enjoyed Hazlitt's principled dissection of *The Excursion*. 'An intense intellectual egotism swallows up every thing',[6] Hazlitt had written:

> The power of his mind preys upon itself. It is as if there were nothing but himself and the universe. He lives in the busy solitude of his own heart; in the deep silence of thought. His imagination lends life and feeling only to 'the bare trees and mountains bare;' peoples the viewless tracts of air, and converses with the silent clouds![7]

This was the thesis by which Keats's view of Wordsworth was conditioned. In February 1818 he informed George and Tom Keats, 'Wordsworth has left a bad impression wherever he visited in Town – by his egotism, Vanity and bigotry – yet he is a great Poet if not a Philosopher' (*L* 1, 237). Hazlitt elaborated further in his *Lectures on the English Poets* (copies of which were on sale by 20 May 1818[8]): '[Wordsworth's] egotism is in some respects a madness; for he scorns even the admiration of himself, thinking it a presumption in any one to suppose that he has taste or sense enough to understand him.'[9] Such an unforgiving critique can only have teased Keats into acknowledging those respects in which his own imaginative powers differed from Wordsworth's. Hazlitt therefore provided not only the goad for Keats to ask how he did *not* resemble Wordsworth, but also the device by which Keats argued the distinction: the ability 'to pass successively through "every variety of untried being" '.

Of Hazlitt's contemporaries Keats was one of few who might accurately be described as a student of his thought. By 1819, how many had read Hazlitt's first book, *An Essay on the Principles of Human Action* (1805)? Few had even held it in their hands, given that a mere 250 copies were published, most of which remained unsold.[10] Yet Keats had done so by 14 September 1817, when he praised Benjamin Bailey in a letter to Jane and Marianne Reynolds: 'He delights me in the Selfish and (please god) the disenterrested part of my disposition' (*L* 1, 160). The eccentric orthography is suggestive. The word was not in quotidian use in 1817, and Keats can have encountered it in few contexts other than Hazlitt's essay. In a letter of January 1818 he would refer to 'that sort of probity & disinterestedness which such men as Bailey possess' (*L* 1, 205)[11] – echoing the regard for such qualities that is the keystone of Hazlittian metaphysics.

If Keats read Hazlitt's *Essay*, how had he obtained it? It is possible he borrowed a copy from the author – the most likely source of that in the possession of their mutual friend Bryan Waller Procter,[12] whose aptitude for philosophy was far less developed than Keats's. As Keats first met Hazlitt in November 1816, he may have been, by autumn the following year, in a position to request the loan. But it may equally well be that Benjamin Bailey, Keats's exemplar of disinterested humanity, was the actual source – Bailey, who lived in a city of libraries, including the Bodleian, where the fugitive title was surely to be found. And it may be that Bailey first drew Keats's attention to Hazlitt's claims as moral philosopher. Hazlitt's *Essay* was, by its author's admission, a 'dry, tough, metaphysical *choke-pear*',[13] and if Keats found himself struggling with its penetralia, he found the ideal guide in its much later recapitulation in the concluding pages of Hazlitt's *Letter to William Gifford Esq.* (1819) – another volume that, even on its first appearance, was hard to find. (It was published at its author's expense and few copies were printed.[14]) By that point Keats had already borrowed Hazlitt's books from their author, who may have supplied that which, as Keats told George and Georgiana Keats on 12 March 1819, 'I have by me at present' (*L* 2, 71), and from which he transcribed many pages of text. Why? In order to illustrate to his correspondents, as he put it,

> The manner in which this is managed: the force and innate power with which it yeasts and works up itself – the feeling for the costume of society; is in a style of genius.
>
> (*L* 2, 76)

More than any other enthusiasm, Keats's application to Hazlitt's precisely-wrought prose betokens the desire to master both its rhetorical intensity and the discipline from which it sprang. Only that could explain the intention, voiced in April 1818, to 'learn Greek, and very likely Italian – and in other ways prepare myself to ask Hazlitt in about a years time the best metaphysical road I can take' (*L* 1, 274). That determination hints that Keats's studies had already reached a respectable level of proficiency under Hazlittian auspices, and that he had received sufficient advice to keep him studying for another year before returning to the only teacher whose advice on 'the best metaphysical road' was to be trusted. This is all the more remarkable given that, as he made this statement, he was working on *Endymion*, which he believed his finest achievement in verse to date.

From the moment Keats took his initial steps down that path, he became more Hazlitt's pupil than anyone else's. The only other person of his acquaintance with anything approaching Hazlitt's level of expertise was Coleridge who, at their only known encounter, failed to distinguish himself as the ideal mentor.[15] And in any case, while admiring aspects of Coleridge's poetry, Keats was not tempted to study at the feet of someone so absorbed by their own ego-fuelled logorrhea. Instead, the spur to analysis, not only of literature but of humanity, was provided by Hazlitt.

> [A]s Wordsworth says, 'we have all one human heart' – there is an ellectric fire in human nature tending to purify – so that among these human creature[s] there is continually some birth of new heroism – The pity is that we must wonder at it: as we should at finding a pearl in rubbish – I have no doubt that thousands of people never heard of have had hearts comp[l] etely disinterested: I can remember but two – Socrates and Jesus – their Histories evince it.
>
> (*L* 2. 80)

In this letter of March 1820, Keats cites Wordsworth's poem 'The Old Cumberland Beggar' – and then, mindful of its author's egotism, makes the point that complete disinterestedness (absent from Wordsworth as a man) was exceptional. The unmentioned connection is Hazlitt, who provides the means by which Keats's lightning-quick imagination moves from Wordsworth to Socrates and Jesus.

Hazlitt's influence was formative – not only of Keats's views of literature but of the world. And Keats went to considerable lengths to pursue him. For instance, on 14 December 1818, two weeks after the death of his brother Tom, he visited Hazlitt in search of the lectures on the comic writers, which Tom's illness had caused him to miss.[16] Hazlitt had been speaking of Cavalier poets, Restoration dramatists, Fielding, and Sterne, subjects which some of Hazlitt's admirers might have considered inessential. If Keats thought otherwise, he could have waited until publication of the lectures, which was to occur on 26 March 1819[17] – that is to say, within months. But he preferred not to; instead he went to the author's house, knocked at his door, and asked for loan of either the manuscript or proof-sheets of the relevant lecture. That in itself reveals a determination to study him. But he did not stop there. When he got Hazlitt's papers home, he copied two lengthy passages into a letter to George and Georgiana Keats – the first 'on account of its being a specimen of [Hazlitt's] usual abrupt manner, and fiery laconiscism' (*L* 2, 24), the second being 'his caracter of Godwin as a Romancer', which Keats deemed 'quite correct' (*L* 2, 25). There was no contemporary whose admiration of Hazlitt extended so far. Hardly surprising, then, that when Keats gave Hazlitt a copy of his final lifetime volume, he scribbled on its flyleaf, 'To Wm Hazlitt Esquire with the Authors sincere esteem'[18] – a heartfelt sentiment.

When in October 1818 Keats wrote his important letter to Woodhouse about negative capability, he revealed that Hazlittian concepts were those with which he had trained himself to think. If we doubt that, one need only return to the letter in which he says, of the poetical character, 'it lives in gusto, be it foul or fair, high or low, rich or poor, mean or elevated'.

This has attracted less attention than might be expected, but it confirms Keats knew 'On Gusto', also reprinted in *The Round Table*, and expected Woodhouse to understand the concept as Hazlitt defined it: 'it is in giving this truth of character from the truth of feeling, whether in the highest or the lowest degree, but always in the highest degree of which the subject is capable, that gusto consists'.[19]

In recent years one or two commentators have suggested that, on the contrary, it was Keats who influenced Hazlitt. But the evidence is overwhelmingly against it. When first they met (in December 1816[20]), Hazlitt was thirty-eight years old, Keats twenty-one. That is to say, not only was Hazlitt the elder man, he was almost twice as old as Keats. That confirms the impression in Keats's letters of his being the disciple to an established, more experienced intellect. For his part, Hazlitt appears to have been generous-spirited, admitting Keats to his home even on inconvenient occasions (as when Keats visited him at York Street shortly before his eviction[21]), ready to lend reading materials when requested. Yet their compatibility as mentor and acolyte did not insure Keats against error. When Keats formulated the idea of the chameleon poet, which seems effortlessly to arise from the contrast between Wordsworthian egotism and Shakespearean genius, he committed what in Hazlittian terms was a solecism: 'it is not itself – it has no self – it is every thing and nothing – It has no character'. That idea – of genius defined by extreme susceptibility to the supervening influence of external things – is Keats's, *not Hazlitt's*; in fact, Hazlitt would have resisted it. For him, the generation of a 'wide range of imaginary reality' comprised an assertion of power utterly distinct from what Keats was describing. In his *Lectures on English Philosophy*, Hazlitt repelled any suggestion the mind was helpless to resist external influences or bodies.

> [T]he mind in these similes is requisite as a merely passive agent, by which I mean a thing perfectly indifferent and nugatory, a mere cypher without any character of its own, that is neither good nor bad, neither deserving of praise nor blame; a chameleon, colourless kind of thing, the sport of external impulses and accidental circumstances, or of a necessity in which it has itself no share. Thus the responsibility of the mind has been taken from it, and transferred to outward circumstances, and all characters in themselves rendered alike indifferent.[22]

Keats had no desire to be an egotist in the Wordsworthian mould and insisted on a different model of creativity, one Hazlitt appeared to endorse in *The Round Table*. But Hazlitt nowhere says Shakespeare was a chameleon – nor would he have done. If in doubt of that, one need only consult 'On Genius and Common Sense', in which Hazlitt defines genius as

> sufficiently exclusive and self-willed, quaint and peculiar. It does some one thing by virtue of doing nothing else: it excels in some one pursuit by being blind to all excellence but its own. It is just the reverse of the cameleon: for it does not borrow, but lend its colours to all about it: or like the glow-worm, discloses a little circle of gorgeous light in the twilight of obscurity, in the night of intellect, that surrounds it.[23]

There is no reason to assume that, as he composed these words, Hazlitt had Keats's formulation in mind, but it is so pitched as to rouse the suspicion he did. Hazlitt's conception of genius was informed by a belief in the inherent power of the individual, an egotistical sublime which he celebrates whenever he writes about art. He would have regarded the opposite view – that is to say, Keats's – as erroneous, especially the claim that genius was other than 'self-willed'.[24] For Hazlitt, power is absolutely central to the creative imagination. Possession of it defines artistic genius – which is why Hazlitt is happy to identify Wordsworth as properly egotistical.[25] If Keats understood Hazlitt's analysis of egotism as condemnatory, he misunderstood him: as Uttara Natarajan observes, 'the power of the Wordsworthian ego [is what] compels Hazlitt's admiration in the first place'.[26]

Why does Keats make that error? The likeliest answer is that he did not realize he had done so. So far as I am aware, he did not read Hazlitt's *Lectures on English Philosophy*, which were in manuscript and would not be published until 1836, and could not have read 'On Genius and Common Sense', which would be published only after his death.[27] What he had read was 'On Posthumous Fame', in which Hazlitt praised Shakespeare for seeming not to have 'an individual existence of his own, but to borrow that of others at will, and to pass successively through "every variety of untried being"'. That was sufficient to prompt Keats's chameleon poet in the belief it was consistent with Hazlittian aesthetics. It would have taken Hazlitt himself to observe that Shakespeare – in this as in so much else – was the exception, not the rule.[28]

There may be another explanation. It is possible Keats understood Hazlitt only too well, and differed with him. In his philosophical thought, as in his poetry, Keats may have been too powerful an intellect merely to imitate. That is to say, he may have recognized Shakespeare as atypical of the Hazlittian argument, yet insisted the idea of the chameleon extended to other writers. That he thereby articulated a vision of imaginative power distinct from that of the man through whose teachings he had inducted himself into metaphysics would have been symptomatic of his originality and genius.

Notes

1 The volume was published on 14 February 1817, six months before. It is hard to believe Keats had not read it, though it was priced at 14 shillings – comparatively steep for a book of this kind.
2 'On Posthumous Fame' in *The Round Table* (1817); *The Selected Writings of William Hazlitt,* ed. Duncan Wu, 9 vols. (London: Pickering and Chatto, 1998) (hereafter Wu), vol. 2, p. 26.
3 This volume is now at Harvard University Library and can be viewed online at http://pds.lib.harvard.edu/pds/view/16001859.
4 Wu, vol. 2, p. 26.
5 Haydon's 'immortal dinner' was described as such by Haydon himself, who was its host. Guests included Keats and Wordsworth. A useful exposition is provided by Stanley Plumly, *The Immortal Evening* (New York: W.W. Norton, 2014).
6 Wu, vol. 2, p. 114.
7 Wu, vol. 2, p. 114.
8 Wu, vol. 2, p. xvi.
9 Wu, vol. 2, p. 316. Even if Keats was not present at the last of the lectures, on 3 March 1818, he may have heard about it. It is described by Wu, *William Hazlitt: The First Modern Man* (Oxford: Oxford University Press, 2008), p. 239.
10 Poor sales of the *Essay* are discussed by Wu, 'Hazlitt's *Essay on the Principles of Human Action*: A Bibliographical Note', in *Metaphysical Hazlitt: Bicentenary Essays* ed. Uttara Natarajan, Tom Paulin and Duncan Wu (Abingdon: Routledge, 2005), p. xvii.
11 Walter Jackson Bate drew attention to Keats's use of disinterestedness in *John Keats* (Cambridge, MA: Harvard University Press, 1963), pp. 255–9.
12 This is now in the possession of the author.
13 'Sir James Mackintosh' in *The Spirit of the Age*; Wu, vol. 7, p. 58.
14 Wu, vol. 6, p. xxiii.
15 John Keats to George and Georgiana Keats, 15 April 1819; *L* 2, 88–9.
16 See *L* 2, 24n2.
17 For full particulars concerning publication, see Wu, vol. 5, pp. xii–xiii.
18 There are at least two versions of the inscription in circulation. Mine is from the letter sent by F. Holland Day to W. C. Hazlitt in 1896, as quoted, Wu, *William Hazlitt: The First Modern Man*, p. 287. The whereabouts of this volume are not known at present.
19 Wu, vol. 2, p. 79.
20 There has been some confusion about the date of the first encounter, but the evidence points unequivocally to late 1816.

21 Wu, *William Hazlitt: The First Modern Man*, pp. 278–9.
22 'Lectures on English Philosophy', *The Complete Works of William Hazlitt*, ed. P. P. Howe, 21 vols. (London: Dent: 1930–4), vol. 2, p. 269.
23 Wu, vol. 6, p. 37.
24 Uttara Natarajan analyses the differences in *Hazlitt and the Reach of Sense* (Oxford: Oxford University Press, 1997), pp. 107–10. The other context in which Hazlitt discussed chameleons was similarly critical: 'On the Qualifications Necessary to Success in Life' (Wu, vol. 8, p. 183).
25 For more, see Natarajan, *Hazlitt*, pp. 98–9.
26 Natarajan, *Hazlitt*, p. 99.
27 'On Genius and Common Sense' was first published in *Table Talk*, vol. 1, published on 6 April 1821.
28 Uttara Natarajan demonstrates that Hazlitt's view of Shakespeare marks him as the exception to his aesthetic principles (Natarajan, *Hazlitt*, p. 110). David Bromwich has also written persuasively on this subject in *Hazlitt: The Mind of a Critic* (New York: Oxford University Press, 1983), ch. 11.

CHAPTER 17

Imagination, Beauty and Truth

Charles W. Mahoney

> A Poet can seldom have justice done to his imagination.
>
> (Keats, annotation to *Paradise Lost*)

Keats's writing is full of 'speculations and surmises' (*L* 1, 185) regarding the imagination. From at least as early as 'Sleep and Poetry' through *Endymion* and the odes of 1819 to such late works as *Lamia* and *The Fall of Hyperion*, as well as throughout the letters, Keats may be found interrogating the workings of the poetic imagination, configuring and reconfiguring its status in relation to other quintessentially Keatsian preoccupations such as beauty and truth, indolence and dreaming, philosophy and 'consequitive reasoning' (*L* 1, 185). While the letters offer pointed, and often cryptic, pronouncements on the imagination, the poems repeatedly debate, even as they stage, the power of the imagination and the poet's shifting relations to it. Critics of Keats long ago recognised the centrality of the imagination to any serious consideration of his work, and in turn the prominence of his 'speculations' on the imagination for any account of the Romantic imagination. To do justice to Keats, that is to say, one must attempt to do justice to his imagination.

Throughout Keats's writing, the imagination bears a conflicted relation to the real, whether understood as the natural world or as the human world of pain and agony. While oftentimes responsive to that which exists in this world, the essential beauty (or truth) that the imagination creates just as often appears to be the product of a dream, of an abandonment of the real for the ideal. Put another way, one of the central tensions informing the Keatsian imagination is that between reality and illusion – or, in terms germane to so much of the poetry, between waking and sleeping, or dreaming. On the one hand, the imagination presents the opportunity for (or perhaps threat of) intoxication, flight and oblivion. In the presence of works of art, the beauty of the natural world, or even the work of poetry itself as it appears to unfold on the page, the poet loses touch with the material world as he gives way to poetic reverie, 'let[ting] winged Fancy wander / Through the thought still spread beyond her' ('Fancy', 5–6). It produces a poetry of romance figured in terms of open casements, windows 'latch'd by fays and elves' ('Dear Reynolds', 50), and faery lands forlorn. This is an imagination which perhaps ought not to be trusted, given its close configuration with dreaming and deception. On the other hand, the imagination increasingly affords the poet the opportunity to immerse himself in the human world of suffering and strife, to attune himself to the painful truth of human experience. Imaginative apprehension in this regard does not turn away from that which has occasioned it, but embraces it, heightening the poet's sense of the ways in which poetry 'should be a friend / To sooth the cares and lift the thoughts of man' ('Sleep and Poetry', 246–7). This version of the imagination does not enchant or deceive but instructs, as when Keats says of the 'Bards of Passion and of Mirth' that 'ye teach us, every day', 'What doth strengthen and what maim' (35, 34). One version, then, of the Keatsian imagination ought to be distrusted in light of its propensity to cheat, to deceive and to delude; another inflection, just as powerful, may be celebrated for its value as an authentic guide to human truth and beauty.

These two strains are not mutually exclusive but, as early as 'Sleep and Poetry', can regularly be heard at work in the same poem. Here the tension is dramatised as that between 'visions' and 'real things'. As entranced as the poet is by his vision of a charioteer who can animate the natural landscape into 'Shapes of delight, of mystery, and fear' (138), he feels himself summoned simultaneously by his sense of 'a nobler life, / Where I may find the agonies, the strife / Of human hearts' (123–4). At the same moment that he indicates his earnest desire to 'know / All that he [the Apollonian charioteer] writes' (153–4), he breaks off:

> The visions all are fled – the car is fled
> Into the light of heaven, and in their stead
> A sense of real things comes doubly strong,
> And, like a muddy stream, would bear along
> My soul to nothingness: but I will strive
> Against all doubtings, and will keep alive
> The thought of that same chariot, and the strange
> Journey it went.
>
> (155–62)

Despite the pressure of 'real things', or what Keats offers in *Endymion* as 'The journey homeward to habitual self' (2. 276), the poet resolves, 'Against all doubtings', to keep the vision before him, a rudder as it were for his own imagination. Thus it is that he then queries, impatiently, why it seems that 'the high / Imagination cannot freely fly / As she was wont of old' (163–5). What, then, is the fundamental responsibility of the imagination? To cultivate flights of fancy? Or to attend to real things and 'the strife / Of human hearts'?

The Romantic imagination is notoriously difficult to define, and impossible to codify according to a consistent set of criteria. Integral to Keats's understanding of the imagination are the claims William Hazlitt makes regarding the natural disinterestedness of the mind. For Hazlitt, the imagination names the ability to 'go out of [one]self entirely and enter into the minds and feelings of others', and is exemplified by Shakespeare, who 'was nothing in himself; but he was all that others were, or that they could become... He had only to think of any thing in order to become that thing'.[1] Sympathy is the decisive attribute of the imagination for Hazlitt, and a priority which resonates throughout Keats's own preoccupation with the poetics of the imagination and the disinterestedness of the poetical character. The movement Hazlitt outlines, from 'thinking' to 'becoming', represents an ideal of self-effacement which would allow Keats in turn to write that 'if a Sparrow come before my Window I take part in its existence and pick about the Gravel' (*L* 1, 186).

Keats's own 'speculations' concerning the imagination are indebted to Hazlitt on numerous scores. He probably read Hazlitt in 1817 during his time in Oxford, attended nearly all of his lectures on the English poets in the winter of 1818, quoted him more often than any other writer in his letters, and considered his 'depth of Taste' one of the 'three things to rejoice at in this Age' (*L* 1, 203). Hazlitt's imprint is perhaps nowhere so legible as in Keats's thoughts on 'Negative Capability', and his subsequent delineations of the function of poetry and the poetical character. Writing to his brothers George and Tom in December, 1817, Keats explains that during a 'disquisition' with his friend Charles Dilke,

> [S]everal things dovetailed in my mind, & at once it struck me, what quality went to form a Man of Achievement especially in Literature & which Shakespeare posessed [*sic*] so enormously – I mean *Negative Capability*, that is when man is capable of being in uncertainties, Mysteries, doubts, without any irritable reaching after fact & reason.
>
> (*L* 1, 193)

'Nothing in himself', Shakespeare exemplifies 'Negative Capability', the ironic ability to abjure resolution in favour of irresolution (to 'be' uncertain), whether considered in relation to 'fact & reason' (a highly circumscribed version of 'truth') or dramatic character; it names the ability of any poet to project himself beyond the confines of personal identity to that which is of abiding interest beyond himself. As a criterion for the 'poetical character' to which Keats aspired, it is to be distinguished from 'the wordsworthian or egotistical sublime; which is a thing per se and stands alone' (*L* 1, 387). Rather, the 'camelion Poet' esteemed by Keats 'is not itself – it has no self – it is every thing and nothing ... A Poet is the most unpoetical of any thing in existence; because he has no Identity – he is continually in for – and filling some other Body' (*L* 1, 387). This ability to elide oneself constitutes the central aspect of the sympathetic imagination. It is precisely what Keats had in mind when he observed in the margins of his copy of *Paradise Lost* that 'One of the most mysterious of semi-speculations is ... that of one Mind's imagining into another'.[2] And it is integral to the increasingly dramatic character of Keats's imagination in his later work.

Beyond the power Negative Capability has as an explanatory mechanism for imaginative self-effacement, it also brings to the fore the entangled status of 'truth' and 'beauty', which are at once to be understood as products of the imagination and as decisive criteria according to which to evaluate the work done by the imagination. The relative value of truth in particular is scrutinised in the eschewal of certainty under the heading of Negative Capability. In distancing the work of the imagination from the 'irritable reaching after fact & reason' – after truth understood in terms of certainty or that which needs to be striven for and explained rather than sensed or intuited – Keats privileges 'half knowledge' over certainty and makes possible a kind of truth that does not depend on intellectual knowledge. Coleridge is singled out here as someone who is unable to remain 'content with half knowledge' (*L* 1, 194), as in a later letter Dilke is. As 'a Man who cannot feel he has a personal identity unless he has made up his Mind about every thing', Dilke represents the antithesis of the imaginative freedom brought into play by Negative Capability; instead, he resembles a decidedly non-poetical character who is imaginatively as well as intellectually confined by his insistence on the egotism of identity and certainty. To counter this cabining of the imagination, Keats proposes that 'The only means of strengthening one's intellect is to make up ones [*sic*] mind about nothing – to let the mind be a thoroughfare for all thoughts' (*L* 2, 213). The poet needn't be certain about anything (except the value of uncertainty). As Keats elsewhere remarks to Bailey with a similar freedom, 'I have not one Idea of the truth of any of my speculations – I shall never be a Reasoner because I care not to be in the right' (*L* 1, 243).

The truth of the imagination is closely aligned with beauty, variously understood in relation to the ideal (oftentimes made available, whether for a poet or an Endymion, in a dream) and the real (apprehensible via the human senses when awake and to be perceived in 'all things'). Take for example the valorisation of 'intensity' – the 'excellence of every Art' – as a matter of the intimacy of 'Beauty & Truth' (*L* 1, 192). Whatever beauty and truth may discretely promise, the point here is that the highest iteration of poetry can only be achieved when they are both legible and working in concert with one another. Keats cryptically aligns beauty and truth on three other occasions in his writing: in his letter to Bailey of 22 November 1817, with its dazzling pronouncement that 'What the imagination seizes as Beauty must be truth' (*L* 1, 184); in a December 1818–January 1819 journal letter to George and Georgiana Keats in which he writes that he 'never can feel certain of any truth but from a clear perception of its Beauty' (*L* 2, 19); and most notoriously in the climactic pronouncement of the 'Ode on a Grecian Urn' that '"Beauty is truth, truth beauty"' (49). At stake in each of these provocative formulations is the possibility of some sort of equivalence between essential beauty (however allied with sensation, the material world and the ideal) and imaginative truth.

In the autumn of 1817, Keats was at work on the third book of *Endymion*. Regarding a long poem as a both test of invention ('the Polar Star of Poetry, as Fancy is the Sails, and Imagination the Rudder', *L* 1, 170) and a trial of his 'Powers of Imagination' (*L* 1, 169), Keats embarked upon another 'trial' of the powers of the imagination in his crucial letter to Bailey. It contains Keats's earliest and in some ways most daring statements regarding the 'authenticity' of the imagination, all of which provide important insight into both his own poetic practice and the most pressing imperatives of poetry as he was beginning to conceive them. '[M]ounted on the wings of Imagination so high' (*L* 1, 185), Keats breathlessly sets forth two of the most cited and puzzling moments in his letters:

> O I wish I was as certain of the end of all your troubles as that of your momentary start about the authenticity of the Imagination. I am certain of nothing but of the holiness of the Heart's affections and the truth of Imagination – What the Imagination seizes as Beauty must be truth – whether it existed before or not – for I have the same Idea of all our Passions as of Love they are all in their sublime, creative of essential Beauty ... The Imagination may be compared to Adam's dream – he awoke and found it truth. I am the more zealous in this affair, because I have never yet been able to perceive how any thing can be known for truth by consequitive reasoning. (*L* 1, 184–5)

Central to Keats's claim is the agency which he assigns to the imagination, here not a passive faculty which receives impressions from the external world but an active agent responsible for making that world. It is imperative to note the energy of this creation: the imagination 'seizes' beauty. It arrests and takes possession of beauty, 'whether it existed before or not', and whatever thus impresses itself irresistibly on the imagination 'must' be truth. Truth is to be understood here as produced by the imagination. Acting on a real, material world apprehensible by the senses (the world that 'exists' and is perceived through 'sensations'), the imagination modifies or as Wordsworth says in 'Tintern Abbey, 'half-creates' the world around it. More radically, anticipating that which does not yet exist ('that which exists *or not*'), the imagination envisions a truth that is otherwise not yet perceptible: the imagination creates, or 'prefigures', its own truth. This second inflection dominates Keats's consideration. Like all our passions at their most sublime (that is to say, intense), the imagination is 'creative of essential Beauty'. As if lost in a dream, oblivious both to himself and to the world around him, the poet then awakens to find that what he has envisioned in his dream as beauty is now true – just as Adam awoke from his vision of Eve to 'behold her, not far off, / Such as I saw her in my dream' (*Paradise Lost* Book 8, lines 481–2). This truth is not confined by the operations of logic, of 'consequitive reasoning', but is empowered by the beauty of what the imagination sees and seizes.

The overwrought alignment of beauty and truth is nowhere more intensely or cryptically brought to the fore than in the 'Ode on a Grecian Urn'. As an unrivalled, and 'still unravish'd' work of art (1), the urn represents an ideal of the beautiful. It can tell 'A flowery tale more sweetly than our rhyme' and its 'unheard' melodies are sweeter than the heard melodies of human poetry (4, 11). As Hazlitt noted of Greek statuary, 'In their faultless excellence they appear sufficient to themselves. By their beauty they are raised above the frailties of passion or suffering. By their beauty they are deified … their forms are a reproach to common humanity'.[3] Another aspect of this self-sufficiency comes to the fore in the urn's singular, enigmatic dictum that 'Beauty is truth, truth beauty' (49). Even in his audacious letter to Bailey, Keats doesn't equate the two terms as unequivocally as he appears to do here. When considering the figurative logic of the chiasmus, however, beauty emerges as the controlling term, suggesting that truth can only be understood in its (and in terms of its) beauty: without beauty, no truth. (This is demonstrably not true, of course: the agonising death of Tom Keats, aged nineteen, the previous December was true, but in no way was it beautiful.) The beauty that 'Ye know on earth' (50), however, is something altogether different: real, painful and mutable rather than ideal, passionless and immutable.

Integral to what we 'know on earth' is suffering, pain and death. The truth about human beauty is that it is transient, and Keats increasingly emphasises the essential necessity as well as difficulty of our apprehending this melancholic truth of the beautiful. In 'On Visiting the Tomb of Burns', Keats writes that 'All is cold beauty; pain is never done', wondering if anyone 'has mind to relish … / The real of beauty, free from that dead hue / Sickly imagination and sick pride / Cast wan upon it' (8, 9–12). The 'real' or unadorned truth of beauty consists in our knowledge of its brevity, untainted by the colorings of a dissimulating imagination that is here not to be trusted. Beauty is cold (akin to the 'cold Pastoral' of the urn) and pain (with all the weight of the Wordsworthian 'burden of the mystery') is never done. We hear a similar lament, and a similarly plangent reading of beauty, throughout the odes. The 'real' of beauty, and of the here-and-now that the speaker of the 'Ode to a Nightingale' cannot finally flee, is similarly characterised by 'The weariness, the fever, and the fret' of a world

> where men sit and hear each other groan;
> Where palsy shakes a few, sad, last gray hairs,
> Where youth grows pale, and spectre-thin, and dies;
> Where but to think is to be full of sorrow
> And leaden-eyed despairs,
> Where Beauty cannot keep her lustrous eyes,
> Or new Love pine at them beyond to-morrow.
> (23–30)

This world of heartache and of death is precisely what the nightingale does not and cannot know; it is the real which the poet seeks to flee, whether 'by Bacchus and his pards, / [Or] on the viewless wings of Poesy' (32–3) in pursuit of the ideal of beauty represented by the nightingale's equally enchanting and oblivious song. Beauty does not seem capable of surviving, of keeping her lustrous eyes, in the mortal world that frames the poem, but may be accessible to us, imaginatively if transiently, through the inscrutable song of the nightingale, a 'light-winged Dryad' (7) more at home in faery land than in this world of sorrow and despair.

Keats's later poetry is increasingly wary of the frailty of human beauty ('Beauty that must die', in the 'Ode on Melancholy', 21) and of the potentially dangerous lures of the unfettered imagination. In the 'Ode to Psyche', Keats simultaneously interrogates the imagination and presents it as querying itself, its allegiances and its abilities, a prospect brought into play by the liminal status of Psyche as neither exactly a goddess nor a mortal. Occupying a purgatorial space between the ideal and the real, she allows

Keats to debate the imagination's allegiances to both. Pledging himself to be Psyche's 'priest, and build a fane / In some untrodden region of my mind', the poet imagines that

> A rosy sanctuary will I dress
> With the wreath'd trellis of a working brain,
> With buds, and bells, and stars without a name,
> With all the gardener Fancy e'er could feign.
> (50–1, 59–62)

Telling here is the rhyme of 'fane / brain / feign': the working brain, or imagination, is at once the site of the proposed temple and the means of creating it. What is at stake is the register in which we read 'feign'. A matter of invention, of fashioning or forming, it is to be celebrated as something akin to the fundamental sense of 'poiesis' as making; but if we inflect 'feign' in terms of forgery, deception and contrivance, it ought instead to be distrusted as the delusive activity of a treasonable imagination.

Fancy is a complicated word for Keats, with an uncertain relation to the imagination. Whereas in 'To Fancy' it appears either to be a faculty distinct from the imagination (operating in a lesser register) or as a denigration of the more dubious potentialities of the imagination, in both the 'Ode to Psyche' and the 'Ode to a Nightingale' it resonates with the freight of imaginative labour. The crucial moment in the 'Ode to a Nightingale' occurs when the poet is violently wrenched from the realm of the nightingale, of poesy and 'faery lands forlorn' (70) by the very word he has just enunciated:

> Forlorn! the very word is like a bell
> To toll me back from thee to my sole self!
> Adieu! the fancy cannot cheat so well
> As she is fam'd to do, deceiving elf.
> (71–4)

Ambiguously feigning in the 'Ode to Psyche', the imagination is now denounced outright for its penchant for delusion: ironically, despite her reputation for deception, she cannot cheat so well as she is reputed to do – or ought to do. This in turn brings to a head Keats's distrust of its propensity to 'freely fly' and entice the poet into a delusory world in which he loses sight of his first priorities as they pertain to the 'sole self' and the relation of this poetic self to human life and human agonies, rather than to the idealisations of goddesses, urns and songbirds. All three of these odes position the imagination as questioning itself, and all three finally undermine the validity of the imagination's visions: the truth to which one awakens from these dreams is not the truth of the imagination, but the truth that the imagination is unreliable. (The poet cannot in the end depend on 'a regular stepping of the Imagination towards a Truth', *L* 1, 218.) Its destabilising effect is such that in the concluding lines of the poem, the poet is lost in a surmise he can in no way resolve: 'Was it a vision, or a waking dream? / Fled is that music: – Do I wake or sleep?' (79–80).

Keats does not overtly organise his thoughts on the imagination under this trajectory from confidence to scepticism. Unlike other Romantic writers, Keats nowhere provides a systematic account of how the imagination operates, how it functions as the 'rudder' for his poetry. He does, however, in a typically Keatsian fashion, offer a few speculations in a letter – in this case the verse epistle to Reynolds of March, 1818. Here, moving uneasily from a meditation on dreaming to a venture in philosophising, Keats interrupts himself to announce:

> Things cannot to the will
> Be settled, but they tease us out of thought.
> Or is it that imagination brought
> Beyond its proper bound, yet still confined, –
> Lost in a sort of purgatory blind,
> Cannot refer to any standard law
> Of either earth or heaven?
> ('Dear Reynolds', 76–82)

What finally is the proper bound of the imagination? Is the imagination to confine itself to the realm of dreaming? Or is there a role for it as the voice as well of 'High reason, and the lore of good and ill' (75)? Put another way, is the imagination to take its bearings from heaven, from the visionary imagination and its 'empyreal reflection' (*L* 185)? Or from earth, from the 'sense of real things' in the context of mortal human life? These questions, like the imagination itself, persistently tease Keats out of and back into thought. There may not be, finally, any standard law for the Keatsian imagination. But in 'pursu[ing] his imagination to the utmost' (as he remarked of Milton),[4] Keats recognised in it not only an indispensable aspect and 'essential beauty' of the poetic process, but also the critical faculty for understanding our 'World of Pains and troubles' if the poet, as 'a sage; / A humanist, physician to all men' (*The Fall of Hyperion*, 1. 189–90), is 'to school an Intelligence and make it a soul' (*L* 2 102).

Notes

1 *The Complete Works of William Hazlitt*, ed. P. P. Howe, 21 vols. (London: Dent, 1930–4), vol. 1, p. 39, vol. 5, pp. 47–8.
2 Beth Lau, *Keats's 'Paradise Lost'* (Gainesville, FL: University Press of Florida, 1998), p. 74.
3 *Works*, vol. 5, p. 11.
4 Lau, *Keats's 'Paradise Lost'*, p. 142.

CHAPTER 18

The Poetical Character

Seamus Perry

Keats's account of the poetical character comes in a letter of 27 October 1818, to his friend Woodhouse:

> As to the poetical Character itself, (I mean that sort of which, if I am any thing, I am a Member; that sort distinguished from the wordsworthian or egotistical sublime; which is a thing per se and stands alone) it is not itself – it has no self – it is every thing and nothing – It has no character – it enjoys light and shade; it lives in gusto, be it foul or fair, high or low, rich or poor, mean or elevated – It has as much delight in conceiving an Iago as an Imogen. What shocks the virtuous philosop[h]er, delights the camelion Poet. It does no harm from its relish of the dark side of things any more than from its taste for the bright one; because they both end in speculation. A Poet is the most unpoetical of any thing in existence; because he has no Identity – he is continually in for – and filling some other Body – The Sun, the Moon, the Sea and Men and Women who are creatures of impulse are poetical and have about them an unchangeable attribute – the poet has none; no identity – he is certainly the most unpoetical of all God's Creatures.
>
> (*L* 1, 386–7)

Woodhouse had written to bolster Keats after the *Quarterly* had rubbished *Endymion*, offering some supportive remarks about the genuine poet, like Keats, 'the true born son of Genius, who creates for himself the world in which his own fancy roams'.[1] The imagination described and deployed in Keats's response is a handsome gesture of his gratitude; but he also takes the opportunity tactfully to correct Woodhouse, whose thoughts about what poets do are, for Keats, as wrong-headed as they were well-meaning. Like many poetry-lovers, Woodhouse thinks to praise poets by claiming that they create and inhabit worlds of their own. It is a common sort of praise;[2] and it can be meant profoundly, as by Coleridge, say, in *Biographia Literaria* (1817), when he chose to attribute such genius to Milton, a poet who 'attracts all forms and things to himself, into the unity of his own IDEAL. All things and modes of action shape themselves anew in the being of

MILTON'. Keats evidently took a very different view about what constituted 'poetical character': indeed, he thought that one main problem with contemporary verse was that each of its authors presided over a world of their own, 'like an Elector of Hanover governs his petty state' (*L* I, 224). Keats's poet, contrarily, evades anything resembling a private universe and enters instead the diversity of the world without. As it happens, Coleridge sometimes thought in those terms about some poets too – those, of course, who did not resemble Milton in idealising genius. Coleridge attributed such mental activity exemplarily to Shakespeare, who, he said, 'darts himself forth, and passes into all the forms of human character and passion, the one Proteus of the fire and the flood';[3] and it is possibly Coleridge whom Keats is following, though probably a Coleridge who has been mediated through Hazlitt.[4] 'He was the least of an egotist that it was possible to be', Hazlitt said of Shakespeare: 'He was nothing in himself; but he was all that others were, or that they could become'.[5] That is marvellous: it was not unusual to celebrate Shakespeare as a hero of the sympathetic imagination, his genius distributed among the brilliantly realised individualities of his characters while he remained invisible himself like an immanent god, but Hazlitt did it memorably well. Likewise, Keats's contradistinction with 'the wordsworthian or egotistical sublime' grew from Hazlitt's deeply tendentious, highly charismatic account of Wordsworth's imagination as a thing which stands repellently alone and gathers everything into the unity of its own ideal: 'An intense intellectual egotism swallows up every thing', said Hazlitt of Wordsworth's philosophical blank verse, which he thought manifested 'an evident repugnance to admit any thing that tells for itself, without the interpretation of the poet, – a fastidious antipathy to immediate effect, – a systematic unwillingness to share the palm with his subject'.[6]

Hazlitt readily grants Wordsworth's imagination its intensity, as Keats allows it sublimity, while both imply its relation to a failing like selfishness or a heedlessness to others; but then the 'poetical character', delighting in things that would appal a moralist, evidently runs a risk of its own – that of having 'no character', in the sense in which (for instance) Coleridge meant when he wrote *Aids to Reflection in the Formation of a Manly Character* (1825). Keats sets out upon his definition of the poetical character with a paradox which is playful and perhaps not far from a joke: for there is something very puzzling in beginning a definition of anything with the observation that 'itself … it is not itself', and then going on to say that this 'character' has 'no character', is something identifiable by having 'no Identity', and gets to be 'poetical' through being 'the most unpoetical of all God's creatures'. He was often drawn by the thought of something which was itself but not itself: 'Our bodies every seven years have completely fresh-materiald', he was excited and troubled to report, making us like the endlessly re-patched garments of a saint, 'the same and not the same' – 'T is an uneasy thought', he touchingly adds, 'that in seven years the same hands cannot greet each other again' (*L* 2, 208, 208–9).

But to say of something, especially of a personality, that it is 'not itself' is not usually to claim an advantage for it: when Iago says of himself, 'I am not what I am' (*Othello*, 1. 1. 65), he identifies with frightening clarity a lack of self-coincidence that underlies moral catastrophe. The failure to be oneself need not be so abysmal, of course, but it is never less than discomposing: Troilus is reported to be undone by love: 'Himself?' says Pandarus, 'no, he's not himself. Would a were himself!' (*Troilus and Cressida*, 1. 2 70-1). That example is close to Keats's letter for only a few lines previously Shakespeare has Cressida's manservant remark of Ajax, a man who is clearly wholly and nothing but himself, 'They say he is a very man *per se* / And stands alone' (1. 2. 15–16), lines that Keats marked in his own copy, and which obviously lie behind his characterisation of the Wordsworthian counter-principle to 'poetical character'.[7] *Troilus* was still in his mind a few lines later, as his editor notes:

> It is a wretched thing to confess; but is a very fact that not one word I ever utter can be taken for granted as an opinion growing out of my identical nature – how can it, when I have no nature? When I am in a room with People if I ever am free from speculating on creations of my own brain, then not myself goes home to myself: but the identity of every one in the room begins [s]o to press upon me that I am in a very little time annihilated – not only among Men; it would be the same in a Nursery of children.
>
> (*L* 1, 387)

In the play Achilles remarks about self-obliviousness: 'Nor doth the eye itself, / That most pure spirit of sense, behold itself, / Not going from itself', and draws the moral that 'speculation turns not to itself / Till it hath travelled and is mirrored there / Where it may see itself' (3. 3. 100–2; 104–6). Adam Smith would have agreed that we come to know ourselves through imaginatively experiencing ourselves as the objects of someone else's experience, and he wrote of a human spectator endeavouring 'to put himself into the situation of the other, and to bring home to himself every little circumstance'.[8] The 'poetical character' grows out of that culture of feeling, but extends and enhances it: for one thing, not just people fall within the scope of Keatsian sympathy, but all sorts of things animate and inanimate, including sparrows and billiard balls (*L* 1, 186, 389), both of which Keats buoyantly offers as test cases of the imagination's reach.

But as his account suggests, Keatsian empathy is also much more emotionally complicated than the tradition normally allows, capable of being both 'burden and release'.[9] Being in a room with other people turns out to be much more fraught, more to be endured, than Smith's citizenly and assiduous cultivation of fellow feeling: the idea of another person's identity *pressing* upon you feels especially striking and individual, though it may have had one poetic precedent in Coleridge's 'Christabel', in which the heroine is undone by a 'forced unconscious sympathy'.[10] He recounts the experience several times in the letters: of his dying brother Tom, whom Keats nursed devotedly, 'His identity presses upon me' (*L* 1, 369); and by contrast, writing to his sister-in-law about his younger sister Fanny, whose character being 'not formed', Keats finds, 'her identity does not press upon me as yours does' (*L* 1, 392). This Keatsian sense of identity as exposed and vulnerable and under pressure is a remarkable development upon eighteenth-century tradition: 'he was especially audacious', as Christopher Ricks remarks, 'in believing that the healthy strength of a sense of identity depends paradoxically upon t risk and openness and not upon self-protection'.[11] *Troilus and Cressida* ran so deeply beneath these preoccupations in the Woodhouse letter, perhaps, because the climax of that play is nothing but an imponderable and agonising crisis of identity, something being at once itself and not itself: 'This is and is not Cressid' (5. 2. 146).

Woodhouse took the point to be that Keats kept company with Shakespeare: 'he may lose sight of his identity so far as to give him a habit of speak[in]g generally in an assumed character … Shak[e]sp[ea]r[e] was a poet of the kind above ment[ione]d – and he was perhaps the only one besides Keats who possessed this power in an extr[aordinary] degree so as to be a feature in his works' (*L* 1, 390). Woodhouse was not wrong, although as it happens Keats's Shakespearean gifts did not translate into anything like effective drama. Critics often borrow another famous piece of his phrase-making, '*Negative Capability*', to name this self-transformative Keatsian gift: 'Negative Capability, the power to fill other bodies', says John Jones, its most eloquent commentator, 'reveals him invading countless privacies, imagining sheer innernesses of feel'.[12] What name critics give to imaginative powers is not of much importance, to be sure; but, actually, '*Negative Capability*' in its only Keatsian appearance does not seem to be quite that empathetic power itself (even if it is its precondition): it is, rather, 'when man is capable of being in uncertainties, Mysteries, doubts, without any irritable reaching after fact & reason' (*L* 1, 193). That seems more like a disposition or a cast of consciousness, an attitude of the mind towards experience, as though some basic imponderability itself might serve as the haunt and main region of one's song. To return to the 'poetical character' letter, the point there, similarly, is not merely the wonderful chameleonic power of imagination (something that many commentators might have routinely praised) but also the way that the 'poetical character' is drawn to a conflicting diversity and contradictoriness that is constitutive of human experience, one which other modes of perception were only going to miss. That thought is something else for which Keats may have owed Hazlitt a debt, for Hazlitt had praised Shakespeare especially for the sheer heterogeneity and differentness of the elements which his verbal imagination brought together: 'The more the thoughts are strangers to each other, and the longer they have been kept asunder, the more intimate does their union seem to become'.[13]

The virtuous philosopher is outraged less by the imagination's pleasure in impersonating villainy than by its simultaneous readiness to impersonate villainy and virtue, relishing 'the dark side of things' as much as 'the bright one'. That a fictive philosopher should take against this all-inclusive attitude towards experience is telling. Keats was repeatedly prone to the belief that he should grow up, leaving behind an apprenticeship of 'poetic ardour' and attaining a maturity of 'more thoughtful and quiet power' (*L* 2, 209), and he was in love with a mighty abstract idea of philosophy, one to the detriment of poetry, which was, he said, 'not so fine a thing as philosophy – For the same reason that an eagle is not so fine a thing as a truth' (*L* 2, 81).[14] (And what reason is that, exactly?) At one point he thought to ask Hazlitt for his advice on 'the best metaphysical road I can take' (*L* 1, 274); but the singularity of that 'road' suggests why philosophy was not, in the end, a Keatsian vocation. 'Can it be', he asked his friend Bailey, 'that even the greatest Philosopher ever arrived at his goal without putting aside numerous objections': such would not be the case with the innately self-interruptive sort of intelligence that he calls, later in the same letter, 'a complex Mind – one that is imaginative and at the same time careful of its fruits' (*L* 1, 185, 186). For poetry to 'surprise by a fine excess and not by Singularity' (*L* 1, 238) is for it to resist the attraction of a more exclusive philosophical rigour and not to set countering thoughts to one side on the way to a goal: 'The only means of strengthening one's intellect is to make up ones mind about nothing', he rephrased in more robust spirits the earlier apercu about '*Negative Capability*' (*L* 2, 213). 'I feel more and more every day, as my imagination strengthens, that I do not live in this world alone but in a thousand worlds' (*L* 1, 403): that experience might possess some innately informing principle of hybridity or plurality, more of an intuition than a position to be deliberated, is the very stuff of Keatsian imagination, 'light and shade … foul or fair, high or low, rich or poor, mean or elevated'. Poetry written within this dispensation would certainly not answer to what De Quincey called a 'poetry of knowledge', but might perhaps be, in its way, a poetry of 'half knowledge' (*L* 1, 194).[15]

The plurality found out by the poetical character is often experienced in his poems, as in his life, as the imposition of other 'pressing' selves or experiences; at other times, the awareness of simultaneous kinds of reality that accompany whatever reality is presently in hand can be felt more serenely or numinously: the attractions of elsewhere are sometimes experienced in a romantic spirit of forlorn desire – 'Ever let the Fancy roam, / Pleasure never is at home' ('Fancy', 1–2). But more characteristically, Keats works an intricate sort of negative imaginative logic by which counter-thoughts acquire a strangely resonant actuality through the act of being ruled out. Bishop Butler – in a work which Hazlitt admired profusely and of which Keats certainly knew – said famously: 'Every thing is what it is, and not another thing'.[16] As the dance of negatives in the 'poetical character' letter suggests ('not itself … no self … nothing … no character') the thought that something might be *not* something was a matter of no small consequence to the Keatsian imagination. As though finding an unexpected imaginative potential within the robust English sense of Butler's remark, a Keatsian thing may be itself and not another thing, and yet that other thing may play a central role in the workings of the poetical character, a negative spirit always alert to what itself it is not. 'Where are the songs of Spring? Ay, where are they? / Think not of them, thou hast thy music too, –' ('To Autumn', 23–4): the songs of Spring are emphatically not within the acoustic range of an ode 'To Autumn', and yet they can hardly have a more memorable hearing in English verse, as though exemplifying Keats's observation, 'Heard melodies are sweet, but those unheard / Are sweeter' ('Ode on a Grecian Urn', 11–12). Such melodies are not themselves: the lines are pure Keats in the way they imagine 'unheard' as though it were, not the annulling of 'heard', but another variant form of it, alongside 'clearly heard', 'faintly heard', or 'misheard'. 'Nothing ever becomes real till it is experienced', he wrote (*L* 2, 81); but his poetry is full of things that are as real as anything else and are either not experienced or experienced only in the most precarious way: things heard going unheard, or felt going unfelt, are hallmarks of the idiom – 'The feel of not to feel it' ('In Drear Nighted December', 21). No wonder, then, that he should have been so haunted by the moment in *King Lear* when Edgar, disguised, asks his blinded father: '"Do you not hear the Sea?"' In truth, there is no sea: the cliff-top on which they find themselves is wholly the work of words, 'a sea heard', as John Bayley said, 'in the mind only';[17] and so it is at once a fiction and yet, since the poetry does indeed momentarily make it heard in the mind, it has a sort of truth too, a mixture which Gloucester's answer manages brilliantly to convey: 'No, truly'.

That Keats twigged the pregnant negative life of the imagination in such moments is nicely implied by his misquotation, noted by Christopher Ricks: for in Shakespeare, Edgar actually asks 'Hark, do you hear the sea?' (*King Lear*, Conflated Text, 4. 6. 4).[18] Empson remarked memorably of the opening lines of the 'Ode on Melancholy' – 'No, no, go not to Lethe, neither twist / Wolf's-bane, tight-rooted, for its poisonous wine' – 'somebody, or some force in the poet's mind, must have wanted to go to Lethe very much, if it took four negatives in the first line to stop them'.[19] It is an example of the effect best described by Coleridge, 'the imagination called forth, not to produce a distinct form but a strong working of the mind still producing what it still repels & again calling forth what it again negatives'.[20] That feels like a reminder of the mind's powers, but it is not far from describing something uncomfortable too, and the way that experience is entwined with its alternative experience can come across as troubling, as in the lines he wrote to Reynolds:

Things cannot to the will
Be settled, but they tease us out of thought.
Or is it that imagination brought
Beyond its proper bound, yet still confined, –
Lost in a sort of Purgatory blind,
Cannot refer to any standard law
Of either earth or heaven? – It is a flaw
In happiness, to see beyond our bourn, –
It forces us in summer skies to mourn;
It spoils the singing of the nightingale.
('To J.H. Reynolds, Esq.', 76–85)

The vision glimpsed beyond the predicted bourn of the poem in this case (Keats 'cannot speak it', 87) is a Malthusian horror of 'eternal fierce destruction' (97), a markedly different sort of poetry that undercuts the loveliness of the lyric sea and so, perhaps, 'spoils' its song. But at other, more intricate moments of Keatsian practice, the alertness of the poetical character to 'the dark side of things' does not merely spoil, but enriches.

The singing of the nightingale in the great ode is shadowed but certainly not spoilt by dark things which the bird itself 'hast never known', but for which its poem finds space, at its greatest moment through the purely speculative agency of a 'perhaps' –

> Perhaps the self-same song that found a path
> Through the sad heart of Ruth, when, sick for home,
> She stood in tears amid the alien corn;
> ('Ode to a Nightingale', 65–7)

At which point, as Barbara Everett says, 'the Ode moves beyond the bounds of the romantic-personal and translates itself into other selves'.[21] Similarly, in the 'Grecian Urn' ode, the poised and serene aesthetic loveliness of the pot is importantly defined by other experiences, pressing around its edges, which it is not:

> What little town by river or sea shore,
> Or mountain-built with peaceful citadel,
> Is emptied of this folk, this pious morn?
> And, little town, thy streets for evermore
> Will silent be; and not a soul to tell
> Why thou art desolate, can e'er return.
> ('Ode on a Grecian Urn', 35–40)

An initially counter-factual movement of the mind enables the inclusive poetical character to contemplate a human world as though it were an alternative kind of fact; its loss is the unexpected price of beauty. In a poem which ends by enunciating 'Truth' as a stirring singularity, the poem allows at this point for a fine excess of different truths; but the effect is of polyphony rather than a settled hierarchy of truth-claims: there is no sense in which one vision trumps or undercuts the other. The desolate village without witnesses to speak for it presses in upon the periphery of the urn-world: the poem can hardly be the 'thoroughfare for *all* thoughts' that Keats recommended at one point in a negatively capable spirit (my italics; *L* 2, 213), but its greatness derives from its openness to the pressure of other thoughts – making an imaginative virtue of being 'weak-sided' (*L* 2, 174), the thing that Keats, battle-hardened by bad reviews, said he wanted to avoid. And so the poem ends up larger than the subject matter it set out with, achieving a version of 'fine excess' and forgoing the tidier pleasures of 'Singularity': it is the multi-perspectival work of one, to use a winning phrase of Keats's own, 'in too huge a Mind for study' (*L* 2, 12).

Notes

1 Woodhouse had originally written 'Imagination' for 'fancy': *KC* 1, 49.
2 See David Bromwich, 'Why Authors Do Not Create Their Own Worlds', in *A Choice of Inheritance. Self and Community from Edmund Burke to Robert Frost* (Cambridge, MA: Harvard University Press, 1989), pp. 247–63.
3 S. T. Coleridge, *Biographia Literaria*, ed. James Engell and Walter Jackson Bate, 2 vols. (Princeton: Princeton University Press, 1982), vol. 2, pp. 27–8; 27.
4 Hazlitt and Keats are brought together in this matter by Walter Jackson Bate, *Negative Capability: The Intuitive Approach in Keats* (1939; [n.p.]: Contra Mundum Press, 2012), p. 28.
5 'On Shakespeare and Milton', *Lectures on the English Poets*, in *The Complete Works of William Hazlitt*, ed. P. P. Howe, 21 vols. (London: Dent, 1930–4), vol. 5, p. 47.
6 'On Mr Wordsworth's Excursion', *The Round Table*; Hazlitt, *Works*, vol. 5, pp. 113, 114. For Keats's response to Hazlitt's idea of Wordsworth, see Stuart M. Sperry, *Keats the Poet* (1973; Princeton: Princeton University Press, 1994), pp. 181–2.
7 Caroline Spurgeon, *Keats's Shakespeare. A Descriptive Study Based on New Material*, 2nd edn (London: Oxford University Press, 1929), p. 150.
8 Adam Smith, *The Theory of Moral Sentiments*, ed. D. D. Raphael and A. L. Macfie (1976; Indianapolis: Liberty Fund, 1982), p. 21.
9 Michael O'Neill, *Romanticism and the Self-Conscious Poem* (Oxford: Clarendon Press, 1997), p. 189.
10 'Christabel', line 609; in S. T. Coleridge, *Poems*, ed. John Beer, rev. edn (London: Everyman, 1999).
11 Christopher Ricks, *Keats and Embarrassment* (Oxford: Clarendon, 1974), p. 25.
12 John Jones, *John Keats's Dream of Truth* (London: Chatto & Windus, 1969), p. 21. And cp. John Bernard, *John Keats* (Cambridge: Cambridge University Press, 1987), 53.
13 'On Shakespeare and Milton'; Hazlitt, *Works*, vol. 5, p. 54.
14 The best account of this aspiration, as of much else in Keats, remains the chapters in John Bayley, *The Uses of Division: Unity and Disharmony in Literature* (London: Chatto & Windus, 1976), esp. pp. 109–14.
15 'The Poetry of Pope', in *De Quincey as Critic*, ed. John E. Jordan (London: Routledge and Kegan Paul, 1973), p. 269.
16 Bishop Butler, 'Preface' to *Fifteen Sermons (1726): Fifteen Sermons Preached at the Rolls Chapel and a Dissertation Upon the Nature of Virtue*, ed. W. R. Matthews (London: Bell, 1967), p. 23. Hazlitt said in *An Essay on Human Action*, which Keats possessed (*KC* 1.254), 'I do not know of any work better worth the attention of those who would learn to think' (Hazlitt, *Works*, vol. 1, p. 50).
17 John Bayley, *Shakespeare and Tragedy* (London: Routledge and Kegan Paul, 1981), p. 7.

18 Christopher Ricks, 'Keats's Sources, Keats's Allusions', *The Cambridge Companion to Keats*, ed. Susan Wolfson (Cambridge: Cambridge University Press, 1992), pp. 152–69, 166.

19 William Empson, *Seven Types of Ambiguity*, 3rd edn (London: Chatto & Windus, 1953; 1973), p. 205.

20 S. T. Coleridge, *Lectures 1808–1819: On Literature*, ed. R. A. Foakes, 2 vols. (Princeton: Princeton University Press, 1987), vol. 1, p. 311.

21 Barbara Everett, *Poets in Their Time* (1986; Oxford: Oxford University Press, 1991), p. 144.

CHAPTER 19

The Senses and Sensation

Stacey McDowell

When meeting one of Fanny Brawne's friends, Keats had failed to be duly delighted by her performance on the piano, as he afterwards observed cattily: 'she plays the Music without one sensation but the feel of the ivory at her fingers' (*L* 2, 13). We might expect the words 'sensation' and 'feel' to be switched around here. Keats ironically reverses them to suggest what is missing when feel (in a typically Keatsian contraction for feeling) is reduced to sense perception alone, to the touch of ivory keys. That Keats would hear in the music the pressure on the fingertips felt by the player is a mark of his quick imagining of the sensory experience at work in the aesthetic. While the feel of ivory and the business of fingers on keys is vital if any sound is to be produced at all, Keats's criticism of music played 'without one sensation but the feel' reveals that something more is needed, that sensation is something plural. His remark gestures towards without needing to specify the other kinds of sensation and feel we can intuit there ought to be: emotional responsiveness, imagination, sensibility. No sensation but in feeling, then, but sensation at once alert to the immediate perception of things, of sound or touch, say, and feelingly responsive to the range of emotions and ideas bound up with aesthetic experience.

The interchanging of the words 'sensation' and 'feel' in Keats's remark also points up the more general difficulty of isolating the meaning of 'sensation' amidst a tangle of associated terms ('the senses', 'sensibility', 'sensitivity', 'sensuousness', 'sensuality') – not to mention the various inflections of the single word 'sense' (sensory perception, meaning, intuition, reason, sound judgment). Still, as William Empson reminds us in his chapter on sense in *The Structure of Complex Words*, 'this theoretically odd connection of meanings is a normal one for the human mind'.[1] Keats make use of this familiar cluster, playing on the meanings of 'sense', 'sensation' and 'the senses' to invoke or exclude their various cognates. His use of individual terms, however, perhaps tells us less about what they mean to him than the fact of the sheer number of sensory descriptions he includes in his poetry. In the descriptions of what can be seen and heard, the scents and tastes, the attentive recounting of feel and touch, Keats is engaged in reflecting upon the means by which sensory experience can be represented or recreated as aesthetic experience, and how, through his poetry, words could be made to give sound, shape, form, even palpable feeling, to sensation.

Everyone seems to agree that Keats is 'a poet of the senses'. The characterisation gained currency during the Victorian period, with critics by turns fascinated and disconcerted by his poetry's luxuriating delight in sensory experience. The question persisting throughout Keats's reception history, however, is whether his is a poetry of nothing but sensation. 'A merely sensuous man' is how Matthew Arnold described him (before going on to defend Keats from the charge implicit in that 'merely').[2] Later critics have stressed how the senses in Keats's poetry variously relate to reality (John Bayley); or truth (John Jones); or philosophy (Stuart Sperry reads Keats's poetry within the context of eighteenth and early nineteenth century philosophy, while Shahidha Bari sets his verse alongside more recent theoretical thinking).

In defining such contrasts and their possible reconciliation, these critics (as well as others) are responding to the tussle of artistic and moral impulses, ambition and obligation articulated by Keats in his poetry and letters, a tussle outlined most famously and most starkly in the letter to Benjamin Bailey in November 1817: 'O for a Life of Sensations rather than of Thoughts!' (*L* 1, 185). Such an appeal could only have been uttered by someone who knew what it was to be harried by the buzzing of thoughts. Yet Keats can still be taken at his word, since what animates his verse is not only his compulsion as a poet to give life to sensory experience, but also his continual questioning of how or how far such an approach can be made to form part of the realities of life, or the life of thought. Arthur Hallam seems merely to rehearse Keats's predicament when he labels him (along with Shelley) a poet 'of sensation rather than reflection', yet his essay goes on to identify the interdependence of sensation and thought for both poets: 'so vivid', he writes, 'was the delight attending the simple exertions of eye and ear, that it became mingled more and more with their trains of active thought, and tended to absorb their whole being into the energy of sense'.[3] It is this 'energy of sense' that places a 'demand on the reader for activity', Hallam continues, calling upon them to respond in kind.

The early works ('Calidore', 'Sleep and Poetry', 'I stood tip-toe upon a little hill' and *Endymion*) offer a rush of sensory descriptions with an enthusiastic urgency which, if it does not demand, at least hopes that the reader will be delighted in turn. As well as delicately observed sights and sounds, the so-called lower senses of smell, taste, and touch are in Keats's verse some of those most carefully attended to. And beyond the traditional 'five senses', his sensitivity to hot and cold (so-called thermoception) makes for intimately precise details: the 'sigh-warm kisses' promised in *Endymion*, for instance, or the refreshing chill of apples in the night air when the moonlight has 'cool'd their cheeks deliciously' (*Endymion*, I. 967; 3. 148). One of the things that characterises the sense perceptions of the early poems is this surprising preciseness, as if Keats is eager not only to draw attention to minute details (the 'vermeil rimm'd' tip of a daisy petal, for example (*Endymion*, I. 50), but to convey in words what something really looks or smells or tastes or sounds or feels like, so that thought and meaning take on the substantiality and immediacy of sensations.

W. T. Arnold noted of Keats's poetry that it communicates 'a sort of appeal to the reader, a tacit question whether he has not noted the same thing, and felt the same pleasure from it'.[4] In book 1 of *Endymion* during the festival of Pan, a priest entreats the Latmians to consider their various pastoral bounties: 'Are not our lowing heifers sleeker than / Night-swollen mushrooms?', he asks (I. 214–5). It is an analogy that may not have struck them before, but one that, upon reflection, seems peculiarly fitting. Calling upon a shared recognition in the reader, the combined oddity and specificity (not just mushrooms but 'night-swollen mushrooms') makes it seem as though no other comparison could work quite as well. What else has that strange silkiness of feel? More so than with the 'silken flanks' (34) of the heifer in the 'Ode on a Grecian Urn', where the concision and consonance might sound better, it is the accuracy of touch and the surprise of recognition that is vital in *Endymion*.

In a letter defending the attractions of a long poem, Keats had asked, 'do not the Lovers of Poetry like to have a little Region to wander in where they may pick and choose?' (*L* 1, 170). This principle offers a good account of the generosity of sensory descriptions in *Endymion*, as well as in some of Keats's shorter narrative poems. Setting out an inventory for his poetic wanderings in 'Sleep and Poetry', Keats imagines himself in 'the realm of Flora', where, he anticipates, he will

sleep in the grass,
Feed upon apples red, and strawberries,
And choose each pleasure that my fancy sees;
Catch the white-handed nymphs in shady places,
To woo sweet kisses from averted faces, –

Play with their fingers, touch their shoulders white
Into a pretty shrinking with a bite
As hard as lips can make it:

(102–9)

Keats's poetry is all 'palates and fingertips', John Jones has noted wryly.[5] Here, as well as invoking a hypersensitivity to taste and touch, the 'energy of sense' (in Hallam's words) relates also to the way that the motion of picking and choosing each pleasure is traced along the lines, making the movement of syntax almost palpable. The catching of hands leads to kisses, leads the reader imaginatively to 'Play with their fingers, touch their shoulders', moving from 'fingers' to 'touch' across the caesura, the breath held as if in wait for the roaming caress of hands, before it turns out that that touch is ventured, more thrillingly because more unexpectedly, with the mouth. And as the amorous biting recalls the earlier feeding on fruit, the 'bite / As hard as lips can make it' turns on the urge to sink one's teeth hard into an apple and the gentle lipping of a strawberry. While moving through modes of sensory experience, from tasting to touching to biting, from hands and fingers to mouths and lips, the verse slips indistinctly between what could be an actual, everyday sensory experience (sleeping in grass, eating fruit) and an erotic or aestheticised imagining (wooing nymphs and wandering in realms of flora). These realistic-mythic sensations, involving the granting of sensory immediacy to imagined scenarios (or what Keats in *Endymion* calls presenting 'immortal bowers to mortal sense' (2. 438)), work to perplex the limits between a poetic life of sensations and external reality.

Often what seems to begin as fanciful daydream turns out to have the bite of sensory immediacy, which is just the moment when Keats begins to worry about what other realms of experience and knowledge are elided through this absorption in the senses. Immediately following these lines in 'Sleep and Poetry', Keats shakes himself into insisting that this realm of Flora must be passed up for a 'nobler life', one which would confront 'the agonies, the strife / Of human hearts' (123–5). No sooner has Keats voiced this resolution than a vision of Apollo bursts into appearance, only for the vision to fade and for reality to reassert itself, where reality is felt now as an encroachment on poetic vision as 'a sense of real things comes doubly strong' (157). Only, the undefined 'real things' and the only intimated 'sense of' them seems somehow less real than the imagined sensations of the previous amatory daydream and brilliant vision of Apollo. As John Bayley has observed, Keats's ambitions 'never sound so unreal … as when he is striving for some new image of reality'; rather, his verse is at its most real when his language aims at the primary grasp of sense perception, when his 'passion for the real strives to make words give the feel of physical experience to imaginary longing'.[6] In poems such as 'Sleep and Poetry', *Endymion*, *The Eve of St. Agnes* and *Lamia*, Keats seeks to confront readers with sensory experiences whose mimetic accuracy strives to feel what is real, even while it warns that giving oneself up to such sensations might be an indulgence or shying away from more pressing or darker realities.

The Glaucus episode in book 3 of *Endymion* is important for what it tells us about Keats's anxiety about the seductions of sensory imaginings and the fantasy, as tantalising as it is terrifying, whereby words could not just describe but create a sensory experience to overwhelm one's grasp of reality. When Glaucus recounts the story of his enthrallment by Circe, he tells how 'with honey-words she wove / A net' (3. 426–7). Like Lamia, whose words come 'as through bubbling honey', it is Circe's voice rather than any mythic potion that charms. If, she coaxes,

> thou art fond
> Of soothing warmth, of dalliance supreme;
> If thou art ripe to taste a long love dream;
> If smiles, if dimples, tongues for ardour mute,
> Hang in thy vision like a tempting fruit,
> O let me pluck it for thee.' Thus she link'd
> Her charming syllables, till indistinct
> Their music came to my o'er-sweeten'd soul;
> (3. 438–45)

Circe's list of enticements reads almost like a parody of the sensory pleasures to be found elsewhere in Keats's poetry. Dalliances and dimples make up some of his more formulaically erotic lines: 'soft dimpled hands, white neck, and creamy breast, / Are things on which the dazzled senses rest' (16–17, 'Woman! when I behold thee flippant, vain'), and *Endymion* itself could be described as a poem spun out of the desire for the ripe tasting of one 'long love dream'. Circe's 'charming syllables' reveal what Keats's sensuous writing is sometimes on the verge of becoming. If this is self-parody, then parody's knack for cutting to the quick of things invites us to read the episode as a commentary on Keats's own anxiety about loading one's words too consciously or calculatedly with sense. For the odd thing about so brazenly seductive a speech ('O let me pluck it for thee' is hardly subtle) is that we need to be told how seductive it is, in a rhetorical move which only points up how much Circe's speech lacks the arresting, even disconcerting, sensuousness that Keats's verse achieves at other times.

'Thus she link'd / Her charming syllables', Glaucus recounts, 'till indistinct / Their music came to my o'ersweeten'd soul'. Playing upon the relationship between sound and sense, Circe's 'charming syllables' speak a poetry that seeks to overwhelm with sensation rather than communicate sense (in terms of meaning) through 'link'd' words that produce 'indistinct / Their music'. In Keats's draft, 'my o'er-sweeten'd soul' had read 'my o'er-sweeten'd sense'.[7] The latter might be the more expected choice, since it is able to suggest both sensuous excess or overstimulation and overwhelmed reason or judgement. Glaucus later names Circe 'this arbitrary queen of sense', and in the version of the story that Keats would have read in Sandys's translation of the *Metamorphoses*, Circe's victims are those 'who forsake that faire *Intelligence,* / To follow *Passion*, and voluptuous *Sence*'.[8] By revising 'sense' to 'soul', Keats avoids the familiar associations of sense and therefore the possible distinctions between them. 'Soul' cannot be confined to just physical sensation or sensuousness or judgement; rather, it is used unusually to encompass all of these things at once, resisting the common distinctions between body and soul or morality and passion, 'the squabble between soul and sense' (in Robert Browning's words).[9] That Keats intuited a link between the two is suggested as well by an allusion in *The Eve of St. Agnes*, where Othello's line to Desdemona, 'the sense aches at thee' (*Othello*, 4. 2. 68), becomes in Keats, 'my soul doth ache' (279), as Porphyro beholds Madeleine. In *Endymion*, even while the mawkish surfeiting of 'o'er-sweeten'd' undoes something of the loftiness of 'soul', Keats's soul-sense feels the effect of Circe's music as a response that absorbs every range of sensation, feeling, understanding.

The friend who had played the piano 'without one sensation but the feel of the ivory at her fingers' could never have overwhelmed the sense or soul of her listeners. However, in the earlier poem 'To Charles Cowden Clarke', which recalls how his own friend's piano playing boasted everything that Fanny's friend lacked, Keats had begun to set out a different way of thinking about the relationship between sound and sensation:

> But many days have past since last my heart
> Was warm'd luxuriously by divine Mozart;
> By Arne delighted, or by Handel madden'd;
> Or by the song of Erin pierc'd and sadden'd:
> What time you were before the music sitting,
> And the rich notes to each sensation fitting;
> (109–14)

The notion of 'fitting' sound to sensation seems slightly forced here, the rhymes are self-consciously artless and stretch the metre with feminine endings, as if flexing against the assumption that music could be cut and measured according to certain emotions. Earlier in the same poem, though, Keats suggests how the patterns of sounds in poetry produce sensations which feel somehow fittingly appropriate, but never 'fitted'. The memory of Clarke's piano playing in the verse epistle comes on the back of a recollection of Clarke's introducing Keats to a variety of poetic styles and forms:

> Spenserian vowels that elope with ease,
> And float along like birds o'er summer seas;
> Miltonian storms, and more, Miltonian tenderness;
> Michael in arms, and more, meek Eve's fair slenderness.
> Who read for me the sonnet swelling loudly
> Up to its climax and then dying proudly?
> Who found for me the grandeur of the ode,
> Growing, like Atlas, stronger from its load?
>
> (56–63)

The image of Atlas, as he is often depicted in statuary groaning under the weight of the globe, is a remarkably apt figuring of a form gaining a kind of self-sufficient integrity through the burden of its own grandeur. The lines give no real detail about the ode: Horatian or Pindaric, for instance, subject matter or addressee. Instead of being descriptive or illustrative, Keats's verse seeks to convey what it feels like, in creatively perceptual terms, to read an ode. The account of his early encounters with poetry in the epistle to Clarke identifies a fascination that runs throughout his writings with how a poem produces sensation – not just through accurate descriptions of sensory experience (although that remained vital, too), but also by producing sensations less easy to define or anticipate, in ways that register the mind's imaginative and emotional responsiveness.

In 'I stood tip-toe upon a little hill', Keats holds that

> In the calm grandeur of a sober line,
> We see the waving of the mountain pine;
> And when a tale is beautifully staid,
> We feel the safety of a hawthorn glade:
>
> (127–30)

What does it mean to hear in a way of telling the feeling of safety in a hawthorn glade? Though they risk fancifulness, and the tale's being 'staid' not 'said' or 'told' might be toying, these lines seem quite serious and assured in having hit upon the most fitting sensation. The same perceptual responsiveness informs Keats's remark, upon reading Milton, that 'there is a cool pleasure in the very sound of vale'.[10] His looking to analogies in physical sensation to describe the effect by which poetry seems to 'translate' words into palpable feeling raises questions about how the mind interprets physical sense impressions, which for Keats has as much to do with poetry as philosophy.

In the eighteenth and early nineteenth centuries, philosophical enquiries into how external stimuli entered the consciousness and became assimilated with feeling and emotion raised questions, too, about how to talk about or describe sensations. Disputing a view of the mind as an impressionable surface to be imprinted by external forms or pressures, the philosopher and poet James Beattie archly enquired, 'does the roar of a cannon bear any resemblance to the ball, or to the powder in shape, in weight or in magnitude? What figure has the pain of the toothach?', he asks, 'is it triangular, or circular, or of a square form?'[11] That such questions could be ventured was proof for Beattie of 'the absurdity of the theories that lead to them'.[12] Such a line of thinking may not have struck Keats as absurd though; or, if it did, it was a kind of absurdity that could be enjoyed as a prompt for imaginative ways of reconceiving sensation in language (the sound of a word that feels cool, for example).

So the impulse to communicate and express sensation in Keats's poetry can be divided loosely into two related modes: the first aims to depict sensory experience with mimetic accuracy, calling upon the reader to notice and recollect in the light of their own experience, as W. T. Arnold described; the second looks to produce a sensation that is more associative. The difference might be between an appeal to sensation that would notice and enter into the feeling of ivory keys beneath a musician's fingers, and the kind of sensation that would hear in poetry the feeling of floating on calm seas, or coolness, or safety in a hawthorn glade. One seeks to produce a literal, the other a perceptual reality.

In Keats's language of sensation, the difference can be seen in *The Eve of St. Mark* between the description of Bertha, as she rises from the fireside to press her forehead ''gainst the window-pane' (49), with the immediate recollection of coolness it evokes, and Keats's remark, written in a letter to his brother upon completing the poem, 'I think it will give you the sensation of walking about an old county Town in a coolish evening' (*L* 2, 201). Half-assured and half-hopeful, Keats's 'I think it will' intimates how this kind of sensation works by suggestion. It may be prompted by, though it is not directly related to, the early lines of the poem:

> The City streets were clean and fair
> From wholesome drench of April rains,
> And on the western window panes
> The chilly sunset faintly told
> Of unmatur'd green vallies cold,
>
> (4–8)

Keats's remark to his brother seems to offer the most perceptive commentary one could ask for to describe the effect of those lines.

The perceptual sensations that Keats's poetry produces in readers are necessarily partly associative and partly subjective, yet they still take their cue from the intimately precise, mimetic descriptions of sensory experience that his verse, even or perhaps especially at its most imaginative, seeks to make real. This dual working of sensation and the senses forms a characteristic quality of feeling across Keats's work, but the effect is most fully combined and condensed in the ode 'To Autumn'. The poem tacitly calls upon the reader to notice and feel pleasure in the way a season registers on the senses, to see ripeness in the bending of a tree, to hear the passing of time in the adjective 'moss'd' (5) or drawn out in the cyder-press's 'last oozings hours by hours' (22). In Keats's ode, the music of Autumn conveys both an immediacy of sense perception as well as the kind of aesthetic sensibility that could observe, 'somehow a stubble plain looks warm – in the same way that some pictures look warm' (*L* 2, 167), as Keats wrote in response to the sight of the Wiltshire landscape that prompted the poem. That warmth is also the warmth that his poem seeks to make felt. What the ode makes felt, too, is the sensation of fecundity and fulfilment in the sights, sounds and tactile pleasures that usher in a season; or the sensation of all life collecting itself, felt in an instant between the gathering and twitter of swallows.

In the early letter that had called for 'a Life of Sensations', Keats went on to distinguish his own approach from the workings of 'a complex Mind – one that is imaginative and at the same time careful of its fruits – who would exist partly on sensation partly on thought' (*L* 1, 186). But his poems display precisely this kind of complexity, and though that carefulness might look more like subsisting than the luxuriating in sensation more readily associated with Keats, it is also a kind of cherishing, which, as in 'To Autumn', becomes a loading and blessing in which thought and sensation conspire together.

Notes

1 William Empson, *The Structure of Complex Words* (London: Chatto & Windus, 1964), p. 254.

2 Matthew Arnold, *Complete Prose Works*, ed. R. H. Super, 11 vols. (Ann Arbor: University of Michigan Press, 1960–77), vol. 9, p. 207.

3 Arthur Hallam, 'On Some of the Characteristics of Modern Poetry, and on the Lyrical Poems of Alfred Tennyson', *The Writings of Arthur Hallam*, ed. T. H. Vail Motter (New York: MLA, 1943), pp. 182–98.

4 W. T. Arnold, *The Poetical Works of John Keats* (London: Kegan Paul, 1888), p. xxvii.
5 John Jones, *John Keats's Dream of Truth* (London: Chatto and Windus, 1969), p. 35.
6 John Bayley, *The Uses of Division* (London: Chatto and Windus, 1976), p. 109.
7 *P* 175n.
8 Quoted in Miriam Allott, ed. *The Poems of John Keats* (London: Longman, 1970), p. 225n.
9 Robert Browning, *The Ring and the Book*, *The Poetical Works of Robert Browning Volume IX*, ed. Stefan Hawlin and Tim Burnett (Oxford: Oxford University Press, 2004), XI. 816.
10 Beth Lau, *Keats's Paradise Lost* (Gainesville, FL: University Press of Florida, 1998), p. 77.
11 Quoted in Stuart Sperry, *Keats the Poet* (Princeton: Princeton University Press, 1973), p. 12.
12 James Beattie, *Dissertations Moral and Critical*, 2 vols. (Dublin, 1783), 2. 14.

CHAPTER 20

Prosody and Versification in the Odes

Michael O'Neill

In Walter Jackson Bate's 1945 monograph *The Stylistic Development of Keats*, still an essential companion to the poetry, Bate sees Keats's poetry as bound up with his responsiveness to 'the distinctive meaning and individuality of the particular'. This responsiveness is evidenced in the poet's delight 'in a sparrow or even a billiard-ball'. It prompts phrases such as 'the *moist scent* of flowers' in *The Fall of Hyperion* (I. 404) or it finds expression in the stress-bunching revision of '*drooping* lamp' to '*chain-droop'd* lamp' in *The Eve of St. Agnes* (357).[1] In the light of the work of Bate and others, the present chapter offers some brief thoughts on Keats's prosody and versification (including the mingling of sense and sound) in his odes.

As has often been noted, the great breakthrough of the odes is their dismantling and reconstruction of the sonnet. In 'If by dull rhymes our English must be chain'd' Keats writes an anti-sonnet sonnet; he protests against constraints of rhyme imposed by traditional schemes. He proposes and in the poem itself enacts 'Sandals more interwoven and complete / To fit the naked foot of Poesy' (5–6). The odes reap the benefit of this experimentation to find 'Sandals' that will 'fit Poesy's naked foot', a comparison that wittily undercuts itself since the pun on 'foot' (implying metrical form as well as limb) complicates the metaphor of clothing. After the varied stanzas forms of 'Ode to Psyche' they settle into the fixed, magically mutable pattern of quatrain followed by sestet typical of the Spring odes ('To Autumn' plays a variation by adding a line). The result does much to make possible 'lyric debate'.[2] The quatrain often begins a train of thought that is new but associatively related to the previous stanza; the sestet spreads, pervades, ramifies, a six-line fantail of suggestions.

Dialogue, re-orchestration, cross-ply rehearsals and returns, unexpected spacious evolvings: all are enabled by this structural device, as is the balance between warring impulses which from Coleridge to I. A. Richards has been seen as a hallmark of poetic equilibrium. Not that Keats's balances are ever less than precarious, even as they are always more than mere balancing acts. A question, 'Who are these coming to the sacrifice?' ('Ode on a Grecian Urn', 31), tells us implicitly that the poet has shifted his attention from individual lovers to a collective group; the line's prosody is even in its emphases and searching in its secondary stresses on 'Who' and 'these', while 'sacrifice' gains in weight and resonance through its contrast with shorter words and its occupation of the rhyme position. The stanza's close tells us that the true answer to that opening question is that there is no answer, since there is no witness:

> And, little town, thy streets for evermore
> Will silent be; and not a soul to tell
> Why thou art desolate, can e'er return.
> (38–40)

In the crucial first two feet of the lines, the prosody is regular. The writing achieves pathos through successive strong pauses after the fourth syllable in those first two lines and after the sixth syllable in the third. Pathos also derives from the 'management of open & close vowels', which Benjamin Bailey recalled as 'one of Keats's favorite topics of discourse': 'Keats's theory was, that the vowels should be so managed as not to clash with one another so as to mar the melody, – & yet they should be interchanged, like differing notes in music to prevent monotony.'[3] In the case of 'Ode on a Grecian Urn', this variety avoids aesthetic 'monotony' by implying a curve of feeling and the tonelessness of aftermath. The 'interplay' of the vowels – between, for example, the 'desolate' quality that attaches to the short *e* of 'tell' and 'desolate', and the yearning that surrounds the repeated sounds in 'town' and the personifying 'thou' – track, in miniature, the passage of 'unheard' (11) melodies into an eternal lifeless silence.

Silence in line 2 of the poem promised discoverable mystery; here Keats discovers the silence of temporal desolation, the word 'silent' taking an appropriately prominent position in line 39. The poet's speaking voice emerges audibly in the near-endearment 'little town', a town that precedes (35) and follows its possible location 'by river or sea shore, / Or mountain-built with peaceful citadel' (35–6). Its location may be uncertain; what is certain is that the town is 'emptied of this folk, this pious morn' (37). As the very sounds of 'mountain' and 'morn' chime with and against the 'town', they, along with the gesturing repetition of 'this', suggest the poet's imagination as it breathes life into what may have inspired but has eluded the craftsman's hand (the town is not to be seen on the urn's surface). The fact that 'not a soul can e'er return' is doubly felt because of the impulse to return evident in the poem's sounds, of which the rhyme involving 'return' is one, a word that holds within itself, in an 'overlooked pun', the 'urn' that cannot enable return.[4]

'Ode on a Grecian Urn', like 'Ode on Melancholy' and 'To Autumn', does not use shorter lines; 'Ode to a Nightingale' and 'Ode to Psyche' do. 'Ode to Psyche' concludes by building towards a rebuilt extended sonnet, its final two stanzas consisting, respectively, of fourteen and eighteen lines. Keats's management of these stanzas is strenuously playful. In the penultimate stanza, his rhymes almost mock the sonnet, in accord with his belated stance as one 'Too, too late for the fond believing lyre' (37). An alternately rhymed quatrain (Shakespearean) is followed by the envelope quatrain rhyme (*abba*) associated with the Petrarchan octave, before the poem allows two lines – 'So let me be thy choir, and make a moan / Upon the midnight hours' (44–5) – to be rhyme-free after a key line, 'I see, and sing, by my own eyes inspired' (43), even if they virtually reword in antiphonal form lines in the previous stanza (30–1). Then the stanza concludes with an alternately rhymed quatrain with two trimeters that have a jaunty feminine rhyme:

> Thy voice, thy lute, thy pipe, thy incense sweet
>   From swinged incense teeming;
> Thy shrine, thy grove, thy oracle, thy heat
>   Of pale-mouth'd prophet dreaming.
>
> (46–9)

Yet because of the extra stresses in 'pale-mouth'd prophet' the rhyme is not naively jaunty. Keats half-mocks yet wholly adopts the quasi-priestly role implied by 'teeming' and 'dreaming', as comes to the fore in the first line of the final stanza: 'Yes, I will be thy priest' (50), less a different note of music than a crashing chord.

In the final stanza, Keats makes fane-building, poem-construction, his topic; the poem builds its dome in air, or in 'some untrodden region of my mind' (51). The final stanza's first fourteen lines base themselves, as Bate notes, on the form of 'an exact Shakespearean sonnet, with the couplet removed from the end and placed after the octave to break the flow of the continual alternate-rhyming' (the stanza then appends a further quatrain).[5] The expressive effect of that couplet displacement is to place the gesture of achievement before rather than at the close of the poem. The lines in question, 'And in the midst of this wide quietness / A rosy sanctuary will I dress' (58–9) might almost have done for a conclusion. But Keats finishes less with an assertion of the creative will than with a testing of its hopes and aspirations; he brings in doubt along with affirmation. His 'fane'

(50) will depend on what he can 'feign' (62), the words glancing a little suspiciously at one another by virtue of being in the rhyme position. Psyche will receive 'all soft delight / That shadowy thought can win' (64–5), where, in 'shadowy', the flicker of an extra syllable casts a shade over 'thought'. Finally, bravely, Keats brings the poem round to its mythic source, and invokes 'A bright torch, and a casement ope at night, / To let the warm Love in!' (67–8). After the rallying stresses on 'bright' and 'torch', the last line turns like a key in a lock, freeing the poem from the cell of potential solipsism. What is allowed 'in' ('warm Love') can assist the attaining of all that 'shadowy thought can win'; the rhyme sings by its own ears inspired.

Bate draws attention to the cluster of technical devices that Keats uses in the odes to achieve greater richness and intensity of texture. They include a rejection of Latinate words in favour of words 'more native in origin', and a greater use of 'bilabials' and spondees (two consecutive strong stresses).[6] The spondaic point is one that might be paused over in relation to an example he helpfully supplies: the close of the 'Ode to a Nightingale'. The opening of this last stanza is often quoted, accruing brilliant commentary, as in Geoffrey Hill's austerely empathetic remark about the echo of 'forlorn': 'The echo is not so much a recollection as a revocation; and what is revoked is an attitude towards art and within art.'[7] The moment makes us realise that this apparently unpremeditated ode has just eavesdropped on itself, listened to and replayed a semantically shifting rhyme word in 'faery lands forlorn' (70). But one hears less about these lines:

> Adieu! adieu! thy plaintive anthem fades
> Past the near meadows, over the still stream,
> Up the hill-side; and now 'tis buried deep
> In the next valley-glades.
>
> (75–8)

Marking the spondees in '*near mead*ows', 'still stream', 'hill-side' and '*next val*ley' (emphases added), Bate argues that the 'distinctive use of scattered spondees, together with initial inversion, lend an approximate phonetic suggestion of the peculiar spring and bounce of the bird in its flight'.[8] Possibly so; but the lines also articulate an unwillingness fully to identify the bird-song with 'the fancy' (73) as a 'deceiving elf' (74). If body is given to the bird's winged departure, emphasis is also given to the poet's tracking of its departure and uncertain but half-yearning location of it in 'the next valley-glades'. Keats knows he has been in an enchanted place or state. He hopes by speaking of his experience and its catalyst as though they were a quotidian matter of meadow, hill and valley that they might be recapturable. The spondees help steady the poem; it regains its poise; the notion that 'the fancy' did not 'cheat' (73) at all must surely be one allowable implication of the wandering final questions: 'Was it a vision, or a waking dream? / Fled is that music: – Do I wake or sleep?' (79–80).

These lines mark a return to the use of a mid-line pause (caesura), employed a few times earlier in this poem of endlessly self-adjusting movements. The mid-line caesura reinforces the exultant ambiguity of 'Already with thee! tender is the night' (35) or the seductive allure of the song that 'Charm'd magic casements, opening on the foam / Of perilous seas' (69–70). Thanks to a well-judged revision – the draft read 'Was it a vision real or waking dream?' (*P* 372n) – the final lines of the ode puzzle the reader into seeking to resolve and reformulate the difference between a 'vision' and 'waking dream'. The result is an enriching quandary, complicated further by the final line's repetition of stress on the syllable 'wake'.

One thing that is sure, and accepted with elegiac nobility, is the fact that 'Fled is that music': the nightingale's and the poem's. The line's precursor passage in 'Sleep and Poetry' invites comparison:

> The visions all are fled – the car is fled
> Into the light of heaven, and in their stead
> A sense of real things comes doubly strong,
> And, like a muddy stream, would bear along
> My soul to nothingness…
>
> (155–9)

The phrase 'doubly strong' strikes the passage's key note, here, as the steady, even steadfast iambics enact a bracing recognition, 'A sense of real things'. The pause after 'nothingness' is momentary but marked, glimpsing how the poet's 'soul' might be borne along to 'nothingness'. The ode, returning to these lines, crystallises and compacts them; it takes from 'fled' the burden of supplying a rhyme word, positioning it at the start of the line, where it sheds a valedictory music, marked by a reversed stress. Using a medial caesura, this last line pivots and tilts halfway through, causing itself and the poem to spin on the question, 'Do I wake or sleep?'.

Spondee in the odes is a metrical vehicle of absorbed discovery, and among the discoveries made in 'Ode to a Nightingale' is the importance for poetry of the maligned 'sole self' (72). The phrase takes a spondaic pause at the close of the opening lines of the final stanza: 'Forlorn! the very word is like a bell / To toll me back from thee to my sole self!' (71–2). Keats's decision to bring out the soleness, the singular uniqueness, of the self shows in his revision from the draft's 'from thee unto myself' (see *P* 371n): 'sole self' intensifies 'myself', and suggests the significance of the self without whose presence and tensions there would be no flights of imagination. Through its versification, the last stanza lays bare the conditions that enable poetic activity, and in it the spondaic is Keats's marker of his own 'inscape' as Gerard Manley Hopkins, one of his major inheritors, will call it, and by extension that of any individual.[9]

The Keatsian prosodic signature involves wheelings and returns: 'Ay, in the very temple of Delight / Veil'd Melancholy has her sovran shrine' ('Ode on Melancholy', 25–6); 'Where are the songs of spring? Ay, where are they? / Think not of them, thou hast thy music too. –' ('To Autumn', 23–4). In these two exemplary odic turns, the rhythms move, in Middleton Murry's sure-footed phrase, 'towards a complete acceptance of a peculiar kind'.[10] The writing accommodates oppositions, latent and manifest; it offers and is attuned to an equable if sorrowing music. Prosodically, the iambic holds its own even as it is beaten into a sword of finer temper through initial stresses (apparent in all four lines) and regroupings (the reinforcing 'ay' and 'thou'). These rhythms suit a poetry that 'marks the before unapprehended relations of things, and perpetuates their apprehension', as Shelley has it in *A Defence of Poetry*.[11]

The lines quoted from 'Ode on Melancholy' attain a note that might, in one of Keats's own coinages, be termed 'high-sorrowful' ('Ode on a Grecian Urn', 29). They do so because the poem's third and final stanza in which they occur forsakes the commands and adjurations of the first two stanzas in favour of statement. The poem that intrigued and delighted with imperatives now offers the difficult balm of near-paradoxical declaration. The poem opens with a flurry of urgent monosyllabic negatives: 'No, no, go not to Lethe, neither twist / Wolf's-bane, tight-rooted, for its poisonous wine' (1–2). The lines win a complex melody from what feels like contending, even mutually obstructing impulses: both the rejection of oblivion and drug, and the attraction of these things, are marked in the clustering stresses of, say, 'Wolf's-bane, tight-rooted'. Stanza two depicts 'the melancholy fit' (11) as a force of nature, falling 'Sudden', as a reversed foot at the start of the line has it, 'from heaven like a weeping cloud' (12). The fit is also a humorously sardonic version of traditional Christian ideas of grace as it falls from 'heaven'. And yet the recollection is more than sardonic: if the 'weeping cloud' of the simile suggests lamentation, it quickly becomes an agent of restoration 'That fosters the droop-headed flowers all' (13).

Here and elsewhere in the ode, prosodic art is at the service of a concentrated array of suggestions, the droopiness of the flowers, for instance, granted full presence by the fifth syllable's additional beat. The stanza retains an element of play through its compilation of melancholy instances and how best to respond to them, concluding with the high-spirited aestheticism of feeding 'deep, deep upon' the mistress's 'peerless eyes' (20). Yet as Keats imagines that strangely non-reciprocal gaze he senses, in an electrifying transition that recalls effects in Donne (the third stanza of the 'The Sun Rising' is a case in point), that 'She' (both mistress and melancholy) 'dwells with Beauty – Beauty that must die' (21). The entire poem and the near-series of which it is part come to a rest and a focus in this line. It is central to Keats's prosody and versification that he can shape objective correlatives for this awareness. But the line itself seems far more than doctrine painfully proved on the pulses; it has the character of memorable dramatic utterance, as Keats seems to reach down to deep levels of the iambic tradition. His voice delays on 'dwell' and the repeated 'Beauty', giving both words their moment in the spotlight, before the conclusive force of 'must die', a spondaic hammer blow. But by realising the entwinement of beauty and dying, Keats is able to advance to the embittered, dignified vision of the end. There, he or his surrogate is rewarded and defeated in virtually the same poetic breath, as a stoically resolved iambic rhythm and echoic sound-patterning recognise: 'His soul shall taste the sadness of her might, / And be among her cloudy trophies hung' (29–30).

In 'To Autumn', as Keats comes to terms with what it is to be alive after Waterloo and indeed Peterloo, he writes a poetry that has foresuffered all and makes newly fortified and fortifying discoveries, as is shown by the remainder of that final stanza:

> Then in a wailful choir the small gnats mourn
> Among the river sallows, borne aloft
> Or sinking as the light wind lives or dies;
> And full-grown lambs loud bleat from hilly bourn;
> Hedge-crickets sing; and now with treble soft
> The red-breast whistles from a garden-croft;
> And gathering swallows twitter in the skies.
> (27–33)

Reversed feet cluster in the opening two stanzas with their intent movements of near-bodily involvement: 'Seasons of mists' (1), 'Close bosom-friend' (2), 'Drows'd with the fume of poppies' (17), 'Steady thy laden head' (20). By the time of the third stanza, there is a change; such stresses diminish. If they reappear, they do so in an elegiac minor key, as in 'Then in a wailful choir' or 'Hedge-crickets sing', to quote two phrases that go in different directions, the first the nearest thing to a tragic note in the stanza, or mock-tragic: it is 'the small gnats' who 'mourn'; the second the disciplined marker of a gathering up, a composing. Or they migrate, beautifully, to the middle of the line, as in the stress on 'bloom', a transitive verb that helps put a soft colour into the cheeks of dying.[12]

Helen Vendler argues finely that the poem's close, its 'glance that rises to the skies', 'is purged of self-referential pathos and nostalgia for the past. The Ode has floated free of its occasion, and ends poised in the sound of song, sufficient unto itself.'[13] That self-sufficiency, however, flowers out of a poem's search for what will suffice, a search embodied in the poem's versification, as Paul D. Sheats notes in relation to the line that haunts the poem through its double act of miming and exposing poetic and human hopes: 'Until they think warm days will never cease' (10):

> The line that exposes the ironic effect of summer's generosity (10) is made to conspire in this generosity, by forming a couplet that prolongs the stanza's closing cadence (cdecDDe). Here, in Keats's one readjustment of the May stanza, meter functions as a formal, nonsemantic analogue to the passage of time.[14]

In the ode, metre functions not only as 'a formal, nonsemantic analogue', but also as part of the poetry's achieved meanings. In 'To Autumn', as in the odes as a whole, prosody and versification shape and guide the relationship between poet and reader. Our sole selves blend, as a result of Keats's technical and expressive skill, with that of the poet, with whom we participate in the knowledge of 'other woe / Than ours', hoping to make of art a 'friend' ('Ode on a Grecian Urn', 47–8, 48).

Notes

1 See Walter Jackson Bate, *The Stylistic Development of Keats* (1945; Abingdon: Routledge, 2014), pp. 7, 6, 4, 2; italics in quotations are Bate's.

2 Walter Jackson Bate, *John Keats* (1963; London: Hogarth, 1992), p. 500.

3 *KC* 2, 277.

4 James L. O'Rourke, *Keats's Odes and Contemporary Criticism* (Gainesville, FL: University Press of Florida, 1998), p. 81.

5 Bate, *Stylistic Development*, p. 130. The Shakespearean sonnet form is present also in lines 1–14 and elsewhere in the poem (see Bate, *Stylistic Development*, p. 129).

6 Bate, *Stylistic Development*, pp. 134, 135.

7 Geoffrey Hill, 'Poetry as "Menace" and "Atonement"', in *The Lords of Limit: Essays on Literature and Ideas* (London: Deutsch, 1984), p. 4.

8 Bate, *Stylistic Development*, p. 139.

9 For Hopkins on 'inscape', see his letter to Robert Bridges, 15 February 1879, in Gerard Manley Hopkins, *The Major Works*, ed. Catherine Phillips (Oxford: Oxford University Press, 2002), p. 235.

10 John Middleton Murry, *Keats and Shakespeare: A Study of Keats' Poetic Life from 1816 to 1820* (London: Oxford University Press, 1925), p. 129.
11 *Percy Bysshe Shelley: The Major Works*, ed. Zachary Leader and Michael O'Neill (Oxford: Oxford University Press, 2003), p. 676.
12 See Jon Silkin, *The Penguin Book of First World War Poetry*, ed. with intro Jon Silkin (Harmondsworth: Penguin, 1979), pp. 66–7.
13 Helen Vendler, *The Odes of John Keats* (Cambridge, MA: Harvard University Press, 1983), p. 261.
14 'Keats and the Ode', in *The Cambridge Companion to Keats*, ed. Susan J. Wolfson (Cambridge: Cambridge University Press, 2001), p. 98.

PART IV

Poetic Contexts

CHAPTER 21

Poetic Precursors (1): Dante and Shakespeare

Chris Murray

When he visited the Isle of Wight in 1817, Keats found his guesthouse decorated with likenesses of historical figures. In correspondence he reports rearranging these images as a hierarchy, with William Shakespeare at the apex as the intended 'Presider' over Keats's genius (*L* 1, 142). Such tangible sense of his predecessors' presences is also a factor likely to have drawn Keats to a work that elaborates the affinity as physical companionship: in Dante Alighieri's *The Divine Comedy* (c. 1320) the elder poet, Virgil, leads Dante through hell and purgatory. These authors affected Keats profoundly, yet he hoped for practical results from his reading too. His friend Benjamin Bailey directed Keats towards Shakespeare and Dante, and the young poet adopted Bailey's ideas on literary influence as spiritual experience. Keats sought furthermore to extract real guidance from these exemplars on how to go about the business of professional authorship. Hence, his responses to Shakespeare are often personal and instinctive, but Keats also looked to Shakespeare for models to write sonnets, narrative poems, and plays. Although Dante's influence is less pervasive in Keats's oeuvre, its importance becomes evident from synopses of Keats's poems that equally describe the trajectory and episodic structure of the *Comedy*. In *The Fall of Hyperion*, the narrator is granted access to the divine realm by a female figure with godly qualities. The poet-speaker in 'La Belle Dame sans Merci' enjoins a shade to recount how he came to haunt a desolate spot. Such evidence for direct textual influence corroborates the idea of private communion with his predecessors. Yet Keats's reading is inseparable from a variety of other contexts in which he encountered the works of Shakespeare and Dante, including critical discourse, social dialogues, popular entertainment, and refraction in texts by other authors.

The high status held by Shakespeare and Dante was newly attained in Keats's lifetime. The idolisation of Shakespeare (Bardolotry) and his popular adoption as a national author gained momentum in the late eighteenth century. A pivotal event was actor David Garrick's 1769 Jubilee, a three-day festival devoted to Shakespeare which made Stratford-upon-Avon a site of pilgrimage. Amongst a smaller audience of literati, Dante's British reception underwent a favourable rehabilitation in the early nineteenth century. Ugo Foscolo authored two long articles on Dante for the *Edinburgh Review* in 1818. In particular, Dante's fortunes were revived after Samuel Taylor Coleridge took interest in Henry Cary's translation of *The Divine Comedy*, which had been neglected since Cary printed it privately in 1814. Impressed by Cary's text – the first complete, English version of the *Comedy* – Coleridge persuaded Taylor and Hessey to publish a new edition, which appeared in 1819.

While Shakespeare was known to readers of Keats's time as a comprehensive genius, a master of diverse literary forms, Dante's work was read partially and cautiously in Britain. Anglophone audiences were likely to know of *The Divine Comedy*, but not Dante's other works. Of the *Comedy*, the *Inferno* was read more widely than the *Purgatorio* and *Paradiso* canticles, and individual episodes attracted attention rather than Dante's journey itself, particularly the story of the adulterous lovers Paolo and Francesca, and the starvation of Ugolino and his children in Ruggieri's tower. Keats may have known paintings of scenes from the *Comedy* by Joshua Reynolds (1773) and Henry Fuseli (1806); certainly he knew the artist Moses Haughton, who engraved Fuseli's depiction of the Ugolino episode. Keats enthused over Taylor and Hessey's arrangement with Cary (*L* I, 296), and Leigh Hunt adapted the Paolo and Francesca episode as a narrative poem, *The Story of Rimini* (1816). Both Coleridge and William Hazlitt included analyses of Shakespeare and Dante in their lectures on literature.

The reputations of Shakespeare and Dante had started to take the shapes by which we now know them – as giants of the canon – but these authors were also discussed in ways that made them current and exciting during the Romantic period. Accordingly, novelty animates Keats's initial responses to Shakespeare. His first serious reading of Shakespeare followed Keats's resignation of medicine in favour of poetry. Keats had subsequently acquired a new literary circle; to quote Shakespeare in correspondence was communication in a special, shared language. Epistolary references to authors show Keats revelling in his social setting, and his eagerness to demonstrate literary credentials. Keats's early letters to Taylor and Hessey are dense with such allusions. He quotes from *The Merchant of Venice* (I. I. 154) to apologise for having 'wound about with circumstance' in a shy request for money (*L* I, 148). Keats tells Haydon that visiting the bank is 'worse than any thing in Dante' (*L* 2, 32). The many references to these predecessors in Keats's poetry – from direct borrowings to fainter echoes – must also be interpreted with his social context in mind. In his use of allusion, Keats presumes a literary readership.

Keats's first intense readings of Shakespeare and Dante occurred in similar circumstances. He brought Shakespeare's works to the Isle of Wight, and took Cary's translation of the *Comedy* on his walking tour of Scotland in 1818. Therefore these were doubly journeys into new realms; the encounter with new landscapes coincided with deep exploration of literature. Furthermore, Keats assigned a creative purpose to each journey. He travelled to the Isle of Wight primarily to compose *Endymion*. From the Scottish excursion, Keats hoped to acquire a repository of natural imagery. Hence the landscape inspired him to write that 'I shall learn poetry here' (*L* 1, 301). Keats's poetic responses to Shakespeare and Dante often recall the environments and sense of purpose in which he read them. 'On the Sea' (1817), a Petrarchan sonnet, alludes to Keats's contemporaneous reading of *King Lear* in its address to 'ye who have your eyeballs vext' (9). The 'wideness of the Sea' surveyed from the Isle of Wight is a metaphor for the intimidating scale of Shakespeare's achievement. The poem's final exhortation to 'brood / Until ye start as if the Sea Nymphs quired' articulates an uneasy contemplation of the ocean, and intimates Keats's need to 'start' to compose ('quire') in light of Shakespeare's example (13–14). Comparably, while Keats did not draft 'La Belle Dame' until 1819, the Dantescan encounter occurs in a 'wither'd' locale (3) that evokes Keats's impressions of 'dreary' Mull in 1818 (*L* 1, 346).

Two further sonnets capture Keats's intentions to equip himself, and subsequently to create, using materials sourced in the works of his predecessors. 'On Sitting Down to Read *King Lear* Once Again' (1818) dismisses the ease of 'golden-tongued Romance, with serene Lute' (1). Instead, the poet must embrace the literature of discord:

> Adieu! for, once again, the fierce dispute
> Betwixt damnation and impassion'd clay
> Must I burn through.
>
> (5–7)

In the sestet, Keats invokes Shakespeare with Dantescan imagery. The poet exhorts Shakespeare to guide him. As Dante does in the *Comedy*, he fears perdition in symbolic woods. From Shakespeare's example, the fires of 'torment' forge the poet. In conclusion, the sonnet expresses Keats's wish for rebirth as a significant poet. He implores Shakespeare to bestow 'wings' upon him. The imagined ascent of his talents recalls phoenix imagery that figures political resurgence in *Richard Duke of York* (*Henry VI* Part 3), I. 4. 36–7:

> When through the old oak forest I am gone,
>   Let me not wander in a barren dream:
> But, when I am consumed in the fire,
> Give me new phœnix wings to fly at my desire.
> (11–14)

The desired poetic flight occurs explicitly in a sonnet from the following year, 'As Hermes once took to his feathers light'. This vision is so powerful that the poet is almost effaced from the octet. In his dream journey, the speaker travels to Dante's Inferno, and witnesses the torment of Paolo and Francesca:

> that second circle of sad hell,
> Where in the gust, the whirlwind, and the flaw
> Of rain and hail-stones, lovers need not tell
>   Their sorrows.
> (9–12)

This is a more confident voice than that which responded to *Lear*. Because the lovers' grief is intuitive to the poet, he discards the Dantescan device of reported speech. Instead, Keats offers a Shakespearean experience of Dante's vision, in which the poet enters the minds of his subjects, sharing their sin, bliss, and torment. While the personal pronoun occurs thrice in the final three lines, its usage does not communicate a fixed identity, but signals the power of the poetic imagination to shift between perspectives:

> Pale were the sweet lips I saw,
> Pale were the lips I kiss'd, and fair the form
> I floated with, about that melancholy storm.
> (12–14)

Initially the poet speaks, but he becomes Francesca's lover Paolo, and joins her in the whirlwind. Keats draws on Shakespeare and Dante, but finally asserts his own vision, in which ecstasy can endure the Inferno.

Some of Keats's most important aesthetic and philosophical reflections are indebted to reading Shakespeare and Dante, but respond more specifically to contemporary discussions of those authors. He conceives of the 'camelion Poet', a mind of self-conscious impersonality that chooses to forget its own identity and assume others in order to relate their experiences (*L* 1, 387). This idea is influenced by Hazlitt, whose lectures Keats attended in 1818:

> [Shakespeare] was the least of an egotist that it was possible to be. He was nothing in himself; but he was all that others were, or that they could become … By an art like that of the ventriloquist, he throws his imagination out of himself, and makes every word appear to proceed from the mouth of the person in whose name it is given.[1]

Similarly, Keats writes that 'a Poet […] has no Identity – he is continually in for – and filling some other Body' (*L* 1, 387). In practice, Keats struggled with these principles. His assured endorsement of the 'camelion' in 1818 may implicitly repent of naivety in his earlier poems. Moreover, Keats felt that he could not abandon his identity entirely. To an author, money necessitated recognition. Hence in an 1820 letter to Percy Bysshe Shelley, Keats claims that '*an artist* must serve Mammon – he must have … selfishness perhaps' (*L* 2, 322–3). Therefore it would be exaggeration to infer that Keats forges a poetic credo from Hazlitt's criticism, although undoubtedly the discussion of Shakespeare is a key influence on Keats's fluctuating concept of authorship.

Keats's responses to Dante are consistent with philosophical interests among contemporaries such as Byron and Shelley, but run against the grain of the Italian poet's popular reception in Britain. British engagements with particular episodes in the *Comedy* reflect a commonplace disapproval of the poem as a whole. Dante originates the idea of a systematic afterlife. The respective inhabitants of hell, purgatory, and heaven are punished, penanced, or blessed in accordance with their behaviour on earth. Anglophone critics commonly found Dante's vision too Catholic, and complained especially that the torments of hell were too macabre. Considered representative of primitive values, the *Comedy* was dismissed on the same grounds as Gothic fiction. In his preface to *The Story of Rimini*, Leigh Hunt laments the 'melancholy absurdity of [Dante's] theology'. To Hunt, a strength of Francesca's love-narrative is that we 'lose sight' of Dante's Inferno.[2] On reading *Rimini*, Keats composed an appreciative sonnet, 'This pleasant tale is like a little copse' (1817). As Keats had probably not read the *Comedy* at this time, presumably it is fortuitous that his sonnet provides an allegory for the superficiality of Hunt's adaptation: the 'little copse' corresponds to Hunt's 'pleasant tale', in place of the gloomy wood where Dante experiences spiritual crisis at the outset of a metaphysical epic. By contrast with Hunt, it is clear from Keats's sonnet on Paolo and Francesca, with its absorption into the punitive whirlwind, that he became interested in Dante's comprehensive view of the afterlife.

Keats demonstrates a deep response to Dante's vision in his philosophical speculations. He theorises 'the gradations of Happiness even like a kind of Pleasure Thermometer', a tiered system evoking the circles of Dante's Inferno, the pavilions of Purgatory, and the spheres of Paradise. Keats elaborates in this note to Taylor, enclosed with an insertion to *Endymion* in 1818, that he perceives realisation of such a philosophy as the basis of his artistic development: it 'is my first Step towards the chief Attempt in the Drama' (*L* 1, 218–19). The idea of the gradated 'Pleasure Thermometer' appeals so greatly to Keats that he appears to realise its secondary, metaphorical application as he writes: he outlines a Dantescan system of progression, then proposes that such an invention could itself be part of a greater journey of professional development from philosophy, to poems, to drama. Keats compares 'human life to a large Mansion of Many Apartments' in a letter written later that year (*L* 1, 280). Here, Keats allegorises the development of consciousness as a passage between chambers of diverse experience. The 'vale of Soul-making' letter of 1819 summons a Dantescan image of massed shades. To traverse such terrain, Keats says, is educative: 'Do you not see how necessary a World of Pains and troubles is to school an Intelligence and make it a soul?' (*L* 2, 102). Adumbrating Dante's journey in this correspondence, Keats's contemplation of the soul recalls more specifically the cosmological discourses of *Paradiso*.

Keats's two attempts at Shakespearean stage tragedy, both from 1819, must be interpreted in light of contemporary critical discussion and theatrical production. Keats and Charles Brown intended their collaborative drama, *Otho the Great*, as a vehicle for Edmund Kean (1787–1833), the most acclaimed tragic actor of his generation. Keats knew the quirks of their intended leading man. In 1817 he wrote an article for *The Champion* to celebrate Kean's return to the stage after illness. Here, Keats credits Kean as a hierophant, who makes worldly the 'spiritual' aspects of Shakespeare's works. By quotation, Keats likens the eloquent Kean to Mark Antony (*Julius Caesar*, 5. 1. 34–5):

> The spiritual is felt when the very letters and points of charactered language show like the hieroglyphics of beauty: – the mysterious signs of an immortal freemasonry! … The sensual life of verse springs warm from the lips of Kean, and to one learned in Shakespearean hieroglyphics, – learned in the spiritual portion to which Kean adds a sensual grandeur: his tongue must seem to have robbed 'the hybla bees, and left them honeyless'.[3]

Keats quotes from Cary's translation of the *Comedy* to portray Kean 'sole apart retir'd, the Soldan fierce!' (4. 126). Dante sees the Sultan Saladin on the plains of Limbo, where he stands at a distance from groups that include Electra, Aeneas, and Julius Caesar. By this citation Keats praises Kean's distinguished acting, but it is also a barbed usage: notoriously, Kean declined to share the stage with actors who might be talented enough to steal his limelight.

Kean's performance was a version of Shakespearean tragic acting suited to an age that favoured melodrama and spectacle. Keats reports 'an indescribable gusto in his voice', and an 'intense power of anatomizing the passion of every syllable'.[4] Like the reference to Shakespearean 'hieroglyphics', these ideas are indebted to Hazlitt. In his essay 'On Gusto' (1816), Hazlitt defines the concept as 'giving … truth of character from the truth of feeling' in order to 'excite [the audience] by affinity'. However, unlike the sustained 'intense power' that Keats attributes to Kean, Hazlitt claims that Shakespeare's gusto is measured, 'not intense, but discursive'.[5] Hence it is clear that *Otho the Great* was not written solely to emulate Shakespearean tragedy, but to suit a forceful actor of whom Coleridge claimed, 'To see him act, is like reading Shakespeare by flashes of lightning'.[6] With Brown providing the plot, Keats composed verse intended to showcase Kean's tragic range. By turns, the main character, Ludolph, displays the eccentricity of Hamlet, the jealousy of Othello, the malice of Richard III, and the impetuosity of Lear. Ludolph learns that his fiancé, Auranthe, has a lover. When he misses an opportunity for revenge, and seems destined to die in the wilderness, Ludolph recalls the 'Must I remember?' of the anguished Hamlet (1. 2. 143), the 'melancholy boughs' of *As You Like It* (2. 7. 110), and Othello's wish for 'suffocating streams' (3. 3. 394). Keats assembles these Shakespearean phrases in a staccato pile-up fashioned for Kean's declamatory style:

> Must I stop here? Here solitary die?
> Stifled beneath the thick oppressive shade
> Of these dull boughs, – this oven of dark thickets, –
> Silent, – without revenge, – pshaw! – bitter end, –
> A bitter death, – a suffocating death, –
> A gnawing – silent – deadly, quiet death!
> Escap'd? – fled? – vanish'd? melted into air?
> She's gone! I cannot clutch her! no revenge!
>
> (5. 1. 18–25)

In his death throes, Ludolph's speech retrieves the image of resurgence that Keats used in the *King Lear* sonnet:

> this prince was gull'd and cheated,
> But from the ashes of disgrace he rose
> More than a fiery dragon, and did burn
> His ignominy up in purging fires!
>
> (5. 5. 133–6)

The draft of *Otho* uses 'Phœnix' for 'dragon'; closer still to the *King Lear* sonnet, and evidence that Keats's professional anxieties continued to permeate his work. Keats identified *Otho* as crucial to his livelihood: 'Whether I shall at all be set affloat upon the world depends now upon the success of the Tragedy' (*L* 2, 229). Despite his best efforts, *Otho* was not accepted for performance at the Theatre Royal, Drury Lane. Cruelly, this news followed earlier indications that the theatre would take *Otho* (*L* 2, 237). Although notice of this disappointment came from stage manager Robert William Elliston, the final decision was probably made by Drury Lane's tyrannical star, Edmund Kean. Rejection ensued from Covent Garden.

Soon after he completed *Otho* in August 1819, Keats commenced a new drama. He composed only four scenes of *King Stephen*, another tragedy conceived as a vehicle for Kean. The play begins in the aftermath of the Battle of Lincoln in 1141. Overrun by forces under the Holy Roman Empress Matilda, Stephen refuses to concede defeat. *Macbeth* is the primary influence on the brisk opening scenes, in which reports from the battlefield establish Stephen's character:

He sole and lone maintains
A hopeless bustle 'mid our swarming arms;
And with a nimble savageness attacks,
Escapes, makes fiercer onset, then anew
Eludes death, giving death to most that dare
Trespass within the circuit of his sword …
(1. 2. 10–15)

Stephen is a sufficiently conflicted figure for tragedy. His bravery verges on insanity. Stephen impresses his enemies in battle and charms his captors with eloquence. He was also a practical choice of subject: the resemblances to *Macbeth*, *Richard III*, and Shakespeare's history plays guaranteed that Drury Lane would already own the scenery and props needed to stage the play well. Yet Keats resigned *King Stephen* quickly. He may have been discouraged by rumours that Kean intended to leave London for America (*L* 2, 248).

Keats's two incomplete narrative poems on the fall of the Titans express his preoccupation with Shakespearean tragedy the same year, and his roughly contemporaneous re-reading of *The Divine Comedy*, this time in Italian (*L* 2, 212). Although Milton's influence dominates *Hyperion: A Fragment*, the disempowered Saturn also evinces Keats's lasting attention to *King Lear* and the *Comedy*:

tell me if this feeble shape
Is Saturn's; tell me, if thou hear'st the voice

Of Saturn; tell me, if this wrinkling brow,
Naked and bare of its great diadem,
Peers like the front of Saturn. Who had power
To make me desolate? whence came the strength?
(1. 98–103)

Keats responds to Dante by inverting the condition of the fallen. Identity persists amongst Dantescan shades, whose former existences are commemorated in the conditions of their immortality, and the narratives they supply. In contrast, Keats's Saturn intimates disassociation from his body, and wonders whether he is recognisable without the symbol of his past, the diadem. Comparably dispossessed by his children, Lear wonders, 'Does any here know me? This is not Lear' (*King Lear* [Conflated Text], 1. 4. 201). Although Keats does not imitate Dante formally, a manner of embedded *terza rima* is evident in certain three-line encapsulations that occur in his blank verse, such as this Dantescan declaration of ineffability:

Meanwhile in other realms big tears were shed,
More sorrow like to this, and such like woe,
Too huge for mortal tongue or pen of scribe.
(1. 158–60).

Keats uses this type of formulation several times in *Hyperion* (1. 34–6, I. 53–5, I. 65–7, and 2. 244–6).

Abandoning *Hyperion*, Keats commenced a new poem on the same theme. In addition to Keats's repeated reading of Dante over the previous few years, the favourable reception of Cary's second edition may have encouraged him to use the *Comedy* as a model for *The Fall of Hyperion*. The Dantescan pilgrimage is clearly a better means to consider a central question of Keats's *Hyperion* project: what becomes of fallen gods? This model allows the pilgrim to encounter the gods in stasis and engage sympathetically with their grief. The tension between the traveller and his guide, and the poet's tentative transition into the visionary realm, compensates for the Titans' inactivity. In addition, the salient features of *The Divine Comedy* are curiously appropriate to Keats's personal concerns in 1819. Dante's steps to the tiers of Purgatory become a figure for the ascent to poetic achievement, trepidatious in Keats's *Fall*, and perhaps especially so in light of his wait for Elliston's verdict on *Otho* that autumn. To 'ascend' or 'die' is the ultimatum before the poet (1. 107–8). In *The Fall*, Moneta takes the place of Beatrice, Dante's lost love and his guide to Paradise. Both adopt quotidian language and lead the respective poets to deeper perspicacity. Yet the priestess Moneta is a more ambiguous figure than Beatrice, consistent with the problematic female characters in Keats's contemporaneous narrative poems, and suggesting his anguish over Fanny Brawne. The gods of *Hyperion: A Fragment* debate whether to resist or rally, but *The Fall of Hyperion* offers a bleak vision of resignation, a transition redolent of Tom Keats's final illness and death in December 1818.

Keats's most accomplished poetry of 1819 manifests his deeper assimilation of influences. While the genres of tragedy and epic compel him towards imitation in the *Hyperion* project, Keats finds his original voice in *The Eve of St. Agnes*: influences are detectable but not restrictive. Aspects of the language are Shakespearean, while the plot hints at *Romeo and Juliet* and *Cymbeline*. Earl R. Wasserman in 1953 interpreted the poem as an allegory for spiritual ascent, comparable to the 'Mansion of Many Apartments' letter. *The Eve of St. Agnes* can be read in this light as evidence of Keats's growing dissatisfaction with Hunt. In response to the facility of Hunt's *Rimini*, Keats restores a Dantescan metaphysical framework to the forbidden love tale. *Rimini* as stimulus for a more sophisticated narrative poem resembles the departure from Hazlitt's view of Shakespearean gusto in Keats's assessment of Kean.

There is comparable reinvention of sources in the 1819 odes. These can be read as interrelated texts, which pursue poetic conceits to the depths exemplified by Shakespeare's sonnets. Moreover, these poems are haunted by the ghost of Hamlet's father. The speaker articulates a poetic vocation, troubled because it is unfulfilled. Four of the six 1819 odes recall *Hamlet*'s spectre by use of the word 'adieu' (*Hamlet*, 1. 5. 91–112). Psyche and Cupid, the three figures of 'Ode on Indolence', and the eponymous nightingale and Grecian urn inspire the speaker, but also prompt self-reproach for poetic failure, a version of Hamlet's inaction. Yet in 'To Autumn', such uncertainty subsides. Autumn, which can 'fill all fruit with ripeness to the core' (6), signifies poetic maturity, with a confident acknowledgement of influences. The phrase reverses Edgar's philosophy of dying in *King Lear*, 'ripeness is all' (Conflated Text, 5. 2. 11). Keats's counterintuitive presentation of ripeness – proceeding inwards from without – communicates his absorption and transformation of literature into something new. Undoubtedly Keats's reactions to Dante and Shakespeare follow intense reading, but he calibrates his responses to various personal and cultural contexts.

Notes

1 *The Selected Writings of William Hazlitt*, ed. Duncan Wu, 9 vols. (London: Pickering and Chatto, 1998), vol. 2, pp. 209–11.

2 *The Selected Writings of Leigh Hunt*, ed. John Strachan, 6 vols. (London: Pickering and Chatto, 2003), vol. 5, p. 165.
3 *John Keats, The Oxford Authors*, ed. Elizabeth Cook (Oxford: Oxford University Press, 1990), pp. 345–6.
4 Cook (ed.), *Keats*, p. 346.
5 *Selected Writings of William Hazlitt*, vol. 2, pp. 79–81.
6 *The Collected Works of Samuel Taylor Coleridge: Table Talk*, ed. Carl Woodring, 2 vols. (Princeton: Princeton University Press, 1990), vol. 1, p. 41.

CHAPTER 22

Poetic Precursors (2): Spenser, Milton, Dryden, Pope

Beth Lau

The literary movement we call Romanticism was shaped in significant ways by a rejection of Augustan and celebration of Renaissance poetry and aesthetics. Throughout most of the eighteenth century, Pope, Dryden, and their followers were considered the exemplars of excellence in English poetry, superior in their correctness to the luxuriant but undisciplined poetry of earlier eras. In the late eighteenth and early nineteenth centuries, however, the Renaissance began to be lauded as the golden age of English literature, its poetry considered more natural and imaginative than that of the tame Augustans. One of the developments that made possible the 'Renaissance Revival' in the Romantic period was the abolishment of perpetual copyright in 1774, which resulted in a proliferation of cheap reprints and anthologies of older works that previously had been inaccessible to all but the wealthy classes. Most of the major Romantic poets – including Keats – saw themselves as heirs to the Renaissance poetic tradition and defined their aesthetic principles and practice in reaction to eighteenth-century neoclassical verse, whose chief representative was Alexander Pope.

According to the Romantic view, Pope's polished, satiric verse, written in regular heroic couplets, had sacrificed passion for mere sense and correctness. He was often accused of being more French than English, in that his poetry followed literary rules proposed by French critic Nicolas Boileau. Satire was regarded as an inferior genre of poetry in that it was 'public, worldly, [and] aggressive', in contrast to the new aesthetic that defined poetry as personal, subjective, emotional, and idealising.[1] Because Pope's subjects in poems such as *The Rape of the Lock* and *The Dunciad* were the affairs of prominent people in contemporary society, his work was considered artificial, not inspired by the natural world and 'universal' human feelings.

Most of the people in Keats's circle subscribed to these views, and none more outspokenly than Keats's earliest mentor, Leigh Hunt. Hunt believed that Augustan poetry represented a decline in English literary history from its golden age in the sixteenth and seventeenth centuries. He particularly found fault with Pope's couplets, which he refers to as 'cuckoo-song verses, half up and half down'.[2] In a note to this passage, Hunt states that Spenser, Milton, and Ariosto are superior to 'Pope, Boileau, and their followers' of 'the French school', for 'the former will teach us to vary our music and to address ourselves more directly to nature'. In his Preface to *The Story of Rimini* (1816), Hunt declares that 'Pope and the French school … have known the least on the subject [of versification], of any poets perhaps that ever wrote. They have mistaken mere smoothness for harmony … their ears were only sensible of a marked and uniform regularity', unlike his own poetry which employs 'a freer spirit of versification' that he encourages others to follow.[3]

Keats at the beginning of his poetic career enthusiastically embraced Hunt's teachings. According to Henry Stephens, who shared lodgings with Keats when both were medical students at Guy's Hospital in 1816, Keats maintained that Pope 'was no poet, only a versifier' (*KC* 2, 209). The longest and most ambitious poems in Keats's first volume (1817), 'I stood tip-toe upon a little hill' and 'Sleep and Poetry', are written in the loose rhymed couplets Hunt advocated, which deviate from Pope's model by containing many run-on lines and varying the placing of pauses or caesuras, often after an unstressed syllable in the second half of the line instead of after a stressed syllable in the first half.[4] In 'Sleep and Poetry', moreover, Keats sketches a history of English literature that conforms to Hunt's views. Keats refers to an earlier age of English poetry when 'the Muses were nigh cloy'd / With honors', which was followed by 'a schism / Nurtured by foppery and barbarism' when poets 'sway'd about upon a rocking horse, / And thought it Pegasus' and 'were closely wed / To musty laws lined out with wretched rule / And compass vile' in obedience to 'Boileau' (178–9, 181–2, 194–6, 206). Keats goes on to express his belief that contemporary poetry, especially that 'upstirr'd / From out its crystal dwelling in a lake', by which he meant Wordsworth and other 'Lake Poets', has entered 'a fairer season' that promises to revive the spirit of the Renaissance (224–5, 221).

This passage in 'Sleep and Poetry' had a significant impact on Keats's critical reception. Although many literary people shared Hunt's and Keats's belief that Pope and his followers represented an unfortunate decline in English verse, others continued to champion Pope and deplore new schools of poetry that deviated from his example. From 1806 to 1826, an impassioned debate that came to be known as 'the Pope Controversy' played out in various periodicals and other publications, in which numerous supporters and detractors of Pope argued the merits of his poetry.[5] This debate informed many of the reviews of Keats's (as well as Hunt's) work. John Wilson Croker begins his dismissive review of *Endymion* in the *Quarterly Review* by identifying Keats as a 'disciple' of Hunt, who in his Preface to *The Story of Rimini* had expressed his 'contempt of Pope, Johnson, and such like poetasters and pseudo-critics'. Croker particularly faults Keats's versification, which deviates from neoclassical verse in that 'There is hardly a complete couplet inclosing a complete idea in the whole book', and Croker later quotes passages that he refers to sarcastically as 'specimens of [Keats's] prosodial notions of our English heroic metre'.[6] John Gibson Lockhart in his infamous 'Cockney School of Poetry' article on Keats in *Blackwood's Edinburgh Magazine* singles out Keats's treatment of Pope in 'Sleep and Poetry' for special condemnation, calling it 'a long strain of foaming abuse against a certain class of English Poets, whom, with Pope at their head, it is much the fashion with the ignorant unsettled pretenders of the present time to undervalue'. Although Lockwood actually shared the belief that 'Pope was not a poet of the same high order with some who are now living', such as Wordsworth, he felt 'uneducated and flimsy striplings' like Hunt and Keats were not entitled to denigrate Pope.[7] Even Byron, who shared Hunt's and Keats's political views and whose poetry, as he himself recognised, participated in the new Romantic aesthetic, sided with the defenders of Pope and attacked Keats for his denigration of Augustan writers in 'Sleep and Poetry'.

Sympathetic reviewers of Keats's poetry, by contrast, often expressed their agreement with his opinions of Augustan and Renaissance poetry. Peter George Patmore's review of *Endymion* praises the 'freedom, sweetness, and variety' of the poem's 'melody', and counsels readers that 'To judge of the comparative extent of this praise, turn at random to Pope's Homer, or even Dryden's Virgil, and read two or three pages'.[8] John Hamilton Reynolds in his review of Keats's 1817 volume declares 'Sleep and Poetry' 'the most powerful and the most perfect' poem in the collection and singles out for praise the passages conveying Keats's 'opinion of the Elizabethan age, – of the Pope's school,–and of the poetry of the present day'.[9]

If Pope was an anti-model for the young Keats, Spenser was his first love and positive role model or 'Presider' (*L* 1, 142). Charles Brown states that 'It was the "Faery Queen" that awakened [Keats's] genius', and Charles Cowden Clarke left a memorable account of the occasion when Keats first borrowed Clarke's copy of *The Faerie Queene* and went through it 'as a young horse would through a spring meadow – ramping!'.[10] Keats's first extant poem, 'Imitation of Spenser' (1814), consists of four of the nine-line stanzas Spenser used for his *Faerie Queene* (rhymed ababbcbcc), and many of Keats's other early poems such as 'Specimen of an Induction to a Poem' and 'Calidore' allude to Spenser's works.

Keats's first major attempt at a long poem, his *Endymion: A Poetic Romance*, is indebted to Spenser in a number of ways, including the genre announced in its subtitle. Although he is a Greek shepherd rather than a Medieval knight, Keats's protagonist, like many of Spenser's heroes, is engaged in a quest; he particularly resembles Prince Arthur who like Endymion is seeking a beautiful woman who appeared to him in a dream (see *The Faerie Queene*, Book 1, canto 9, stanzas 13–15). Despite many Spenserian elements, the poem is not written in Spenserian stanzas but in the loose, run-on couplets Hunt advocated. Keats may have been further influenced by Hunt's belief that Spenser's stanza is not 'pleasing now-a-days' except in 'humorous or satirical' works.[11]

Keats was dissatisfied with *Endymion*, and after he finished the poem he was determined to adopt new styles and poetic role models. A sonnet written in January 1818 indicates which writer Keats turned to at this point. In 'Lines on Seeing a Lock of Milton's Hair' Keats extols Milton's poetry as a 'temple of sweet noise' (12) and refers to himself as a worshipper 'Who, to thy sacred and ennobled hearse, / Would offer a burnt sacrifice of verse' (8–9). Milton was a towering figure for all the major Romantic poets. His *Paradise Lost* was regarded as the greatest epic poem in English, worthy to stand alongside those of Homer and Virgil. On the one hand, Milton was inspiring to later writers, as he offered a model of the poet as an almost Godlike being that others might emulate. On the other hand, it was easy to feel intimidated by Milton's example and fear one could not measure up to it.

In the winter and spring of 1818, however, Keats was determined to learn from the greatest literary masters, and he embarked on an intense study of Milton that is documented by the extensive notes and markings he made in his copy of *Paradise Lost*, which survives at Keats House. The fruit of his engagement with Milton in 1818 was *Hyperion*, written in the fall of that year. Keats did not complete his Miltonic epic, however; he abandoned it at 136 lines into Book 3. Critics have explored various reasons why Keats gave up *Hyperion* (and his later rewrite, *The Fall of Hyperion*). These reasons range from the idea that the poem was too closely imitative of *Paradise Lost* to the opposite problem – that it was not Miltonic enough. Jonathan Shears, for example, claims that *Hyperion* lacks the action and coherence of *Paradise Lost* and reads as 'a series of lyrical moments … rather than a sustained narrative'.[12]

In January 1819, Keats turned from Milton back to his first love Spenser for inspiration in writing *The Eve of St. Agnes*, his first poem in Spenserian stanzas since *Imitation of Spenser*. *St. Agnes* is generally considered Keats's most successful narrative poem and the first of the major works of 1819 for which he is best known. Greg Kucich says *St. Agnes* 'seems both quintessentially Spenserian and utterly modern at the same time'.[13] It is also quintessentially Spenserian and utterly Keatsian. *St. Agnes* conveys Keats's ability to draw extensively upon another writer but create a work uniquely his own.

By the summer of 1819 Keats was feeling beleaguered. He was short of money and confronting the fact that his first two books had not sold well and had been ridiculed in harsh reviews. He was also in love but aware that he could not marry without the means of supporting a wife and family. If he could not make a living by writing poetry, he might have to revert to his medical training for employment; he considered becoming a ship's surgeon (*L* 2, 112–17). In the end, however, he could not bear to give up poetry and so left London for the Isle of Wight and then Winchester, where he was determined to write popular, marketable works. One of these was a play, *Otho the Great*, which he composed in collaboration with Charles Brown, who had previously written a comic opera that enjoyed a successful run at Drury Lane Theatre. Another project was the poem *Lamia*, which Keats believed contained 'that sort of fire … which must take hold of people in some way – give them either pleasant or unpleasant sensation', for 'What they want is a sensation of some sort' (*L* 2, 189).

Keats adopted the story of *Lamia* from Robert Burton's *Anatomy of Melancholy*, but its verse form derived from Dryden's poetry. Charles Brown states that Keats wrote the poem 'with great care, after much study of Dryden's versification' (*KC* 2, 67), and Richard Woodhouse after hearing Keats recite the poem told John Taylor that 'The metre is Drydenian heroic – with many triplets, & many alexandrines' (*L* 2, 165). For the first time since *Endymion*, Keats composed a major poem in heroic couplets, but not in the loose, enjambed style of his early verse. Nor did he model his couplets on the 'cuckoo-song verses' of Pope (Hunt, *Feast*, line 18) that he had disparaged in 'Sleep and Poetry'. Dryden offered a middle ground between these two extremes, for his heroic couplets followed Augustan practice but were considered more varied and flexible than Pope's. Hunt in fact cited Dryden as a model for the 'freer spirit of versification' he employed in *The Story of Rimini*.[14]

Hunt claims that *Rimini* differs from Dryden's work in that it conveys more 'sympathy with the tender and the pathetic',[15] but when he wrote *Lamia* Keats wanted to eschew sentiment, which he felt would provoke ridicule in reviews. 'It is possible,' he tells Woodhouse, 'to write fine things which cannot be laugh'd at in any way', and he believes 'There is no objection of this kind to Lamia' (*L* 2, 174). One reason Keats is likely to have turned to Dryden is that the latter's work was frequently characterised as bold and masculine. Hunt describes Dryden's versification as 'vigorous'.[16] William Cowper praises the 'manly rough line' of Dryden, and John Gibson Lockhart approves Dryden's 'masculine wit and good sense'.[17] William Hazlitt claims Dryden is 'a bolder and more varied versifier than Pope. He was a more vigorous thinker, a more correct and logical declaimer, and had more of what may be called strength of mind than Pope.'[18] Dryden was even criticised for the sexual license in some of his poems, but this aspect of his work would also have appealed to Keats at this time. In September 1819 Keats wished to make *The Eve of St. Agnes* more sexually explicit, and when Woodhouse objected, declared that 'he does not want ladies to read his poetry: that he writes for men' (*L* 2, 163).

Keats, who had been characterised as effeminate and juvenile in the hostile reviews of *Poems* and *Endymion*, apparently wished to adopt Dryden's vigorous, masculine style and outlook in *Lamia*. He frequently employs a knowing, worldly wise tone about women and love, as when the narrator declares at the opening of Part 2, 'Love in a hut, with water and a crust, / Is – Love forgive us! – cinders, ashes, dust … That is a doubtful tale from faery land, / Hard for the non-elect to understand' (2. 1–2, 5–6). Part I of *Lamia* begins

> Upon a time, before the faery broods
> Drove Nymph and Satyr from the prosperous woods,
> Before King Oberon's bright diadem,
> … … … … … … …… … … … … … … …
> Frighted away the Dryads and the Fauns
> … … … … … … …… … … … … … … …
> The ever-smitten Hermes empty left
> His golden throne, bent warm on amorous theft.
> (I. 1–8)

Robert Gittings believes these lines are indebted to Dryden's modernisation of Chaucer's *Wife of Bath's Tale*: 'In Days of Old, when *Arthur* fill'd the Throne … The King of Elfs and little fairy Queen / Gamboll'd on Heaths, and danc'd on ev'ry Green' (1–4).[19] Another source may have been the opening lines of *Absalom and Achitophel*, one of the passages in Dryden's work often condemned as immoral.[20]

> In pious times, ere priestcraft did begin,
> Before polygamy was made a sin,
> When man on many multiplied his kind,

Ere one to one was cursedly confined;
... ...
Then Israel's monarch, after heaven's own heart,
His vigorous warmth did variously impart
To wives and slaves.

(1–9)

Keats's poem waxes nostalgic about an earlier age when the promiscuous god Hermes could freely satisfy his lust, as Dryden praises patriarchal times when King David could 'impart' his 'vigorous warmth' to many women.

The supernatural serpent-woman Lamia is often read as a metaphor for the visionary imagination, and she dies when the empirical philosopher Apollonius exposes her as a dangerous illusion. She is similar to the beautiful but deceptive Spenserian figure of Romance that Keats banishes in favour of Shakespearean tragedy in 'On Sitting Down to Read *King Lear* Once Again'. In *Lamia*, the style of poetry preferred to entrancing but false romance is not Shakespearean tragedy but urbane, rational, Drydenian verse. Apollonius in fact resembles Dryden as described by Hazlitt: a 'vigorous thinker', 'logical', with great 'strength of mind'. This reading is complicated, however, by the fact that Lamia is presented sympathetically and Apollonius unsympathetically in the poem's conclusion, and Lycius dies when he is deprived of his supernatural lover. If Keats wished to be as manly, rational, and unsentimental as Dryden, he did not quite succeed in *Lamia*, which retains a fondness for the opposing qualities.

In the fall of 1819, Keats composed a poem that can be considered even more Augustan than *Lamia*. *The Jealousies* is a satire of contemporary political and literary figures, after the manner of Pope, Dryden, and Byron, whose *Don Juan*, Cantos 1 and 2, had recently appeared. The poem depicts a promiscuous fairy King Elfinan who has a passion for mortal women that is considered a crime in his kingdom, and he has reluctantly agreed to marry the fairy Princess Bellanaine at the urging of his parliament. These incidents parallel the affairs of the Prince Regent, a notorious womaniser who had illegally married a Catholic and who reluctantly agreed to marry Caroline of Brunswick in 1795 at the behest of his father the king, in exchange for having his debts paid by Parliament. George the Prince Regent never liked Caroline and separated from her in 1796. In 1819 their marriage was much in the news as George was seeking grounds to divorce his wife. Keats participates in the public debate over the royal couple in his burlesque of an undignified fairy prince and a pampered princess.[21]

One might think that Keats would have composed his first full-fledged satire in heroic couplets, especially since he had recently imitated Dryden's versification in *Lamia*. Instead, the poem is written in Spenserian stanzas. It was not uncommon for Spenser's stanza to be used for satire, as Pope did in 'Spenser. The Alley', a mock heroic description of squalid urban neighborhoods. We recall that Hunt believed the stanza was most appropriate for 'humorous or satirical' works. But by employing this stanza and borrowing other elements from Spenser, such as the name Elfinan (from *FQ* 2. 10. 72) and the setting in a fairy kingdom, Keats may also have intended to satirise Spenser. Or rather, Keats may be satirising his earlier self, the young poet who had adored the lush imagery and enchanted world of *The Faerie Queene*. In fact, *The Jealousies* is filled with parodic references to other Keats poems, including *The Eve of St. Mark*, *The Eve of St. Agnes*, and 'Ode to a Nightingale', almost as if Keats had taken on the persona of the hostile reviewers who attacked his earlier works. Moreover, around the time Keats composed *The Jealousies* he was considering earning a living by writing for periodicals (see *L* 2, 174, 176–81). As Steven Jones says, Keats planned 'a sacrificial shift … from poetic romance to journalistic satire' in a dramatic reversal of his initial aesthetic principles and literary role models.[22]

The Jealousies remained unfinished after Keats became ill in February 1820, and from that point on he wrote no more poetry. Joseph Severn, however, reports that when he and Keats were travelling to Italy the latter told him of a poem he wished to write. 'It was Keats [*sic*] intention', Severn told John Taylor, 'to make a long Poem upon the Story of Sabrina' from Milton's *A Mask* or *Comus*; 'he mentioned this many times to me … he intended Sabrina to be modelled on Spencers Una – or its principal to have been moral Beauty'.[23] Sabrina was made tutelary goddess of the Severn River after she leaped into its waters to escape being killed by her stepmother. In *Comus*, she is summoned by the Attendant Spirit to break the spell cast on The Lady because 'maid'nhood she loves, and will be swift / To aid a Virgin, such as was her self / In hard besetting need' (855–7).[24] Una is the pure lady and representative of the one true faith in Book 1 of *The Faerie Queene*, and Sabrina's story is also told in *FQ* 2. 10. 17–19. At the end of his life, Keats reverted to Spenser and Milton as his presiders and even embraced the 'moral beauty' of their praise of female chastity. He no longer sought to imitate the worldly, satirical style of Dryden and other Augustan writers but returned to his Romantic roots, which drew nourishment from the great Renaissance poets.

Notes

1 Steven E. Jones, *Satire and Romanticism* (New York: St. Martin's, 2000), pp. 8, 5–6.
2 Leigh Hunt, *The Feast of the Poets* (1814 ed.), line 18, in *The Selected Writings of Leigh Hunt*, vol. 5, ed. John Strachan (London: Pickering and Chatto, 2003).
3 Hunt, *Selected Writings*, pp. 54, 167.
4 See Walter Jackson Bate, *The Stylistic Development of Keats* (1945; New York: Humanities Press, 1962), pp. 19–28.
5 See Upali Amarsinghe, *Dryden and Pope in the Early Nineteenth Century: A Study of Changing Literary Taste 1800–1830* (Cambridge: Cambridge University Press, 1962), pp. 130–4, 222–3.
6 Donald H. Reiman, ed., *The Romantics Reviewed*, Part C, 2 vols. (New York: Garland, 1972), vol. 2, pp. 768, 769.
7 Reiman, *Romantics Reviewed*, vol. 1, p. 91.
8 Reiman, *Romantics Reviewed*, vol. 2, p. 559.
9 Reiman, *Romantics Reviewed*, vol. 1, pp. 261–2.
10 *KC* 2, 55; Charles and Mary Cowden Clarke, *Recollections of Writers* (London: Centaur Press, 1969), p. 126.
11 *Feast of the Poets*, in Hunt, *Selected Writings*, p. 58.
12 Jonathan Shears, *The Romantic Legacy of 'Paradise Lost'* (Farnham: Ashgate, 2009), p. 178. For an analysis of the *Hyperion* poems, see also Susan Wolfson's 'Epic and Tragedy' essay in this volume.
13 Greg Kucich, *Keats, Shelley, and Romantic Spenserianism* (University Park: Pennsylvania State University Press, 1991), p. 209. Kucich provides the most thorough study available of Keats's poetic dialogue with Spenser.
14 Preface, *Story of Rimini*, in Hunt, *Selected Writings*, p. 167; *The Autobiography of Leigh Hunt*, ed. J. E. Morpurgo (London: Cresset, 1949), p. 258.
15 *Autobiography*, p. 258.
16 *Autobiography*, p. 258.
17 Qtd. in Amarsinghe, *Dryden*, pp. 81, 120.
18 'On Dryden and Pope', *The Selected Writings of William Hazlitt*, ed. Duncan Wu, 9 vols. (London: Pickering and Chatto, 1998), vol. 2, p. 238.
19 Robert Gittings, *John Keats: The Living Year* (London: Heinemann, 1954), p. 224.
20 See Amarsinghe, *Dryden*, p. 11n. 1. John Dryden, *Selected Poems*, ed. Paul Hammond and David Hopkins (Harlow: Pearson, 2007).
21 See Jones, *Satire*, p. 127.
22 Jones, *Satire*, p. 127.
23 Joseph Severn, *Letters and Memoirs*, ed. Grant F. Scott (Aldershot: Ashgate, 2005), p. 190; see also p. 172.
24 *The Complete Works of John Milton, Vol. 3: The Shorter Poems*, ed. Barbara Kiefer Lewalski and Estelle Haan (Oxford: Oxford University Press, 2012).

CHAPTER 23

Contemporaries (1) (and Immediate Predecessors): Tighe, Radcliffe, Southey, Burns, Chatterton, Hunt, Wordsworth

Michael O'Neill

Keats drew from a great range of contemporary poetry in ways which are in accord with a poetry that is open to interpretation, often ambivalent, and riddling. Anne Mellor persuasively sees him as a poet who experiences 'discomfort with being aligned with the feminine', but who plays out in his work forms of 'cross-gendering', such cross-gendering being apparent, for her, at the end of 'Ode to Psyche', where Keats identifies with both male and female perspectives.[1] The ode reveals a veiled debt and implicit tribute to the influence of Mary Tighe and her narrative poem in Spenserian stanzas, *Psyche*, and Keats's ear was attuned to the work of female poets. Jane Stabler has shown how patterns of structure and phrase in poems by Ann Radcliffe such as 'Morning, on the Sea-Shore' leave their impression on 'Ode to a Nightingale' and 'Ode on a Grecian Urn'.[2]

Yet the influences on 'Ode to Psyche' are multiple. It is suffused with echoes of Wordsworth, as Keats imagines building a temple 'In some untrodden region of my mind' (51), a temple which will attract to itself 'shadowy thought' (65). Those 'thoughts' are begotten by Wordsworthian 'shadowy recollections' (152) in his 'Ode: Intimations of Immortality'. They bear witness to Keats's recognition that, like Wordsworth in the Prospectus to *The Recluse*, part of the Preface to *The Excursion*, he 'must tread on shadowy ground' (28).[3] In general, Keats, this chapter will argue, is a poet of remarkable openness to the work of his contemporaries and immediate forebears.

Wordsworth will attract the lion's share of attention. But his influence on Keats is inseparable from Keats's reaction to other poets (his responses to Coleridge, Byron, and Shelley are the subject of the following chapter). Keats associates awareness of sorrow and grief with Wordsworth, a poet concerned with 'the "burden of the Mystery"' (*L* 1, 281), and these states take centre-stage in the opening depiction of Saturn in the first *Hyperion*, stilled, fallen, and 'realmless' (1. 19), as Keats's loss-magnetising adjective has it.[4] Yet the poem also draws stylistic sustenance from Wordsworth's contemporaries. Two crucial lines rework a passage from Southey's *Thalaba*, in which reader and hero meet a damsel that 'seemed sorrowful, but sure / More beautiful for sorrow' (Bk. II, lines 383–4).[5] Twinning words, 'sorrow' and 'beauty', close to his poem's thematic heart, Keats exclaims, describing Thea's face, 'How beautiful, if sorrow had not made / Sorrow more beautiful than Beauty's self' (I. 35–6). His retentive memory conjures up Southey's lines, and his imagination shapes them into a form that redefines the meaning, in context, of the shopworn 'beautiful'.

Robert Burns and Thomas Chatterton stayed with Keats as exemplars of 'mighty Poets in their misery dead' (123), in Wordsworth's phrase from 'Resolution and Independence'. Burns is the subject of meditation about the relationship of a poet's life to his work in Keats's writing during his northern walking tour. A possible catalyst is that Burns had become the centre for such meditation after Wordsworth's *A Letter to a Friend of Robert Burns* (1816), which, as Beth Lau points out, was owned by Benjamin Bailey, Keats's friend, and referred to in critical terms by Hazlitt in his lecture of February 1818 'On Burns, and the Old English Ballads'.[6]

'Tam o' Shanter' is the point of departure for a bout of admiring verbal mimicry in Keats's description of a country dance that was 'indeed "no new cotillon fresh from France." No they kickit & jumpit with mettle extraordinary, & whiskit ... & stampt it, & sweated it, tattooing the floor like mad' (*L* I, 307). This evocation is in prose, but, in its mixture of vigour and a more cerebral idiom ('mettle extraordinary'), it captures an essence of Burns's style. And yet Burns's 'Misery is', Keats comments a little later, 'a dead weight upon the nimbleness of one's quill' (*L* I, 325).

Burns and his native Scotland provoke Keats to reflect on the conflicted and possibly dubious nature of poetic achievement in another sonnet, 'On Visiting the Tomb of Burns', which sponsors the thought, running from octave to sestet, that 'All is cold beauty; pain is never done / For who has mind to relish, Minos-wise, / The real of beauty' (8–10). This riddling wording comes close to suggesting that the 'real of beauty' is to be 'cold', a 'shadowy thought' that preoccupies later poems by Keats, especially 'Ode on a Grecian Urn' and *The Fall of Hyperion*. At the same time, 'relish', with its urge to confront the 'real' in a spirit of savouring appreciation, anticipates 'Ode on Melancholy'. Burns's 'Misery', to which even relatively playful poems such as 'To a Mountain-Daisy' bear witness, is a presence in the rhyming septenaries, possibly influenced by Wordsworth's 'Star Gazers', of 'There is a joy in footing slow across a silent plain'.[7] The poem concludes with a 'prayer / That man may never lose his mind on mountains bleak and bare' (45–6). And Burns leaves his mark on 'La Belle

Dame sans Merci', 'the cold hill's side' (26, 44) recalling Keats's response to Burns.[8] Surprised by the beauty of Burns's 'native place', Keats writes: 'the Idea I had was more desolate, his rigs of Barley seemed always to me bur a few strips of Green on a cold hill – O prejudice!' (*L* 1, 323). Yet that prejudiced 'Idea' re-emerges in the 'desolate' landscape of the ballad.

If Keats was conscious, in his response to Burns, of wishing to 'refine the true beauty of the older poet's achievement without sentimentalising or obscuring the actual pain or hardship of his career', his reaction to Thomas Chatterton was less guarded.[9] Chatterton earns Keats's praise throughout his short career. *Endymion* is 'INSCRIBED TO THE MEMORY OF THOMAS CHATTERTON'. When Keats turns away from Milton in 1819, Chatterton is the poet to whom he has recourse in his belief that 'English ought to be kept up' (*L* 2, 167). Keats writes: 'He is the purest writer in the English Language. He has no French Idiom, or particles like Chaucer<s>– 'tis genuine English idiom in English words' (*L* 2, 167). Although there is an unintended irony in the association of Chatterton, shrewd faker of a past that never was, with the 'genuine', the relevance of Keats's remark to the lexical choices in 'To Autumn', with its preference for concrete words uninfluenced by 'French idiom', is evident. An example is the echo in 'To bend with apples the mossed cottage-trees' (5) of Chatterton's *Aella* (1777), 'When the fayre apple, rudde as even skie, / Do bend the tree unto the fructyle ground' (184–5).[10] Keats has dispensed with Chatterton's more abstract adjective 'fructyle' and made the movement of the line enact the bending of the trees under their load of fruit. Chatterton also enchanted Keats's ear; Benjamin Bailey reports how the young poet would recite, or *chant*, in his peculiar manner the following stanza of the 'Roundelay sung by the minstrels of Ella';

> *Come with acorn cup & thorn,*
> Drain my hertys blood away;
> Life & all its good I scorn;
> Dance by night or feast by day.
> (*KC* 2, 276)

The interlaced vowels and mingling of feelings – death-drawn and joyously hedonistic – find their way into Keats's poetry.

Leigh Hunt showed Keats how to write in an apparently improvisatory, brisk, sensuous, politically liberal, and sociable style. He is the single most important figure in Keats's emergence as a poet in his 1817 *Poems* and *Endymion*, an influence not missed by contemporary reviewers. Bate supplies the needful technical analysis of Hunt's effect on Keats's early sonnets and couplets.[11] Technique provides the quill with which self writes the world, and Keats drank eagerly from the heady brew of Hunt's challenges to Augustan prosodical precepts and practice. Bate points to Keats's Huntian preference for pauses after the seventh syllable, supplying as an example: 'Kind Hunt was shut in prison, (x) yet has he, / In his immortal spirit, (x) been as free' ('Written on the Day that Mr. Leigh Hunt Left Prison', 2–3; see also lines 9–10 in the same poem).[12] This heterodox use of the pause is in keeping with the poem's celebration of what it is to be 'free'. Bate finds traces of Shakespeare, Milton, and Wordsworth in these Hunt-influenced sonnets: Keats was determined to find his own voice by studying and imitating the practice of writers other than his most obvious literary patron and champion.[13]

In a couplet poem such as 'I Stood Tip-toe upon a Little Hill', placed first in Keats's 1817 *Poems*, and with an epigraph from Hunt's *The Story of Rimini*, the reader hears echoes of the Huntian manner, with its fresh, sparkling, jaunty diction, feminine rhymes and swiftly refocusing enjambments. Yet Keats outgrows his teacher, displaying an uncanny grasp of the ways in which words might body forth the real. In the following lines from Hunt's *The Story of Rimini* –

> 'Tis nature, full of spirits, waked and springing –
> The birds to the delicious time are singing,
> Darting with freaks and snatches up and down,
> Where the light woods go seaward from the town.
> (I. 15–18)[14]

the light, brisk tone is managed adroitly, the poet's field of vision accommodating and moving between the relatively close-up and the far-off, but the diction obeys Imlac's prohibition against numbering 'the streaks of the tulip', in Samuel Johnson's phrase.[15] Keats's 'I Stood Tip-toe upon a Little Hill' exudes the same good will towards the natural world:

> Sometimes goldfinches one by one will drop
> From low hung branches; little space they stop;
> But sip, and twitter, and their feathers sleek;
> Then off at once, as in a wanton freak:
> Or perhaps, to show their black, and golden wings,
> Pausing upon their yellow flutterings.
> (87–92)

But the difference in linguistic richness and sensuous fullness is immediately apparent. The verbs here – in, say, 'sip, and twitter, and their feathers sleek' – have an eye-on-the-object intentness, and the rhythms are tremblingly sensitive, alert to slowings, speedings, and a mixture of the two in the unexpected balance of the final line, where 'flutterings' quiver in the act of 'Pausing'.

The same poem shows a young poet using but outdoing Hunt's manner in the process of beginning to embrace Wordsworthian matter: this process extends beyond the rewording, say, of Wordsworth's 'tidings of invisible things' (*The Excursion*, 4. 1142) as 'Shapes from the invisible world' (186).[16] It embodies the idea, as Wordsworth puts it in the fourth book of *The Excursion*, in Miriam Allott's paraphrase, that 'Myths and legends originate in imaginative response to the beauties of nature'.[17] Indeed, in the 1815 edition of *The Feast of the Poets*, Hunt's witty, discursive take in poetry and prose on the contemporary literary scene, Wordsworth, for all Hunt's criticisms of his self-absorption, is still described as 'the Prince of the Bards of his Time!'[18] In short, Hunt is, ironically, a major influence on Keats's discovery of Wordsworth. Wordsworth contributes to Keats's wish to throw off Hunt's influence as a person (and poet) 'who does one harm by making fine things petty and beautiful things hateful' (*L* 2, 11).

Keats may well have read Hunt's long notes to *The Feast of the Poets* which object to the alleged monotony of accent and pauses in Pope, and urge attention to the attainment of an unaffected variety in versification.[19] In *Endymion* Keats goes beyond Hunt in his use of run-on lines.[20] From his study of Hunt and trust in his own imagination, Keats finds a mode of writing adequate to convey the eager momentum of 'our searching' (1. 11) and the concomitant trust that 'Some shape of beauty moves away the pall / From our dark spirits' (1. 12–13). If he accepts, in an echo of Wordsworth's 'Ode: Intimations of Immortality', line 189, that 'years should bring the philosophic Mind' (*L* 1, 186), he sustains a sense of the 'holiness of the Heart's affections' (*L* 1, 184) that subtly differs from the older poet's.

This is a question of the colouring given by each poet to their images and descriptions, and of the final object of 'affections'. Keats's natural instinct is to lose himself in the object; Wordsworth's to use the object to seek to find himself. When Wordsworth sees the hare at the start of 'Resolution and Independence' as 'running races in her mirth' (11) and raising 'a mist' (13) 'from the plashy earth' (12), he evokes a creaturely image with kinetic, playful tenderness; his hare allows him to enjoy a brief liberation from the cares of consciousness. But those cares will absorb the image a few stanzas later: 'And I bethought me of the playful Hare: / Even such a happy Child of earth am I' (30–1), he asserts, seemingly and affectingly less than wholly convinced by his own insistence. Wordsworth returns to the self at the lyric's heart, and the hare dwindles into exemplum. Keats's hare in the first stanza of *The Eve of St. Agnes* is simply there, its living identity vouched for by a rhythm that seems to mime the cold ache with which it 'limp'd trembling through the frozen grass' (2). Its meaning is its being; it is justified in the poem's structure by virtue of being a cohabitant of its vision. Keats gives the slip to any sense of the 'palpable design' (*L* I, 224) to which he takes exception in Wordsworth by dwelling with unequalled imaginative intensity on the poem's special simulacrum of our common physical existence. The poem exhibits Keats's fascination with a reality in which pulses beat and blood rushes, in which cold, age, and death challenge and yet tie an inextricable knot with sex and longing.

Not that Keats is unaware of himself as a poet, shaper of his own fictive world. The final stanza's adieu to the romance brings out openly a dimension of self-consciousness about his poetic fashioning that pervades the poem. Keats, as he brooded on Wordsworth's poetry, has two fundamental responses. On the one hand, Wordsworth is redefining modern poetry, gifting or weighing it down with the theme of 'the heart [*written over* 'head'] and nature of Man', revealing in a poem like 'Lines Written a Few Miles above Tintern Abbey' a 'Genius' which is 'explorative' of the 'dark Passages' that lead beyond the 'Chamber of Maiden Thought' (*L* I, 281). On the other hand, Keats senses a major difference between Wordsworth and himself, as is made clear by the distinction he draws in the 'poetical Character' letter of 27 October 1818 to Woodhouse between 'the wordsworthian or egotistical sublime' and 'the camelion Poet' (*L* I, 387). Keats's poetic explorations will reveal to him the difficulty of shedding the 'egotistical', 'sublime' or otherwise.

This tension, in part derived from his conflicted response to Wordsworth, between self-awareness and self-forgetfulness, between concern with suffering and the desire for beauty, inflects itself in Keats's finest poetry. Even when, as in 'Ode to a Nightingale', the 'sole self' (72) emerges as a principal actor in the poem's drama, 'sole' takes on an impoverished inflection because of the poem's moments of rapt communion, through language, with otherness: whether located in a 'glass of vintage' (11), 'Fast fading violets' (47), 'the sad heart of Ruth' (66), or 'faery lands forlorn' (70). Wordsworth may conjure up 'the silence of the seas / Among the farthest Hebrides' ('The Solitary Reaper', 15–16). Yet the effect of absolute if momentary self-forgetfulness, typical of Keats, does not occur in Wordsworth. The concerns of the flowing couplets in 'The Solitary Reaper' are ready to be reeled in by the poem's master spinner as quickly as they are unspooled, and, sure enough, the next stanza begins, 'Will no one tells me what she sings?' (17).

Keats wears any Wordsworthian borrowings with a distinct difference.[21] The younger poet's 'hungry generations' (62) in 'Ode to a Nightingale' distinguish themselves from the 'countless generations of Mankind' (4. 758), their likely source in Wordsworth's *Excursion*. They make an intensified appeal to our capacity for identification (and, indeed, recoil) through the change of 'countless' to 'hungry'. Wordsworth's adjective is that conferred by a poet assuming the narrative perspective of a relatively detached if sympathetic looker-on. Keats's is that bestowed by an author who captures the appetitive drive central to continued, fated, and dissatisfied existence, and relies on the reader's greeting spirit to work in co-operation with the poet. In the same passage from *The Excursion*, the Wanderer sparks Keatsian responses in his line 'While Man grows old, and dwindles, and decays' (4. 757), which leaves its traces on 'When old age shall this generation waste' (46) in 'Ode to a Grecian Urn' and 'Where youth grows pale, and spectre-thin, and dies' (26) in 'Ode to a Nightingale'. Setting the lines beside one another points up Keatsian departures. For the Wanderer 'man grows old'; for Keats's speaker, 'old age' is a more actively destructive force that will 'waste' a generation. Again, Keats gives a shocking, almost sardonic twist to the Wanderer's description of a gradual, inevitable passage into old age; in the ode, 'youth grows pale … and dies'.

The *Hyperion* project represents Keats's most sustained attempt to be what he tries out as a possible description of Wordsworth: a poet of 'epic passions' who 'martyrs himself to the human heart, the main region of his song' (*L* 1, 278–9). Wordsworth, in the lines from the Prospectus to *The Recluse* to which Keats alludes, refers to 'the Mind of Man, / My haunt and the main region of my Song' (39–40). Yet he is also the poet of 'the human heart', most memorably at the close of the Intimations ode, where he offers 'Thanks to the human heart by which we live' (203) before asserting the singleness – and singularity – of his imaginative powers: 'To me the meanest flower that blows can give / Thoughts that do often lie too deep for tears' (205–6). The 'main region' of Keats's song in the first *Hyperion* is the confrontation with loss and downfall through the depiction of the fallen Titans in Book 1, the attempt to assert a trust in process, through the deliberated wisdom of Oceanus's speech in Book 2, and the beginnings of a miniature *Prelude* (not that Keats knew the poem) in Book 3, in which Apollo's dying into life as a newly incarnated god (or poet) takes centre-stage.

If the poem is Keats's answer to *The Excursion* – the first-named item in one of 'the three things to rejoice at in this Age' (*L* 1, 203), it both benefits and may suffer from not fully wishing to turn itself into a poem of sustained conversational disputation. Keats's imaginative investments are at their most compelling in moments that are arrested, liminal, poignant with actual or virtual meaning: Saturn silent in his vale, Hyperion looking at the stars before he dives down to the earth. In *The Fall of Hyperion* Keats seeks to rid his language of its Miltonic pomp and bring it closer to a barer, post-Wordsworthian idiom. Concern with the role of the poet prompts a manner that is strikingly subjective, showing a superbly intelligent grasp of what Wordsworth has bequeathed to modern poets. Ironically, as he fights for his own space among the poets of his time, Keats rejects in his encounter with Moneta 'large self worshipers' (1. 207), a plural category that serves to name a solitary, formidable figure: Wordsworth. The contempt of the moment only points up the riven, intimate, and creative nature of Keats's relationship to the older poet.

Notes

1 Anne K. Mellor, *Romanticism and Gender* (New York: Routledge, 1993), pp. 180, 182.
2 'Ann Radcliffe's Poetry: The Poetics of Refrain and Inventory', in *Ann Radcliffe, Romanticism and the Gothic*, ed. Dale Townshend and Angela Wright (Cambridge: Cambridge University Press, 2014), pp. 197–8.
3 See Patrick J. Keane, *Emerson, Romanticism, and Intuitive Reason* (Columbia, MO: University of Missouri Press, 2005), pp. 146–7. Wordsworth is quoted from *21st-Century Oxford Authors: William Wordsworth*, ed. Stephen Gill (Oxford: Oxford University Press, 2010).
4 See Stuart M. Sperry, *Keats the Poet* (1973; Princeton: Princeton University Press, 1994), p. 181.
5 Noted in *The Poems of John Keats*, ed. Miriam Allott (London: Longman, 1970), p. 399n, from where Southey is quoted.
6 *Keats's Reading of the Romantic Poets* (Ann Arbor: University of Michigan Press, 1991), pp. 16–17. Lau notes the possibility that Keats 'may have accepted Hazlitt's condemnation of the essay and not have bothered hunting it down' (17).
7 Miriam Allott, 'Keats and Wordsworth', *Keats-Shelley Memorial Bulletin* 22 (1971): 30.
8 Nicholas Roe, *John Keats: A New Life* (New Haven: Yale University Press, 2012), pp. 314–15
9 Sperry, *Keats*, p. 144.
10 Noted in *Poems*, ed. Allott, p. 651n, from where Chatterton is quoted.
11 Walter Jackson Bate, *The Stylistic Development of Keats* (1945; London: Routledge, 2015), pp. 9–19, 192–6 (sonnets), 19–27, 199–201 (couplets).
12 Bate, *Stylistic Development*, p. 15. The caesural markers are Bates's.
13 Bate, *Stylistic Development*, p. 19.
14 Leigh Hunt, *Selected Writings*, ed. with intro. David Jesson Dibley (1990; Manchester: Carcanet, 2003).

15 *The History of Rasselas: Prince of Abissinia*, ed. J. P. Hardy (1988; Oxford: Oxford University Press, 1999), p. 26.
16 See Lau, *Keats's Reading*, p. 57. Lau's book contains invaluable tabulations of suggested echoes of Wordsworth in Keats, alongside those critics who have suggested them.
17 *The Poems*, ed. Miriam Allott, p. 91n.
18 See Lau, *Keats's Reading*, pp. 21, 19, from which Hunt is quoted.
19 Bate, *Stylistic Development*, p. 20.
20 Bate, *Stylistic Development*, pp. 22–3.
21 See Lau, *Keats's Reading*, p. 28.

CHAPTER 24

Contemporaries (2): Coleridge, Byron, Shelley

Jane Stabler

The Examiner captures the relative standing of Keats, Shelley, Byron and Coleridge in 1816, the year that Leigh Hunt introduced Keats and Shelley to the public as 'Young Poets'. Keats was twenty-one and Shelley just three years older; Coleridge, then in his mid-forties, was established as 'the sage of Highgate', but this did not save him from *The Examiner*'s ferocious reviews of his 1816 volumes, *Christabel, Kubla Khan and The Pains of Sleep* and *A Statesman's Manual.* Hazlitt (the reviewer) attacked Coleridge for poems and political sermonising whose effects seemed interchangeable in that they left the faculties in a state of suspension:

> Innumerable, evanescent thoughts dance before him, and dazzle his sight, like insects in the evening sun … He is without a strong feeling of the existence of any thing out of himself; and he has neither purposes nor passions of his own.[1]

A few weeks later, *The Examiner* saluted the twenty-eight-year-old Byron as 'a Noble Poet' who 'feels most powerfully, and has opinions as well as an experience of his own. His character therefore as a poet is also his own'.[2] The idea of a poet's self-possession or poetical character in relation to his contemporaries obsessed Keats. Like many young writers, he was preternaturally anxious about not finding his voice, or losing it, or being over-influenced: 'I refused to visit Shelley, that I might have my own unfetterd Scope –' he told Bailey in a letter of 8 October 1817 (*L* 1, 170). His reason for steering clear of other poets is evident in remarks he made to George and Georgiana Keats in September 1819: 'Men who live together have a silent <p> moulding, and influencing power over each other – They interassimulate' (*L* 2, 208). One of Keats's famous mis-spellings here merges the ideas of assimilation or blent identity with simulation or acting. Between 1816 and 1821 his urgent work of self-definition was informed by continual interrogation of points of kinship with and difference from his contemporaries. 'A Man is like a Magnet, he must have a repelling end'

(*L* 2, 240), he observed in January 1820. Opposite forces of attraction and repulsion exert a constant pressure when he finds himself in proximity to another poet:

> the fact is [Hunt] & Shelley are hurt & perhaps justly, at my not having showed them the affair officiously & from several hints I have had they appear much disposed to dissect & anatomize, any trip or slip I may have made.
>
> (*L* 1, 214)

Critical anatomy conditions Keats's own relationship with his contemporaries. His letters recurrently classify other minds in order to measure his own growth. Keats's eager probing of the strengths and weaknesses of his fellow-writers was matched by the smart he felt about criticism. He maintained a keen scrutiny of his social superiors, Shelley and Byron; Keats was more able to marvel at Coleridge, perhaps because Coleridge was older and vulnerable to 'debt and embarrassment'.[3]

Keats requested *Sibylline Leaves* (issued in August 1817) from Dilke in November 1817. It included all of Coleridge's major poetry not in the 1816 volume: the revised and re-glossed 'Rime of the Ancient Mariner', other lyrical ballads rejected by Wordsworth after 1798, and corrected versions of sonnets, odes and blank verse poems from the intervening years. The visions of the *Christabel* volume were fragments rescued from oblivion, but *Sibylline Leaves* (appearing in the same month as *Biographia Literaria*) showed Coleridge re-organising and anatomising his own creative faculty. Keats's verdict on Coleridge the poet in 1818 was almost the opposite of Hazlitt's review of 1816:

> at once it struck me, what quality went to form a Man of Achievement, especially in Literature & which Shakespeare possessed so enormously – I mean *Negative Capability*, that is, when man is capable of being in uncertainties, Mysteries, doubts, without any irritable reaching after fact & reason – Coleridge, for instance, would let go by a fine isolated verisimilitude caught from the Penetralium of mystery, from being incapable of remaining content with half-knowledge.
>
> (21 December 1817; *L* 1, 193–4)

'Half knowledge' is what Hazlitt had lamented in the two 1816 volumes. After *Sibylline Leaves* and *Biographia Literaria*, Keats could categorise Coleridge as a fussy logician, preparing fastidious glosses and errata sheets to clip the wings of imaginative flight. Keats's sketch of his encounter with Coleridge in 1819 is often read as a musical interlude in which Keats lets the monologue of the older poet wash over him like the voice of a nightingale.

Certainly Coleridge the oracular public speaker is present, but we can also hear Keats registering (and resisting) Coleridge's tendency to catalogue:

> In those two Miles he broached a thousand things – let me see if I can give you a list – Nightingales, Poetry – on Poetical Sensation – Metaphysics – Different genera and species of Dreams – Nightmare–a dream accompanied <with> by a sense of touch – single and double touch – A dream related – First and second consciousness – the difference explained between will and Volition – so m[an]y metaphysicians from a want of smoking the second consciousness – Monsters – the Kraken – Mermaids – southey believes in them – southeys belief too much diluted – A Ghost story – Good morning – I heard his voice as he came towards me – I heard it as he moved away – I had heard it all the interval – if it may be called so.
>
> (*L* 2, 88–9)

'Different genera and species … single and double touch … First and second consciousness… the difference explained': Keats picks up the fine slicing of critical distinction which he always found too methodical when someone else was wielding the scalpel.

Shelley also lectured Keats on Hampstead Heath, as Keats recalled, rather wryly, in August 1820 ('I remember you advising me not to publish my first-blights', *L* 2, 323). When Keats first met him in December 1816, Shelley had published several pamphlets and *Queen Mab* with its controversial prose notes, which classified him as a 'striking and original thinker'.[4] 'Shelley's poem is out', Keats wrote about *Laon and Cythna*, '& there are words about its being objected too, as much as Queen Mab was. Poor Shelley I think he has his Quota of good qualities, in sooth la!!' (*L* 1, 194),

While implying that Shelley has a decent share, 'quota' is also a measured assessment; Keats is sympathetic, but detached. Shelley asked Ollier to send *Rosalind and Helen* to Keats in 1819 (see *L* 2, 311), but Keats had not rushed to read *The Revolt of Islam*: 'I have not yet read Shelly's Poem', he wrote, two months after it came out (*L* 1, 237).[5] It was not until Shelley invited him to Italy in 1820 that Keats produced any detailed response to Shelley's verse, partly elicited by Shelley's comments on having re-read *Endymion* with 'a new sense of the treasures of poetry it contains, though treasures poured forth with indistinct profusion. This', Shelley said, 'people in general will not endure, & that is the cause of the comparatively few copies which have been sold'.[6] Keats's response was cryptic and defensive:

> I received a copy of the Cenci … There is only one part of it I am judge of; the Poetry, and dramatic effect, which by many spirits now a days is considered the mammon … *an artist* must serve Mammon – he must have "self concentration" selfishness perhaps. You I am sure will forgive me for

> sincerely remarking that you might curb your magnanimity and be more of an artist, and 'load every rift' of your subject with ore. The thought of such discipline must fall like cold chains upon you, who perhaps never sat with your wings furl'd for six Months together. And is not this extraordina[r]y talk for the writer of Endymion? whose mind was like a pack of scattered cards – I am pick'd up and sorted to a pip. My Imagination is a Monastry and I am its Monk – you must explain my metap[es] to yourself.
>
> (16 August 1820; *L* 2, 322–3)

This sounds like an instinctive, thrusting reaction against Shelley's view that *Endymion* should have carried a little less freight. The image 'rich metal loaded every rift' is from Spenser's Cave of Mammon whose 'portentous massiness' was praised by Hazlitt in his 1818 lecture.[7] To suggest that Shelley should be more grounded, massy and present in his own work, that he might try 'self-concentration' or 'selfishness perhaps', inclines towards the egotistical sublime and away from the negatively capable; however, as A. C. Bradley suggests, both poets were equally troubled by the sense of being set apart and too much a part of the material universe. Keats wrote little about Shelley's poetry, but he seems to have thought his way through much more of it, as his borrowing of Shelleyan phrases indicates.

Bradley points out that 'self-concentration' in Keats's letter of 16 August 1820 is probably a misquotation from the Preface to *Alastor* (just as *Endymion* is influenced by an earlier reading of *Alastor*), and that both poems are responses to the portrait of solitude in The *Excursion*.[8] In Bradley's reading, Keats's allusion to 'Hymn to Intellectual Beauty' in the letter to Bailey 13 March 1818 (14–15 *Examiner* version; *L* 1, 243) reveals clear affinities between Shelley and Keats with regard to their search for the principle of beauty; nevertheless, Keats's use of the word 'consecrates' still seems to incline to 'the holiness of the Heart's affections' (*L* 1, 184), or 'the burgundy mark on the bottles of our Minds' (*L* 1, 243) rather than to an abstract sanctity. For Keats the mention of consecration comes as part of a comparison of 'Things real – things semireal – and no things' (*L* 1, 242–3), in which poetry might belong under all three heads. The force of 'consec[r]ates' for Keats (especially writing to the soon-to-be-ordained Bailey) would seem to reside in the laying of hands on bread and cup, the physical proof of a broken body, and an awareness of how the experience of suffering might become part of the pursuit of truth (as Keats was working out this relationship, his brother Tom 'had a spitting of blood' [*L* 1, 244]). Bradley allows that despite his resemblance to Shelley, 'the idealism of Keats is much more concrete'.[9] In *Adonais* Shelley will lovingly dispense with things real and semi-real before effecting a different kind of consecration.

When discussing the poetic embodiment of personality that was Lord Byron, Keats's tendency to think through apposition turns the worldly into something paradoxically lacking in substance, something 'theatrical and pantomimical' (*L* I, 395). Byron famously impugned Keats's masculinity when he suggested that susceptibility to criticism was womanish: 'a man should calculate upon his powers of *resistance* before he goes into the arena'.[10] Less often noticed are Keats's descriptions of Byron in feminine terms. He imagines Byron's influence on women readers as pervading Byron to the core. Likening Byron to one of Cleopatra's serving women (removing aristocracy and manliness together) in Shakespeare's *Antony and Cleopatra*, Keats contemplates the attraction of 'rich talk':

> This they call flirting! they do not know things. They do not know what a Woman is. I believe tho' she has faults – the same as Charmian and Cleopatra might have had … for there are two distinct tempers of mind in which we judge of things – the worldly, theatrical and pantomimical; and the unearthly, spiritual and ethereal – in the former Buonaparte, Lord Byron and this Charmian hold the first place in our Minds; in the latter John Howard, Bishop Hooker rocking his child's cradle and you my dear Sister are the conquering feelings. As a Man in the world I love the rich talk of a Charmian; as an eternal Being I love the thought of you. I should like her to ruin me, and I should like you to save me.
>
> (14–31 October 1818, *L* I, 395–6)

Playing the part, one suspects, of the roué to his concerned sister-in-law; Keats admits the appeal of being courted or ravished by sensuous performance. Our natures can be swayed, he suggests, by something which is itself yielding and momentary. The enchanting siren – who might be somebody's sister or 'the witch poesy' – haunts Keats's poetry as with Coleridge (Geraldine), Byron (Medea, the witch of the Alps) and Shelley (the witch of Atlas, the magnetic lady). The pervasive power of something that is soft and diffusive is addressed in Keats's 'To Lord Byron': 'thou thy griefs dost dress' (l. 7), he writes, likening Byron's vaunted sorrows to clouds that veil the moon:

> Through the dark robe oft amber rays prevail,
> And like fair veins in sable marble flow.
>
> (11–12)

Here, the erotic image of a golden, glowing body under a dark robe is chiastically anatomised into fair veins in marble, taking us into the realm of fine art, but the sonnet remains caught between distant homage and the lurking thrill of imagined physical touch. Like the mingled texture of 'amber rays', 'sable marble' modifies stone with the fluid ripple of a pelt, streaming over the line ending with the verb 'flow'. Although Keats's call to Byron to 'warble' on (13) might remind us of his patient listening to Coleridge, this sonnet swells with the possibility of being darkly possessed by another being.

The phenomenal success of Byron's *Childe Harold* and the Turkish Tales (1812–16) made verse romance and epic appear to be the most significant literary forms of the day. Keats felt that he had failed to write the long poem that would guarantee immortality, but, as H. J. Jackson discerns, Keats's shorter lyrics turned out to be much more marketable in the longer term.[11] Keats and his contemporaries competed in ballad stanzas, rhyming couplets, Miltonic blank verse, odes, sonnets, tragedy, letters, dream visions, wars waged in prefaces, fragments; they pledged public allegiance to Homer, Spenser, Shakespeare, Milton, Dante, and partook of a less publicly flaunted enjoyment of popular theatre and 'Damosel Radcliffe' (*L* 1, 245). To grasp the ways in which Coleridge, Byron, Shelley and Keats shared a formal context, we can compare their different uses of the same romance motif. In choosing their treatment of kissing, I take my cue from Christopher Ricks, whose brilliant summation of what made Keats's voice distinctive depends partly on a comparison with Byron.[12] Kissing involves temporary inter-assimulation (as Keats called it), but eventual pulling apart. Kissing focuses the micro-world of rhyme and the macro-world of the self realised in relation to another in which Keats was so engaged.

Ricks demonstrates that what contemporary critics perceived as 'bad taste' in Keats's writing could become avant-garde artistic veracity, speaking to the future even as it appalled its first readers. The moralistic caution that would lead publishers to request revisions to *The Eve of St. Agnes* and *Laon and Cythna* are internalised by Coleridge. His sole use of the bliss-kiss rhyme occurs in: 'Ah why refuse the blameless bliss? / Can danger lurk within a kiss?'.[13] Crosscurrents of thought furrow this attempt at seduction. 'Bliss' is shadowed by ideas of refusal and blame. Instead of persuading its recipient to grant a kiss, the poem sways uneasily towards guilt-stricken foreboding. 'Love's Sanctuary' makes Coleridge's religious monitoring of bliss more explicit:

> This yearning heart (Love! witness what I say)
> Enshrines thy form as purely as it may,
> Round which, as to some spirit uttering bliss,
> My thoughts all stand ministrant night and day
> Like saintly Priests, that dare not think amiss.[14]

The resolution of 'bliss' with 'kiss' is here walled off by ranks of 'saintly Priests' that 'dare not think' of the obvious rhyme. By contrast, Keats's Porphyro will exultingly combine the roles of lover and religious devotee: 'Ah silver shrine, here will I take my rest / After so many hours of toil and quest, / A famish'd pilgrim' (337–9). Coleridge's poetic kisses are troubled by questions of classification. In the Sonnet 'To a friend who asked, how I felt when the Nurse first presented my Infant to me' (*Sibylline Leaves*), even Coleridge's moving admission of emotional ambivalence is compartmentalised by his inveterate habit of comparison and qualification:

> Then was I thrill'd and melted, and most warm
> Impress'd a Father's kiss: and all beguil'd
>   Of dark remembrance and presageful fear,
>   I seem'd to see an angel-form appear –
> 'Twas even thine, beloved woman mild!
>   So for the Mother's sake the child was dear,
> And dearer was the Mother for the Child.
>
> (8–14)

The rhyme scheme helps Coleridge to rationalise the trauma that is mutual dependency, but the impulse to 'melt' – and the lovely ambiguity about whether 'most warm' refers to his impulse or the first brush with his baby's skin – is quickly checked by the reinstatement of paternal identity: the 'Father's kiss' is 'impress'd' and is, therefore, a token of acceptance that imposes absolute separation from both wife (now imagined as non-physical) and infant son.

Equally estranged from the mothers of their children, Byron and Shelley were much less inhibited when it came to kissing. Although they shared an enlightened classical outlook on idealised free sexual union, Shelleyan eros is conceptualised within a wider Greek frame of reference, which means that Shelleyan kissing usually takes place in a highly rarefied atmosphere. While Ricks celebrates the moisture content of Keats's 'slippery blisses', the physicality of Shelley's kisses resides in an intellectual glow. In *Prometheus Unbound* (which Keats said should have been written more slowly, even before he had read it), the kiss/bliss rhyme makes a fleeting appearance in Act I when a spirit tells how

> On a poet's lips I slept
> Dreaming like a love-adept
> In the sound his breathing kept;
> Nor seeks nor finds he mortal blisses,
> But feeds on the aerial kisses
> Of shapes that haunt thought's wildernesses.[15]

Surrounded by the sound of breathing, the spirit resembles a Popean sylph at first, cradled in the curve of the poet's lip. Any chance that the poet might 'feed' in a human way vanishes with the succeeding image of the poet feeding on air, kissing ethereal shapes (not mouths). A more tangible kiss occurs in Act 2, within Panthea's dream:

> for when just now
> We kissed, I felt within thy parted lips
> The sweet air that sustained me, and the warmth
> Of the life-blood, for loss of which I faint,
> Quivered between our intertwining arms.
> (2. 1. 102–6)

Prometheus dreams himself 'within' the space of Panthea's 'parted lips', and the breathing pauses of blank verse allow us to hear human suspiration as well as the incoming throb of 'warmth' pulsing over the line end and ushering in a tide of 'life-blood'. Poised between states of consciousness, Shelley's lines render the kiss as the meeting point, not just of brother and sister, but past and future worlds. Their imagined touching is erotic, but it is an eroticism of cosmic radiance, searingly chaste despite being (as with *Laon and Cythna*) incestuous.

Byron claims that the irresistibility of the 'kiss/bliss' rhyme is part of life, but he also revels in the sensuous reciprocity of life and art. In *Don Juan* Canto 2, Byron devotes several *ottava rima* stanzas to Juan and Haidee's first kiss. Like pairs of rhyming words, the two lovers are in sight before they meet; 'and, beholding this', the narrator tells us at the end of stanza 185, 'Their lips drew near, and clung into a kiss'. In Byron's manuscripts the word 'kiss' was followed by a mixture of stops and dashes, which became a semicolon in the first edition. A dash, however, still seems the most appropriate form of punctuation to carry the oscular 'clinging' that lasts to the couplet of stanza 187.

> A long, long kiss, a kiss of youth, and love,
>   And beauty, all concentrating like rays
> Into one focus, kindled from above;
>   Such kisses as belong to early days,
> Where heart, and soul, and sense, in concert move,
>   And the blood's lava, and the pulse a blaze,
> Each kiss a heart-quake, – for a kiss's strength,
> I think, it must be reckon'd by its length.
>
> By length I mean duration; theirs endured
>   Heaven knows how long – no doubt they never reckon'd;
> And if they had, they could not have secured

> The sum of their sensations to a second:
> They had not spoken; but they felt allured,
> As if their souls and lips each other beckon'd,
> Which, being join'd, like swarming bees they clung –
> Their hearts the flowers from whence the honey sprung.[16]

Christopher Ricks argues that, unlike Keats, Byron never implicates us in the 'hot tinglings of sensation'; the 'limpidity and lucidity' of his style 'act as a *cordon sanitaire* against contagious embarrassment'.[17] The shifting tones of *Don Juan,* however, might incite a fuller range of affect. Byron offers the throwaway: ' "Kiss" rhymes to "bliss" in fact as well as verse – / I wish it never led to something worse' (6. 59), but the disturbing image of the swarming bees invites the reader to imagine the amorphous shape of mouths and souls meeting with the wordless moaning of uncensored passion. Byron experimented with other possibilities for the last line of stanza 187: 'And one was innocent, but both too young' is a knowing reminder of Juan's earlier affair with Julia; 'And mixed until the very pleasure stung' is an uncomfortable reminder that this is Haidee's first sexual encounter (Byron will re-use the image when Dudù explains that she cried out because she dreamt of a bee sting); another option was 'With sometimes more within them than one tongue'. Like the honeyed stickiness of the couplet Byron finally chose, the 'clung/tongue' rhyme risks the embarrassing language of physical frankness. Byron revised his image of tongues two stanzas later into a more Pentecostal image of love's universal language, but throughout *Don Juan*'s scenes of kissing, we can detect an interplay of Keatsian physicality, Shelleyan immateriality and Coleridgean second thoughts.

Concluding his *Examiner* review of *Christabel,* Hazlitt scrutinised with distaste his own curiosity about what happens in Coleridge's poem: 'The mind, in reading it, is spell-bound' Hazlitt remarked, but 'There is something disgusting at the bottom of his subject'.[18] Keats almost certainly read this review. He could not have read Shelley's elegy *Adonais,* in which the kiss between Urania and the poet longs for Keats to 'live', 'survive' and be again 'alive', then makes this happen in verse:

> Kiss me, so long but as a kiss may live;
> And in my heartless breast and burning brain
> That word, that kiss, shall all thoughts else survive,
> With food of saddest memory kept alive.
>
> (227–30)

From spellbound disgust to ascension into high art, Keats and his contemporaries contested, in isolated verisimilitude, those points and all the space between.

Notes

1 *The Examiner* 8 September 1816, p. 572.
2 *The Examiner* 22 September 1816, p. 603.
3 Samuel Taylor Coleridge, *Biographia Literaria*, ed. James Engell and W. Jackson Bate, 2 vols. (Princeton: Princeton University Press, 1983), vol. 2, p. 157.
4 *The Examiner* 1 December 1816, p. 761.
5 Michael O'Neill's identification of a possible echo of *The Revolt of Islam* (9. 4. 31–2) in 'Ode to a Nightingale' (65–6) (made in editorial correspondence) suggests that Keats had read Shelley's poem by May 1819.
6 Shelley, *The Letters of Percy Bysshe Shelley*, 2 vols (Oxford: Clarendon Press, 1964), vol. 2, p. 221.
7 William Hazlitt, *The Complete Works*, ed. P. P. Howe, 21 vols. (London: J. M. Dent, 1930), vol. 5, p. 42.
8 A. C. Bradley, *Oxford Lectures on Poetry* (London: Macmillan 1909; repr. 1926), pp. 209–44, especially pp. 227, 240–4).
9 Bradley, *Oxford Lectures on Poetry*, p. 232.
10 Lord Byron, *Letters and Journals*, ed. Leslie A. Marchand, 13 vols. (London: John Murray, 1973–94), vol. 8, p. 103.
11 H. J. Jackson, *Those Who Write for Immortality: Romantic Reputations and the Dream of Lasting Fame* (New Haven: Yale University Press, 2015), pp. 114–30.
12 Christopher Ricks, *Keats and Embarrassment* (Oxford: Oxford University Press, 1974), pp. 69–114.
13 'The Kiss' (1796), lines 3–4; S. T. Coleridge, *Poems*, ed. Ernest Hartley Coleridge (Oxford: Clarendon Press, 1912).
14 First published from MS in 1893.
15 Lines 737–42. Percy Bysshe Shelley, *The Major Works* ed. Zachary Leader and Michael O'Neill (Oxford: Oxford University Press, 2003).
16 Stanzas 186–7. Lord Byron, *The Complete Poetical Works,* ed. Jerome J. McGann, vol. 5 (Oxford: Oxford University Press, 1986).
17 Ricks, *Keats and Embarrassment,* p. 83.
18 *The Examiner* 2 June 1816, p. 349.

CHAPTER 25

Ballad, Romance and Narrative

Andrew Bennett

Keats regularly wrote narrative poems that regularly failed to be the kinds of poems that he originally set out to write. His most successful non-epic narratives – the romance poems *Isabella; or the Pot of Basil* (1818), *The Eve of St. Agnes* (1819) and *Lamia* (1819), and the ballad 'La Belle Dame sans Merci' (1819) – tend to be successful just to the extent that they fail in terms of their ostensible generic allegiances, just to the extent that they fail to fulfil the ambition of their form. It is not simply that the poems can be understood to be mixed, 'composite' or hybrid forms, but that they are profoundly impelled by an argument with their own formal and generic parameters.[1] Keats's narrative poems mark a distance from the genres with which they seem to identify through often rather subtle narrative, metrical, thematic, rhetorical and tonal deformations – deformations and deviations from convention that are often so slight that they are commonly misidentified as resulting from the *gaucherie* of youthful enthusiasm, from class or educational deficiency, or from simple ideological impurity (Keats is too reactionary or too seditious; his poetry exudes overly masculinist tendencies and assumptions or is emasculated, even effeminate, in tone). In particular, the narrative trajectories of such poems characteristically involve distortions or distensions of temporality and causality, while the narrative voice is complicated by and diffracted through an array of distancing effects – not the least of which are the complex ironies involved in generic self-reflection itself. These are poems that resist their own narrative impulse, that is to say, and that also thereby refuse fully to commit to the fictions that they invent and in which they invite readers to indulge. In this chapter, I will examine the interplay between genre and narrative rhetoric that characterises the challenge to his readers that Keats presents in his ballads and romance poems.

Keats's excessively long, digressive, rambling, unfocused and, for that reason alone, formally dissonant four-book *Endymion* (1818) carries its own explicit marker of genre in its subtitle, *A Poetic Romance*. The subtitle implicitly points to the poem's distance from the increasingly popular mode of prose romance – the plot-driven gothic, historical, and domestic novels of writers such as Ann Radcliffe, Charlotte Smith, Fanny Burney, and Walter Scott – as it does from the epic tradition of Milton's *Paradise Lost* (1667) and from the allegorical romance tradition of Spenser's *The Faerie Queene* (1590–6). If, as Karen Swann argues, *Endymion* is an 'almost perfect failure' as an enterprise that is designed to 'commodify' Keats as a modern poet,[2] the poem may be said to constitute an exception to the rule that generic dysfunction leads to literary success. Indeed, consequential upon *Endymion*'s failure to engage its audience are the later rhetorically and narratologically tighter, more clearly focused, and generically sceptical narrative poems of Keats's relative maturity. Readers and critics are divided over the merits of Keats's allegorical-epic-romance poem and on what is ultimately to be gained by reading its 4,050 lines, but the contemporary verdict was sometimes virulent in its condemnation. On its first publication in May 1818, the poem received some excoriating reviews, not least by the well-known critic John Gibson Lockhart in *Blackwood's Edinburgh Magazine*. In a highly politicised article, part of a series on the 'Cockney School of Poetry', Lockhart identified Keats as a young acolyte of Leigh Hunt – political radical, editor, ex-political prisoner (he spent two years in Surrey Gaol in 1813–15 for libelling the Prince Regent) and author of *The Story of Rimini* (1816) – before describing Keats's alleged mentor as 'the meanest, the filthiest, and the most vulgar of the Cockney poetasters'. Lockhart argues that Keats had been afflicted by what he calls '*Metromanie*' or 'poetical mania' and has produced a poem of 'imperturbable drivelling idiocy' governed not only by vulgarly aspirational, lower-class 'cockney' language and poetics but also by the 'sedition' of crypto-revolutionary politics (*CH* 99, 97, 98, 109). John Wilson Croker followed up the *Blackwood*'s attack in September in the Tory *Quarterly Review* by declaring that despite 'superhuman efforts' he had been unable to read the poem beyond its first book: the poem is 'more unintelligible' and 'twice as diffuse' as Hunt's *Rimini*, and 'wanders from one subject to another' in pursuit of sound association rather than any consequential train of ideas (*CH* 110–12). Two years later, *Endymion* was still being attacked, when Francis Jeffrey (erstwhile scourge of William Wordsworth's 1807 *Poems, in Two Volumes* and *The Excursion* [1814]), commented on the poem's 'florid wreaths' of language and on a narrative that goes 'rambling and entangling' itself everywhere, 'like wild honeysuckles' (*CH* 203). There is a sense for such critics that the poem is, if anything, *too* poetic, too concertedly wedded to allegorical and metaphorical dilation, verbal abundance, and rhetorical experimentation, almost as if it is Jacobinical just in its excesses and its defiance of poetic order and decorum. Keats has thrown into the poem 'everything that occurred to him in the shape of a glittering image or striking expression', Jeffrey remarks, 'cover[ing] his pages with an interminable arabesque of connected and incongruous figures' (*CH* 203). As the narrator of Keats's much more compact *Isabella* puts it, there is a desire for 'the gentleness of old Romance, / The simple plaining of a minstrel's song' (387–8) that remains emphatically unfulfilled in *Endymion*. Instead, Keats's poem throws at the unsuspecting reader what one mid-century critic describes as a 'fantastic exuberance of ornament and decoration', and what the early twentieth-century biographer Sidney Colvin characterises as a 'bewildering redundance and intricacy of detail'.[3]

In fact, even as he wrote the poem, Keats was aware of the problems that his readers would encounter. Somewhat unusually, he was even prepared to say as much publicly. In an effort to defuse the critical attacks that were nevertheless launched, the narrator of *Endymion* comments on his own poetic deficiencies, declaring wearily at the end of Book 3 that ''tis a very sin / For one so weak to venture his poor verse / In such a place as this': 'O do no curse, / High Muses!', he pleads, but 'let him hurry to the ending' (937–40). Indeed, Keats insisted on including a remarkably open and notably self-'castigating' Preface in which he announces that the poem he is presenting to the public should not in fact be presented to the public: he introduces the poem with 'a feeling of regret' because it includes 'every error denoting a feverish attempt, rather than a deed accomplished' (*P* 102). In an assertion with which some of his contemporaries clearly concurred, Keats perhaps unwisely declared that none of the four books are 'of such completion as to warrant their passing the press' (*P* 102.).

Keats, we might surmise, learned from his mistakes. *Endymion* is about a young man falling in love both with the moon-goddess Diana and with an 'Indian maid', and eventually resolves in the revelation that the two are one, mortal/immortal, human/god. His other romance poems and 'La Belle Dame sans Merci' also focus on illusions of love, but in each case the delusional nature of love is emphasised and indeed moved to the centre of the narrative. In other words, the later poems are *structurally* sceptical of the possibility of the theme of transcendent, redemptive romantic love – by contrast with *Endymion*, where the transcendental or extra-terrestrial and the sublunary are finally unified and resolved. In Keats's version of a tale from the fourteenth-century Italian writer Giovanni Boccaccio, Isabella falls for a young man, Lorenzo. Her brothers disapprove of the relationship and murder Lorenzo, after which Isabella finds and disinters her dead lover's severed head, re-buries it in a basil pot, and weeps over it; ultimately, she wastes away and 'die[s] forlorn' (497) when the brothers steal the pot and disappear. 'La Belle Dame sans Merci' concerns a medieval knight who has been transfixed and abandoned by a mysterious, 'fairy' woman on a hillside along with other victims of the eerily enthralling *femme fatale*. In *The Eve of St. Agnes*, Porphyro breaks into the castle of a rival family to hide in a young woman's closet, spy on her while she undresses, and enter her bed as she dreams (implicitly also entering both her dream and her body), before fleeing with her into the wintry night. In *Lamia*, Lycius falls for a serpent disguised as a beautiful young woman, only for her true identity to be revealed by the philosopher Apollonius. At the thematic centre of each poem, there is an unveiling of romantic love as deceptive, coercive, unreasonable, deadly, fleeting or delusory. But these common concerns also have striking formal consequences: the ironising of and scepticism towards the conventional love-plot also entails formal and rhetorical divagations from the convention of romance form. As Stuart Curran argues, in coming late to the 'generic development' of romance, Keats is able to 'build on the logical possibility inherent' in the form such that irony becomes Keats's 'characteristic rhetorical mode'.[4]

The inherent possibility in modern poetry of generic ironisation is also evident in 'La Belle Dame sans Merci: A Ballad', which adopts and radically modernises the traditional ballad form that it announces in its title:

O what can ail thee, knight at arms,
  Alone and palely loitering?
The sedge has wither'd from the lake,
  And no birds sing.

O what can ail thee, knight at arms,
  So haggard and so woe-begone?
The squirrel's granary is full,
  And the harvest's done.

I see a lily on thy brow
  With anguish moist and fever dew,
And on thy cheeks a fading rose
    Fast withereth too.

I met a lady in the meads,
  Full beautiful, a fairy's child;
Her hair was long, her foot was light,
    And her eyes were wild.

I made a garland for her head,
    And bracelets too, and fragrant zone;
She look'd at me as she did love,
    And made sweet moan.

I set her on my pacing steed,
    And nothing else saw all day long,
For sidelong would she bend, and sing
    A fairy's song.

She found me roots of relish sweet,
    And honey wild, and manna-dew,
And sure in language strange she said –
    I love thee true.

She took me to her elfin grot,
    And there she wept, and sigh'd full sore,
And there I shut her wild wild eyes
    With kisses four.

And there she lulled me asleep,
    And there I dream'd – Ah! woe betide!
The latest dream I ever dream'd
    On the cold hill's side.

I saw pale kings, and princes too,
    Pale warriors, death pale were they all;
They cried – 'La belle dame sans merci
    Hath thee in thrall!'

I saw their starv'd lips in the gloam
    With horrid warning gaped wide,
And I awoke and found me here
    On the cold hill's side.

And this is why I sojourn here,
    Alone and palely loitering,
Though the sedge is wither'd from the lake,
    And no birds sing.

[stanza numbers are omitted]

The poem's anachronisms, its explicit archaisms, are already marked by a title that repeats that of a poem by the fifteenth-century French poet Alain Chartier (or by Richard Ros's Medieval English version of Chartier's poem).[5] And yet, in spite of its medievalist diction and accoutrements – a long-haired, wild-eyed, 'Full beautiful' lady who is also not a lady but a 'fairy's child', together with a knight, a garland, sedge, a 'zone' (a belt or girdle), a steed, an 'elfin grot', and kings and princes – the poem is also thoroughly modern, taking its lead from the era's resurgence of interest in the ballad and in medievalism more generally. A comparison with Keats's other, less well-known ballad is enlightening in this respect.[6] 'La Belle Dame sans Merci' was written in London in April 1819, but ten months earlier, during a walking tour of Scotland with his friend Charles Brown, Keats included in a letter to his fifteen-year-old sister a hastily written ballad following a pilgrimage to Robert Burns's cottage and grave in Ayrshire. Although the earlier ballad has largely been overlooked in Keats's reception, it might credibly be understood to have established the groundwork for Keats's later, more famous poem. The Scottish ballad is based on a character from Sir Walter Scott's hugely popular novel *Guy Mannering* (published anonymously in 1815). Keats had not read the novel, but as a keen theatre-goer he is likely to have attended a dramatised version – a 'musical play', by Daniel Terry from 1816 – that had been regularly performed at the Theatre Royal in Covent Garden between December 1817 and February 1818.[7] In a journal of the tour of Scotland published in 1840, Brown recalls that he recounted the plot of Scott's novel after which Keats wrote his response:

> Old Meg she was a gipsey,
>   And liv'd upon the moors;
> Her bed it was the brown heath turf,
>   And her house was out of doors.
>
> Her apples were swart blackberries,
>   Her currants pods o' broom,
> Her wine was dew o' the wild white rose,
>   Her book a churchyard tomb.
>
> Her brothers were the craggy hills,
>   Her sisters larchen trees –
> Alone with her great family
>   She liv'd as she did please.
>
> No breakfast had she many a morn,
>   No dinner many a noon,
> And 'stead of supper she would stare
>   Full hard against the moon.
>
> But every morn of woodbine fresh
>   She made her garlanding,
> And every night the dark glen yew
>   She wove and she would sing.

And with her fingers old and brown
    She plaited mats o' rushes,
And gave them to the cottagers
    She met among the bushes.

Old Meg was brave as Margaret Queen
    And tall as Amazon:
An old red blanket cloak she wore;
    A chip hat had she on.
God rest her aged bones somewhere –
    She died full long agone!

Although 'Old Meg' concerns a solitary elderly gypsy rather than a ghostly meeting between a knight and a fatal young woman, there are a number of details that link the two ballads: both are set 'out of doors' and both involve a quasi-mystical relationship between characters and natural surroundings; both share the imagery of roses, garlands, hunger (or not eating) and singing; and both seem to resolve in death (or in a form of death-in-life, a death-like suspended animation, in the case of 'La Belle Dame sans Merci'). It is clear, from a cursory reading of 'Old Meg' that it would not have been written without the models of Thomas Percy's *Reliques of Ancient English Poetry* (1765), and of modern ballads by writers such as the 'ballad-monger' Robert Southey, by co-authors William Wordsworth and Samuel Taylor Coleridge in their *Lyrical Ballads* (1798) and by Mary Robinson in her *Lyrical Tal*es (1800), as well as by more obscure poets such as Anne Taylor (the sister of Keats's publisher John Taylor), who published a poem remarkably similar in theme, technique, and tone in 1810.[8] But while Keats's poem has a certain rhetorical *brio* in its substitutive figuring of natural items for the gypsy's family and possessions, and a certain shock-value in its ending, what it lacks is the suggestiveness of the concertedly undecidable narrative logic of 'La Belle Dame sans Merci', which works, not least, by arousing in the reader a sense of permanent hermeneutic suspense. Who is this lady and who is the knight?, we might ask. What is the knight doing here, and who are these kings and princes? What, beyond her beauty, is the lady's power – or is her beauty itself her power?

While Keats's earlier ballad follows the conventional rhythmical pattern of four-line stanzas with alternate four-beat and three-beat lines (iambic tetrameters and iambic trimeters), in 'La Belle Dame sans Merci', Keats challenges readers' expectations by slightly modifying the conventional pattern (three tetrameters followed by one trimeter). The earlier poem has a rhetorically simple form that focuses almost exclusively on the utter destitution and solitude of the Gypsy and that hints at and resists certain magical or mystical properties (she stares at the moon instead of eating; she makes 'garlands' while singing, as if making a spell; she has an animistic relationship with her surroundings). By contrast, 'La Belle Dame sans Merci' manages to produce a circular form (the first stanza is largely repeated in the last) while also being decidedly open-ended, both in form (the questioner in the frame-narrative of stanzas 1–3 does not return at the end) and hermeneutically (the poem finally and emphatically leaves the reader in a state of conceptual and interpretative suspense). The contrast between the two ballads, in other words, is striking, and it is the fact that the later poem offers the familiar pleasures of the ballad form while at the same time restricting or withholding them – formally and in terms of the poem's meaning – that produces the extraordinary, permanent power of Keats's ballad.

'La Belle Dame sans Merci' may be said to have emerged out of *The Eve of St. Agnes*, which Keats had composed in January and February of 1819, since it is name-checked in the earlier poem at a crucial moment. Having found his way to Madeline's chamber, watched her undress and go to sleep before loading her table with exotic food-stuffs, Porphyro 'muses', 'entoil'd in woofed fantasies', on her sleeping face. He then rouses himself and plays 'an ancient ditty, long since mute, / In Provence call'd, "La belle dame sans mercy"' (288, 291–2). It is a distinctly odd moment that, along with the exorbitant lines describing the lovers' private feast, seems designed to disrupt or delay narrative progression and at the same time challenge credibility (is this really the moment to pick up your lute and sing? Is it really opportune, now, to set out a feast of 'candied apple', 'jellies soother than creamy curd', 'lucent syrops' and other treats [265–7]?). But it is also an assertively self-involved moment that seems to draw attention to the poem's own fictionality as well as to the parallels between music, poetry, and sexual desire.

One of the poem's most controversial stanzas follows hard on the heels of this retrospectively and proleptically intertextual moment. In stanza 36, Porphyro seems to melt into Madeline's dream:

> Beyond a mortal man impassion'd far
> At these voluptuous accents, he arose
> Ethereal, flush'd, and like a throbbing star
> Seen mid the sapphire heaven's deep repose;
> Into her dream he melted, as the rose
> Blendeth its odour with the violet, –
> Solution sweet: meantime the frost-wind blows
> Like Love's alarum pattering the sharp sleet
> Against the window-panes; St. Agnes' moon hath set.
> (316–24)

Shortly after making some relatively minor revisions to the poem in September 1819 (including to this stanza), Keats was famously confronted by his friend, Richard Woodhouse, who was also the legal advisor to his publisher. Woodhouse challenged Keats to explain what the former saw as the shockingly lewd suggestiveness entailed by the recent revisions (*L* 2, 162–3). Apparently distracted by the idea that Keats had revised the poem to imply pre-marital sex, and perhaps misled by the intense metaphoricity of the lines, Woodhouse seems to have overlooked the fact that in the original version, Porphyro not only gets into Madeline's bed but at the critical moment appears to be aroused to a state of fervent tumescence by her 'voluptuous accents' (he 'arose', we read, 'impassion'd', 'flush'd and throbbing'), and seems to have been blind to the fact that there is talk of melting, of blending, and of a suggestively sexual 'Solution sweet', as well as an implication of not entirely oneiric penetration ('Into her dream he melted' implies not only a melting of one cognitive state into another – sleep into wakefulness or vice versa – but also of one body into another).

The fact that Keats's first close-reader, Richard Woodhouse, can both attend to the implicitly sexualised *anti*-romance implications of the poem and at the same time overlook them is indicative of the complexity and uncertainty of its rhetoric and tone. In fact, the poem announces its resistance to romance assumptions early on. Stanza 5 foregrounds and dismisses romance, not least by the way that the mode is identified with the hollow and indeed aggressive 'revelry' of the castle's hostile inhabitants:

> At length burst in the argent revelry,
> With plume, tiara, and all rich array,
> Numerous as shadows haunting fairily
> The brain, new stuff'd, in youth, with triumphs gay
> Of old romance. These let us wish away,
> And turn, sole-thoughted, to one Lady there,
> Whose heart had brooded, all that wintry day,
> On love, and wing'd St. Agnes' saintly care,
> As she had heard old dames full many times declare.
> (37–45)

While the narrator of *Isabella* yearns for 'the gentleness of old Romance', in *The Eve of St. Agnes* 'old romance' is identified with the idea of a young brain being 'stuffed' with phantasmatic fairy 'shadows': such 'triumphs gay' are spurned and the reader is instructed to turn away from them sole-thoughtedly towards the broodingly waiting Madeline. The poem is a romance, therefore, that also at the same time distances itself from the codes, conventions and assumptions of its own mode. There is a distinct equivocation in the poem's language between a kind of spiritualism marked by a rhetorical religiosity on the one hand (the opening stanzas concern a 'holy man'; Madeline is brooding on St Agnes's 'saintly care' [44]; Porphryo later describes himself as a 'pilgrim' [339] and so on), and a gothic rhetoric of theft, violence, voyeurism, deceit, death and illicit sexual acts, on the other ("Mid looks of love, defiance, hate, and scorn' Madeline is 'Hoodwinked with faery fancy' [69–70]; the inhabitants of the castle are, to Porphyro, 'barbarian hordes, / Hyena foemen, and hot-blooded lords' [85–6]; the poem ends with the mention of witch, demon and 'coffin-worm', and with one servant dying 'palsy-twitch'd' with 'meagre face deform[ed]' and the other 'For aye unsought for' sleeping 'among his ashes cold' [374–8]). The poem is poised between these two conceptions of romance, as it is between sleep and wakefulness, sentimentality and a kind of knowingness, life and death, and the real and what might be imagined. It is precisely this instability of rhetoric, tone, and genre – one that is generated, not least, in response to cultural and political contexts that Keats's early romance poem *Endymion* was unable successfully to negotiate – that makes *The Eve of St. Agnes* so richly suggestive and therefore, we might conclude, so endlessly open to reading and interpretation.

Notes

1 Stuart Curran highlights the importance of 'composite orders' in the Romantic period in *Poetic Form and British Romanticism* (New York: Oxford University Press, 1986), ch. 8, commenting that they are dependent on the 'sense of formal possibilities that marks the age of British Romanticism' (p. 203).
2 Karen Swann, '*Endymion*'s Beautiful Dreamers', in Susan J. Wolfson, ed., *The Cambridge Companion to Keats* (Cambridge: Cambridge University Press, 2001), p. 20.
3 *CH* 350; Sidney Colvin, *John Keats: His Life, and Poetry, His Friends, Critics and After-Fame* (New York: Scribner's, 1917), p. 172.
4 Curran, *Poetic Form*, pp. 146, 150.
5 See J. Caitlin Finlayson, 'Medieval Sources for Keatsian Creation in *La Belle Dame sans Merci*', *Philological Quarterly* 79 (2000): 225–47.
6 While 'The Eve of St Mark' (1819) adopts the iambic tetrameter metre characteristic of the traditional ballad, it is usually seen not as a ballad but as a 'companion piece' to *The Eve of St. Agnes*. (See Stuart Sperry, *Keats the Poet* [Princeton: Princeton University Press, 1974], p. 221.)
7 See Claire Lamont, 'Meg the Gipsy in Scott and Keats', *English* 36 (1987): 139–40.
8 On Southey as 'ballad-monger', see Byron, 'English Bards and Scotch Reviewers', in Jerome J. McGann, ed., *Lord Byron: The Major Works* (Oxford: Oxford University Press, 2000), line 142; on Taylor, see Lynette Felber, 'Ann Taylor's "The Maniac's Song": An Unacknowledged Source for Keats's "La Belle Dame sans Merci"', *ANQ: A Quarterly Journal of Short Articles, Notes, and Reviews* 17 (2004): 29–36.

CHAPTER 26

Epic and Tragedy

Susan J. Wolfson

Adieu to Romance

If poetic manhood is tragedy and epic, aspirant Keats had his work cut out for him. *Endymion: A Poetic Romance* (1818), the longest work he'd ever write or publish, was neither. Its 4,000 lines, Keats conceded, was a space for readers' wandering, to pick and choose to their liking. An epic demands argument, and tragedy a hero, and Endymion was no model: always passive, variously despairing, enchanted, infantilised, then suddenly spiritualised into erotic success.

'On sitting down to read *King Lear* once again' is Keats's signal of 'determination' for better credentials. This was how he titled a sonnet composed in January 1818 while reading page proofs for *Endymion.*[1] With the stage held by Nahum Tate's romance revision of the play (1681), Keats's 'read' is significant. But it's not just reading, it's re-reading, 'once again' against the seductions of 'Romance': a 'serene' 'melodizing' of the 'far-away', figured as a golden-tongued, 'Fair plumed Syren' (Keats's poetry is quoted from *K*, unless indicated otherwise). Keats underlined 'Helen's golden tongue' in *Troilus and Cressida.*[2] The *Adieu!* is as fond as it is insistent. No wonder: *Lear*'s 'fierce dispute / Betwixt Damnation and impassion'd clay' synonymises 'read' with 'burn through'. While the hope is rebirth – 'When I am consumed with the fire, / Give me new Phœnix-wings to fly at my desire' (13–14) – the trope is only prospective, and implicates cyclical repetitions. There is warp in the metre of this last line, a hexameter born out of pentameter. Hexameter is the last line of the Spenserian stanza that builds *The Faerie Queene.* If Keats talks tragedy, he lingers in a form of Romance.

Hyperion's Endeavour

Keats wanted to leave the 'sentimental cast' of *Endymion* for 'a more naked and grecian Manner' and an 'undeviating' 'march of passion and endeavour'. Unlike the 'mortal ... led on, like Buonaparte, by circumstance', new hero, Apollo, 'being a fore-seeing God will shape his actions like one' (23 January 1818; *L* 1, 207; K 88). The simile is historically resonant. Vanquished at Waterloo (June 1815), Napoleon left the progressive hopes of a generation in shambles, rendering 'more harm to the life of Liberty than any one' Keats said (*L* 1, 397). What would a regime change look like in the actions of a foreseeing, 'enlighten'd' hero?

Yet Keats would always title the poem for Hyperion, a god foreseeing his own doom in his fallen brothers. When Keats toured the north in summer 1818, it was to return find his own brother Tom dying, painfully. Sitting down to write *Hyperion,* he felt a horrible contradiction. The plan was to hail Apollo, 'Father of all verse' (3. 13), but life had made him 'father of' that 'tremendous' knowledge 'that the World is full of Misery and Heartbreak, Pain, Sickness and oppression' (he wrote back in May). 'I wish I could say Tom was any better', he sighs in September; 'His identity presses upon me so all day that I am obliged to go out' or 'to write, and plunge into abstract images to ease myself of his countenance his voice and feebleness' (*L* 1, 368–9; *K* 200). 'I have left / My strong identity, my real self', is the voice he writes for dethroned Saturn (1. 113–14).

In October Keats theorises a 'camelion' poetics of conceptual power (including what it's like to be this Saturn) in imagining oneself into 'some other Body' (*L* 1, 387; *K* 214). Proximate to Tom, however, this 'other Body' presses on him with such pain that 'ease' gets betrayed to disease. 'I live now in a continual fever', Keats tells a friend, caught between having to 'suffer' with Tom, and the 'crime' of aspiring to 'fame of poetry'. 'Imagine 'the hateful siege of contraries' (*L* 1, 369; *K* 200), he writes, summoning a phrase he had underlined in Satan's survey of an Eden he can only ruin.[3] 'I am sorry to give you pain', he apologizes to this friend, 'but I really have not self possession and magninimity [*sic*] enough to manage the thing otherwise' – no junior Apollo, he. Poetry is 'feverous relief' next to 'Poor Tom' (*L* 1, 370; *K* 201). Keats underlined this naming in *King Lear,* painfully dating it October 4. Even the poetry of Apollo's deification falls into physical convulsion – its pain, struggle, anguish, imprinted with intimate knowledge of dying bodies. Tom's last days were of 'a most distressing nature', Keats says, as he returned to an epic he was now calling 'the fall of Hyperion'.[4]

Fluxes of passions, sieges of thought and feeling, shape *Hyperion* into a 'lyrical epic'.[5] Book I opens after the action of revolt, to audit the defeated Titans – stunned, confused and aching – then shifts to Hyperion's agonised premonitions, before he descends to earth, in Book 2, to view his fallen comrades. Keats turns Book 3 to Apollo, awakening to divinity, but he stopped writing, mid-sentence, in April 1819, after only 135 lines. This wasn't Apollo's march after all. For any story of loss, *Paradise Lost* (*PL*) was the paradigm, most sublime in Satan's ruining into a 'glory obscured; as when the sun new risen / Looks through the horizontal misty air / Shorn of his beams' (*PL* 1. 594–6). Keats's angle was to dispel Milton's theology into Wordsworthian 'dark passages' where 'we see not the ballance of good and evil' (*L* 1, 281; K 130), letting even Milton's Satan escape the balance, on the dramatic power of his 'epic passions' (*L* 1, 278; *K* 129): 'round he throws his baleful eyes" (1. 56). Keats underlines this and its extended sequel (*K* 226):

At once, as far as Angels' ken he views
The dismal situation waste and wild:
(1. 59–60)

sights of woe,
Regions of sorrow, doleful shades, where peace
And rest can never dwell, hope never comes
That comes to all
(1. 64–7)

With no ritual invocation to a muse, Keats launches his epic with a one-sentence stanza of relentless intensifications, layer by layer, line by line, word by word. Its fourteen lines shape a sonnet that now truly rereads King Lear:

DEEP in the shady sadness of a vale
Far sunken from the healthy breath of morn,
Far from the fiery noon, and eve's one star,
Sat gray-hair'd Saturn, quiet as a stone,
Still as the silence round about his lair;
Forest on forest hung about his head
Like cloud on cloud. No stir of air was there,
Not so much life as on a summer's day
Robs not one light seed from the feather'd grass,
But where the dead leaf fell, there did it rest.
A stream went voiceless by, still deadened more
By reason of his fallen divinity
Spreading a shade: the Naiad 'mid her reeds
Press'd her cold finger closer to her lips.

In antithesis to inspiration (no breath), the thuds of *Deep in* (sounding *deepen*, echoed in *sunken*) sink into epochal obituary. Repeated words and syllables punctuate a litany of what's lost: light, health, air, song, movement itself. For this dirge, Keats had to coin some subtractions: Saturn's *realmless* eyes (1. 19), versus (to come) Apollo's *gloomless* eyes across the *liegeless* air he's born to rule (3. 80–92). Under 'the full weight of utterless thought', Saturn can riddle no 'reason' for his fall – especially to forces that seemed so 'untremendous' (2. 129–55).

Keats models the council of Book 2 on *Paradise Lost* 2 – but with no judgmental epic narrator. Some of this charge is taken up by Oceanus's lecture (173–243) on the 'course of Nature's law' and generational inevitability: 'A power more strong in beauty, born of us / And fated to excel us.' There's a tradition of hearing Keats's proxy (and not without Keats's help[6]). Yet not for nothing, and with Hazlitt's help, did Keats study Shakespeare's dramatic characters. In Oceanus, Keats creates, camelion-wide, a complacent sophist, exempla and clichés ready at hand. Milton's God is not the godfather, but Milton's poetry, 'godlike in the sublime pathetic' (*K* 231). Praising the 'Magnitude of Contrast' in the rally of the fallen angels, Keats fiercely underlined Milton's line, loving 'The light and shade … the sorrow, the pain, the sad-sweet Melody … the thousand Melancholies and Magnificences of this Page' (*PL* 1. 535–65; *K* 227–9). He underscored Satan's ruining into an 'excess / Of glory obscured; as when the sun new risen / Looks through the horizontal misty air / Shorn of his beams' (*PL* 1. 593–6), bringing it to Hyperion with allusive force: 'Regal his shape majestic, a vast shade / In midst of his own brightness' (2. 372–3; *K* 229). He underscored the Cherubims' 'Millions of flaming swords' that in a 'sudden blaze / Far round illumin'd Hell' (*PL* 1. 664–6), and relayed this into Hyperion's survey of the fallen gods, a 'misery his brilliance had betray'd / To the most hateful seeing of itself' (2. 369–70).

The light to come is Apollo. Milton's 'management' of Books 1–3 Keats deemed 'Apollonian' (*K* 233), the mark of his 'fore-seeing' hero. Yet if Apollo stands for cerebral brilliance (prophesy, philosophy, poetry, music, medicine too), Keats's figuring is notably retro-Endymion: bower-born, accessorised with a mother and a sister, yearning for a 'beauteous star, / And I will flit into it with my lyre, / And make its silvery splendour pant with bliss' (100–102). In no fierce dispute, his 'aching ignorance' wins a 'wondrous lesson' from Muse-Mnemosyne; in an instant, 'Knowledge enormous makes a God of me' (3. 104–13). 'Names, deeds, gray legends, dire events, rebellions, / Majesties, sovran voices, agonies, / Creations and destroyings' (114–16) enter his brain in a march of empty nouns. What's left to say? 'Apollo shriek'd; –and lo! from all his limbs / Celestial glory dawn'd. he was a god!' In *1820*, 'Celestial' is the last word, trailed by fourteen un-symbolic asterisks (p. 199).

The more compelling blaze was the one haunted by shady visions. 'Blazing Hyperion on his orbed fire / Still sat' (1. 166–7). *Still* denotes the temporal *yet;* but as a station, Keats plays into a devastating repetition: 'Sat gray-hair'd Saturn … / Still as the silence' (I. 4–5) is the textual past that twins this moment. Keats's epic similes and analogies thicken the intimations of mortality:

For as among us mortals omens drear
Fright and perplex, so also shuddered he
(I. 169–70)

sometimes eagle's wings,
Unseen before by Gods or wondering men,
Darken'd the place; and neighing steeds were heard,
Not heard before by Gods or wondering men.
(I.182–5)

'Instead of sweets, his ample palate took / Savour of poisonous brass and metal sick' (I. 188–9) is a sensation that would become Keats's own mortal savour. 'The last two years taste like brass upon my Palate', he tells the woman he loved and hoped to marry, Fanny Brawne in August 1820, with less than half a year to live, without her (*L* 2, 312; *K* 423). 'We see the ebb and flow of the feeling, its pauses and feverish starts, its impatience of opposition, its accumulating force when it has time to recollect itself, the manner in which it avails itself of every passing word or gesture, its haste to repel insinuation, the alternate contraction and dilation of the soul': this is Hazlitt on *King Lear*, one of the 'great master-pieces in the logic of passion'.[7] Keats marked a good deal of this sentence in *Characters of Shakespear's Plays*, taking its logic into *Hyperion*. Nightmares invade Hyperion's 'palace bright', aching it with his fever. It 'Glared a blood-red through all its thousand courts, / Arches, and domes, and fiery galleries' (I. 179–80). The very clouds flush 'angerly' (180), hailing Hyperion, 'full of wrath' (213):

His flaming robes stream'd out beyond his heels,
And gave a roar, as if of earthly fire
(I.214–15)

Keats uses *as if* to register not just analogy but a prophecy of Hyperion's doom to earth.

The epic action, 'shady visions come to domineer', is from presences already in the mind.

Why do I know ye? why have I seen ye? …

Saturn is fallen, am I too to fall?
Am I to leave this haven of my rest,

This cradle of my glory, this soft clime,
This calm luxuriance of blissful light,
These crystalline pavilions, and pure fanes,
Of all my lucent empire?
(I. 231, 234–9)

Hyperion sounds the echoes. John of Gaunt's dying hymn to an England lost to internecine usurpation elegises 'this sceptred isle, /... This other Eden, demi-paradise, /... This blessed plot, this earth, this realm, this England' (*Richard II,* 2. I. 40–50). Waking in Hell, Satan realizes 'this the region, this the soil, ... this the seat / That we must change for Heav'n, this mournful gloom / For that celestial light' (*PL* I. 243–5).

Hyperion falls first in dread, scanning a realm 'Deserted, void, nor any haunt of mine'; it dies in his eyes: 'I cannot see – but darkness, death and darkness' (I. 239–42). For this assault from within, Keats rewrites Satan's insinuation into Eden. Satan enters 'wrapt in a mist / Of midnight vapour', finding cover inside a sleeping serpent. Underlining this passage,[8] Keats mobilizes it for Hyperion's 'horrors' (I. 175):

A mist arose, as from a scummy marsh.
At this, through all his bulk an agony
Crept gradual, from the feet unto the crown,
Like a lithe serpent vast and muscular
Making slow way, with head and neck convuls'd
From over-strained might.
(I.258–63)

What a cruel wrench is *crown* – from empire to imperiled body. Keats closes Book I on Hyperion's course downward to darkness: 'Forward he stoop'd over the airy shore, / And plung'd all noiseless into the deep night' (I. 356–7) – *noiseless* also meaning *still.* This is the 'sublime pathetic' at its darkest: grand and silent.

For the 'dethronement of Hyperion ... by Apollo' and 'the war of the Giants for Saturn's reestablishment', there were only 'very dark hints' in the mythologies; the 'incidents would have been pure creations of the Poet's brain'.[9] Keats gave up 'in a sort of qui bono temper, not exactly on the road to an epic poem' (*L* 2, 42). *Qui bono/cui bono: for whose benefit?* The rise of Apollo over Hyperion had not been an undeviating march after all. And Keats's unanticipated equivocation was all the more powerful for this. His publishers insisted on having *Hyperion, A Fragment* in the 1820 volume – allotting more than a quarter of its pages. Shelley thought it 'astonishing ... the very highest style of poetry', elevating Keats to one of 'the first writers of the age'.[10]

Sitting Down to Reread *Hyperion* Once Again; or *The Fall of Hyperion, A Dream*

Returning the project in fall 1819, Keats made Hyperion's agony an epic poet's qualifying exam: a dream, in agonising degrees of sensation, of his own death. Wrought in the shadow of Dante's *Purgatorio* and the doom of Milton's *Paradise Lost,* Keats's *Fall of Hyperion* has no Apollo-god of poetry – just this human poet, told he is no poet, merely a useless, fevered dreamer. This sentence is pronounced by the Titan-survivor Moneta, who sets that death test, and gives its proof in the theatre of her memory. It's Keats's memory, too: her memory is his *Hyperion.*

In *Hyperion* the Titans' fall gave epic syntax to mortal knowledge; in the revision, a mortal poet bears this knowledge. This is a theme Keats sketched out in the spring of 1819 for mortal life: a 'vale of Soul-making', for which 'human heart [is] the hornbook'. A soul ('identity') is formed as the heart is schooled, made to 'feel and suffer in a thousand diverse ways'. It's 'a grander system of salvation than the chrystain religion' because it makes human sense of suffering (21 April; *L* 2, 102–3; *K* 251). What Keats couldn't figure out in *Hyperion* – an experiential philosophy for Apollo's victory – becomes his premise in *The Fall of Hyperion:* a 'poet' challenged to earn this identity from the hornbook obliquely punned into Moneta's 'horned shrine' (I. 137). A 'vale of Soul-making' imprints the recovery in *The Fall* of the text of *Hyperion*: 'Deep in the shady sadness of a vale' (I. 294). This vale will become the poet's for 'A long awful time' (384) as he bears, on an acute sympathetic register, the suffering that *Hyperion*'s poet-godling Apollo rehearses in rapid transit.

The stakes are spelled out at the opening. 'Fanatics have their dreams' and so do savages, but 'bare of laurel', these 'shadows of melodious utterance' can only 'die' (I. 1–7):

> For Poesy alone can tell her dreams,
> With the fine spell of words alone can save
> Imagination from the sable charm
> And dumb enchantment.
>
> (I. 8–11)

If Keats plays a promising chime from *vell*um to *mel*odious to lau*rel* to *tell* to *spell,* every one of Poesy's claims will be tested – both in the poet's dream, and for the poem subtitled *A Dream:*

> Whether the dream now purposed to rehearse
> Be poet's or Fanatic's will be known
> When this warm scribe my hand is in the grave.
>
> (I. 16–18)

Not just genre but narrative logic is in question: is the dream-rehearsal the distillation of memory (Mnemosyne embodied) or the writing uncertainly to come (Moneta its medium)? Is *now* (lettered inside k*now*n) post-dream or the present of writing? The question entails its scribe: 'this warm scribe' and the fear of the *Hyperion* poet that his subject may be 'Too huge for mortal tongue or pen of scribe' (I. 160) are the sole events of *scribe* in Keats's poetry. It was a critical self-assignment.

A spell of words and a warm hand figure into the ordeal at Moneta's shrine, a site exceeding the mere 'faulture' of worldly ruins (I. 70) – a great Keats-coinage evoking faultline and failure. At the end of a 'patient travail' of 'innumerable degrees' (91–2), the dreamer tells how

> suddenly a palsied chill
> Struck from the paved level up my limbs,
> And was ascending quick to put cold grasp
> Upon those streams that pulse beside the throat
> … the cold
> Grew stifling, suffocating, at the heart.
> And when I clasp'd my hands I felt them not
> (I.122–5, 129–31)

This agony, formerly the force that suffocates Hyperion, is *The Fall*'s authority. The poet has 'felt / What 'tis to die' and then 'live again' (141–3), in order to see others die – so Moneta describes a passport to vision that is indistinguishable from a curse.

On this pulse, Keats wrote and rewrote an extended debate between this poet and Moneta about his (or any poet's) claim to vocation: is a poet clear-eyed about 'the miseries of the world', or does he want 'thoughtless sleep' (I. 148–53)? Is he one of those who 'Labour for mortal good', or one of the 'dreamers weak', impotent 'vision'ries' unable to 'benefit … the great world' and too restless for any 'haven' of relief (154–71)? Keats drafted another twenty-seven lines (184–210^{II}) to get this far: 'The poet and the dreamer are distinct, / Diverse, sheer opposite, antipodes' (200–202). It's no conclusion. Written *A Dream,* the poem's logic is a conundrum. And its muse defies its very medium:

> I had no words to answer for my tongue,
> Useless, could find about its roofed home
> No syllable of a fit Majesty
> To make rejoinder to Moneta's mourn.
> (I.228–31)

Keats found a syllable, *-less*, to write of her 'eyes visionless entire … Of all external things' (I. 267–8). It is Moneta who rejoins, with a test of aesthetic logic that entails aesthetic ethics: 'My power, which to me is still a curse, / Shall be to thee a wonder' (I. 243–4), 'Free from all pain, if wonder pain thee not' (I. 248). This *if* is more than casual codicil. Her 'wan face' is 'bright blanch'd / By an immortal sickness which kills not' (I.256–8) – a sublimity beyond capable imagination:

deathwards progressing
To no death was that visage; it had passed
The lily and the snow; and beyond these
I must not think now, though I saw that face–
(I. 260–3)

'I must not think now' halts at this unending present. To the medical term, 'mortal sickness', Keats fits a new syllable, and writes the genesis of the 'high tragedy / In the dark secret Chambers of her skull' (I.277–8): 'Then came the griev'd voice of Mnemosyne, / And griev'd I hearken'd' (331–2). Editors usually mark a slip for 'Moneta' here, but Keats, whose dreamer has hailed a 'Shade of Memory!' (282), wanted Mnemosyne, her 'griev'd voice' remembered in 'griev'd I'.

The text of *Hyperion* returns with grieving revision. The poet is no *spectator ab extra,* but a camelion-witness, with a vengeance:

Moneta silent. Without stay or prop
But my own weak mortality, I bore
The load of this eternal quietude,
The unchanging gloom, and the three fixed shapes
Ponderous upon my senses a whole moon.
(I.388–92)

Ponderous upon has mental weight, physical sensation and poetic consequence all at once:

For by my burning brain I measured sure
Her silver seasons shedded on the night,
And every day by day methought I grew
More gaunt and ghostly.
(I. 393–6)

In 'the vale / And all its burthens' (397–8) – burthens on the gods, on their witness, on poetic measure – the dreamer undergoes and, forever it seems, relives his soul-making into a tragic poet.

Keats ends his first (only complete) Canto at a threshold to test any reader:

– And she spake on,
As ye may read who can unwearied pass
Onward from the Antichamber of this dream

> Where, even at the open doors awhile
> I must delay, and glean my memory
> Of her high phrase – perhaps no further dare. –
> (1.463–8)

Poet and reader may be distinct, diverse. Or not: *ye may* rhymes with *I* ... *delay.* Canto II opens the doors, and when the dream resumes, 'Now in clear light I stood, / Reliev'd from the dusk vale' (2. 49–50), it's a short lease of relief, because this dreamer knows 'What 'tis to die' (1. 141–2).

His memory is now the muse, and Keats recalls a scene in *Purgatorio* for this doubled knowledge. At the gates of Purgatory, Dante glanced a marble stair so 'polish'd, that therein my mirror'd form / Distinct I saw' (9. 86–7).[12] Keats turns this mirror to Mnemosyne – 'the polish'd stone / ... reflected pure / Her priestess-garments' (2. 51–3) – so that, in a feint of syntax, the god's motion in *Hyperion* ('On he flared, / From stately nave to nave, from vault to vault'; 217ff.) gets a mirror in the dreamer's eyes:

> My quick eyes ran on
> From stately nave to nave, from vault to vault,
> Through bowers of fragrant and enwreathed light
> And diamond paved lustrous long arcades.
> Anon rush'd by the bright Hyperion;
> (2. 53–7)

In the run of reading, the predicate from 53 makes a claim on line 57. While line 58 – 'His flaming robes stream'd out' – aligns the grammar (Hyperion rushed by the eyes, not the eyes rushed by Hyperion), its Latinate syntax allows line 57 a double grammar, for the moment figuring a 'camelion Poet ... in for – and filling some other body' (*L* 1, 387; *K* 214): Hyperion's. It is such a poet (not guide Moneta) who, in the dream-form of *The Fall,* authorizes the already-ruining 'comparison of earthly things' (2.3). Hyperion's flaming robes

> gave a roar, as if of earthly fire,
> That scar'd away the meek ethereal hours
> And made their dove-wings tremble: on he flared –
> (2. 59–61)

The words are the same as *Hyperion*'s (1. 215–17), but the revision's mainframe gives them new sounds. In *flared* Keats recalls Canto I's last doubtful note, *dare,* then hits an exact rhyme here, on the regime-burning *scar'd.* Yet from this chord, the very last words of Keats's latest effort, 'on he flared–' pause at a dash, to inscribe, with a sympathetic warm hand, a stand-alone, three-stress dramatic propulsion into the unwritten future: epic, tragic and severely modern.

Notes

1 Autograph ms, 'Jan[y] 22–1818,' on a blank page opposite page 1 of *King Lear* in Keats's facsimile of the first folio (Keats House, Hampstead). Keats states his 'determination' to his brothers in a letter first published in R. M. Milnes, *Life, Letters and Literary Remains of John Keats* (London: Edward Moxon, 1848), vol. 1, pp. 96–7.
2 Caroline Spurgeon, *Keats's Shakespeare* (London: Oxford University Press, 1928), p. 151.
3 *Paradise Lost* 9.121–2; Beth Lau, *Keats's 'Paradise Lost'* (Gainesville, FL: University of Florida Press, 1998), p. 150.
4 16–18 December 1818 (*L* 2, 4, 14).
5 Hartman, 'Spectral Symbolism and Authorial Self', in *The Fate of Reading* (Chicago: University of Chicago Press, 1975), p. 60 – an essay also sharp on the relay of ease and disease in Keats's compositional siege.
6 'I never can feel certain of any truth but from a clear perception of its Beauty', he wrote on 31 December 1818 (*L* 2, 19).
7 William Hazlitt, 'Lear', *Characters of Shakespear's Plays* (London: R Hunter, 1817), p. 157.
8 *PL* 9. 158–9, 179–91; Lau, *Keats's 'Paradise Lost'*, pp. 152–3.
9 Richard Woodhouse's annotations on *Endymion*, April 1819; H. B. Forman, *The Poetical Works of John Keats* (New York: Crowell, 1895), p. 314.
10 W. M. Rossetti, 'Memoir,' *The Poetical Works of Shelley* (London: Edward Moxon, 1870), pp. cxxxiii–iv.
11 Keats meant to cancel these, but modern editions include them.
12 Henry Francis Cary's translation, *The Divine Comedy*, 3 vols. (London: Taylor and Hessey, 1814), which Keats owned, and took with him to read on his walking tour with Charles Brown in the summer of 1818.

CHAPTER 27

Lyrical Genres

Christopher R. Miller

In May of 1816, a sonnet titled *To Solitude* appeared in Leigh Hunt's periodical, *The Examiner*. This minor literary event might have been utterly forgotten if the poem, credited to 'J.K.,' had not marked the print debut of a young medical student named John Keats. Soon enough, the budding poet was participating in Hunt's sonnet-writing contests; but just as quickly, he would chafe under his mentor's influence, not to mention the formal rules of the sonnet itself. Even as he worked in longer narrative genres, however, Keats continued to write sonnets, using the form for both general themes and particular occasions, both impromptu jotting and meticulous craft; and in the course of his brief career, he composed over sixty of them. Despite (and even because of) its constraints, the sonnet played an indispensable role in Keats' development as a lyric poet. In short, the practice of writing sonnets kept Keats grounded in the structural economy of a brief lyrical form, even as he expanded on that form in his odes.

The idea of development has been a durable motif in scholarship on Keats, for a variety of reasons: it marks the astonishing growth of his poetic powers over the course of just a few years; it tallies with his own emphasis on stages of maturation and his metaphor of life as a 'Mansion of Many Apartments' (*L* 1, 280); it describes the imaginative process by which he assimilated his reading and experience; and it tracks his deliberate movement through literary influences (Hunt, Spenser, Shakespeare, Milton) and genres (sonnet, ode, epic, romance). The sonnet makes an especially apt focus for investigating Keats's artistic evolution, because the poet conspicuously adapted it for his own purposes, and because he keenly observed its felicities and limitations.

In a letter to his brother George in 1819, Keats faulted the Petrarchan sonnet for its 'pouncing rhymes' (the two couplets nestled in the octave), and the Shakespearean because 'the couplet at the end of it has seldom a pleasing effect' (*L* 2, 108). Having written some 2,000 heroic couplets in

Endymion, he was surely wearied by what Milton in the Preface to *Paradise Lost* had dismissed as artistic 'bondage' imposed on the poet and aural 'jingling' inflicted on the reader. And yet Keats could not reject rhyme outright, despite his venture into the Miltonic blank verse of his 'Hyperion' poems. Instead, he salvaged elements from the two major sonnet forms and repurposed them for his odes. The typical eighteenth-century 'great ode' was loosely Pindaric in structure – irregular in lineation, stanza length, and rhyme scheme – but Keats preferred the more orderly features of the sonnet. Four of his odes feature ten-line stanzas in iambic pentameter, consisting of a Shakespearean quatrain sutured to a Petrarchan sestet; the other two contain variations on this pattern. Through this prosodic alchemy, Keats almost entirely purged his odes of the dreaded couplet – leaving only a vestigial trace of it in the eleven-line stanzas of *To Autumn*, perhaps in emphasis of its theme of dilatory lingering.

For Keats, the sonnet was not only an organizing structure, however; it was an ongoing poetic exercise that vitally confirmed his sense of poetic vocation. It was the form that he used to pay tribute to poets both living (Byron) and dead (Chatterton), and to herald an artistic new age of 'great spirits'. It was also the ground on which Keats matched his talents against other members of Hunt's circle, including the elder and more prominent Percy Shelley. The brevity and strict rules of the form were well suited to Hunt's timed writing competitions on set themes – from which Keats emerged as the clear winner with 'On the Grasshopper and the Cricket', and as a respectable contender with 'To the Nile'.

Hunt's contests, as well as Keats's associations of the sonnet with lightness and spontaneity, affirmed the Renaissance value of *sprezzatura* – the art of making virtuosity seem effortless. Keats articulated that ethos in an 1817 letter to his friend J. H. Reynolds, in which he remarked that Shakespeare's sonnets 'seem to be full of fine things said unintentionally – in the intensity of working out conceits' (*L* 1, 188). Here, Keats distills his ideal of a poem that seems casually offhand while performing deliberate work. The word 'intensity' – with its Latin root denoting something stretched or strained – aptly conveys both the passionate feeling and the verbal compression that go into writing a sonnet.

In writing his own sonnets, Keats drew on several models: not only Shakespeare's meditations on mutability and immortality but also Milton's early reflections on poetic ambition and achievement, and the late eighteenth-century work of poets such as Charlotte Smith and William Lisle Bowles. Often grouped under the stylistic heading of 'Sensibility', these later poems typically featured solitary speakers, situated in twilit landscapes, and expressing emotions of melancholy, nostalgia, or loneliness. Though Keats began writing a few decades after the height of Sensibility, several of his early poems, including his debut effort, reflect its crepuscular afterglow. In particular, he might have been emulating Smith's *Elegiac Sonnets* (1785), which included a poem addressed to Solitude, and he certainly knew a seminal poem that lay behind it: Milton's *Il Penseroso*, whose speaker prefers a life of seclusion with the allegorical figure of Melancholy.

Keats departs from these precursors in notable ways: rather than wishing to live with Solitude, he begins with a grudgingly conditional statement: 'O Solitude! if I must with thee dwell, / Let it not be among the jumbled heap / Of murky buildings' (1–3). From his position in a dreary Southwark flat, he insists on one kind of isolation (pastoral retreat) over another (urban alienation), but in the sestet he stubbornly asserts a higher preference for the 'sweet converse' (10) of 'two kindred spirits' (14). Here, we have an early glimpse of Keats's play with the expressive possibilities of Petrarchan structure: through a formally motivated contrast, the poet arrives at a redefinition of solitude.

Even during his early Petrarchan apprenticeship, Keats was striving for the ideal of Shakespearean development. 'On First Looking into Chapman's Homer' (1816) exemplifies the working out of conceits that he had in mind. Only the title identifies the literal experience; the rest of the poem translates the act of reading into a symbolic language of discovery. In the past, reading books was like a traveller's voyages to distant realms; but in the present, the thrill of encountering a sixteenth-century English edition of Homer requires a stronger metaphorical vocabulary of astonishment – hearing the voice of the translator, seeing a previously unknown planet, gazing in mute wonder at the Pacific alongside fellow explorers. Each trope represents a new attempt to convey some essential quality of an experience: a night of reading Homer with a friend was like communing with the dead and patiently scanning the heavens, but it was even closer to the feeling of discovering something in the company of others.

Beginning in 1818 with 'When I Have Fears', Keats adopted the Shakespearean sonnet – and its characteristic reckoning with mortality – into his repertoire. In many ways, the poem emulates Shakespeare's Sonnet 12: it is structured by the syntax of 'When / then'; it turns from expressing a general meditation to addressing a specific listener; and it offers a series of metaphors for its central concern – the labour of literary production. Here, the working out of conceits is itself devoted to envisioning future *work*.

The effort of imagining this labour had to find a conclusion, a way of rounding off a seemingly endless course of thought. All poems pose the aesthetic challenge of closure, but the strictures of the sonnet compel that task with particular salience; and in this poem Keats finds an open-ended solution that looks ahead to his later lyrics. Though he duly ends his poem with a couplet, he blunts its epigrammatic effect through the relentless pace of two enjambments: 'then on the shore / Of the wide world I stand alone, and think / Till love and fame to nothingness do sink' (12–14). Here, he avoids making definitive claims about Love or Fame; rather, he renders a stoic report on seeing (or not seeing) them slip from view.

Typically, Keats's sonnets commemorate completed experiences, or they refer to a generalised or habitual present, but there are several notable exceptions. These might be called 'real-time' sonnets, in that they describe an event as it happens, or constitute a mental event unto itself. In dramatic terms, they are akin to soliloquies, in which a character reflects on his own thoughts and emotions as they pass; in narrative terms, they adopt the mode of what Samuel Richardson called, in reference to his own epistolary novels, 'writing to the moment'.[1] Several of these poems articulate feelings of creative frustration. In 'On Receiving a Laurel Crown from Leigh Hunt', for example, Keats attempts a Petrarchan sonnet about crowning himself with a symbol of poetic supremacy associated with Petrarch himself; and he keenly feels the pressure of that grandiose gesture. In effect, the sonnet's fourteen lines measure a wait for inspiration that never arrives.

Keats confronted a similar dilemma in the spring of 1817, when he went to see the Elgin Marbles at the British Museum. Under the expectant gaze of Haydon, he felt unequal to the task of writing about the sublimity of the experience, and in two sonnets, he professes feelings of dizziness and fatigue. Instead of depicting the objects he came to see, he represents his own psychosomatic response to them. Here, the sonnet serves as both a reassuringly bounded container and a frustratingly arbitrary horizon: though the sonnet offers a definite structure, Keats feels he has no time to 'speak / definitively' (1–2) about his encounter.

The real-time sonnet proved useful a year later on Keats's walking tour of northern England and Scotland. In the 1780s, Bowles had framed his site-specific sonnets as a traveller's notes in a memorandum book, and Keats's Scottish poems serve a similarly diaristic purpose. Like any tourist, Keats had begun his trip with idealised expectations, so he inevitably expresses some disappointment – most acutely in the sonnet he wrote about visiting Robert Burns's cottage, 'This Mortal Body of a Thousand Days'. Instead of a holy shrine, he finds a tourist site selling drams of whiskey; and in the absence of any numinous literary presence, he dwells on concrete physical details. Having become literally drunk on the place's offerings, he feels reduced to a pulsating and dizzy body – awkwardly impaired and yet triumphantly alive.

While the 'thousand days' of the title sounds proverbially large, its diurnal unit of measurement reduces life to a poignantly finite series, and the sonnet form aptly conveys that sense. Keats's circumscribed movement inside a cottage is echoed by the prosodic paces within the sonnet's narrow form, as the living poet asserts his own presence in the void left by a dead one: 'Yet can I stamp my foot on thy floor' (9); 'Yet can I ope thy window sash' (10); 'Yet can I think of thee' (12); 'Yet can I gulp a bumper to thy name' (13). Ordinarily, only one coordinating conjunction would suffice to enable a Petrarchan *volta* from octave to sestet, but here the flurry of defiant *yet*s animates something other than a rhetorical turn. They serve as both a contrastive *but* and a temporal *still*, and in their sheer repetition, they mark an interval of restless movement and creative ferment. (The function of that *still* would later be inverted in the 'Ode to a Nightingale', when the poet contemplates his own death while the bird blithely continues on: 'Still wouldst thou sing, and I have ears in vain', 59.) In conveying bodily vitality and temporal flux, these physical and mental gestures anticipate the odes, with their self-positioning between a knowable past and an uncertain future, and between death and life.

In the odes of the following year, Keats would never again mention a specific poet or site by name, but the function that Burns had served – as presiding spirit, as precursor, as emblem of immortality, as historical reference-point – would be taken up by a procession of symbolic figures. Wordsworth had famously condemned personification as bloodless artifice, but Keats disproves the charge by treating allegorical figures (Psyche, Indolence, Melancholy, Autumn) and non-human things (an artefact, a bird) with a striking warmth and intimacy, running through a dialogical range of feeling from tender affection to ardent questioning to cold disenchantment.

In turning to the ode, Keats adopted a form that was regarded in eighteenth-century theory and practice as the highest species of lyric: a worthy peer to epic, a secular version of sacred hymn, and an expansive medium for unfettered genius. Poets such as William Collins and Joseph Warton had harked back to the genre's ancient roots in musical performance, and in that vein, Keats often invokes the idea of a song. Earlier, he had written interpolated songs for *Endymion* (a 'roundelay' on sorrow, a Hymn to Pan), and a ballad about an enchantress who attracts young knights with her siren's lays ('La Belle Dame sans Merci'); and on his Scottish tour, he attempted a folk ballad ('Old Meg She Was a Gypsy').

Always fascinated by the idea of the poet as spellbinding bard, Keats was nevertheless temperamentally unsuited to writing earnest ballads in the tradition of Wordsworth and Burns. His interest in lyricism, then, found a new expressive outlet in the odes. While they make no pretence to be songs, they persistently explore the power of music, both verbal and nonverbal, both real and imagined: in the 'tuneless numbers' devoted to Psyche, in the trilling of a nightingale as it takes shape in the minds of human listeners, in the 'unheard melodies' played by a musician depicted on an urn, and in the ambient 'music' of birds and insects heard on an autumn evening.

One of the chief advantages of the ode was that it had no prescribed length or form, so it gave Keats freer rein to register a range of feelings, and to alternate between immediate perception and mental abstraction. A few poetic examples will demonstrate this difference. In 1818, Keats wrote 'Lines on Seeing a Lock of Milton's Hair', on the occasion of viewing a prized possession of Hunt's. Ordinarily, Keats might have composed a sonnet about the relic (Hunt himself had written three), but he wrote a quasi-ode instead. This formal choice can be seen as a gesture of defiance against Hunt, but it also shows Keats deliberately subordinating a single occasion to a larger meditation on poetic achievement – as if the glimpse of Milton's hair had merely startled Keats into confessing his deepest ambitions. What might have been a brief occasional poem contains what Shakespeare's Cleopatra calls 'immortal longings' (*Antony and Cleopatra* 5. 2. 272).

The sonnet 'To Sleep', written in the spring of 1819, further demonstrates what Keats gained by adopting the longer form of the ode. In many ways, the poem strives to be an ode: it addresses its subject with vocative epithets ('O soothest Sleep!'); it describes itself as a 'hymn' that closes with a drowsy 'Amen'; and it asks for the boon of 'forgetfulness divine' (5, 6–7, 4). (Indeed, the poem echoes Mark Akenside's 1745 ode *To Sleep*, which begged the titular deity for both relief from insomnia and inspiration in dreams.) The vocational ambitions of an ode are too grand for the scale of a sonnet, however, and Keats takes wry advantage of that mismatch: he plays on the tension between the agonisingly indefinite wait for sleep and the reassuringly bounded nature of the sonnet, between the unruliness of human experience and the artifice of poetic form. In suggesting that Sleep might arrive 'in midst of this thine hymn' (6), he knows that, even without that blessed interruption, the poem, if not the poet's own eyes, will close at line 14. The imposed brevity and closure of the sonnet, then, was both a boon and a vexation: it brought shape to a formless vigil but accentuated the artifice of the exercise.

Among the odes, 'Psyche' most closely mimics the eighteenth-century conceit of the sublime ode as cultic hymn, but it also expands on that premise. Before raising a hymn to the goddess, Keats grounds the poem in a putatively eyewitness account of happening upon Psyche ensconced with Cupid in a forest bower; and in the end, he recasts the myth of this amorous union as an allegory of the soul's connection to the world. Instead of 'holy' (38) boughs in a sacred grove, there are only the mind's own 'branched thoughts' (52) reaching into the world. The poem can thus be tracked as a series of scenes: a dream vision of Psyche, a resolution to establish a cult and temple devoted to the goddess, and finally a virtual 'fane' (50) installed within a 'working brain' (60), with a window open to let in light and love.

This progression could be called a 'working out of conceits', but here the mental work requires more space to develop than a sonnet would allow: the imaginative amplitude to stage a fantasised scene of surprise and recognition, to reiterate and redescribe, to tell a story and explore its allegorical meaning. In a letter, Keats remarked that 'Psyche' was 'the first and the only [poem] with which I have taken even moderate pains'; but he also insisted that he wrote the ode in a 'leisurely' fashion, in 'a more peaceable and healthy spirit' (*L* 2, 106). By emphasising leisure, he can be understood to mean both the frame of mind in which he wrote and the wider framework of the odes themselves, as an unfolding series of stanzas. Within that slower pace, Keats could pursue the anti-closural effects of gradual fading or withdrawal that had shaped the end of 'When I Have Fears': the departure of a bird in the 'Ode to a Nightingale'; the festival procession away from a little town in 'Ode on a Grecian Urn'; the banishment of the 'phantoms' of Love, Ambition, and Poesy in the 'Ode on Indolence'; the faltering evening light of 'To Autumn'. In that context, the conclusion of 'Psyche' inverts that pattern, with its expectant vigil for the arrival of 'warm Love' (67) rather than its disappearance.

The 'Ode to a Nightingale' elaborates on the premise of the sonnet 'To Sleep' in a different way: not as a hymn to a goddess but as a nocturnal meditation suspended between states of sleep and wakefulness. In the vein of earlier real-time sonnets, this ode purports to be the spontaneous report of an internal condition; but here Keats has more room to explore the mental contours of his vigil. Indeed, he finds himself in the midst of a reverie without knowing how it will end, and he expresses deeply conflicted feelings about sleep and what Shakespeare called its 'second self', death. He begins by reporting a sensation of 'drowsy numbness' (1) akin to the effects of a poison; he confesses the suicidal fantasy at the root of that metaphor; he recoils from the sobering implications of that desire; and he concludes in an uncertain limbo between dreaming and waking.

In a perceptually intensified version of Keats's real-time sonnets, the 'Ode to a Nightingale' purports to be simultaneous with the birdsong it describes. The duration of its utterance is shaped by the arc of the nightingale's flight, as the bird moves from a nearby tree to a more distant glade. Keats might have learned this technique from Coleridge's conversation poems, in which the course of the speaker's thought runs in parallel with the events of the phenomenal world. These inner and outer worlds intersect when Keats utters the word 'forlorn' (70) and then emphatically repeats it (71), as if he has been startled by his own voice. In that echo, the word functions not as transparent semantic medium but as a sudden sound breaking in on an interior meditation. Keats had used various forms of reiteration in his sonnets, but not with the dramatic force of this self-overhearing. Even as it participates in the fiction of spontaneous speech, the wayward word registers the spatial extension of odal form: it reappears not across successive lines but across the blankness of a stanza break.

Like the 'Ode to a Nightingale', the 'Ode on a Grecian Urn' represents an extended moment of perception, but here, Keats becomes a disembodied viewer posing questions to an ancient artefact; and the scenes depicted on its surface take on a vivid imaginary life that eclipses his own physical presence. Departing from the Elgin Marbles sonnets, he does not represent himself as a visitor in a museum gallery or report his own bodily sensations. Rather, it is the figures on the urn who swell into vivid life, while the poet's own physical presence is only fleetingly suggested in the 'burning forehead' and 'parching tongue' (30) that belong to human beholders who love and strive outside the cool precincts of the urn's marmoreal perfection.

Keats had favoured the perennial Shakespearean theme of mutability in his sonnets, and in the odes on the nightingale and the urn, he contemplates the relationship between permanence and flux with new urgency. It is telling that he uses the word 'generation' in both of these poems: he means it to denote a human population born at a particular historical moment, but he associates it less with birth than with disappearance; one generation is always being superseded by the next. The experience of hearing the nightingale's song on a passing night is ephemeral, and yet from a biological perspective, it is the same avian code echoing through the ages, even as successive eras of human listeners hear different meanings in it. The urn, on the other hand, is a deliberately wrought thing with an original context and set of meanings, never to be fully retrieved. The artisan who made the urn would not have seen it in pathetic terms as a 'foster child of silence and slow time' (2); and he would not have seen its three depicted scenes as an allegory of art's capacity to arrest and immortalise a single moment. It is the nineteenth-century poet, standing across an unbridgeable generational divide, who sees the urn within this interpretive context.

As a series, the odes are striking for the variety of ways in which they situate a lyric speaker – ranging from the first-person sensory experiences in the 'Ode to a Nightingale', to the elliptical self-references in the 'Ode on Melancholy', to the near-total self-effacement in the ode 'To Autumn'. In his chameleonic way, Keats moves among different time-schemes and focal lengths, and between the occasional specificity of the sonnet and the generality of the ode. There is no better example of this fluidity than the unusual path traced by the first stanza of Keats's last ode, 'To Autumn': while it begins in the suspended present of a hymnal invocation ('Season of mists and mellow fruitfulness'), it ends with the indicative statement of an accomplished fact (the declaration that 'summer has o'er-brimmed' (11) the bee hives). Nowhere does the speaker reveal himself amid this seasonal copia; instead, the world itself seems infused with intentionality, in mental acts of conspiring, maturing, and setting. It is the bees, not the poet, who are said to think.

Here and elsewhere in the odes, Keats works variations on the kind of intensity that he had admired in Shakespeare's sonnets – that paradoxical ideal of dilation and containment, leisure and labour. It is a particular kind of negative capability that embraces intermixture and simultaneity, in ways that go beyond Petrarchan binarism or the quatrain-by-quatrain unfolding of Shakespearean conceits. In the 'Ode to a Nightingale', the poet expresses feelings of both pain and happiness; he is 'half in love with easeful death' (52) even as he absorbs the sensory abundance of the world. In the 'Ode on a Grecian Urn', he sees both a tangible object and an illusionistic space of real people; he considers scenes representing three aspects of human endeavour; and he expresses both envy of and superiority over the visual stasis of the urn. In the 'Ode on Melancholy', he discovers the inseparability of Joy and Melancholy, beauty and pain. Rather than adopting a binary structure of describing depression and its banishment, he finds ways of representing time-lapse metamorphosis: a gloomy cloud that drops life-fostering rain, a lover fondly gazing into angry eyes, a bee turning nectar into poison, the figure of Pleasure always waving goodbye – but never quite leaving for good.

Note

1 *Selected Letters*, ed. John Carroll (Oxford: Clarendon Press, 1964), p. 329.

PART V

Influence

CHAPTER 28

Tennyson to Wilde

Herbert F. Tucker

Shelley's magnificent elegy *Adonais* (1821) presciently frames how Keats would influence his Victorian successors. 'He is made one with Nature: there is heard / His voice in all her music' (370–1): Keats's writing has so rearticulated the world that the 'plastic stress' of his imagination persists to compel 'All new successions to the forms they wear' (381–3). 'Forms' here indicates both the Gestalt-changing shift in mere phenomenal perception that a deep reading of Keats can induce and, where the reader is a poet, a secondary-imagination preference for Keatsian structures of verse and phrase, trope and argument, that with practice become second Nature. In major poetry, moreover, the disposition of such a technical legacy can foment brilliant permutations of creative conflict:

When lofty thought
Lifts a young heart above its mortal lair,
And love and life contend in it, for what
Shall be its earthly doom, the dead live there
And move like winds of light on dark and stormy air.
(392–6)[1]

To see what successive nineteenth-century generations of 'young hearts' made of Keats is to encounter formative early phases of an ongoing reception history in which poets uplifted by thought, when they grapple with this predecessor, are grappling with something in themselves. This chapter's concern will be influence as it transpires at the granular level where allusion lives, where in textual detail poets join their precursors in complex filiations of continuity and strife.

With Keats, more than with other poets comparably influential, the force of example is felt and negotiated *verbally*: the provocation he issues to those who must rewrite him not only begins in language but also tends to stay there – rather than in the images or concepts that poetic words happen to name – as it gets reprised in the answering poet's audible echo. Most

Victorian poems influenced by Keats *sound* Keatsian. That in turn lets rhymed and metered nineteenth-century verse – already a tissue of repetition – serve, under the strain of Keats, as a ready figure for the ambivalence with which his influence is expressed, along a gamut from rechanting his song to recanting it. Quite apart from the extraordinary beauty that must strike every generation of readers, two qualities in Keats's handling of language persistently condition the locally engaged Victorian responses that we shall consider. First, the language that does not just convey thought discursively but poetically embodies it (the beauty that is truth?) is irreducibly artificial; the body Keats's sensuous poetic invites us to assume is prosthetic. Second, the binary registers of space and time tend in Keats to prove poetically interconvertible: image and story, diction and syntax, substantive and tense are modalities only superficially distinct within the Keatsian verbal chronotope. Their deep affinity underwrites both Keats's uncanny power to make a description *tell* and the complementary tendency of his plots to implode, or to reinstate the status quo ante, which in the end is not so much altered as it is roundly grasped anew. When these two qualities of language are wielded by a poet so conspicuously disenchanted as Keats, they engender an arresting effect of physical presence, which they simultaneously conspire to undo; that the fancy can cheat, but only so well, is a major burden of Keatsian art. This complex legerdemain a poet deeply influenced by Keats might or might not forgive, but could never forget – and accordingly aspired to rival, along the spectrum from less to more sophisticated idiosyncrasy to which we now turn.

At sophistication's bottom rung Keats acquired an emulator of Borgesian fidelity in Thomas Hood, a cockney poet nearly his age who made an early Victorian mark as a writer of light and topical verse, and whose plodding imitations 'Ode: Autumn' and 'Ode to Melancholy' (1827) need detain us no further than to mark a limit case of minimal if flattering ambition. A rung or two higher, and distributed widely across the century and the talent pool, stands the practice of Keats-browsing. This is most often exercised by way of the hyphenated epithet, which may be either cherry-picked for authentic flavour or synonym-modified with a view to decent self-respect. Anyone paying attention when Wilde in 'Panthea' (1881) mentions his beloved's 'crimson-stainèd mouth' (128) will remember Keats's 'purple-stained' one from the 'Nightingale' ode (18), the more easily since some stanzas earlier Wilde has owed his 'purple-lidded sleep' (42) to an 'azure-lidded' original in *The Eve of St. Agnes* (262).[2] As D. G. Rossetti had been fond of the same manoeuvre, we may credit both Aesthetes with threading their allusive micro-enactments of Keats into the fabric of a frankly avowed belatedness. And their having done so may serve notice that something of the kind was already at play in Keats. Quintessentially Keatsian epithets are built on the past passive participle: a verbal form characterising the noun it modifies as one to which something has been done, encoding an anterior history, and thus rendering at molecular scale the Keatsian chronotope discussed above. So does an allied trick of Keats's style that Victorian poets regularly performed, the repurposing of nouns and verbs and adjectives to take each other's places. Under cover of neologism this grammatical synaesthesia (so to call it) let Hopkins, like the early Tennyson, loosen the grip of routine reference and one-way progressive signification. When Hopkins says, in 'Spring' (1877), 'The glassy peartree leaves and blooms' (6), and for the twinkling of an image the last two nouns seem verbs, the Keatsian effect condenses whole seasons, even generations, into a punctual event at whose recurrence the hand is ever at the lips bidding adieu.[3]

Victorian poets did such things because they wanted to sound like Keats: to claim an affiliative resemblance, yes; but also to earn it by doing on their own, if also on the cheap, a kind of thing that Keats had done. Such behaviour exploited affordances that recent developments in verse-craft had placed into the public domain: the price of fame, paid out in the wages of what Browning ironically called, in an 1855 poem à propos that ends with the name John Keats, 'Popularity'. Browning's poem appeared within a few years of the Spasmodic craze of the mid-century – preceded by Monckton Milnes's 1848 *Life, Letters, and Literary Remains of John Keats* – when a rash of young writers issued book-length poems, some bestsellers among them, whose plot was little more than a display space for striking special effects of phrase and image. The Spasmodics thus drew a second line for navigating Keats's Victorian influence, perpendicular to Hood's but likewise sustained by the manufacture of poetic articles eliciting brand recognition pretty automatically. Keatsianism on this order was a reproducible result, appropriated as less a human than a natural resource, and entraining little of the Romantic poet's suspicion that the natural was itself a deeply compromised cultural effect.

Poetic influence is rarer, and more interesting, where it turns into argument. Here instead of reproducing Keats for his own sake the Victorian poet begs (or borrows) to differ, establishing a Keatsian position so as to outflank it or take it en passant, or hijacking a Keatsian trajectory and steering it elsewhere. This manoeuvre is especially frequent with Hopkins, who from the start made it the habit of perfection to indulge a recognisably Keatsian sensuous sonority on the way to renouncing it. Priestly sonnet after sonnet celebrates the natural world with ecstatic enthusiasm, only to convert ecstasy into piety by affirming nature's status as Creation. Time and again, at or near the sonnet's volta the 'brute beauty' of the physical world 'buckles' (thus a famous textual crux from 'The Windhover', 1877) under stress of the metaphysical, which takes up into the Word, and takes off the poet's shoulders, the burden of unassisted creativity that Keats vested in human language. Much of the abiding appeal of these poems inheres in the spectacular way their verbal scapes and stresses in the octave adjust Hopkins's word into the divine Logos; and the energy released during this reaction shines back upon the dialectics of nature and artifice that galvanise language in Keats. This is so despite the orthodox simplification that waits in a Hopkins sestet. The end-times agon, for example, that in 'Spelt from Sibyl's Leaves' (1885?) conclusively winds life 'all on two spools… black, white; right, wrong' (11–12) heightens the unpropped Keatsian intensity of the personified vision of 'Evening' that precedes it – 'her earliest stars, earl-stars, stars principal, overbend us, / Fire-featuring heaven' (3–4) – and that may derive from the vision in *Hyperion*, 'upon a tranced summer-night', of 'Tall oaks, branch-charmed by the earnest stars' (1. 72–3). Each passage animates the other with the magic hand of chance – and whether or not the poet holds that God plays dice with the universe.

The very strictness of his confessional faith licenses in Hopkins fixed feasts of joy that Keats had to temper on secular grounds. The Victorian's apprehension of the transiency named in titles like 'To What Serves Mortal Beauty?' and 'Spring and Death' came to him as a problem to which he knew (even if he candidly could not always feel) the orthodox solution; the Romantic had to meet that rooted contrast in the improvisations of paradox instead. Thus 'Spring and Fall', where for once Hopkins checks his dogma at the door, becomes the most maturedly Keatsian of his lyrics, with its autumnal 'worlds of wanwood leafmeal' and its gentle concession that existential questions must find their answers by ghostly guesswork in the vale of soul-making. Influence flows both ways between the experimental odes Keats wrote for pagan goddesses and the coupleted hymns Hopkins wrote for the Virgin Mary. When we juxtapose 'The May Magnificat' (1878) and 'The Blessed Virgin Compared to the Air We Breathe' (1883) with Keats's 'Maia' and 'Psyche', unexpected likenesses subtend the obvious doctrinal difference. Lovely in herself and gratifying to her filial votary, the earth goddess who is also mother to a god graces springtide for both poets, each bemused to praise beauty as humankind's most merciful dispensation. Both poets revive the Venus that lies, by whatever name, in the *veneration* of a common sensuous endowment: by association Hopkins emerges as a mythmaker lost in wonder, while Keats's 'pigeon tumbling in clear summer air' ('Sleep and Poetry', 93) comes into fresh focus via Hopkins as the dove descending within a lower-case magnificat.

Tennyson's broad menu of responses to Keats includes a quotient of corrective revisions like those engrossing Hopkins. The Laureate typically lodged the redirected energies of Keatsian embodiment not at church, though, but at home. When basing his idyll 'Dora' (1842) on the book of Ruth, he found an icon ready made in Keats's image of the homesick biblical protagonist who 'stood in tears amid the alien corn' ('Nightingale' 66–7). Repeated imagery of harvest reapers, braided flowers, and a cry vanishing overland leaves Dora alone to weep in secret – until at last a patriarch relents and the house is reconciled. Again, two lyrics embedded in *The Princess* (1847) epitomise that work's homing instinct. In 'O Swallow' the summoned bird undertakes an autumnal Keatsian emigration only in order to nest like the Prince, who wants a beloved straight out of the 'Bright Star' sonnet to 'lay me on her bosom, and her heart / Would rock the snowy cradle till I died' (4. 85–6).[4] In 'Come Down, O Maid' Tennyson bends all the domestic gravitas he can muster towards securing Love with Plenty in the valley, by the hearth and nursery, where time and even death are blessed by familial continuity: 'Myriads of rivulets', 'The moan of doves', and 'murmuring of innumerable bees' (7. 205–7) acknowledge respectively Keatsian flux, desire, and mortality, but embrace them all in the bosom of bourgeois domesticity. The Victorian resolutions that thus gave shelter to an initially Romantic deprivation show by contrast how remarkable was the chronic irresolution towards which Keats drove his poems. For poets at their most Victorian, that negative capability of his required an affirmative rejoinder; they had to reckon it only half the story, which should be completed with the advance of more years, and stanzas, than Keats had been able to afford. After 'Adieu, adieu' tolls like a bell (and in quotations marks too) to close lyric 56 from *In Memoriam* (1855), the next lyric pivots on 'those sad words' and promises to 'abide a little longer here' and 'take a nobler leave', for the common good.

The revisionary correction that licensed Victorian poets to drink deeply of beauty with Keats, on condition that they then depart on other errands, takes full-blown form in the poems of Arnold. The early 'Strayed Reveller' goes round and round in 'eddying forms' (lines 5, 296) but otherwise goes nowhere.[5] Arnold's need to work free from the loops of sensation found leverage in modes of intellectual critique that proved, in the end, incompatible with poetry as he could imagine wielding it, and he accordingly devolved from a poet into a critic. The most enduring poems he did write stage confrontations between the critical intellect and a generative fancy whose register he consistently marks as Keatsian – albeit in a mode whose reduction of poetry to mere image and feeling breaks faith with the fusion that Keats's own best writing sustains between those qualities and a penetrating sceptical reflection. In the second act of *Empedocles on Etna* (1852) Keats, renamed Callicles, pipes lyrics from a leafy hollow upslope to the bare volcanic summit where Arnold's listening proxy then voices them over with unrhymed commentary, whose increasingly depressing burden finally impels him over the rim of the crater to death. Arnold quickly reprobated this dead end in a famous 1853 preface that excoriated contemporary poetry for being, in effect, too spasmodically Keatsian; still, poetic detours around it were not easy to chart. 'The Scholar-Gipsy' (1853) attempts an intriguing variant that fights Keats with more Keats. Arnold loads with lush (Keatsian) descriptiveness every rift of its ten-line (Keatsian) stanzas on the Scholar, then breaks off this dream of ease with (Keatsian) interjections – 'But what – I dream!' (131), 'No, no, thou hast not felt the lapse of hours!' (141). And then, having anatomised the commercial triviality and spiritual inconsequence of Victorian philistinism, Arnold recruits the Scholar anew, under the banner no longer of luxuriant indolence but now of the marginalised cultural avant-garde, whose ascetic singleness of purpose earns, of all things, a magically chastened power to read Keats better than ever: 'listen with enchanted ears, / From the dark dingles, to the nightingales!' (219–20). This ambitious lyric thus comes the long way round to sponsor, as its own hard-won discovery, a severity that is always latent in Keats but that Arnold has but half heard.

Listening better is the project of a third Arnoldian essay in corrective recuperation, 'Dover Beach'. A night-time setting turns down vision in favour of audition, lending an ear to numerous Keatsian borrowings – from 'Psyche' and 'Nightingale', *Eve of St. Agnes*, 'On the Sea' – which wash across the text like waves across shingle. That oscillation underscores dimensions of verse form with which this poem does its deftest work. The first strophe comprises fourteen lines, whose break after line 6 sets a pattern executed more firmly in the six-line and eight-line strophes that follow. The bulk of the poem, then, comprises two sonnets that are traveling incognito: stacked upside down (6:8) in contravention of ordinary sonnet structure, irregularly rhymed and, while iambically metered, nicked into as many tetrameters and trimeters as pentameters, inducing a deprivation-anxiety arguably learned from Keats's curtailed stanza in 'La Belle Dame sans Merci'. Keeping such awkward faith, under duress, with traditional versification lets Arnold put Victorian belief on trial: the 'withdrawing roar' of culturally steady 'Faith' (21–5), and, in one last free-form strophe, the compensatory hope that interpersonal fidelity, once love itself is gone (33), may cushion the hostility of the real. Keats knew a lot about that hostility; overcoming an abidingly critical reluctance to credit Keats with such knowledge forms the deeper allusive agenda here for Arnold the poet dallying with despair.

'Dover Beach' not only does sonnet form backward, twice; it also runs in reverse the imagery, and the breathtakingly swooping perspectivism, of one sonnet in particular, 'Bright Star'. The infantine undulation in which Keats's sestet cozies up to its end characterises the periodic cradling of the surf with which Arnold begins. His casement opening on the foam ('Come to the window') discloses, through the moment's 'sweet', an 'eternal note of sadness' (6, 14), amplified through a Sophoclean megaphone into 'misery' (18), which interpoetically seems to come out of nowhere until we realise how the last, sonnetoid octave derives its imagery from the octave in Keats. There fidelity has taken shape in the splendid isolation of a star that looks down, 'stedfast' but unmoved, upon earth's 'moving waters' – which moreover, as Arnold's odd figure of the coastline as a 'girdle furled' (23) can teach us to discern in Keats's 'pure ablution round earth's human shores', have served as primary care providers for a titanic telluric body (1–6). Keats's ailing Mother Earth needs not just surveillance but therapy, as she may also need the cosmetic application of snowfall in order to 'mask' (7) what might not otherwise be a pretty sight. This cosmetology Arnold makes it his mission to strip away for the rest of the poem; meanwhile, the allusive form of his endeavour reveals what concessions to a harsher outlook have lurked in Keats's lines all along. 'Dover Beach' thus goes up the down staircase of 'Bright Star' to join 'the high, white star of Truth' ('Stanzas from the Grande Chartreuse' [1855], line 69): a disenchanted vantage from which acknowledged isolation must be its own comfort, as it has painstakingly ruled out every other.

We have seen how Arnold neutralises Keats, Tennyson domesticates him, Hopkins converts him. These several strategies of containment all attest a Victorian anxiety about the dangers of seduction by a joy at once irresistible in prospect and yet, in the event, either inaccessible or impermanent. Goblin fruit? Christina Rossetti thought so, and her famous rendition of the insatiability of modern wants in 'Goblin Market' suggests that the hope and fear that her peers projected onto Keats bespoke a widespread Victorian ambivalence about desire as such. True Keats-love, like every human resource Keats touched, had a way of turning any 'solution sweet' (*St. Agnes*, 322) – love included – back into a tart open question.

That may be why the most strenuous Victorian encounters with Keats depart from the reproductive and revisionary models of influence we have been considering. Encounters of this third kind are openly dialectical: they invite Keats into a poem for dialogue, as a kind of consultant on a problem still pending, which his example may help to formulate and explore. They are harder to parse and interpret than a borrowing or correction is, yet they are if anything more important to recognise if we are to appreciate influence, with Shelley in *Adonais*, as creative transaction with a living hand. I accordingly propose in closing a handful of allusive complexes from the Victorian canon that are unmistakably Keatsian but remain unfinished business for the literary history we have yet to write. Each instance is a compound that evokes a plurality of texts so as to invoke the spirit of Keats behind them; and each desires Keats's company in order to cope with refractory vagaries of desire itself.

1. In 1838 Elizabeth Barrett Barrett published in 'The Soul's Travelling' a poem of desultory ambition that arrives at orthodox confession, Hopkins-like, after passing in sections 7–10 into a 'grassy niche / Hollowed in a seaside hill', a 'cavelike nook' (127–36) that becomes in meditation a valley of the shadow whose presiding spirit is Keats: La Belle Dame's grot made dainty in the lines just quoted, followed up in series by a pastoral catalogue of flowers, an audition of breaking waves made mythic (as in Keats's 'On the Sea'), and an interval of silence 'culled' into language and by that verbal incarnation imbued with the 'deathly odor' of mortality (167–75).[6] At this point EBB crosses into section 10 with a dramatic act of self-reading: 'on its deathlessness alway. // Alway! alway? must this be?' (176–7). The parallel is striking with the final stanzas of 'Nightingale', and its poetic effect outlasts the rather rote Christian chastisement of vanity with which EBB ties her poem off. That nook abides as a fertile but untilled resource to which, and not to orthodoxy, she will return in the Keatsian intervals that punctuate *Aurora Leigh* (1857).

2. Early in 'The Stream's Secret' (1870) D. G. Rossetti yearns to know (what that long poem never does decipher) the message Love entrusted to the stream at its wellhead, 'Murmuring with curls all dabbled in thy flow / And washed lips rosy red' (11–12).[7] In form this word not writ but spoken in water comes from a bower in *Endymion*, where the shepherd-hero can't tell whether Proserpine rests and 'her tender hands / She dabbles', or whether Echo 'sits / And babbles thorough silence' (1. 945–8). It is, even for Keats, a redundantly echoic passage, where internal rhyme cascades over the couplets in a shimmering analogue of the Narcissan delight, and

plight, that structure his wayward romance. It was for this dilemma, and the ambiguous erotic promise of beholding 'The same bright face I tasted in my sleep, / Smiling in the clear well' (1. 889–96), that Rossetti enlisted Keats's scene of erotic reverberation here and also in the first 'Willowwood' sonnet from *The House of Life* (1870). There Love keeps his divine secret as jealously as ever, but brokers the revelation in another watery mirror of the beloved: 'And as I stooped, her own lips rising there / Bubbled with brimming kisses at my mouth' (13–14). At this point the crisscross of images is doubled by that of Keats allusions: 'With beaded bubbles winking at the brim, / And purple-stained mouth' comes uppermost from the 'Nightingale' ode (17–18), making good on those 'rosy red' lips from 'The Stream's Secret' and entraining the ode's trenchant, reciprocating contraries: a critique of illusory escapism, together with an inventory of what ills there are from which to crave escape. How love might escape the orbit of self-love rests, for now, suspended in the Keatsian intertext that Rossetti's career tirelessly rewove.

3. Among Victorian heirs of Keats, Tennyson exhibited the most versatility, never more pointedly than when soliciting guidance, or fellowship at least, along the verdurous glooms of the lost heart. One way to measure Tennyson's own immense influence is to note that it was usually through him that later poets made their way back to Keats. His various rehabilitations of 'Nightingale' alone might occupy a chapter of this length, from 'Recollections of the Arabian Nights' (1830) across 'Lancelot and Elaine' (1859) to 'The Ancient Sage' (1885). At the most arresting of these frequent junctures the great ode brings with it other texts by Keats to enrich, by perplexing, the articulation of what the heart struggles to know: 'To Autumn' in 'Tears, Idle Tears' (1847); 'Ode on Melancholy' in *In Memoriam*'s lyric 88 ('Wild bird'); 'When I Have Fears' in the gorgeous eighteenth lyric of *Maud* (1855). But let the last word here go to 'Demeter and Persephone', a poem published in 1889 as a senior's valediction to the classicism in which Tennyson had been educated yet which in practice he nearly always reproduced in Romantic terms that were principally Keats's. Demeter ends her monologue three times on its final page, in a magniloquent yet also awkward Keatsian bow that expresses both Tennyson's reluctance and his bafflement at the end of the Victorian era. First, in a harvest *hommage* right out of 'To Autumn', the goddess blesses her negotiated agreement to share Persephone with Hades on a schedule guaranteeing the seasonal cycle (121–5). But such secular paganism always gave Tennyson worries, which his Demeter here shares as she looks past it, 'ill-content' (126), to the

promise not of stability but of improvement. This is figured in the rhetoric of Oceanus from *Hyperion*, 2. 181–231, whence comes in all but words Demeter's forecast of 'younger kindlier Gods to bear us down, / As we bore down the Gods before us' (129–30). And yet, to the perennial credit of Tennyson's deep reading of Keats, this feel-good meliorism sticks at the last in the goddess's throat. She concludes not with 'the worship which is Love' (146) but with a blank verse quatrain admitting harder truths about suffering, guilt, and strife in which – as Keats had long taught Tennyson to remember, much though Demeter hopes to forget – Love's worship trains its votaries. We see last, to the stately commemoration of a Keatsian music, just what she and Persephone hope to 'see no more' yet cannot refrain from imagining:

> The Stone, the Wheel, the dimly-glimmering lawns
> Of that Elysium, all the hateful fires
> Of torment, and the shadowy warrior glide
> Along the silent field of Asphodel.
>
> (147–51)

Notes

1 *Percy Bysshe Shelley: The Major Works*, ed. Zachary Leader and Michael O'Neill (Oxford: Oxford University Press, 2003).
2 Oscar Wilde, *Complete Poetry*, ed. Isobel Murray (Oxford: Oxford University Press, 1997).
3 *Gerard Manley Hopkins: The Major Works*, ed. Catherine Phillips (Oxford: Oxford University Press, 2002).
4 *The Poems of Tennyson*, ed. Christopher Ricks (London: Longman, 1969).
5 *Poetical Works*, ed. C. B. Tinker and H. F. Lowry (London: Oxford University Press, 1950).
6 *The Poetical Works of Elizabeth Barrett Browning* (London: Smith, 1897).
7 Dante Gabriel Rossetti, *Collected Poetry and Prose* (New Haven: Yale University Press, 2003).

CHAPTER 29

Hardy, Edward Thomas, Stevens, Bishop, Heaney

Michael O'Neill

In late September 1819, Keats, who looked 'upon fine Phrases like a Lover' and found that 'Shakspeare and the paradise Lost every day become greater wonders to me' (*L* 2, 139), turned on Milton and sent him packing as he abandoned the *Hyperion* project (including the revised version of that poem): 'Miltonic verse', he wrote, 'cannot be written but in an artful or rather artist's humour. I wish to give myself up to other sensations' (*L* 2, 167). However fair or unfair to Milton, the remark illustrates how Keats looked to be influenced at this late stage of his short career. Rejecting the exploitation of someone else's style in order to create 'the false beauty proceeding from art', he sought to speak with 'the true voice of feeling' (*L* 2, 167).

Many of the finest poets who write in response to Keats find such a 'voice' in his work and seek to shape an answerable, kindred utterance within their own compositions. This chapter considers some representative examples. Thomas Hardy's 'At the Pyramid of Cestius near the Graves of Shelley and Keats' is, ultimately, for all its interest in Cestius's lack of fame, a poem of what Jeffrey C. Robinson identifies as 'the enshrining temperament' evident in many poems that honour Keats.[1] His 'At Lulworth Cove a Century Back', however, suggests the houseless, elusive nature of poetic genius:

> Had I but lived a hundred years ago
> I might have gone, as I have gone this year,
> By Warmwell Cross on to a Cove I know,
> And Time have placed his finger on me there:
>
> '*You see that man?*' – I might have looked, and said,
> 'O yes: I see him. One that boat has brought
> Which dropped down Channel round Saint Alban's Head.
> So commonplace a youth calls not my thought.'
>
> '*You see that man?*' – 'Why yes; I told you; yes:
> Of an idling town-sort; thin; hair brown in hue;
> And as the evening light scants less and less

He looks up at a star, as many do.'

'*You see that man?*' – 'Nay, leave me!' then I plead,
'I have fifteen miles to vamp across the lea,
And it grows dark, and I am weary-kneed:
I have said the third time; yes, that man I see!'

'Good. That man goes to Rome – to death, despair;
And no one notes him now but you and I:
A hundred years, and the world will follow him there,
And bend with reverence where his ashes lie.'[2]

Starting with a seemingly chance allusion to Macbeth's feigned but deeply felt lament after the discovery of Duncan's murder, 'Had I but died an hour before this chance / I had lived a blessed time' (2. 5. 87–8), Hardy leaves us to wonder whether he would have been any different from those who, while Keats was alive, noticed only 'an idling town-sort'. He senses, one feels, that he would not have realised he was living in 'a blessed time'. The poem uses the technique of 'time-switching' that Nicholas Roe identifies as Keatsian.[3] Its theme has a metapoetic dimension: in a sense, all good poems find themselves a century back, in a dialogue, often disputatious, with Time.

'*You see that man?*' Time asks three times, as Hardy broaches a Keatsian theme found in the induction to *The Fall of Hyperion*: that poetry can be written by anyone and can only be written by a unique individual. Hardy's poem loiters round the edges of Keats's career, downplaying in order finally to affirm. It alludes, as a note to the poem has it, to the supposed fact that 'Keats, on his way to Rome, landed one day on the Dorset coast, and composed the sonnet, "Bright star"'.[4] Hardy mimics indifference to 'So commonplace a youth', and imagines making three unsatisfactory answers. The curtailed allusion to Peter denying Christ three times helps to explain why the ending is so powerful, suggesting Keats's own via dolorosa as the poem's place-names shift from Warmwell Cross and Saint Alban's Head to the eternal city: 'That man goes to Rome – to death, despair'.

In the same breath, Time charitably allows the poet to be privy to its own knowledge, 'And no one notes him now but you and I', before the final two lines with their prophecy of future fame. Charitably, because Hardy cannot but be ignorant as an imagined contemporary of what Keats will do with his star-gazing, that is, write (or rewrite) 'Bright star'. Hardy once asserted that 'Romanticism will exist in human nature as long as human nature itself exists'.[5] Romanticism lives again in the frugal spareness of the lines that signal the coming into being of 'Bright star': 'And as the evening light scants less and less / He looks up at a star, as many do.' Hardy suggests that many may have looked at a star, but that only one poet made from that looking up the poem that wins 'reverence' from future generations.

In 'The Darkling Thrush' Hardy pays homage to Keats's 'Ode to a Nightingale', even as he almost caricatures the earlier poem. For Keats's bird that 'Singest of summer in full-throated ease' (10), Hardy substitutes, in his seeming lament for 'The Century's corpse outleant' (10), 'An aged thrush, frail, gaunt, and small' (21): pitiably unglamorous, fated to be read in human terms. Against the dire omens of gloom the bird sings out. Hardy is not exactly ready to say to his bird, as Keats says to his, 'I will fly to thee' (31). But he takes cautious heart from the bird's apparently motiveless rapture. The impassioned organ notes of Keats's ten-line stanzas have given way to a cunningly diminished music in Hardy's eight-line stanzas; they keep the pentameter severely at bay. And yet the bird is granted the capacity to have 'chosen thus to fling his soul / Upon the growing gloom' (23–4), as though throwing down a gauntlet. The bird, one might hazard, is the spirit of poetry embodied in Keats's ode, come back to haunt a disbelieving age, an age so disbelieving it doubts whether doubt itself be doubting. Keats stresses what human beings know and the bird does not: he longs to 'quite forget / What thou among the leaves hast never known' (21–2). Hardy's speaker finds in the very lack of apparent cause for the bird's joyous song possible evidence of 'Some blessed Hope, whereof he knew / And I was unaware' (32–3).

The thrush speaks to the sceptical idealist in Hardy. For Keats, the bird is desired other and rival poet, its song twining itself round the poet's own voice, but always distant from it, even as it is what the poet bewitchingly ventriloquises. A single syllable encapsulates this fusion and dualism, the sound of 'or', which enters the poem, in effect, in the line, 'Now *more* than ever seems it rich to die' (55); develops momentum in the account of the bird seductively '*pour*ing forth thy soul' (57); passes over into the recognition of the gap between poet and bird, 'Thou was not *born* for death, im*mort*al Bird!' (61); transfers itself to the poignant glimpse of Ruth as 'She stood in tears amid the alien *corn*' (67); finds a lamenting afterlife for the imagination's journey in the two syllables of the repeated word '*forlorn*' (70, 71); and finally emerges as the pivot of the entire poem in the conjunction 'or' which undergirds the blurring alternatives of the close. For his part, Hardy learns lessons from Keats's manipulation of sound; the rhyme between 'sky' and 'I' pursued in the first two stanzas suggests the element of subjectivity, pathetic fallacy, as does the reworking of the Keatsian phrase 'spectre-thin' (25) in 'spectre-gray' (2). Hardy's vision is bifocal, at once late Victorian and disillusioned, and Keatsian: hence the incongruities of tone and diction which bear witness to a strain only finally calmed by the gracefully iambic movement of the close.

Edward Thomas says of Keats that he was, 'though a lover of the moon, a most sublunary poet, earthly, substantial and precise, a man, but for his intensity, singularly like his fellow-men'.[6] Keats as a lunar poet shows himself in his yearning to be on proximate terms with 'the Queen-Moon' ('Ode to a Nightingale', 36), to depict moonlight throwing 'warm gules on Madeline's fair breast' (*The Eve of St. Agnes*, 218), and to sense in Moneta's face a moonlike, slightly inhuman serenity. For Thomas in 'Liberty', moonlight stands for a state of beyondness, and yet, as in a Keats ode, there are secret sympathies between the poet and symbolic object:

> It is as if everything else had slept
> Many an age …
> and but the moon and I
> Live yet …
> Both have liberty
> To dream what we could do if we were free
> To do some thing we had desired long,
> The moon and I.
> (4–5, 7–8, 9–12)[7]

The repeated twosome, 'The moon and I', relishes its oddness. Thomas is on colloquially intimate terms, it would seem, with the object of Endymion's longing gaze. If Keats evokes yearning, Thomas, a poet of 'as if' and qualifications, does not so much express as analyse processes of virtual dream and desire, in lines that revolve around irresoluteness, possibly about the worth of an action such as 'joining an army' which the poet had done a few months earlier.[8] The poem is wholly Keatsian, however, in the way in which it sets going a train of reflection, then concerns itself with its value, as in the to-and-fro movement of the second stanza of 'Ode on a Grecian Urn': 'Heard melodies are sweet, but those unheard / Are sweeter; therefore, ye soft pipes, play on' (11–12). The opening 'Platonic' assertion has a hushed, forced quality, as though the poet were urging himself to believe, and yet within a phrase, 'soft pipes', his allegiance to the non-sensuous starts to crumble.[9]

Thomas, comparably, weighs up and finds wanting the value of hours such as 'this one passing' (16), discreetly lifted from 'this passing night' ('Ode to a Nightingale', 63), which is contrasted with less self-conscious ones, when he has 'forgot' (again using a key word from the Nightingale

Ode) 'To wonder whether I was free or not' (18). Yet the final four lines backtrack:

> And yet I still am half in love with pain,
> With what is imperfect, with both tears and mirth,
> With things that have an end, with life and earth,
> And this moon that leaves me dark within the door.
> (24–7)

One recalls the rescue-act Keats performs in the final, strictly hedged-in affirmation of the 'Ode on a Grecian Urn', where the concluding aphorism is spoken by the urn. The aphorism's circularity is a function of the urn's own perfected being, yet it is spoken in the context of the poet's awareness of realities that challenge the confidence of art. Keats sets out the opposition with starkly antithetical eloquence: 'When old age shall this generation waste, / Thou shalt remain … a friend to man' (46–7, 48). Thomas twists and turns, his eddying rhymes catching up with themselves. He is 'half in love with pain' (24), recalling how Keats was 'half in love with easeful Death' ('Ode to a Nightingale', 52), but this half-love remains, steadily present within the circle of shadow traced by the speaker's self-awareness. Keats is traceable in the poem's final movement, even as it remains typical of Thomas: the 'mirth'/ 'earth' chime picks up a rhyme Keats uses in the second stanza of 'Ode to a Nightingale' (12, 14). Thomas reverses the rhyme, grounding 'mirth' in the 'earth', 'with things that have an end', a line that suggests the influence of 'To Autumn', even if Keats uses his art often to resist the inevitable consequence of process. Thomas, too, does not end with an end, but with 'this moon that leaves me dark within the door'; his sole self looks as Keats listens, 'Darkling' ('Ode to a Nightingale', 51) and 'forlorn', yet ready for further encounters, further wrestlings of the spirit.

Keats gluts his 'sorrow on the salt-sand wave' ('Ode on Melancholy', 15), distilling, arresting, slowing. Thomas disperses then gathers, moving between the expertly exploratory and the stoic, even noble posture of the poem's last line. Both control time and let it flow. Keats appeals to a future age to judge him 'When this warm scribe my hand is in the grave' (*The Fall of Hyperion*, I. 18). Thomas adapts Keats's image of the scribal hand at the close of 'The Long Small Room', when the restless writing self participates in and is at the mercy of the processes it tries, by recording, to resist:

> One thing remains the same – this my right hand
>
> Crawling crab-like over the clean white page,
> Resting awhile each morning on the pillow,

Then once more starting to crawl on towards age.
The hundred last leaves stream upon the willow.
(12–16)

Hints of transience gather force in the streaming leaves on the willow, yet the way they 'remain' in the very moment in which they threaten to vanish from the clean white page pays a profound tribute to the poet whose hand is in the grave. Two post-Keatsian ways of imagining process are at work here. One is the sense of flow, caught in the participles; one is the recognition, embodied in the verb 'stream', that the moment can be made to stay, arrested in the perpetual present-tense of the poem, the 'outward scene' made 'accessory to an inner theatre', as F. R. Leavis has it.[10]

Keats generates a wealth of responses in twentieth-century American poets, as is also discussed in Chapter 30. Two preliminary examples must suffice here. One is Wallace Stevens's 'Sunday Morning', the other Elizabeth Bishop's 'Large Bad Picture'. 'Sunday Morning' is a majestic response to Keats's 'To Autumn'. Helen Vendler is surely right that Keats creates his autumnal music through the use of 'beautiful implicit meanings', while Stevens is 'homiletic and doctrinal'.[11] Stevens's poem recognises that Keats's success is virtually impossible to reproduce; and depends in its last stanza on an absorption in the sounds of autumn, not excluding feeling and mood, but allowing them to exist – equably, calmly, almost heart-breakingly – within the larger natural scene in which process is all.

Stevens's poem capitalises on this aspect of Keats's ode, a perfect example of a poem serving as an illuminating form of literary criticism. It finds access to a voice sponsored by a woman, Stevens's equivalent to the female presences who grace Keats's odes in sometimes disturbing ways as inspiring muses. Keats's odes allow for the romance between poet and anima, but they also suggest that romance can turn sour. For his part, Stevens's female figure is negatively capable in her hearing of a voice that is ambiguously secular and post-Christian as it rejects 'spirits lingering' for the assertion: 'It is the grave of Jesus, where he lay'.[12] This female hearing passes over into the poet's own more declarative accents: declarative though not exactly doctrinally anti-religious since Stevens offers us, as Vendler notes, 'a choice among truths' in his series of 'or' constructions.[13]

We live in an old chaos of the sun,
Or old dependency of day and night,
Or island solitude, unsponsored, free,
Of that wide water, inescapable.

The movement of Stevens's own blank verse is at once 'free' and 'inescapable', in accord with his post-Keatsian vision of the human predicament. Stevens opens Keats's poem to the experience of a new continent, almost in fulfilment of Keats's own imagining at the close of his sonnet 'On First Looking into Chapman's Homer'. If Keats, thrusting Balboa to one side, assumes for himself the conquistadorial role of 'stout Cortez' (11), depicted as 'Silent, upon a peak in Darien' (14), Stevens looks at a place where 'Sweet berries ripen in the wilderness', his American rewriting of 'While barred clouds bloom the soft-dying day' (25). Stevens's deer and quail occupy the place of full-grown lambs and quintessentially English redbreast. Adjectives tell us about chaos and the artistic will to order. When 'the quail / Whistle about us their *spontaneous* cries' (emphasis added), Stevens makes us aware, by contrast, of the poet's art as he readapts the exquisite control of tempo that marks the close of Keats's ode. The American poet's own rhythm sweeps eloquently outwards, and yet sinks 'Downward':[14]

> And, in the isolation of the sky,
> At evening, casual flocks of pigeons make
> Ambiguous undulations as they sink,
> Downward to darkness, on extended wings.

The word 'casual' dismisses causality from the natural scene, though not from the poem. The poem is able to name and enact its own 'Ambiguous undulations', settling for the pigeons, unglamorous substitutes for Keats's 'gathering' (33) swallows, as 'they sink, / Downward to darkness, on extended wings'. Just as 'gathering' allows for agency in 'To Autumn', so the phrase 'extended wings' qualifies too bleakly sombre a close. The phrase has a gracefully intertextual implication. It suggests how Keats has permitted a later traveller on poetry's viewless wings to find those wings 'extended'.

Elizabeth Bishop's 'Large Bad Picture' 'can be read', in Susan McCabe's words, 'as a kind of response to Keats's "Ode on a Grecian Urn"'.[15] A poem about a work of art, as is Keats's ode, 'Large Bad Picture' takes as it its subject 'a big picture' that 'a great-uncle painted'. Despite the title, the poet honours as well as mocks the great-uncle's nostalgia for 'the Strait of Belle Isle or / some northerly harbor of Labrador'.[16] The series of 'or' sounds suggests an element of Keatsian influence, his unusual attentiveness to the intimacy between sound and meaning, here creating an effect of questing tentativeness. The poem has a stealthy reticence coupled with a descriptive generosity that is at once characteristic of Bishop and a lesson taught by Keats, very much a poet for which the object is the adequate symbol. Here the painting speaks of the great-uncle's longing for realism and delight in the ongoing present ('hundreds of fine black birds / hanging in *n*'s in banks'), hints of covert emotion, the impulse to arrest life in a perfectly stilled image ('On the middle of that quiet floor / sits a fleet of small black ships'), and the desire to orchestrate nature so that the viewer of his work can consume a beautiful sunset.

The last lines concede, as Keats does in his description of the urn, that there is always something that eludes the shaping spirit of imagination. Describing ships reaching their goal, Bishop writes: 'It would be hard to say what brought them there, / commerce or contemplation'. 'What the Imagination seizes as Beauty' turns out to be not so much 'truth' (*L* I, 184) as a dithering between alternatives, 'commerce or contemplation', Bishop's wry version of Keatsian 'ors' at the end of 'Ode to a Nightingale'. Ships, uncle and poet all fail to know what impels them; yet the fact that the ships can be thought of as desiring 'contemplation' can be read as a final tribute to the artist's capacity to provoke thought, much as Keats arrives, as noted above, at a strictly qualified affirmation at the close of 'Ode on a Grecian Urn'.

Keats is among the singing masters of Seamus Heaney's poetic soul, as is shown by 'The Harvest Bow'. The poem celebrates harvest bows tied by the poet's father. With Keatsian sympathy for the physical and wordless, Heaney represents himself as every inch in the family tradition; like his father, but in his own way, the poetic son is engaged in 'Gleaning the unsaid off the palpable'.[17] This line works as Heaney's tribute to his father, as a celebration of his own art, and as a restatement of a Keatsian poetry that keeps its head steady like a gleaner. Heaney's rhyming, wobbling unstably between true and off, suggests that affirmation will not have an easy time in the poem any more than it ever does in Keats's work. If Keats's urn warrants the description 'Cold Pastoral', Heaney's harvest bow is a 'frail device', much as the poem about it is. 'The end of art is peace / Might be the motto of this frail device', in the final stanza, are lines fraught with a double meaning: art aims at peace; peace means art could no longer continue. The poem reimagines the alien corn as brought into the house and pinned on the deal dresser, but as retaining a wildness since the bow feels like a slip knot recently burnished by the corn's spirit. That tension seeks, as so many poems in the Keatsian tradition do, to reject the false beauty proceeding from art in favour of the true voice of feeling, a rejection that is Keats's repeated gift to his poetic heirs and admirers.

Notes

1 *Reception and Poetics in Keats: 'My Ended Poet'* (Basingstoke: Macmillan, 1998), p. 18.
2 *Collected Poems of Thomas Hardy* (London: Macmillan, 1932).
3 *John Keats: A New Biography* (New Haven: Yale University Press, 2013), p. 291.
4 *Collected Poems of Thomas Hardy*, p. 84. It would appear that Keats first composed the poem in 1819, then produced a further copy in 1820 for Severn. (It is this second copy that Hardy supposes was the poem's original version): see *P* 638.
5 *The Life and Work of Thomas Hardy*, ed. Michael Millgate (Basingstoke: Macmillan, 1989 corr.), p. 151.
6 Edward Thomas, *Keats* (1916; Cheltenham: Cyder, 1999), p. 39.
7 Edward Thomas, *The Annotated Collected Poems*, ed. Edna Longley (Tarset: Bloodaxe, 2008).
8 Thomas, *Annotated*, p. 261.
9 See John Jones, *John Keats's Dream of Truth* (London: Chatto & Windus, 1969), p. 222.
10 *New Bearings in English Poetry: A Study of the Contemporary Situation* (London: Penguin/Chatto & Windus, 1972 reissue), p. 55.
11 Helen Vendler, 'Wallace Stevens', in *Part of Nature, Part of Us: Modern American Poets* (Cambridge, MA: Harvard University Press, 1980), pp. 23, 22.
12 Wallace Stevens, *Collected Poetry and Prose*, sel. Frank Kermode and Joan Richardson (New York: Library of America, 1997).
13 'Wallace Stevens', p. 22.
14 'Wallace Stevens', pp. 23–4.
15 Susan McCabe, *Elizabeth Bishop: Her Poetics of Loss* (University Park, PA: Penn State University Press, 1994), p. 52
16 Elizabeth Bishop, *Poems, Prose, Letters*, sel. Robert Giroux and Lloyd Schwartz (New York: Library of America, 2008).
17 Seamus Heaney, *Field Work* (London: Faber, 1979).

CHAPTER 30

American Writing

Mark Sandy

John Keats had thought seriously about visiting the United States and harboured 'hopes' that 'such a stay in America' (*L* I, 343) would benefit his family and health. Although his brother and sister-in-law did emigrate, Keats never went to America. This did not deter him from speculating that one of the 'Children' of George and Georgina Keats 'should be the first American Poet' (*L* I, 398). Nor did it prevent him from recreating the supposed moment when Cortez first espied the mountainous isthmus of 'Darien' ('On First Looking into Chapman's Homer', 14), which conjoins North and South America.[1] The fact that Keats was confined only to imagining as present the vastness of the American coast has not curtailed the variety and array of responses to Keats's own imaginative presence in American letters from the early nineteenth century onwards.

Emerson and Thoreau

This section focuses on the writings of Ralph Waldo Emerson and Henry David Thoreau and traces the conceptual and verbal echoes of Keats's work in their own. Often characterised as the inheritors of Wordsworth and Coleridge, Emerson and Thoreau are equally indebted to Keats's legacy. Emerson praised 'certain lines' in Keats's *Hyperion* for their poetic 'inward skill'[2] and Thoreau had read a range of Keats's poetry; most probably, in *The Poetical Works of Coleridge, Shelley, and Keats in One Volume. Stereotyped by John Howe. Philadelphia [J. Grieg], 1832.*[3] With varying emphases, both Emerson and Thoreau are responsive to the cadences, rhythms, and modulations of Keats's poetical thought and practice. In a core passage from *Nature*, Emerson insists on seeing through, and with, a creative, active, eye:

> Standing on the bare ground, – my head bathed by the blithe air and uplifted into infinite space, – all mean egotism vanishes. I become a transparent eyeball; I am nothing; I see all; the currents of Universal Being circulate through me; I am part or parcel of God.[4]

Here Emerson is attuned to Keats's conception of what it is for the 'I [to] live in the eye; and my imagination, surpassed, is at rest' (*L* I, 301). Alert to Keats's account of the 'poetical Character' (*L* I, 387) as negatively capable and self-annihilating, Emerson stresses a moment of selflessness when 'all mean egotism vanishes'. Emerson's formulation echoes Keats's empathetic ability to enter, unobtrusively, into other states of being and feel those inner psychic and physical spaces beyond ourselves 'upon our pulses' (*L* I, 279). Keats's negatively capable imagination permits the mind to 'take part in [the] existince' (*L* I, 186) of another being's inner spaces, solidity and life.

Emerson's central idea of self-reliance, like Keats's definition of poetical character, opposes 'consequitive reasoning' (*L* I, 185) to advocate a rejection of rationalised thought and habitual thinking in favour of a revelatory state achieved through embracing 'uncertainties, Mysteries, doubts' (*L* I, 193).[5] Such an intuitive disclosure of being as presence, for Emerson, transforms the personal into the impersonal, dissolving habitual frictions between individual and society, subject and object, mind and body, spirit and matter. Recognising the importance of the imaginative capacity to transcend the boundaries of individual selfhood, Emerson succinctly endorses what is, essentially, a mode of Keatsian negative capability when he writes, '[w]e are not strong by our power to penetrate, but by our relatedness'.[6]

Thoreau's own sense of imaginative disclosure tests Keats's suspension of 'a fine isolated verisimilitude caught from the Penetralium of mystery' and, alternatively, delights in the revelation of 'verisimilitude' (*L* I, 194), which flows from the world once mystery has been restored to it. When Thoreau writes of echoes as part of the 'universal lyre', he does so in a mode that recalls Keats's claim that the 'Mind may have its rewards in the repeti[ti]on of its own silent Working' (*L* I, 185):

> The echo is to some extent, an original sound, and therein is the magic and the charm of it. It is not merely a repetition of what was worth repeating in the bell, but partly the voice of the wood, the same trivial words and notes sung by a wood-nymph.[7]

In a swerve away from Keats, Thoreau's own sense of negative capability does not dissipate difference and division or realise a synesthetic blurring of the senses, but instead recaptures a dual poetic vision in which a renewed experience of each sense is felt doubly keenly.[8] Thoreau's sharpened double-sense requires that the act of perception (feeling, hearing, seeing, and smelling) becomes itself perceptive and speaks of what it is to be caught in a given moment of sensation or experience of feeling, seeing, smelling, tasting or (as with the 'echo') hearing.[9]

In some respects, nevertheless, Thoreau is closer to Keats than he may himself have recognised. His echoes of the woods and song of the 'wood nymph' are haunted by Keats's 'leaf-fring'd legend' of 'the dales of Arcady' ('Ode on a Grecian Urn', 5, 7). Thoreau's meditation on quietness, silence, and sound attempts to resolve itself in the contradictory 'ditties of no tone' ('Ode on a Grecian Urn', 14) and to approximate those Keatsian repetitions in 'a finer tone' (*L* I, 185). Thoreau's alertness to 'what was worth repeating in the bell' reimagines Keats's own insistence that 'the very word is like a bell' ('Ode to a Nightingale', 71). Thoreau presses us not to hear the 'repetition' of the repeating sound of the bell, but within that repetition to listen for a new (and yet continually) heard and unheard sound of the 'notes' of the Dryad and the 'voice of the wood' itself.

Recalling Keats's Grecian Urn, Thoreau's 'echo' both occupies and moves across time (memory, history, and myth), place, and space to 'tease us out of thought' ('Ode on a Grecian Urn', 44). Similarly, Emerson as poet sought to revisit and revise aspects of Keats's poetics, reworking the dictum 'Beauty is truth, truth Beauty' ('Grecian Urn', 49) into 'Beauty is its own excuse for being' ('The Rhodora'). For Emerson, the presence of beauty in the ordinary was its own self-justification without, as he may have felt in Keats, the need for any otherworldly or metaphysical underpinnings. In spite of these (re-)negotiations, the poetic practices and theories of Emerson and Thoreau are indebted to Keats's Spring Odes and their distinctive self-conscious artistry which, as does so much of American Romanticism in their wake, ponders the status of poetry and the role of the poet.

Whitman and Dickinson

How the poetry of Walt Whitman and Emily Dickinson engages with Keats's poetic bequest forms the focus of this next section. Two poems in Whitman's *Sea-Drift* are concerned with tragic poetic consciousness. Both poems traverse the threshold of Keats's 'magic casements' to focus on, and distance from us, 'perilous seas, in faery lands forlorn' ('Ode to a Nightingale', 69–70) and their attendant states of confused consciousness. Whitman writes large Keats's 'perilous seas' on the vast canvas of the seascape of America's Eastern Seaboard.

In 'Out of the Cradle Endlessly Rocking', the action of singing recalls Keats's nightingale and serves as a retrospective 'reminiscence' of the decisive event in time and space that created the youthful Whitman into the poet (the 'out-setting bard').[10] Here poetic selfhood has become and still continues to become by the continuation of the 'self-same song' ('Ode to a Nightingale', 65) of a forlorn bird. The song of Whitman's dark songster, recalling Keats's sensuously existential sense in the words 'Darkling I listen' ('Ode to a Nightingale', 51), grieves for its lost mate: '*O night! Do I not see my love fluttering out among the breakers? / What is that little black thing I see there in the white?* ('Out of the Cradle Endlessly Rocking', 79–80, emphasis in original). The Whitmanesque imagination transmutes Keats's Miltonic-inflected 'Darkling' into the desperately hoped for sighting of the 'little black thing' of the missing (or deceased) she-mate somewhere out there on the horizon.

This unfolding tragic love affair of the two birds sets in motion two contradictory ideas: one that the sea finally gives up its dark secret to both poet and bird, and the other that a change within the observing consciousness of the boy would-bepoet grants him access to the tragic secret that the sea has always been whispering. In actuality, this change in the boy's consciousness occurs, simultaneously, within the instance (the moment of perception) that the sea surrenders its 'clew':

> Whereto answering, the sea,
> Delaying not, hurrying not,
> Whisper'd me through the night, and very plainly before daybreak,
> Lisp'd to me the low and delicious word death,
> And again death, death, death, death.
>
> ('Out of the Cradle Endlessly Rocking', 165–9)

Recalling Keats's 'eternal whisperings' ('On the Sea', 1) of the sea, Whitman's contracted phrase 'Whisper'd me' ('Out of the Cradle Endlessly Rocking', 184) breathes the poet into existence out of the womb-like 'embalmed [nocturnal] darkness' ('Ode to a Nightingale', 43). This verbal contraction both registers the vital birth, albeit tragic, of the would-be poet into an existential poetic consciousness and completes the 'destiny of me', as the poet's subjectivity is that which is whispered into a continual state of becoming (and, by implication, singing) as the 'chanter of pains and joy, uniter of here and hereafter' ('Out of the Cradle Endlessly Rocking', 20).

In another of Whitman's twilight coastal poems, 'As I Ebb'd with the Ocean of Life', the specific singularity of purpose and action of a version of Keatsian 'quiet breathing' (*Endymion*, 1. 5) – 'I inhale' (20) – dramatises an illusory sense of an autonomous self-enclosed state of withdrawn isolation. But in the same breath, Whitman's poem also suggests such introspection is susceptible to (if not akin with) an outer landscape of fractured and fragmenting 'wash'd up drift', 'dead leaves', and breaking billows of the mysterious ocean ('As I Ebb'd with the Ocean of Life', 23, 24, 21).

Instantaneously, Whitman endeavours to preserve the boundaries between self – 'the real Me' ('As I Ebb'd with the Ocean of Life', 28) or Keatsian 'sole self' (72) – and world, while he stages a self decentred by the centripetal force of the ocean's gathering power. The merging of Whitman's 'myself' with 'part of the sands and drift' ('As I Ebb'd with the Ocean of Life', 24) is both a wilful enactment of agency and an enforced (by the outer power of the ocean) merger and fracturing of the self. Whitman's perilous romance of the sea, as it does for Keats, encapsulates all elements of life no matter how painful. Whitman shared in Keats's conviction that the intensity of poetic art is 'capable of making all disagreeables evaporate' (*L* 1, 192).

This Keatsian negatively capable poetic intensity is felt through and questioned by the self-reflexivity of Emily Dickinson's poetry. A series of tropes, questioning what is visible or invisible, culminate in the final stanza of 'The Butterfly's Day':

Till Sundown crept – a steady Tide –
And Men that made the Hay –
And Afternoon – and Butterfly –
Extinguished – in the Sea –[11]

In 'The Butterfly's Day', light, life, and the ability to *see* whether with visionary or mundane eyes is called into doubt. After all, the elusive, enigmatic, flight of the butterfly tracks a passage across the sky that marks out its own ephemeral journey from life (emergence from the cocoon) to death as its colourful seen or unseen existence is 'Extinguished' by an implied 'Sea' of darkness.

Dickinson's use of diction and reluctant commitment to certainties in 'The Butterfly's Day' captures something of Keats's hope that 'The poetry of earth is never ceasing' ('On the Grasshopper and Cricket', 9). Her speakers, like many of Keats's, often reflect on the transient nature of existence.[12] In a late poem, 'The Earth has Many Keys', Dickinson contemplates further her own mortality and claims 'The cricket is utmost / Of elegy to me'.[13] Dickinson is again attuned to both Keats's hopeful claim for the cricket's melody and the funereal song of 'To Autumn'. Nature's music, for Dickinson and Keats, mourns our passing and promises the possibility of an afterlife seemingly secured by the eternal rebound of seasonal change.

But Dickinson, after Keats, remains sceptical about the restorative powers of nature. Dickinson's butterfly is a focal centre which absents itself from the visual field and the poem itself. Sensitive to the shifting shades, hues, and tones of Keats's 'camelion Poet' (*L* 1, 387), Dickinson declares, 'I Dwell in Possibility – / A fairer House than Prose – / More numerous of Windows'. She reminds us, as Keats understood, that the 'Mansion' of poetic fiction-making consists of 'Many Apartments' (*L* 1, 280) and is capacious enough to accommodate numerous 'Windows' – possibilities and perspectives (apertures of vision) – which, paradoxically, can also incorporate impossibilities and ways of not seeing.

Dickinson follows Keats in understanding poetic vision as the imagining of what cannot be seen or felt; an immersion in the Keatsian sensation of 'The feel of not to feel' ('In drear nighted December', 21). Conscious also of Keats's weighing-up of Beauty, art, and truth against our mortal realm in 'Ode on a Grecian Urn', Dickinson's poetry tests whether nature and artistic vision are able to compensate us for our transient and contingent existences.

Twentieth- and Twenty-First-Century Novelists

This following section explores post-Romantic responses to Keats in the work of twentieth- and twenty-first-century American novelists. F. Scott Fitzgerald speculated that the indelible 'nostalgic sadness' which marked his own work was a consequence of reading 'Keats a lot'[14] in his youth. For Fitzgerald, Keats was the assured exponent of the compressed verbal phrase capable of lending an exterior solidity and interior sensation to his chosen poetic subject. In the opening of *The Eve of St. Agnes*, a narrative poem in Spenserian stanzas admired by Fitzgerald as 'probably the finest technical poem in English', he found one of many such instances to justify his admiration for Keats's poetic accomplishments:

> A line like 'The hare limped trembling through the frozen grass', is so alive that you race through it, scarcely noticing it, yet it has colored the whole poem with its movement – the limping, trembling and freezing is going on before your eyes.[15]

It is precisely this empathetic ability to dissolve into these momentary inward spaces of feeling, which Fitzgerald identified with Keats's negatively capable poetics and used as a model for his own artistry. In a passage from *The Beautiful and Damned*, Fitzgerald's poetics of transient intimacy and inner feeling reveal their Keatsian provenance:

> Halcyon days like boats drifting along slow-moving rivers; spring evenings full of a plaintive melancholy that made the past beautiful and bitter, bidding them look back and see that the loves of other summers long gone were dead with the forgotten waltzes of their years. Always the most poignant moments were when some artificial barrier kept them apart… [N]ot knowing that they were following in the footsteps of dusty generations but

> comprehending dimly that if truth is the end of life happiness is a mode of it, to be cherished in its brief and tremulous moment.[16]

Fitzgerald's 'plaintive melancholy' and 'forgotten waltzes' re-imagine Keats's 'plaintive anthem' ('Ode to a Nightingale', 75) just as the lost 'dusty generations' derive from the transient 'hungry generations' (62) of the same ode. Fitzgerald recreates 'the loves of other summers long gone' as a poignant and wakeful vision of past and future disappointed love, failed connection, and broken dreams. His central lovers, Anthony and Gloria, are oblivious to the emotional and physical devastation that await them because – as Fitzgerald writes reimagining the spurious circumstances of Keats's composition of the Nightingale Ode at Wentworth gardens – 'both were walking alone in a dispassionate garden with a ghost found in a dream'[17] touched by their own Keatsian 'plaintive anthem'.

That Fitzgerald was intrigued by Keats's adjectival use of 'plaintive' is evident in the final scene of a short story published by Scribner in the autumn of 1922. 'Winter Dreams' was a transitional work, later collected in *All the Sad Young Men* which, consolidating an essential theme of his past and next major work, meditates in its closing pages on the loss of dreams, youth, and love – all of 'these things were no longer in the world'[18] – without ever fully realising the 'mythopoeic' grandeur of the final sentiment of *The Great Gatsby*.[19]

But stylistically, Fitzgerald's description of when '[t]he dream was gone'– and Dexter Green's efforts to rekindle his pure vision of Judy Jones (a prototype for Daisy Fay in *The Great Gatsby*) – achieves a tighter Keatsian precision in the felt, vernal, sensuality of 'her mouth damp with his kisses and her *eyes plaintive with melancholy* and her freshness like new fine linen in the morning'.[20] Fitzgerald's fiction frequently inhabits, as does Keats's speaker at the close of the Nightingale Ode, a world of fled vision and uncertain dreams.

For Saul Bellow's fiction, this fall into the quotidian is given shape and purpose through direct reference to Keats being read aloud. In Bellow's short story, 'Max Zetland: By a Character Witness', the characters find spiritual release from the city and economic hardship when as they row the 'lagoon':

> [W]e read Keats to each other while the weeds bound the oars, Chicago was nowhere. It had no setting. It was something released into American space.[21]

Here reciting Keats's line 'Upon the honeyed middle of the night' (*The Eve of St. Agnes*, 49) offers a near epiphany of self-dissolution into the idyllic 'sky clear green, pure blue'. Such an escape into romance is fleeting as Chicago's 'boring power of a manufacturing center' is only temporarily 'arrested'.[22] In *Seize the Day*, the recollection of hearing read aloud the Indian Maid's song (*Endymion*, 4. 279–84) causes Bellow's Wilhelm to accept that suffering is instrumental in shaping 'Intelligences' or souls into authentic identities through a 'World of Pains' (*L* 2 102). Such a 'medium of a world like this' (*L* 2 102) is vital in Bellow's struggle for the 'heart's ultimate need'.[23] Bellow upholds Keats's 'truth' of the imagination and its power to attest to the 'holiness of the Heart's affections' (*L* 1, 184).

Recently, Philip Roth's *Everyman* took Keats's 'Where but to think is to be full of sorrow' ('Ode to a Nightingale', 27) as a cue to meditate on cardiac failure, ageing, and physical frailty.[24] Recollecting Keats's alluring yet troubled seas of the Nightingale Ode, Roth's novella symbolises our tragic human predicament through the dark rolling ocean. Refracted through Whitman and Stevens, Roth's Romantic motif of the sea is one of Keatsian vital appeal and fatal destruction.

Twentieth-Century Poetry

This final section acknowledges Keats's continued posthumous presence in twentieth-century American poetry. Even Stevens, who insists that the 'romantic must never remain', is willing to concede, in 'The Plain Sense of Things', that the Romantic 'absence of imagination had / Itself to be imagined'.[25] William Carlos Williams tenders a solution to this dilemma with the post-Romantic assertion that there are 'no ideas but in things'[26] only to find that his dictum shares with Keats's negative capability a loss of selfhood and a sense of 'Things real – such as the existences of Sun Moon & Stars and passages of Shakspeare' (*L* 1, 243).[27] Frost also resisted Keats's negative capability by claiming that a poem was a 'momentary stay against confusion'[28] rather than an immersion in doubts and uncertainties. Yet much of Frost's work celebrates a Keatsian poetics of the earth and those possibilities of an 'uncertain / Something more of the depths'.[29]

Poetry and the imagination even, in Stevens's mind, is 'one of the enlargements of life' and has – akin to Keats's notion of 'snail-horn perception' (*L* 1, 265) – the 'power to possess the moment it perceives'.[30] Such a 'moment' occurs in the final stanza of 'The Idea of Order at Key West':

> The maker's rage to order words of the sea,
> Words of the fragrant portals, dimly-starred,
> And of ourselves and of our origins,
> In ghostlier demarcations, keener sounds.

Stevens's closing lines avow and disavow the 'dark voice of the sea', reclaiming as much as they bid adieu to Keats's romance of 'perilous seas, in faery lands forlorn' ('Ode to a Nightingale', 70). Stevens reinforces a desire to move beyond a heap of Romantic tropes that, in his words, are persistently everywhere and 'should not remain'.

This poetic difficulty is restated at the end of Stevens's earlier poem, 'The Snow Man', which 'beholds / Nothing that is not there and the nothing that is'. Stevens's proposition recalls Keats's definition of poetic selfhood as 'every thing and nothing' (*L* I, 387). We are asked to imagine as both there and not there the 'nothing' or 'no thing' which suggestively, but elusively, implies the presence of some thing or something.

Nonetheless whatever that elusive something might be can only be beholden by 'One [that] must have a mind of winter', a mind which is at once a blank (nothing) and a creating consciousness (a something). Whether welcomed or resisted, Stevens's sensitivity to a Romantic nothing that might be a something is illustrative of the subtle and lasting legacies of Keats's negatively capable poetics in the American imagination.

Notes

1 Jeffrey N. Cox, *Keats's Poetry and Prose* (New York: W.W. Norton, 2009), p. 55, fn. 6.
2 Douglas Emory Wilson, ed. and intro. Ronald A. Bosco. *The Collected Works of Ralph Waldo Emerson: Society and Solitude,* vol. 8 (Cambridge, MA: Harvard University Press, 2010), p. 30. Hereafter *CWE.*
3 Robert Sattlemeyer, *Thoreau's Reading: An Intellectual Life with Bibliographical Catalogue* (Princeton: Princeton University Press, 1988), p. 155.
4 Carl Bode, ed. and intro. Malcolm Cowley, *The Portable Emerson,* 2nd edn (Harmondsworth: Viking-Penguin, 1981), p. 11.
5 George Kateb, *Emerson and Self-Reliance*, 2nd edn (Lanham: Rowman, 2002), pp. 29–30.
6 *CWE,* p. 153.
7 Carl Bode, ed. 'Sounds', *Walden, The Portable Thoreau*, 2nd edn (Harmondsworth: Penguin, 1982), p. 375.
8 Dan Beachy-Quick, *Wonderful Meditations: Essays, Meditations, Tales* (Minneapolis: Milkweed, 2012), p. 50.
9 Dan Beachy-Quick, '"The Oracular Tree Acquiring": On Romanticism as Radical Praxis', *The Radical Impulse in the Nineteenth Century and Contemporary Poetic Practice*, ed. Julie Carr and Jeffrey C. Robinson (Tuscaloosa: University of Alabama Press, 2015), pp. 33, 31–45.
10 Francis Murphy, ed. 'Out of the Cradle Endlessly Rocking', *Walt Whitman: Complete Poems* (Harmondsworth: Penguin, 1996).

11 Thomas H. Johnson, ed. *Emily Dickinson: The Complete Poems,* 2nd edn (London: Faber, 1975).
12 Compare with Richard Gravil, *Romantic Dialogues: Anglo-American Continuities 1776–1862* (New York: St Martin's Press, 2000), pp. 191; 187–212.
13 Mary Loeffelholz, *Dickinson and the Boundaries of Feminist Theories* (Illinois: University of Illinois Press, 1991), pp. 145–6.
14 Andrew Turnbull, ed. *The Letters of F. Scott Fitzgerald* (Harmondsworth: Penguin, 1968), p. 547. Hereafter *LFS.*
15 *LSF*, p. 44.
16 F. Scott Fitzgerald, *The Beautiful and Damned* (1922; Harmondsworth: Penguin, 1966), p. 116. Hereafter *BD.*
17 *BD*, p. 116.
18 F. Scott Fitzgerald, *The Collected Short Stories of F. Scott Fitzgerald* (Harmondsworth: Penguin, 1986), p. 383. Hereafter *CSF.*
19 John Kuehl, *F. Scott Fitzgerald: A Study of the Short Fiction* (Boston: Hall, 1991), pp. 67–8.
20 *CSF*, 383, emphasis added.
21 Saul Bellow, *Collected Stories* (Harmondsworth: Penguin, 2001), p. 241. Hereafter *CS.*
22 *CS*, p. 241.
23 Saul Bellow, *Seize the Day* (1956; Harmondsworth: Penguin, 1988), p. 118.
24 Philip Roth, *Everyman*. (London: Cape, 2006).
25 Wallace Stevens, *Collected Poems* (London: Faber, 1984).
26 Walton A. Litz and Christopher McGowan, eds. *Paterson, the Complete Poems of William Carlos Williams*, vol. 1 (New York: New Directions, 1986), p. 264.
27 Barry Ahearn, *William Carlos Williams and Alterity: The Early Poetry* (Cambridge: Cambridge University Press, 1994), p. 156.
28 Mark Richardson, ed. *The Collected Prose of Robert Frost* (Cambridge, MA: Harvard University Press, 2007), p. 132.
29 Edward Connery Lathem, ed. 'For Once, Then, Something', *The Poetry of Robert Frost* (Harmondsworth: Vintage, 1971), lines 9–10.
30 Wallace Stevens, *The Necessary Angel: Essays on Reality and the Imagination* (New York: Knopf, 1951), p. 61.

PART VI

Critical Reception

CHAPTER 31

Contemporary Reviews

Kelvin Everest

Keats's career as a published poet – a handful of magazine publications and just three volumes of poetry – lasted less than four years. Its beginning was an article in the liberal weekly *Examiner* of 1 December 1816, by the paper's editor the well-known radical Leigh Hunt. He grouped Keats together with Shelley and John Hamilton Reynolds as three young writers who promised a 'considerable addition of strength' to a 'new school' of poetry (*CH* 41–2). This was a fateful introduction to public notice, marking Keats's political affiliation as radical, and his poetry as mannered in a style closely associated with Hunt's own verse. The connection with Hunt and his principles in poetry and politics was the dominating factor in Keats's literary reputation during his lifetime, leading to what have come to be seen as the most notorious critical attacks on a living poet in British literary history. It was widely believed for many years that Keats died as a result of these attacks, which was not the case. There is, however, no doubt that they affected him in complicated ways, provoking productive resistance as well as a sense of hurt and humiliation. The attacks also had a profound influence on Keats's critical reception during his lifetime and immediately following his death.

By far the most damaging of the hostile reviews were the attacks on *Endymion* in *Blackwood's Edinburgh Magazine* (vol. 3. 519–24, August 1818) and the *Quarterly Review* (vol. 19, 204–8, dated April 1818 but actually published in September). Both publications were committed to a Tory defence of Church and State, and were defined in opposition to the liberal *Edinburgh Review* at a time when aggressive party politics dominated literary journalism. The *Blackwood's* review was by John Gibson Lockhart, and still after two centuries its toxic mix of social sneering, personal insult and outrageously wilful bias can shock. Lockhart relentlessly satirised Keats's earlier stylistic mannerisms – the attack begins with some swipes at the 1817 *Poems* – before settling to a sustained deriding of 'the calm, settled, imperturbable drivelling idiocy of *Endymion*' (*CH* 98). Just as Keats's style is characterised as Hunt's carried to ridiculous extremes, so *Endymion*'s radicalism exemplifies how the 'bantling' Keats has learned to 'lisp sedition' (*CH* 109) from Hunt's politics. Lockhart reserves a singular disgust for Keats's sensuous eroticism, 'prurient and vulgar … evidently meant for some young lady east of Temple-bar' (*CH* 102).

The *Quarterly*'s attack was a more serious matter, with its much bigger audience and a genuine national influence. Its review was by John Wilson Croker, though for many years it was widely understood to have been by the magazine's editor himself, William Gifford. Croker's attack, unlike Lockhart's, was not overtly political in content, though it mentioned Keats's Hunt connection and the motivation of its prejudice was plain. Croker was contemptuously dismissive in tone, derisively conceding that he had not even troubled to read most of *Endymion*, and he was withering on Keats's perceived technical incompetence, even while acknowledging a modicum of talent, grotesquely misapplied. Croker's attack mocks *Endymion*'s idiosyncratic versification – 'he cannot indeed write a sentence, but perhaps he may be able to spin a line' (*CH* 113) – but it is especially vindictive in dissecting Keats's style of rhyming, to which he attributes the pervasive nonsensical character of the poem: 'he seems to us to write a line at random, and then he follows not the thought excited by this line, but that suggested by the *rhyme* with which it concludes' (*CH* 112).

Croker's attack prompted public objections to its unwarranted severity and obvious bias, by John Scott in the *Morning Chronicle* (3 October 1818) and in a review by Keats's friend John Hamilton Reynolds (*West of England Journal*, 6 October 1818), but the reputational damage was done. It seems probable that Keats himself was not, after the initial shock, too badly affected. His own Preface to *Endymion* had truthfully acknowledged the poem's limitations of immaturity and unreadiness for public criticism, while anticipating better success with future efforts.

In fact from the very outset of his publishing career, commentary both hostile and friendly tended to occupy common ground. Keats's poetry was disconcertingly different for his contemporary readers, and that remains true for new readers in every generation. The contemporary reviews have a persisting value in helping us to focus what is distinctive and challenging in his greatness. Keats's original draft Preface to *Endymion* refers in passing to the critical reception of his first published volume, the 1817 *Poems*: 'About a twelve month since, I published a little book of verses; it was read by some dozen of my friends who lik'd it; and some dozen who I was unacquainted with, who did not' (*P* 739). Most of the known early reviews are by 'friends', but their supportive judgements are surprisingly easy to square with qualities that attracted censure and mockery from less sympathetic critics. Even John Hamilton Reynolds, one of the three new poets of Hunt's *Examiner* announcement, admits in the *Champion* (9 March 1817) that *Poems* is 'not without defects': a 'natural freedom of versification, at times passes to an absolute faultiness of measure'; there is an over-use of 'compound epithets'; he is 'apt occasionally to make his descriptions overwrought'. Reynolds of course spends most of his time extolling Keats's strengths, characterised as a reliance 'wholly and directly on nature', and an ability 'to look at natural objects with his mind, as Shakspeare and Chaucer did'.

This quality is something Reynolds struggles clearly to define, but his account seems to be reaching for a critical language to capture Keats's idiosyncratic intensity in imagining a life for nature: 'his imagination is very powerful...[his poetry] is remarkably abstracted [but] never out of reach of the mind', as if to suggest that it is difficult to articulate what exactly Keats's nature poetry is trying to *say*. The young Keats, unlike 'one or two established writers of the day', does not believe that 'mystery is the soul of poetry – that artlessness is a vice – and that nothing can be graceful that is not metaphysical'. Keats's disconcertingly direct and unmediated natural description consequently avoids trying 'to puzzle the world with a confused sensibility' (*CH* 46–8). Another friend, George Felton Mathew, in the *European Magazine* (May 1817) noted an influence from the Elizabethans, as did an anonymous writer in the *Monthly Magazine* (April 1817). This likeness to Chaucer, Shakespeare, Spenser and the Elizabethans consisted in a roughness of versification combined with coinages and oddly colourful and arresting epithets, castigated by Mathew as a 'slovenly independence of...versification'. Like Reynolds, Mathew pleads Keats's immaturity, managing to describe typifying Keatsian qualities as affectations that will be grown out of. He notes the bad influence of Hunt: the poems 'savour too much...of [Hunt's] foppery and affectation'. Interestingly, Mathew easily avoids the danger of uncritical acclaim, observing that 'too much praise is more injurious than censure', and offers shrewd commentary. Keats's youth 'may be discovered in the petty arguments of his principal pieces', and this weakness of 'argument' is attributed to his 'enmity to the French school, and to the Augustan age of England', producing a principle that 'plan and arrangement are prejudicial to natural poetry'. The difficulty of identifying a coherent frame of thought in the poetry is thoughtfully developed to the perception of a general lack of moral sentiment and recommended virtue, in favour of 'luxuries of imagination' (*CH* 50–4).

Even Leigh Hunt himself, in an unsigned review in *The Examiner* (1 June 1817), notes the apparent lack of an intellectual and reflective dimension.

Keats's 'faults' arise from his great strength, a 'passion for beauties, and a young impatience to vindicate them'. This produces 'a tendency to notice every thing too indiscriminately and without an eye to natural proportion and effect', which we can understand as a reference to the lack of an organising argument. Hunt also joins with others in finding that Keats's 'sense of the proper variety of versification' is executed 'without a due consideration of its principles' (*CH* 57). Perhaps the most insightful of the early reviews is by Josiah Conder in his own publication the *Eclectic Review*. Like most others Conder acknowledges that Keats is clearly a talented writer, but limited by immaturity and by 'not having yet entered in earnest on the business of intellectual acquirement'. This judgement will harden in Conder's review of Keats's 1820 poems into a frank animosity to Keats's lack of Christian moralising. Here there is a forebearance owing to Keats's youth, and a real acuity in reading the early poems as '*all about* poetry… the first efflorescence of the unpruned fancy, which must pass away before anything like genuine excellence can be produced' (italics in original, *CH* 68). This catches, albeit obliquely, the Keatsian preoccupation with his own claims to be a poet, and its consequent constant circling around the question of his own development and emerging place in a tradition. It fixes the abiding question of Keats's leading themes, which in the mature achievement balance so perfectly the limits of transient personal agency against the permanence of great art and its paradoxical representation of fleeting human experience.

Conder is also forthrightly perceptive on the influence of Hunt in the 1817 volume, where 'the affectation which vitiates [Hunt's] style must needs be aggravated to a ridiculous excess in the copyist' (*CH* 67). How should we understand this Huntian influence? As we have seen, for Keats's first readers his metres were loose and idiosyncratic in the manner of the Elizabethan dramatists, and especially later Shakespeare, avoiding end-stopping and entirely without the supposed mechanical regularity of couplets. Keats's earlier published work clearly attempts a deliberate exaggeration of the effect, drawing attention to its own freedom from the Augustan constraint attacked in 'Sleep and Poetry'. Keats's diction was still more emphatically developed from Hunt's practice, and so – particularly for politically hostile readers – manifestly provocative. There is a revelling in prominently novel coinages. Frequent adjectives and adverbs ending in '-y', transferred epithets, and a general clearly deliberate oddity could be read as freshly eccentric or ludicrously bizarre. These qualities form part of the substance of the unusual metrical character of the poetry, constantly skirting what was perceived as an un-Pope-like deviation from the rule.

Keats's rhymes concentrated and exaggerated these qualities, rendering the curious diction more prominent, and often using the 'feminine' ending of an extra unstressed syllable. His rhymes, often seeming chosen for their sound alone, attracted particular criticism for their influence on the 'argument' of his poems, with a perceived tendency to deflect the thought along paths dictated by the exigencies of rhyme rather than sense, and thus subverting any chance of an unfolding logic. It was as if the young poet was struggling incompetently under constant pressure to meet the formal requirement of his own chosen idiom. This alleged 'fault' served a more fundamental criticism, that Keats's poetry lacked 'plan' or 'arrangement'. Even reviewers looking to be supportive noted the apparent absence of argument, finding in Keats a striking succession of imagery in distinctive expression, but not amounting to a coherent intellectual whole. The poems didn't seem to be *about* anything, except perhaps themselves. There was broad agreement that Keats had a sharp detailed eye for nature and an unusually intense and sensuous imagination. Equally general was the view that these abilities were in the service of an immature and experientially limited young writer who needed time to develop, and whose talents were in thrall to the bad model of Hunt.

Perhaps the most suggestive of all the contemporary reviews of *Endymion* appeared unsigned in the *London Magazine* (April 1820). It was by P. G. Patmore (father of the poet Coventry Patmore) and reflected astutely on the poem's resistance to prevailing conceptions of poetry itself. Far from conforming with such notions as formal poetic decorum – Augustan diction, metrical regularity, competent rhyme – Keats's poem called for a different canon of judgement. *Endymion* 'is not a *poem* at all [but] an ecstatic dream of poetry... an involuntary outpouring of the spirit of poetry'. This was a positive inflection of the charge that Keats's poetry lacked plan or arrangement, noting that *Endymion* 'as a tale' was 'nothing', offering 'no connecting interest to bind one part with another' (*CH* 136–7). Like most commentators, Patmore readily conceded that Keats's faults were inextricably bound up with his strengths, but was distinctive in mainly emphasising the power and promise of his originality.

The serious politically motivated critical attacks on *Endymion* in *Blackwood's* and the *Quarterly* were preceded by a piece in the Tory *British Critic* (June 1818) which captured exactly the kind of shocked amusement affected by those who saw Keats as a disciple of Hunt who had taken his mannerisms to a hilarious extreme. The *British Critic* review is genuinely funny in its relentless parade of Keatsian coinages and quirks of phrasing and diction, and reminds us that Keats was for his first audience a vexingly puzzling and strange-sounding poet. It has been argued that Keats's contemporary reception was not on balance one of unjust neglect or victimhood.[1] He received more than fifty notices of one kind or another, many of them positive, and by writers some of whom are today still remembered and read (or at least studied). His death was quite widely reported, and his final volume of 1820 was on the whole favourably received. The general tenor of the reviews of *Lamia...and Other Poems* was to note a gathering strength in the writing, a more positively marked originality of imaginative conception and a welcome lessening of Hunt's influence, though faults of the kind attacked in *Endymion* were still evident, often characterised as 'affectation'. An anonymous writer in the *Monthly Review*, for example, while accepting that the 1820 volume mingled good and bad qualities, observed that Keats was 'continually shocking our ideas of poetical decorum', and pleaded with him to become 'less strikingly original' (*CH* 159). The dominant note however, throughout the public notices of 1820, was a shared impulse to rescue Keats from the appalling injustice of, especially, Croker's *Quarterly* review.

Francis Jeffrey, the doyen of Whig literary criticism in the *Edinburgh Review*, the *Quarterly*'s great adversary, had remained silent in 1818 when the attacks appeared. He came belatedly to Keats's defence in the *Edinburgh* of August 1820, affirming Keats's obvious great talent while implicitly rebuking Croker and Lockhart. But Jeffrey's motivation seems principally not to have been to extol the substance of Keats's promise and originality – there is little insightful commentary on the poems – but rather in a spirit of political enmity to redress the critical wrong done to the young Keats by Jeffrey's own opponents, and this impression is reinforced by most other favourable accounts of Keats's last volume. An anonymous reviewer in the *London Magazine and Monthly Critical and Dramatic Review* (August 1820) offering the usual recognition of talent while castigating 'affectation' opens by lamenting the *Quarterly*'s attack. John Scott in *Baldwin's Magazine* (September 1820) likewise, in a fair and balanced discussion of the 1820 poems, offers stern public rebuke of Croker. It does appear that the attacks of 1818, while resented by Keats at first, and causing him some distress, did not have an immediately damaging effect on his development. But the public perception, articulated in the critical reception of his greatest book, was by the end of 1820 one that greatly reinforced the view that Keats, sharing the fate of Thomas Chatterton and Henry Kirke White (two poets whose recent demise in the wake of harsh public criticism had defined their cultural presence), was a young writer whose career was destroyed by critical malevolence. This view was to shape Keats's posthumous cultural image, particularly through the Victorian period, and more especially when combined with the idea, mistakenly given currency after Keats's death by Leigh Hunt's well-meaning statements,[2] that Keats's social origins were obscure, lowly and impoverished. In Keats's own lifetime, the *Lamia* reviews came too late to help his career, as by the time of their appearance through 1820 Keats's health was rapidly failing, allowing the sense of cruelly and unjustly thwarted promise to grow in him as his hopes of further poetic achievement faded. His early death seemed to his friends to seal a fate in obscurity that had been determined to hunt him down since the Tory reviews of 1818.

Those friends formed a remarkable dimension of his critical readership. Keats was clearly a magnetically attractive personality, inspiring deep affection and loyalty amongst his circle of acquaintance. Some in that circle served his ultimate triumph as a major English poet by their guardianship of memorials to his life, preserving extensive correspondence, unpublished work and an extensive body of related material and reminiscence. Posterity owes a particular debt to Richard Woodhouse, who met Keats through John Taylor and James Hessey, publishers of *Endymion* and the *Lamia* volume. Taylor and Hessey, and Woodhouse himself, shared serious misgivings over what they saw as the dangerous eroticism of the *Lamia* volume (particularly *The Eve of St. Agnes*), a view which, though it seems quaintly blinkered to today's readers, chimed with other and sterner criticisms of Keats's lack of a moral framework (see Conder's interesting review of *Lamia* in the *Eclectic Review* [September 1820: *CH* 232–9]). Woodhouse, however, was convinced that Keats was a genius, and proceeded methodically to collect and preserve a wealth of material by and associated with the poet in order to safeguard his chances of success with posterity. His meticulous care in preparing Keats for a future readership was both selfless and far-seeing, and all readers and scholars owe him a great debt. Woodhouse's collection, together with others preserved by Keats's friends (see *P* 741–52), provided a foundation for later study. Woodhouse probably played some part too in Keats's contemporary critical reception, as the author of a review of *Endymion* in the *Champion* (8 June 1818) which remarkably attempted to feel its way towards an articulation of Keats's doctrine of 'negative capability' as embodied in *Endymion*'s 'dramatic poetry': 'Mr Keats conceives the scene before him, and represents it as it appears' such that we 'identify ourselves with the scene' (*CH* 89).

Keats's circle included of course Hunt, and once his writing career was under way it widened to include major figures such as Hazlitt and Lamb, and others well-known at the time such as Henry Crabbe Robinson, and the painter Benjamin Haydon. He met and was read by Wordsworth, and had a memorable meeting with Coleridge. John Clare knew Keats's work through their shared publisher, and though the two poets never met, Clare recorded thoughtfully appreciative commentary. So it is reasonable to say that Keats had a definite presence in the literary culture of Regency London, albeit one which all who knew him assumed was doomed quickly to fade on his early death. Keats was also acquainted with Shelley, though there seems to have been a certain coolness between them, and more on Keats's part until Shelley's generous offer of shelter in Italy when he learned of Keats's illness in 1820. Shelley and Keats probably only ever met on relatively few occasions, including at least two sonnet-writing competitions with Hunt. Once Shelley left England for Italy in March 1818 they never met again, and Keats does not mention Shelley at all thereafter until his illness. Shelley does mention Keats, declaring a reservedly mixed opinion of *Endymion*, but increasingly impressed by the *Lamia* volume. But Shelley's determination to write an elegy for Keats on learning of his death was to have momentous consequences for Keats's reputation. Shelley's *Adonais* was motivated by powerful converging forces in his own life and career, but there is no doubt that its primary purpose was to celebrate and affirm Keats's claim to classic status as an achieved poet. His chosen idiom was consequently one which is imbued with an elevated and challenging classicism in style and density of reference. These qualities make for a poem of real difficulty, and all generations of readers have found it so. But the poem's manner is in calculated tribute to Keats, who as Shelley understood it had been quite literally hounded to death by pusillanimous and grossly biased public criticism (Shelley was convinced that the true author of the *Quarterly*'s review was Robert Southey[3]). It has been argued that Shelley himself invented this narrative of Keats's fate, in the service of an exercise in self-aggrandisement, conscious or not, whereby Keats's 'weakness' in the face of criticism is etherealised at the expense of his actual tough-mindedness and determination.[4] But while Shelley may well have come to exaggerate somewhat the accounts he had been given of Keats's reaction to criticism, such a view of his great elegy seems completely inappropriate. Many others attributed Keats's illness in part at least to depression at his treatment; and *Adonais* itself is driven and energised by a highly sophisticated appropriation of Keats's own poetry, which pervades Shelley's elegy from start to finish. Shelley's purpose is to establish Keats's place in the firmament of major English poets by a rich density of allusion to Keats's poetry which implicitly places him on the same plane with those other elegising poets that echo through the poem: not simply the Greek pastoral elegists, Bion, Moschus and Theocritus, but Spenser, Milton, even Byron.[5]

Unfortunately *Adonais* has served Keats's critical afterlife in a mixed way. However mistakenly, it has been read by many, right up to the present day, as representing a fraily vulnerable 'feminised' Keats. In that image Shelley's complimentary tribute has reinforced a version of the myth that Keats was ultimately a poet whose promise was blighted by adversity, sufficiently lacking in resilience and self-belief to allow himself to be 'snuffed out by an article'. The phrase is Byron's, from a famous stanza in *Don Juan* (canto 11, stanza 61). This qualified endorsement of Keats's achievement has about it something patronising and disconcertingly trivialising. Byron was wholly unpersuaded of Keats's talent until his judgement was influenced by Shelley's account of his death apparently at the hands of the *Quarterly*, and by his resulting more attentive appraisal of the *Lamia* volume. Before that, his views on Keats were startlingly demeaning, and couched in terms of a 'socio-sexual revulsion', chiming with Tory views we have noted in *Blackwood's* and the *British Critic*, which today seems almost incomprehensible. He attacked Keats's poetry in class terms as 'shabby-genteel', 'vulgar', lacking the 'nobility of thought and of style' characteristic of gentlemen. Byron distinguishes his critical adaptation of such language from actual social superiority – men of Keats's 'School' 'may be … gentlemenly men, for what I know' (*CH* 130) – but the social sneering of a Lord at the pretensions of upstart common humanity pervades his discourse. Byron seems especially disgusted by Keats's sensuality, which he construes as a yearning in Keats for delicious experience that is actually closed to him. He writes of 'Johnny Keats's *p–ss a bed* poetry', and reacts to Jeffrey's defence 'The Edinburgh praises Jack Keats or Ketch or whatever his names are; – why his is the Onanism of Poetry'.[6] These remarks – which go on to a cruelly demeaning comparison with sexual perversion – were made in private correspondence, but their sneering offensiveness, likening Keats's verbal relish for sensual and erotic pleasure to a species of masturbation, marks the extreme hostility to which Keats's supposed social origins and class identity exposed him. But Shelley's has proved by far the most far-sighted of all the contemporary judgements on Keats's standing as a poet, at once predicting his eventual elevation to the canon of English poetry, and himself assisting in that elevation through the brilliance of his poetic tribute to Keats.

Notes

1 See Lewis M. Schwartz, *Keats Reviewed by His Contemporaries* (Metuchen, NJ: Scarecrow Press, 1973), pp. 1–2.
2 In *Lord Byron and Some of His Contemporaries* (London, 1828).
3 For Shelley's neurotically hostile attitude to Southey at the time, see *The Poems of Shelley*, vol. 4, 1820–1821, ed. Michael Rossington, Jack Donovan and Kelvin Everest (London: Routledge, 2014), p. 237.
4 See James A. W. Heffernan, '*Adonais*: Shelley's Consumption of Keats', *Studies in Romanticism* 23 (1984): 295–315, and Andrew Epstein, '"Flowers that Mock the Corse Beneath": Shelley's *Adonais*, Keats and Poetic Influence', *Keats-Shelley Journal* 48 (1999): 90–128.
5 See Kelvin Everest, 'Shelley's *Adonais* and John Keats', *Essays in Criticism* 57 (2007): 237–63.
6 *'Between Two Worlds': Byron's Letters and Journals*, vol. 7, ed. Leslie A. Marchand (London: John Murray, 1977), pp. 200, 217.

CHAPTER 32

Critical Reception, 1821–1900

Francis O'Gorman

John Keats's reputation as a poet was made by the century of his death. His reputation as a man was almost unmade. Criticism had, infamously, not been consistently admiring of his poetry during his life-time. Immediately after his death, a prominent English critic still struggled to perceive what Keats had actually done. William Hazlitt (1778–1830), who had known Keats, was restless: he thought, as he said in *Table-Talk* (1822), there was a 'deficiency of masculine energy of style', a 'want of action, of character, and so far, of imagination'.[1] That helped set some of the gendered critical terms that would dominate Keats's reception throughout the century, a man who risked giving emotion the name of effeminacy. At his most favourable, Hazlitt looked to an impossible future rather than an achieved past: Keats 'gave the greatest promise of genius of any poet of his day' (*CH* 248), Hazlitt said in his controversial anthology *Select British Poets* (1824). A promise of genius: not actual genius. What had happened was that Keats's premature death had deprived readers of the certainty of judgment, leaving a division between what was done and what was hoped for.

Division of other kinds characterised Keats's readers thereafter. The lustre of unfulfilled gifts helped influence judgments on the poet that Keats might have been and – something related happened with Emily Brontë (1818–48) –encouraged scrutiny of what was really known about him. The notion of Keats as unfulfilled promise, as 'nearly almost', was as familiar to the nineteenth century as the twentieth. The appreciative essay on Keats in *The Olio* for 28 June 1828, perhaps by Barry Cornwall,[2] cast in stronger terms Hazlitt's argument about futurity. The article declared that 'if he had lived [Keats] would have proved himself the only mind worthy to be placed side by side with Milton in blank verse and epic genius'.[3] Keats was often to be the poet who was unable to keep his word. He was the man who could write 'the noblest piece of blank verse that has appeared since Milton's',[4] in the judgment of *The Olio*, but not enough of it. Keats had achieved neither the perfection of the life nor of the work.

Even from the first posthumous reviews, Keats's life-story was impossible to separate from his poetry. His early loss placed pressure on those who had known him to remember his personality in compensation for the inadequate record of his achievement. 'John Keats was handsome, indeed his face might be termed intellectually beautiful', said *The Olio,* holding on to precious facts in the absence of warm life: 'it expressed more of poetry than even his poetry does, beautiful as it is, with all its faults, and these are not few'.[5] The lost physical body was akin, even superior, to the lost corpus – which was bedevilled by problems. It was to the problem of how to relate biography to poetry that Richard Monckton Milnes, later Lord Houghton (1809–85), turned with decided views in his *Life, Letters, and Literary Remains, of John Keats*, published in two volumes by Edward Moxon in 1848. This was one of the two most significant volumes on Keats to appear in the nineteenth century. 'To the Poet', Milnes began, 'if to many man, it may justly be conceded to be estimated by what he has written rather than by what he has done, and to be judged by the productions of his genius rather than by the circumstances of his outward life'.[6] That was an important statement that would be argued over with some ferocity. What in practice it meant to Houghton was that elements of Keats's life – he was writing a biographical study after all – had to be passed over, as biographers of Milnes himself would have to pass over elements of his (he kept an enormous secret archive of pornography). Most particularly, tact was required where the poet's letters to Fanny Brawne were involved. 'Where personal feelings of so profound a character are concerned', Milnes said:

> it does not become the biographer, in any case, to do more than to indicate their effect on the life of his hero, and where the memoir so nearly approaches the times of its subject that the persons in question, or, at any rate, their near relations, may be still alive, it will at once be felt how indecorous would be any conjectural analysis of such sentiments, or, indeed, any more intrusive record of them than is absolutely necessary for the comprehension of the real man.[7]

Not everyone agreed with this during the course of the century. This was the era that Henry James, after all, would come to think as the age of publicity when the author's private life became exceptionally scrutinised.[8] The most important event in the period where Keats's privacy was concerned was Harry Buxton Forman's edition of *Letters of John Keats to Fanny Brawne Written in the Years MDCCCXIX and MDCCCXX and now given from the Original Manuscripts* (London: Reeves and Turner, 1878). This, the other most significant Keats's book in the century, was followed five years later by the four volumes of *Poetical Works and Other Writings of John Keats: Now First Brought Together, Including Poems and Numerous Letters not before Published* (London: Reeves and Turner, 1883). These openly challenged Milnes' omissions and, apart from anything else, made the Brawne letters public. Placed on either side of James Anthony Froude's edition of Thomas Carlyle's revelatory *Reminiscences* (1881), which showed the unhappy private life of a public man of letters, Forman's volumes sparked a sequence of questions about the limits of biographical knowledge and about how to relate biography to writing. 'The three final years of Keats's life', Buxton Forman said in his Introduction in 1878:

> are in all respects the fullest of vivid interest for those who, admiring the poet and loving the memory of the man, would fain form some conception of the working of those forces within him which went to the shaping of his greatest works and his greatest woes.[9]

Keats's life was not to be writ in water after all. *The Saturday Review* was vexed, telling its readers that beyond 'what Lord Houghton has chosen to tell of Keats we do no […] understand why any one should seek to pry'.[10] At the centre of the story, the *Saturday* continued, was an unflattering portrait of Fanny as a 'Minx' who prompted 'the most mean and miserable of passions – jealousy'[11] in the personal life of a dazzling poet. This was not edifying. *The Athenæum*, robustly, thought Buxton Forman's 1878 publication 'the greatest impeachment of a woman's sense of womanly delicacy to be found in the history of literature', and concluded without hesitation: 'To publish the love-letters of a dead man who, if he were living, would cry out from the depths of his soul against it, seems to the common understanding of those to whom the affections are more than fame a heinous offence.'[12] Buxton Forman (1842–1917) made his name as a bibliographer, collector and editor – and as a forger. His deceptions, like those of Thomas James Wise (1859–1937), were practised on, among others, the poet and Keats admirer, Algernon Charles Swinburne (1837–1909).

Swinburne, a friend of Houghton, was equally appalled by Buxton Forman's revelations about Fanny, who had died in December 1865. What mattered for Swinburne was the work. In his four sonnets published as 'In Speculcretis' (1884), he repudiated Buxton Forman (with whom, strange to say, he maintained a polite correspondence):

> Shame, such as never yet dealt heavier stroke
>   On heads more shameful, fall on theirs through whom
>   Dead men may keep inviolate not their tomb,
> But all its depths these ravenous grave-worms choke.[13]

Swinburne was, himself, disinclined to appreciate intrusions into his own life and was quite prepared to ditch a friend – Simeon Solomon, the painter – when he tried to sell parts of their correspondence. He defended Keats's right to privacy as implicitly he defended all writers. The biographer and critic Edmund Gosse (1849–1928), enormously admiring of Forman's edition, was conscious that there was some 'subtle feeling of diffidence and shame' in wanting to '[stir] the ashes of this divine memory' and intrude on the private love – Buxton Forman revealed it to be a betrothal – of this 'noble poet and great man'.[14] But Gosse thought, distinctively, that the edition was justified because the finest poems of Keats's life were associated with Fanny and thus she had a place in the critical understanding of 'one of the greatest creative geniuses of all time'.[15] Gosse was graceful in treating Miss Brawne herself, admitting that 'her nature is exposed to a cruel test in being measured by the side of his'.[16] But of her further limitations he would not speak. Gosse was a rare voice in Buxton Forman's support. More characteristically, *The Examiner* thought it a mistake 'that these letters should have been drawn into the light of public print'[17] and the only justification was that the edition freed Miss Brawne from any charge of having betrayed Keats. 'The only thing that can be said to [her] discredit', the reviewer asserted, 'is that she had not sufficient generosity, or sufficient faith in the greatest of her lover, to marry him in spite of his illness and poverty, and in spite of the advice of her friends'.[18] That, perhaps, was a lot to ask.

Swinburne did not appreciate the revelations about Keats's feelings. And as a critic he had some doubts about Keats's manliness. Keats was at once the author of the near perfect 'Ode to a Nightingale' and, Swinburne declared, 'some of the most vulgar and fulsome doggerel ever whimpered by a vapid and effeminate rhymester in the sickly stage of whelphood'.[19] Unevenness in Keats's career, and that lack of masculinity, were significant obstacles: Keats was best known, Swinburne implied, through selections. Such publication – Keats needed an exceptionally good editor – would remove what John Ruskin in 1856 thought characterised both Tennyson and Keats: 'certain expressions and modes of thought which are in some sort diseased or false'.[20] But, for Swinburne, when Keats was great he was almost unsurpassable. And it was Odes, Swinburne said, which marked the apex of the Romantic's lyrical achievement. The two that were

> nearest to absolutely perfection, to the triumphant achievement and accomplishment of the very utmost beauty possible to human words, may be that to Autumn and that on a Grecian Urn; the most radiant, fervent, and

> musical is that to a Nightingale; the most pictorial and perhaps the tenderest in its ardour of passionate fancy is that to Psyche; the subtlest in sweetness of thought and feeling is that on Melancholy.[21]

Swinburne's rapturous language, dwelling on the emotional qualities of Keats's writing, obliquely confirmed an earlier influential critical opinion – that of Tennyson's friend, Arthur Henry Hallam (1811–33) – who gave to Keats (as well as to Tennyson) a label that proved enduring. Writing 'On Some of the Characteristics of Modern Poetry and On the Lyrical Poems of Alfred Tennyson' (1831), Hallam made a crucial distinction. He compared Shelley and Keats and, though he found them different in manner, he said that:

> They are both poets of sensation rather than reflection. Susceptible of the slightest impulse from external nature, their fine organs trembled into emotion at colours, and sounds, and movements, unperceived or unregarded by duller temperaments.[22]

Sensation rather than thought – the terms – as it happens, were Keats's. And they influenced judgment of him (and Tennyson) across the century, persuading readers to perceive Keats primarily as a poet of emotion and not of ideas.

Matthew Arnold (1822–88), critic and poet, was bothered by the love letters too and what they revealed of Keats's masculinity. 'Letters written when Keats was near his end, under the throttling and unmanning grasp of mortal disease, we will not judge',[23] he said in 1880. But Arnold, thinking about Keats's poetry, perceived a writer of sensation differently from Hallam. Sensation for Keats was of a reflective kind. He was a poet, Arnold said, not of the 'sensuous or sentimental' but of the more recognisable masculine virtues of 'intellectual and spiritual passion'.[24] Romanticism here was not about overwhelming let alone unmanning feeling but involved emotion in balance with thought. Brainwork was compatible with loveliness and exquisite verbal form. At the end of Arnold's essay, he spoke of Keats's fame as a poet who had, near the end of his life, felt he had left nothing behind that would ensure immortality. Not so, said Arnold, giving the highest tribute paid to Keats in the nineteenth century:

> Shakespearian work it is; not imitative, indeed, of Shakespeare, but Shakespearian, because its expression has that rounded perfection and felicity of loveliness of which Shakespeare is the great master.[25]

That sense of the mixed achievement of Keats, sometimes described in terms of manliness, remained the template for assessments of the poet's achievement till the end of the century. Swinburne's friend, William Michael Rossetti (1829–1919), returned to gendered vocabulary as he described what he perceived as Keats's faults in his 1887 biography:

> it seems to me true that not many of Keats's poems are highly admirable; that most of them, amid all their beauty, have an adolescent and frequently a morbid tone, marking want of manful thew and sinew and of mental balance[.][26]

There was a cultural, a reading, problem in Keats's achievement. His work involved the association of beauty, poetry and passion with something that was not entirely proper for a man. Keats exposed for a sequence of nineteenth-century writers a problem of sentimentality, of how it was possible to be both red-blooded and well-read; muscular and tender; in training and in love. So even as Rossetti concluded his assessment, thinking of what Keats's demise had done to his reputation, his language was treading a careful line between an acknowledgement of Keats's emotional intensity and a recognition of how close that was to a failure to be robust, a failure to assure readers that it was possible to feel deeply *and* be a man. 'By his early death', William Michael Rossetti said, Keats 'was doomed to be the poet of youthfulness; by being the poet of youthfulness he was privileged to become and to remain enduringly the poet of rapt expectation and passionate delight'.[27] Replacing his early term 'adolescent' with 'youthful' and over-writing morbidity with delight, Rossetti was still trying to solve the problem of what Keats might have done to the masculinity of poetry.

In the centenary year, *The Speaker: The Liberal Review* was thinking of H. Buxton Forman again because, still dedicated to making public private correspondence, he had just published *The Letters of John Keats* (London: Reeves and Turner, 1895). 'Mr Buxton Forman', said the reviewer uncompromisingly, 'can never be forgiven the publication of Keats's letters to Miss Brawne'. And now, in this new collection, the same problem was evident of a youthful writer who was at once not always in control of language and one of the finest poets in English. Here was a version of the Mozart conundrum for biographers with which the playwright Peter Shaffer had such amusement in *Amadeus* (1979). The letters were sometimes good-humoured and sometimes profound. But there was also that other side to Keats, the 'irresponsible youth' who resembled, *The Speaker* said, Robert Louis Stevenson. Keats, like Stevenson, was a 'languid, elegant, affected weakling of art'.[28] A divided man, a divided judgment: these issues had dominated Keats's critical reception in the nineteenth century. And so, aptly, *The Speaker* in 1895 could only end with another divided judgment of both Buxton Forman and the poet whose reputation he had so controversially shaped:

> Here is the Keats whom we honour, the Keats whom we love, and the Keats whose early death is an abiding sorrow and immeasurable loss to English art. For any other Keats – silence and oblivion. It is our deep regret that Mr. Buxton Forman, who has laboured so loyally upon Keats's behalf, and has done him fresh and valuable service in this edition, should not have shrunk from doing him what we thinking a cruel disservice also.[29]

Notes

1 William Hazlitt, *Table-Talk: Essays on Men and Manners* (London: Frowde, 1901), p. 346.
2 'Barry Cornwall', the lawyer, poet and writer Bryan Procter (1787–1874).
3 'A Titan in Spirit' (1828) reproduced in *CH* 256–8 (257).
4 'A Titan in Spirit'.
5 'A Titan in Spirit', p. 256.
6 Richard Monkton Milnes, *Life, Letters, and Literary Remains, of John Keats*, 2 vols. (London: Moxon, 1848), vol. 1, p. 1.
7 Milnes, *Life, Letters, and Literary Remains*, vol. 2, pp. 242–3.
8 See, for instance, Richard Salmon, *Henry James and the Culture of Publicity* (Cambridge: Cambridge University Press, 1997).
9 Harry Buxton Forman, ed., *Letters of John Keats to Fanny Brawne Written in the Years MDCCCXIX and MDCCCXX and now given from the Original Manuscripts* (London: Reeves and Turner, 1878), p. xiv.
10 'Letters of John Keats to Fanny Brawne', *The Saturday Review* 45 (16 February 1878): 216–17 (216).
11 'Letters of John Keats to Fanny Brawne', p. 217.
12 'Our Library Table', *The Athenæum* (16 February 1878), p. 218.
13 The sonnets were first published as 'Post Mortem (Four Sonnets)', *Fortnightly Review* 35 (January 1884): 65–6 and then included in Swinburne's *A Midsummer Holiday and Other Poems* (London: Chatto & Windus, 1884), pp. 134–8 (138).
14 Edmund Gosse, 'Literature' [review of Forman, *Letters of John Keats to Fanny Brawne*], *The Academy*, 301 (9 February 1878): 111–12 (111).
15 Gosse, 'Literature', 112.
16 Gosse, 'Literature'.
17 'Keats's Letters to Fanny Brawne', *The Examiner*, 3654 (9 February 1878): 176–8 (176).
18 'Keats's Letters to Fanny Brawne', p. 177.
19 Algernon Charles Swinburne, 'John Keats', *Miscellanies* (London: Chatto & Windus, 1886), p. 211.
20 *The Library Edition of the Works of John Ruskin*, ed. E. T. Cook and Alexander Wedderburn, 39 vols. (London: Allen, 1903–12), vol. 5, p. 210 (*Modern Painters* 3 [1856]).

21 *The Library Edition of the Works of John Ruskin*, p. 216.
22 *The Poems of Arthur Henry Hallam Together with his Essay on the Lyrical Poems of Alfred Tennyson*, ed. Richard le Gallienne (London: Elkin, 1893), pp. 93–4.
23 'John Keats' (originally the Preface to the Keats selection in Ward's *English* Poets, vol. 4): *Essays in Criticism*, ed. Susan Sheridan (Boston: Allyn and Bacon, 1896), p. 38.
24 'John Keats', p. 40.
25 'John Keats', p. 43.
26 William Michael Rossetti, *Life of John Keats* (London: Scott, 1887), p. 208.
27 Rossetti, *Life of John Keats*, p. 209.
28 'Keats: A Warning', *The Speaker* 12 (21 December 1895): 675–6 (676).
29 Ibid.

CHAPTER 33

Keats Criticism, 1900–1963

Matthew Scott

On New Year's Day, 1903, Henry James recalled Shelley's elegy for Keats in a letter to his friend Urbain Mengin: 'Keats, the child of the Gods! Read over to yourself, but *aloud*, the stanzas of the *Adonais* [...] descriptive of the corner of Rome where they both lie buried, and then weep bitter tears of remorse at having sacrificed them to the terrestrial *caquetage* of A. de Musset!'.[1] Modern readers are likely to be pretty bemused by his contrasting Keats with the earthly cackling of this later French poet, but the general sentiment is clear enough and it comprehends a nostalgic view that was widespread during James's life. His Keats is the Shelleyan Platonist of high Romanticism, otherworldly and ethereal, who fled in death away from a too fleshy reality. Lurking too is the idea of Keats's avowed classicism as a beautiful, escapist mythology, an echo of Wordsworth's slightly churlish remark about his younger contemporary's love of 'pretty [...] Paganism'.[2] It is a conception of Keats as too delicate for reality (or even as somehow unreal) that goes back to Shelley and it is one with which critics of the twentieth century felt they had to wrestle.

Sixty years after James's letter, at the other end of the period covered here, John Bayley described a very different and more distinctly earthy writer in his brilliant Chatterton lecture of 1962, 'Keats and Reality'.[3] Keats's 'vulgarity is his "material sublime"', Bayley maintained in a characteristically ambiguous remark which he meant nevertheless as high praise. The lecture sought to countermand an accusation common among Keats's first readers that he was a vulgar writer. It was by getting things wrong in terms of convention, Bayley decided, that Keats, the 'most disconcerting of our poets', established his individual voice: 'Keats is most fully his poetic self, most wholly involved in what he is writing, when he is, in the usual and technical sense, "bad", or on the edge of "badness"'. 'Disconcerting' is a word that runs through Bayley's appraisal and it is a quality that emerges as a product of Keats's own exercise of Negative Capability. 'The vulgar man is sunk in his own selfhood, and yet is unaware of it', Bayley notes in an intriguing reformulation of that conception of unselfconsciousness. With Keats, he decides, it gives rise to an unmannered 'badness', which is defined as the 'devout, unmisgiving (Hunt's admirable word) acceptance of the first eager brainwave, and a subsequent unawareness that it might be modified or corrected'.[4] For most twentieth-century critics, the Odes were indisputably Keats's greatest achievement; an idiosyncrasy of Bayley's great essay is that he celebrates above all *The Eve of St. Agnes*. A few earlier readers, such as Kenneth Muir (1959), had admired the way Keats in his narrative poems 'luxuriated in the world of romance' as a retreat from reality but Bayley picked up on a lack of polish that threatened to unweave that world.[5] For this reason, he liked those poems best in which the collision between romance and reality is most obvious, when, as Seamus Perry has said (summarising Bayley), Keats folds 'into the rich world of romance some fragment of experience drawn from a world more vividly ordinary'.[6]

Perry has suggested that in focusing attention on the real, Bayley's Keats is the original of such later accounts of the poet as that of his most important recent biographer, Nicholas Roe, for whom Keats is a creature of his edgy cultural moment, keen to reflect the ordinary world around him and respond to its most pressing concerns.[7] From James's escapist aesthete to Bayley's vulgar realist and then on to the highly politicised New Historicism that first emerged in the 1980s, there appears to be a gradual process of diminishing the idealised Keats in order to embed him within the realities of his time. Certainly the most significant period in this regard was the 1960s, when a series of important biographies emerged by Walter Jackson Bate (1963), Aileen Ward (1963), Douglas Bush (1966) and Robert Gittings (1968).[8] Even so, it is wrong to assume either that this was a simple linear development (Keats was after all the one Romantic poet to be unambiguously celebrated through the formalism of the New Critics) or that earlier readers were all politically naïve. An eccentric celebrant of Keats's politics was George Bernard Shaw (1921), who believed him to be a proto-revolutionary, but his was not an isolated interest: H. W. Garrod (1926), Clarence Dewitt Thorpe (1931) and C. L. Finney (1936) all wrote about Keats's connections to the liberal politics of his time, the last of these emphasising the role of radical thought in his intellectual development through first his schooling in Enfield and later his place within the Hunt circle.[9] The New Historicists were therefore building upon a pre-existing tradition rather than establishing a new line of thought. Moreover, during the period covered by this essay, Keats attracted (among others) formalists as well as biographers, manuscript scholars and source hunters, those interested in the mythology of Romanticism as well as Freudians, and critics fascinated by the ways in which his work informed upon the spheres of sex, politics and philosophy. In short, the history of Keats criticism is interesting exactly because, unlike that of lesser writers, it is not a neat evolution towards a single accepted orthodoxy such as the radical Keats of present academic taste.

Unlike his nearest contemporaries, Shelley and Byron, the centrality of Keats to an understanding of English Romanticism was never in any doubt during this period. T. S. Eliot compared the achievements of Keats and Shelley (to the general discredit of the latter), noting that despite his reservations about *Hyperion*, Keats was 'a great poet'.[10] Even F. R. Leavis, writing for *Scrutiny* in an otherwise rather supercilious essay of 1936, admits that Keats was 'gifted to become a very great poet' and attributes this (through a reading of 'Ode to a Nightingale') to his 'un-Byronic' and 'un-Shelleyan' aversion to 'afflatus'; Keats's attitude, he observes imperiously, has 'itself the authenticity of fact'.[11] William Empson in 1930 teased out some of the complexities of Keats's poetry in a few stunning pages to describe the seventh of his types of ambiguity: 'Ode to Melancholy', he writes, 'may show how what is accepted as intelligible poetry may be considered as an association of opposites such as would interest the psycho-analyst'.[12] The notion that Keats worked through a divided poetic consciousness – sensation, imagination, the ideal against thought, philosophy, the real – became a commonplace during this period. D. G. James (1948) built on the idea in an account of the *Hyperion* project, whose failure, he says, was 'the greatest achievement of Romanticism; in it the Romantic mind beheld its own complexity and condemned itself'.[13] James, an associate of Tolkien and Lewis, also produced a very interesting, now little known, study of the Romantic imagination (1937), which places Keats's ideas in the context of the thought of Coleridge and Wordsworth.[14] H. W. Garrod had undertaken a similar task in the opening chapters of his important work *Keats*, the bulk of which is devoted to the Odes. Garrod is fiercely disparaging there about the major attempt of the time to locate Keats within his specific cultural moment, the two-volume biography by Amy Lowell (1925), whom he accuses of poor research and prolixity.[15] This is unfair but it is certainly true that the work is now of predominantly historical interest.

A number of early twentieth-century critics attended to Keats's intellectual development by investigating his sources to discover his reading. Ernest de Sélincourt (1921) and Sidney Colvin (1917) were early pioneers; their work was continued by Robert Gittings (1955, 1956), H. E. Biggs (1946) and F. E. L. Priestley (1944), each of whom aimed to establish the extent to which earlier writers exerted an influence on Keats.[16] John

Middleton Murry combined both biography and critical evaluation in his important *Keats and Shakespeare* (1926), which immediately suggests the extent to which in the century after his death Keats had become indispensable to conceptions of the English literary canon.[17] In fact, that title is somewhat deceptive since Murry is focused less upon allusion, a subject better covered by Caroline Spurgeon (1928), and more upon an intellectual affinity that he found in the two writers.[18] '[Q]uite instinctively we feel that there was in both Shakespeare and Keats a greater richness of the poetic gift, and a greater completeness of common manhood, than in any other of our English poets':[19] modern readers are likely to find Murry's tone highly extravagant and indeed F. R. Leavis (1936) was very rude about it at the time. Nevertheless, in building his argument, Murry subjects Keats's ideas about the poetical character and Negative Capability to very insightful analysis. A little later, Walter Jackson Bate built constructively upon Murry, who had quoted large sections of the most significant letters, in a remarkable essay, written as an undergraduate, on Negative Capability (1939), in which he makes an early attempt to discriminate between Keats's critical theories as they emerge in the letters and his own poetic practice.[20] In anticipation of Bayley several decades later, Bate observes a tension between the imagined and the real in Keats's 'reaching for an intensity imprisoned within the bounds of the concrete'.[21]

Growing interest in the 'real' Keats led in the twentieth century to an increased determination to recreate his biography and, allied to this, there was a sharpening of focus upon the documents that related to his life and circle. In particular, this is true of the letters, the study of which was aided in due course by the emergence in 1958 of the standard edition by Hyder Edward Rollins, who also produced an invaluable sourcebook, *The Keats Circle* (1948). Even before that edition, three of the century's greatest literary critics, A. C. Bradley (1909), T. S. Eliot (1933) and Lionel Trilling (1955), had written very finely on Keats's letters.[22] Bradley's essay began, like Garrod's later study, as one of his lectures as Professor of Poetry at Oxford and he chose the letters, an odd subject for the occasion at first glance, in order to explore the connective, poetical quality of Keats's mind, as well as to detail what was said there about poetic theory. Bradley foreshadows Eliot and Leavis in comparing Keats and Shelley, but finds more common ground. The most interesting part of the essay comes as he wrestles with the connection between beauty and truth in Keats's thought (perhaps the most recurrent and vexed topic in the twentieth-century criticism). For Bradley, it is in the making of beauty that Keats discovers his moral purpose. 'To make beauty is *his* philanthropy' is a particularly evocative apophthegm.[23]

Bradley was the first to take Keats seriously as a thinker who contributed to the philosophical questions that are fundamental to Romanticism and his influence was far-reaching. Of later attempts, the most significant is certainly Lionel Trilling's essay 'The Poet as Hero: Keats in his Letters', which initially appeared as an introduction to his selected edition. The influence of Freud rumbles beneath this powerful essay in which Trilling charts the emergence of Keats as a moral thinker by examining his 'geniality' (a form of intuitive empathy not dissimilar to Bayley's 'vulgarity'). The hallmark of Keats's thought, Trilling concludes, is 'his refusal to be fixed in any final judgment' and he cites the observation, brilliantly paradoxical (perhaps the Keatsian quality *par excellence*), in the letters: 'for ought we know for certainty 'Wisdom is folly'!'[24]

In Eliot's early prose, there are scattered observations about Keats, who gets a brief if rather condescending mention in 'Tradition and the Individual Talent', an essay that does not otherwise sufficiently acknowledge its Romantic antecedents. His earlier disdain for the Romantics had obviously tempered by 1933 but not entirely disappeared. Praise for Keats's poetry extends to the letters – 'the most important ever written by an English poet'[25] – but an odd thing about the lecture is that he spends much longer on Shelley, whom he purports to dislike, than Keats, who is praised for being 'a very different kind of poetic mind' to Wordsworth, Coleridge and Shelley, one 'pretty close to intuition',[26] but then treated in only a few rather suggestive pages. Eliot delivered the lecture at Harvard, which was already and would long remain the most important centre for Keats scholarship in the world. The peerless Harvard Keats collection grew initially out of the gift from Amy Lowell's large private library in 1925 and was expanded by Arthur A. Houghton Jr.: Eliot was preaching to the converted. Later scholars of Keats associated closely with the university include Bate, Douglas Bush, Jack Stillinger and David Perkins, whose highly suggestive essay of 1953 demonstrated some of the ways in which the diction of the letters is gradually reflected in the later Odes.[27]

Perkins (1959), Bate (1963) and Stillinger (1971) all produced extended readings of the Odes, which had become, by the mid-century, the most widely known anthology pieces of the Romantic period, their sources and composition pored over in minute detail.[28] 'Ode on a Grecian Urn', and in particular its closing lines, generated a minor critical industry of its own with Robert Bridges (1895), Arthur Quiller-Couch (1925), I. A. Richards (1929) and T. S. Eliot (1929) slugging it out over whether the lines made the poem great or risked reducing it, as Eliot thought, to meaninglessness.[29] The most influential reading of the poem is that of Cleanth Brooks

(1947), which begins with Eliot's disparaging remarks but quickly offers a way out of the matter that had most troubled the poem's detractors, namely whether the statement 'Beauty is truth, truth beauty' (49) can be said in any sense to be philosophically or scientifically provable, let alone factually verifiable.[30] Brooks instead takes the poem to be an internally coherent poetic drama of which we can only ever ask whether its parts are consistent one with another: the phrase, he writes, 'is a speech "in character" and supported by a dramatic context'.[31] Rather than ask whether beauty can truly be claimed as truth, Brooks considered the kind of truth that the urn might offer within the poem, and this is inevitably a parable about reading. We can intuit that something speaks truly to us without understanding all the facts about it. This is at the heart of the New Critical principle that a work of art cannot ever hope fully to reach out beyond its context as a contained aesthetic artifact – as complete and discrete as the urn itself. It offers a sense of history, but one dispossessed of the mess of facts that cloud the mind of the historicist; hence Brooks's subtitle, 'Keats's Sylvan Historian: History Without Footnotes'. Later accounts by Earl R. Wasserman (1953), Leo Spitzer (1955) and M. H. Abrams (1958) built on and responded to Brooks.[32]

While the Odes and letters received disproportionate attention during the first half of the twentieth century, in the post-war period critics began seriously to reassess the rest of Keats's *oeuvre*, especially the narrative poems. R. H. Fogle (1945), Wasserman (1953) and Bush (1957) were all important but for Jack Stillinger, the author of the most influential reevaluation of *The Eve of St. Agnes*, they had really done little to press the terms of Keats's world of romance beyond those naively accepted by his Victorian readers.[33] Stillinger's 1961 essay revolutionised the way readers understood the sexual politics of that poem and he recast Keats as a realist, who created a modern anti-romance that forced 'a facing-up to' and ultimately an 'affirmation' of the actual.[34] That essay has the quality of thrusting youth about its daring; his more established colleague at Harvard, Walter Jackson Bate, published the stately work two years later that was to become in the eyes of many the single most important ever to be published on the poet. *John Keats* (1963) was dedicated to Douglas Bush, senior among the Harvard Keatsians, and it stands as a summation of that tradition. Bate's achievement is at least twofold. As an establishment of the facts of Keats's life and circumstances, especially of his youth and background, it broke new ground. But the book also represents a triumph in the new variety of psychological life writing that emerged in the second half of the century. Bate penetrates very deeply into Keats's intellectual and social development, and in doing so he builds upon earlier critics such as M. R. Ridley (1933), as well as his own work on the development of Keats's style (1957), to show how the poetry evolved so dramatically.[35] The individual readings of the poems remain vital starting points for students to this day. In the same year as Bate's book, Aileen Ward (1963) had the apparent misfortune to publish her own very accomplished biography. It is the slighter and yet sprightlier of the two works, and hence is acutely Keatsian in its way. Ward arranged her material with a decorous self-assurance and was, not inappropriately, rewarded with the Duff Cooper prize, an award that celebrates erudite and stylish non-fictional prose.

Notes

1 Henry James, *Letters*, vol. 4, ed. Leon Edel (Cambridge, MA: Harvard University Press, 1984), p. 266.
2 William Wordsworth in *KC* 2, 144.
3 John Bayley, 'Keats and Reality', *Proceedings of the British Academy*, 47 (1962): 91–126.
4 Bayley, 'Keats and Reality', pp. 98, 124, 99, 98, 100.
5 Kenneth Muir, ed., *John Keats: A Reassessment* (Liverpool: Liverpool University Press, 1959), cited in Bayley, 'Keats and Reality', p. 93.
6 Seamus Perry, 'Truth, Beauty and Enfield', *Literary Review*, 403 (2012): 9.
7 Nicholas Roe, *John Keats: A New Life* (New Haven: Yale University Press, 2012).
8 Walter Jackson Bate, *John Keats* (Cambridge, MA: Harvard University Press, 1963); Aileen Ward, *John Keats: The Making of a Poet* (New York: Viking, 1963); Douglas Bush, *John Keats: His Life and Writings* (New York: Collier, 1966); Robert Gittings, *John Keats* (London: Heinemann, 1968).
9 George Bernard Shaw, 'Keats', in *The John Keats Memorial Volume* (London: Lane, 1921); H. W. Garrod, *Keats* (Oxford: Clarendon, 1926); Clarence Thorpe, *The Mind of John Keats* (Oxford: Oxford University Press, 1926); Claude Lee Finney, *The Evolution of Keats's Poetry*, 2 vols. (Cambridge, MA: Harvard University Press, 1936).
10 T. S. Eliot, *The Use of Poetry and the Use of Criticism* (London: Faber, 1933), p. 100.
11 F. R. Leavis, 'Revaluations IX: Keats', *Scrutiny* (March 1936): 376–400 (at 399–400).
12 William Empson, *Seven Types of Ambiguity* (London: Chatto, 1930), p. 217.
13 D. G. James, *The Romantic Comedy* (London: Oxford University Press, 1948), p. 126.
14 D. G. James, *Scepticism and Poetry: An Essay on the Romantic Imagination* (London: Methuen, 1937).
15 Amy Lowell, *John Keats*, 2 vols. (Boston: Houghton Mifflin, 1925).
16 Ernest de Sélincourt, 'Introduction', in *The Poems of John Keats* (London: Methuen, 1921), pp. xix–xlviii; Sidney Colvin, *John Keats: His Life and*

Poetry His Friends Critics and After-Fame (London: Macmillan, 1917); Robert Gittings, 'Keats and Chatterton', *Keats-Shelley Journal*, 4 (1955): 47–54; Robert Gittings, *The Mask of Keats: A Study of Problems* (Cambridge, MA: Harvard University Press, 1956); H. E. Biggs, 'Swift and Keats', *PMLA*, 61 (1946): 1101–8; F. E. L. Priestley, 'Keats and Chaucer', *MLQ*, 5 (1944): 439–77.

17 John Middleton Murry, *Keats and Shakespeare* (London: Oxford University Press, 1926).

18 Caroline Spurgeon, *Keats's Shakespeare: A Descriptive Study Based on New Material* (London: Oxford University Press, 1928).

19 Murry, *Keats and Shakespeare*, p. 147

20 Walter Jackson Bate, *Negative Capability: The Intuitive Approach in Keats* (Cambridge, MA: Harvard University Press, 1939).

21 Bate, *Negative Capability*, p. 62.

22 A. C. Bradley, 'The Letters of Keats', in *Oxford Lectures on Poetry* (London: Macmillan, 1909), pp. 209–46; Lionel Trilling, 'The Poet as Hero: Keats in His Letters' (1951) rpt. in *The Moral Obligation to Be Intelligent: Selected Essays* (Evanston, IL: Northwestern University Press, 2008), pp. 224–58.

23 Bradley, 'Letters of Keats', p. 237.

24 Trilling, 'Poet as Hero', p. 245.

25 Eliot, *The Use of Poetry and the Use of Criticism*, p. 100.

26 Eliot, *The Use of Poetry and the Use of Criticism,* p. 102.

27 David Perkins, 'Keats's Odes and Letters: Recurrent Diction and Imagery', *Keats-Shelley Journal*, 2 (1953): 51–60.

28 David Perkins, *The Quest for Permanence: The Symbolism of Wordsworth, Shelley, and Keats* (Cambridge, MA: Harvard University Press, 1959), chs. 7–9; Jack Stillinger, 'Imagination and Reality in the Odes', in *The Hoodwinking of Madeline and Other Essays on Keats's Poems* (Urbana, IL: University of Illinois Press, 1971), pp. 99–119.

29 Robert Bridges, *John Keats: A Critical Essay* (London: Lawrence and Bullen, 1895); Arthur Quiller-Couch, *Charles Dickens and Other Victorians* (Cambridge: Cambridge University Press, 1925), pp. 145–6; I. A. Richards, *Science and Poetry* (London: Kegan Paul, 1926), pp. 58–60; T. S. Eliot, 'Dante' (1929) in *Selected Essays* (London: Faber, 1932), pp. 230–1.

30 Cleanth Brooks, 'Keats's Sylvan Historian: History without Footnotes', in *The Well Wrought Urn: Studies in the Structure of Poetry* (New York: Harcourt Brace, 1947), pp. 139–52.

31 Brooks, 'Keats's Sylvan Historian', p. 435.

32 Earl R. Wasserman, *The Finer Tone: Keats' Major Poems* (Baltimore: Johns Hopkins University Press, 1953), ch. 2; Leo Spitzer, 'The 'Ode on a Grecian Urn', or Content vs Metagrammar', *Comparative Literature*, 7 (1955): 203–27; M. H. Abrams, 'Belief and Disbelief', *University of Toronto Quarterly*, 27 (1958): 117–36.

33 R. H. Fogle, 'A Reading of Keats's "Eve of St Agnes"', *College English*, 6 (1945): 325–8; Douglas Bush, 'Keats and His Ideas', in *The Major English Romantic Poets: A Symposium in Reappraisal*, ed. Clarence D. Thorpe et al.

(Carbondale, IL: University of Southern Illinois Press), pp. 231–45; Jack Stillinger, 'The Hoodwinking of Madeline: Skepticism in "The Eve of St Agnes"', *Studies in Philology*, 58 (1961): 533–55.

34 Stillinger, 'The Hoodwinking of Madeline', p. 466.

35 M. R. Ridley, *Keats' Craftsmanship: A Study in Poetic Development* (Oxford: Clarendon Press, 1933); Walter Jackson Bate, 'Keats's Style: Evolution toward Qualities of Permanent Value', in *The Major English Romantic Poets: A Symposium in Reappraisal*, ed. Clarence D. Thorpe, Carlos Baker and Bennett Weaver (Carbondale, IL: University of Southern Illinois Press), pp. 217–30.

CHAPTER 34

Keats Criticism, Post-1963

Richard Marggraf Turley

Keats takes us to the moon seventy-three times in his poems. Those moonshots include the setting satellite of *The Eve of St. Agnes*, the new moon of *The Cap and Bells* and the Queen-Moon of 'Ode to a Nightingale'. He conjures it, also, through absence, in the bereft skyscape of *Endymion*'s 'moonless night'.[1] These repeated glimpses of, or allusions to, earth's companion tell us something important about Keats's poetic aspirations, evident from his earliest writing. In 1817, just a year after his first published poem appeared in *The Examiner* – fourteen lines on the theme of solitude, signed 'J. K.' – Keats undertook a self-imposed test of invention, *Endymion*, retelling in over 4,000 lines the story of the Greek shepherd beloved by the moon goddess. The critical response was crushing. *Blackwood's* charged Keats with 'metromanie' – poetic lunacy – and a viciously puerilising attack by the *Quarterly Review* battened onto the word 'moon' itself to accuse Keats of playing at *bouts-rimés*, where the sounds of nouns, rather than genuine ideas, generated inexpert phrases such as 'shady boon' (see *CH* 97, 112). Charges of immaturity, ephemerality and jejune shallowness dogged 'Johnny' Keats for the rest of his short career, and were only partially redeemed during his poetic afterlife by Victorian audiences who fetishised a different kind of youth – delicate, doomed, palpitatingly visionary – as depicted in Percy Shelley's elegy for Keats, *Adonais*.

This chapter's survey of more recent critical biases begins a year after another J. K. – John Kennedy – committed the West to a literal lunar challenge. Against the Cold War's ideological escape velocities, the year 1963 witnessed the blue moon of two full-length Keats biographies in the critical firmament, Aileen Ward's *The Making of John Keats* and Walter Jackson Bate's *John Keats*. By then, Keats's poetic reputation had been firmly rehabilitated, boosted by detailed textual studies that traced Keats's creative growth from 'apprentice' to fully fledged master. Both 1963 biographies were inflected by, and cemented, this narrative of steady maturation (development, evolution, craft). Ward traced a trajectory of rapid psychological evolution, and Bate mapped the development of poetic power onto Keats's life, their poet a man hurtling towards the *annus mirabilis* of 1819, and what they saw as the settled accomplishment of the odes.

Stuart M. Sperry's pivotal study, *Keats the Poet* (1973), further instituted this graphline of assured, accelerated technical and creative achievement, sounding pedal notes of psychological development, growth and increasing sophistication. In the same year, Harold Bloom's *The Anxiety of Influence* identified a paradigm of cross-generational agon, in which strong, 'belated' poets like Keats were prompted to 'swerve' around their precursors' works to find their own, confident voices. Keats's oedipal struggle with Milton is the paradigmatic exemplar for Bloom. As Keats's modern reputation took shape in the mid-1970s, the playfulness, paradoxes, contradictions and frequent breaches of stylistic decorum that infuriated Keats's contemporaries were – with important exceptions – no longer seen as a reflection, or function, of character, but rather as separate effects of language. These effects were brilliantly explored in the deconstructive and philosophically oriented readings of Paul de Man and Geoffrey Hartman – the latter's *The Fate of Reading* (1975) included a landmark chapter on 'To Autumn' – and in David Simpson's seminal *Irony and Authority in Romantic Poetry* (1979), which explored Keats's scepticism of determinate meanings and closure. A parallel, if less theoretically driven, critical heuristic applied itself to Keatsian compression, imaginative process and artistic strategies, exemplified by Jack Stillinger's sparkling study, *The Hoodwinking of Madeline and Other Essays* (1971) and Morris Dickstein's *Keats and His Poetry* (1971).

At the same time as Keats was being refashioned as a fully matured author, whose often flimsy early work was to be valued only in so far as it anticipated themes in the major writing, a number of quirky, orthogonally suggestive, counternarratives emerged. Rather than ignoring, or overdubbing, the pubescent voice that led the *Quarterly* and *Blackwood's* to denounce Keats as a callow poetaster, and Byron to label Keats's productions as 'piss-a-bed poetry', Christopher Ricks insisted on returning disruptively adolescent tones to readers' ears.[2] Keats's doggerel, bawdy and late satire were neither, Ricks argued brilliantly in *Keats and Embarrassment* (1974), wince-worthy interruptions to maturation, nor excusable errors. On the contrary, the 'youthful, the luxuriant, the immature' were 'vantage points' (p. 12). The argument was picked up by Marjorie Levinson in her dazzling Marxist and 'New Historicist' study of vulgarity, self-indulgence and 'masturbatory dynamics', *Keats's Life of Allegory: The Origins of a Style* (1988), which located Keats's political challenge to established power precisely in vulgar, jejune breaches of social and poetic propriety. My own

Keats's Boyish Imagination (2004), which read Keats's complicated boyishness as a locus of agency in the letters and poems, derived its conceptual energy from these earlier studies.

When Jerome McGann's new historicist essay 'Keats and the Historical Method' appeared in 1979, the predominant modes of inquiry, from 'new criticism' to Yale poststructuralist formalism, were concerned with style and aesthetics, fragmentation and paradox, rather than socio-historical dimensions.[3] Where 'history' had been largely subordinated to the 'literary text', McGann's remarkable essay, followed in 1983 by his short polemic *The Romantic Ideology*, combined Bakhtin's concept of dialogism with materialist and psychoanalytical inquiry to identify more intricate (re)framings, embeddings, refractions and mutual frictions. McGann's slant lines into the poetry stimulated a substantial move beyond the self-sufficiency of the text towards historiographical and sociological topographies, as well as a *re*turn to the class and social debates that lensed Keats's first critical reception, inspiring two decades of new historicist and cultural materialist critique, whose energies continue to be felt today.

Historicist stratagems for disclosing the topical concerns, discursive entanglements and complex political relocations of Keats's work presented a revitalising corrective to new critical and formalist constructions of a depoliticised, aestheticised poet. Some readers, however, were mistrustful of new historicism's creative license, particularly its reliance on the 'argument from absence', where unheard (political) melodies, rather than heard refrains, appeared to be sweetest. While the method's advocates were happy to be led beyond the page into the Corn Laws, the Six Acts, popular protest and Peterloo, others regarded the approach as antipodal to the internal, more self-sufficing insights literary criticism had traditionally provided. An important testbed was the ode 'To Autumn', long the poster poem of transcendent detachment from the politics of the post–Napoleonic Wars era. A number of exhilarating readings attuned themselves to the ways in which the poem in fact displaced (in McGann's reading), or harboured (in Roe's), a highly developed, sceptical political consciousness. For sponsors of historicity, Romanticism's visionary, transcendent mode was merely a 'self-representation' – ideological smokescreen – to be resisted at all costs. The method was landmarked in a special issue of *Studies in Romanticism*, 'Keats and Politics: A Forum' (1986). (A twenty-fifth-anniversary follow-up, titled 'Reading Keats, Reading Politics', included Jonathan Mulrooney's astute exegesis of historical trauma in the *Hyperion* poems as constitutive of a new kind of aesthetic experience.)[4] Where early discussions in the new historical mode tended to look for traces of Keats's flight from political engagement, the later forms showcased in *Keats and History* (1995), edited by Roe, took for granted Keats's sense of his writing's (coded) relation to radical counterculture and reform. The volume was followed by Roe's widely admired *John Keats and the Culture of Dissent* (1997).

Political analysis also manifested in less polarised/-ising forms. A significant set of new emphases explored Keats's marginalised position vis-à-vis early nineteenth-century print culture and the literary market place. Seminal essays, including Diane Long Hoeveler's on *Isabella*, which read Lorenzo's head as an 'emblem of class', were fingerposts towards exciting new directions, as critics pulled into bold relief Keats's struggles to orient his aesthetic with popular public taste.[5] The ideological dimensions of Croker's and Lockhart's 'Cockney School of Poetry' reviews, which turned any activity by Hunt and his 'acolytes' into new channels of class confrontation, were the focus of resumed interest. Work on Keats's attempts to hail and shape an ideal, deferred audience was also represented by Andrew Bennett's consistently engaging *Keats, Narrative and Audience: The Posthumous Life of Writing* (1994). Subsequent investigations into class and reception included a lively chapter on Keats's first reviews in Andrew Franta's *Romanticism and the Rise of the Mass Public* (2007), while Heather Jackson's elegant book on Romantic afterlives, *Those Who Write for Immortality: Romantic Reputations and the Dream of Lasting Fame* (2014), brought into fascinating apposition Keats's efforts to align his poetry with popular taste and his current hyper-canonical status (by no means as secure, or settled, as we might imagine).

'Cockney' Keats emerged as a key focus of scholarly activity from the mid-1980s onwards, with essays by William Keach and Richard Cronin opening early casements on the politics of 'Cockney' style.[6] The widening recovery of Keats in his Cockney milieu has also supplied valuable apercus into his relation with other London literary figures. *Examiner* editor Leigh Hunt has attracted the lion's share of recent critical attention, but Keats's interfrictions with the Ollier brothers, Hazlitt, Percy Shelley, Byron, Coleridge, Wordsworth, Joseph Severn and Barry Cornwall – the focus of my *Bright Stars: John Keats, Barry Cornwall and Romantic Literary Culture* (2009) – have also received welcome attention. Scholars today have a significantly more nuanced understanding of Keats's associations with editors, reviewers, fellow and rival authors, illustrators, financial backers, dilettantes and musicians in Hunt's extended set. Research into Keats's sociability is well represented by pertinent chapters in Jeffery N. Cox's *Poetry and Politics in the Cockney School* (1998), which explored the artistic and political culture that articulated itself self-consciously through the broad works of the avant-garde coterie grouped around Hunt. The most recent full-length contribution is Gregory Dart's *Metropolitan Art and Literature, 1810–1840: Cockney Adventures* (2012), which deepened understandings of Keats, Hunt and Cockney suburbanism.

Our discipline benefited from a number of historically oriented, referential studies that illuminated the range and depth of Keatsian engagements with the scientific, astronomical, philosophical and medical ideas of the day. Keats's hospital training, in particular, has sustained critically regenerating attention, incorporating a triptych of scholarly volumes on Keats and Romantic epidemiology: Donald C. Goellnicht's *The Physician-Poet: Keats and Medical Science* (1984), Hermione De Almeida's *Romantic Medicine and John Keats* (1991) and Hillas Smith's *Keats and Medicine* (1995). In 2007, James Allard published a chapter-length discussion of Keats's medical experience in *Romanticism, Medicine and the Poet's Body*; Druin Birch offered a detailed evaluation of Keats's dressership at Guy's Hospital in *Digging Up the Dead*; and John Barnard meticulously reconstructed the poet's Guy's schedule in an important *Romanticism* essay, 'The Busy Time'.[7] Most recently in this vein, as noted earlier in the present volume, a *TLS* commentary by Roe in 2015 returned to light fascinating information on the range of Keats's activities as a trainee surgeon, which included being called on to tend to Mrs Jane Hull, shot in the head at close range by her husband (happily, she survived).[8] As a consequence of this continuing interest, critics have a much finer sense of how Keats's poetic and medical ambitions host each other.

Two apparently opposed devotions – formalism's to aesthetic ('feeling', value, art's agency), and historicism's to referentiality – have produced a major animating tension in Romantic criticism over the last five decades, and Keats's writing has provided an important venue for struggles between these two heuristic dispositions. Vendler's *The Odes of John Keats* (1983), a self-enclosing paean to the poet's odal 'perfection', is rightly recognised as a crowning achievement of late formalism. Although published at a time when materialist precepts were beginning to settle into orthodoxy, Vendler's book didn't draw a line under formalist legacies. Stuart Curran's bravura polemic, *Poetic Form and British Romanticism* (1986), applied itself, via enlivening initial discussion of Keats, to the ways in which self-mirroring conceptual structures in Romantic writing permit access to larger cultural debates; and a decade later, Michael O'Neill published a fine, multiauthor study, 'written back' at historicist critics, *Romanticism and the Self-Conscious Poem* (1997), whose broader diagnostics around form, value and 'aesthetic achievement' were advanced by a chapter on the

Hyperion fragments. Synthesising methodologies also emerged at this time, aimed at bringing evaluations of Keats's artistic mastery and the enthusiasms of referential criticism into rapport. A notable landmark in this 'New Formalism', or Neo-formalism, arrived with the fusing modalities of Wolfson's *Formal Charges: The Shaping of Poetry in British Romanticism* (1997), whose 'contextualized formalist criticism' was quickened by a chapter on Keats's late lyrics that explored how Romantic aesthetic representation was ('always already') engaged in social and political interpretation.

A major post-1963 topic of critical focus has been Keats's complex relation to gender identity. In important respects, the questions that gender theorists have asked of Keats's work are the same as Keats posed to himself: how did his writing relate to his female public, to women writers, to the gendered expectations of other male authors? How did his class and social circumstances problematise his claims to a virile masculine aesthetic? Equally, how were his poetic swoons to be assimilated into a literary market place whose gender-normative contours were becoming increasingly apparent to him? Meshing historicist and feminist methodologies, Levinson's *Keats's Life of Allegory* (1988) gathered these areas of self-conscious concern into its recalibrating purview. Following Levinson's (in)famous volume, many feminist issues on Keats became wrapped up in broader concerns with gender codes and cultural reception. A second milestone arrived with Anne Mellor's investigation into the gendered imagination, performativity and complex moments of slippage, *Romanticism and Gender* (1993).

Keats's inwards-spun circuitings around 'Negative Capability' and the 'camelion Poet' have been of consistent interest to critics exploring permeable gender boundaries. Mellor, Philip Cox and Adriana Craciun argued (with various caveats) that Keats self-consciously configured his creativity as feminine, while Karen Swann and Margaret Homans were less inclined to subscribe to the idea of Keats as an 'ideological cross-dresser' (as powerfully conceptualised by Mellor), concluding (with Keats) that Keats wrote for men.[9] For Wolfson, the tensions, instabilities and contradictions between gender forms in Keats are part of his historical meaning.[10] Wolfson's *Borderlines: The Shifting of Gender in British Romanticism* (2006) included an acute, historically attuned discussion of indeterminacy, developing themes earlier rehearsed in her highly influential essay, 'Feminizing Keats'.[11] Other distinguished recent contributions on identity and literary subjectivity include Emily Rohrbach's, whose 2004 essay on temporality and gendered development in Keats prismed the oft-told maturation narrative through feminist theory to suggest that Keats's movement from 'feminine weakness to masculine genuis' was more complex than the linear progression Keats believed his poetry and letters plotted.[12] Rachel Schulkins's *Keats, Modesty and Masturbation* (2014) brings this valuable strand of investigation up to date, centring on the political investments in Keats's substitution of the pleasures of gendered imagination for physical sensations.

Keats's experiments with different masks of masculinity received vibrant attention from the 1990s onwards, lent impetus by Marlon B. Ross's germinal essay, 'Beyond the Fragmented Word'.[13] Keats's attempt, Ross argued, to get around – to move beyond – his imitation of patrilineal discourse in *Hyperion* leads him to develop a more private, oblique idiom. John Whale's *John Keats* (2005) stood out among much excellent subsequent work on sexuality and masculine identity. Another key publication was James Najarian's 'literary history' of Keats's posthumous legacy, *Victorian Keats: Manliness, Sexuality and Desire* (2002), which staged productive intersections with Gay Theory to track Keats's appropriation to later nineteenth-century understandings of male sexuality.

From early source studies, to more recent inquiries into authorship, canonicity, textuality and influence, the richly allusive grain of Keats's writing, its nods and winks and tips of the hat, has proved perennially fascinating. Should we think less of 'Ode on a Grecian Urn' and 'Ode to Melancholy' – and of Keats – knowing that just pages apart in Thomas Nugent's English translation of Etienne Bonnot de Condillac's *Essay on the Origin of Human Understanding* (1756), formulations may be found that read like first drafts of lines from these famous poems: 'Nothing is beautiful that is not true: and yet every truth is not always beautiful'; 'But suppose some sudden fit of melancholy seizes our mind'?[14] Ought we to situate Keats's famous 'Bright Star' sonnet – stranded in manuscript during Keats's lifetime – differently in Romantic literary culture knowing that fellow Hunt protégé, Barry Cornwall, published one of his own, moreover with striking rhetorical similarities ('would I fain be unto thee,/ Stedfast for ever') in 1820?[15]

The answer to both questions is the same: 'of course'/'probably not'. While Romantic ideology presents poets like Keats (especially Keats) as self-sufficient, synchronous geniuses, we've become accustomed to regarding writers as self-enrolled members of extensive communities. Modern studies of literary transmission have given us a much clearer picture of the intertextual webs that describe and locate Keats's creative practice. Martin Aske's *Keats and Hellenism* (1985) presented the influence of classical antiquity on the poet as a psychic drama; Greg Kucich's *Keats, Shelley, and Romantic Spenserianism* (1991) contoured the impact of Spenser, exploring an artistic relationship conducted through echoes, allusions and direct quotations; and R. S. White's *Keats as a Reader of Shakespeare* (2000) explored the stimulus Keats received from his great 'Presider'. In *Keats's Reading of the Romantic Poets* (1991), Beth Lau switched focus to contemporary lexical nodes and crossings, while in *Keats's Paradise Lost* (1998) she returned to the poet's self-staged, self-defining struggle with Miltonic epic. Thomas McFarland's *The Masks of Keats* (2000) explored medieval and classical 'modes' available to the poet. Recently, Jonathon Shears devoted an intelligent chapter to Keats's 'formal misreadings' of Milton in *The Romantic Legacy of Paradise Lost* (2009).

Keats, we are told, went 'again and again' to the British Museum's Temporary Elgin Room, where he gazed at the marbles, 'rapt in revery'.[16] A strong critical tradition attends to the ekphrastic strain in his work, given formative momentum by Ian Jack's *Keats and the Mirror of Art* (1967). Grant F. Scott's *The Sculpted Word: Keats, Ekphrasis, and the Visual Arts* (1994) argued that Keats's word sculptures register unease about gender. In a related argument, Theresa M. Kelley explored the 'hidden complexity and anxiety' of Keats's fair attitudes, reminding us that ekphrastic objects are 'made in time and out of matter', with all the consequences that follow for poets.[17] Evaluating Keats's own influence on futurity, Sarah Wootton's *Consuming Keats: Nineteenth-Century Representations in Art and Literature* (2006) stationed itself productively at the interchange of art criticism, reception and influence studies to explore Keats as an enablingly 'creative reserve' for successive artists and authors (p. 8).

In view of Keats's deep botanical knowledge, his close limnings of rural, urban and suburban landscapes and what Ashton Nichols, in *Beyond Romantic Ecocriticism* (2011), calls his 'eco-sensitivity' (p. xvi), it is surprising that, amid substantive work on the green frequencies of other Romantic writers, ecocritical research centred on Keats is relatively sparse. For sure, his birdsong (or its absence), withered sedge and rose-tinctured tableaux of harvest home are routinely invoked in ecocritical studies, but there remains no full-length book on 'green' Keats. Shorter recent contributions include Alan Bewell's pioneering 1992 essay, 'Keats's Realm of Flora', which explored Keats's poems 'as a textual equivalent to a garden';[18] Roe's essay, 'John Keats's "Green World"' (2000), which looks at how Keats's 'proto-ecological awareness' is inseparable from his wider reformist ideas;[19] and Jonathan Bate's discussion of 'To Autumn' and air quality in *The Song of the Earth* (2000). Most recently, in *Food and the Literary Imagination* (2014), the interdisciplinary team of Archer, Marggraf Turley and Thomas explored Keats's representation of worked land in 'To Autumn', relocating the ode's arable poetics from Winchester's water meadows to the (then) recently planted St Giles's Hill cornfield. As we prepare to deal with the consequences of anthropocentric climate change, Keats's writing has much still to tell us about the mutually constitutive relationship between humans and environment, and equally, in Bate's words, about 'why poetry continues to matter'.[20]

The relays, dislocating shifts and self-recursions of Keats's language, rejected by the poet's first reviewers as an 'uncouth', preposterous 'jargon', tainted by association with Hunt, have attracted sustained critical attention from scholars of all theoretical stripes. Notable recent contributions include James O'Rouke's *Keats's Odes and Contemporary Criticism* (1998), indebted to deconstructive methodologies; Garrett Stewart's essay, 'Keats and Language' (2001), which attended to Keats's 'phonetic drifts' and 'kaleidoscopic shuffles', his 'language in action';[21] Jack L. Siler's *Poetic Language and Political Engagement in the Poetry of Keats* (2008), which focused more expansively on the relations of 'word to world, poetry to society, art to life' (p. 1); and Magdalena M. Ostas's article, 'Keats and the Impersonal Act of Writing' (2010), on the 'formal workings' of Keats's poetry.[22] Marcello Giovanelli's innovative *Text World Theory and Keats's Poetry* (2013) addressed Keats's turns of phrase through cognitive linguistics, and most newly, in *Reading John Keats* (2015), Susan Wolfson returned to the 'actions' of Keats's language, showing how these 'activate' us as readers (p. x).

As a consequence of these rich debates and critical legacies, a more complexly attuned, finely calibrated and finally more human figure has emerged. As we peer at futurity, what role do we perceive for our field as it continues to embolden its repertoires? In his letters, Keats envisaged a 'grand march of intellect'. Perhaps we might do more to demonstrate the ways in which his writing annotates today's so-called real-world problems, asserting its relevance beyond the habitual realms of literary criticism to such defining challenges as climate change, food and water security, mass surveillance, demagoguery, neo-slavery and corporatocracy. Perhaps hybrid modes of critique – forms willing to embrace creative enactments alongside political and aesthetic analysis and science, ethics and technology alongside hermeneutics – will be most suited to demonstrating to the shadows of magnitudes that await us the pertinence of John Keats and the discipline he inspires.

Notes

I am indebted to Greg Kucich's aerial view, 'John Keats', in *Literature of the Romantic Period: A Bibliographical Guide*, ed. Michael O'Neill (Oxford: Clarendon Press, 1998), and to Mark Sandy's fine summary, 'Twentieth- and Twenty-First-Century Keats Criticism', *Literature Compass*, 3 (2010), pp. 1320–33.

1 *Endymion*, 4. 156.
2 Byron, letter dated 12 October 1820.
3 'Keats and the Historical Method', *Modern Language Notes*, 94 (1979): 988–1032.
4 'How Keats Falls', *Studies in Romanticism*, 50 (2011): 251–73.
5 'Decapitating Romance: Class, Fetish and Ideology in Keats's *Isabella*', *Nineteenth-Century Literature*, 49 (1994): 321–38.
6 Richard Cronin, 'Keats and the Politics of Cockney Style', *Studies in English Literature, 1500–1900,* 36 (1996): 785–806; William Keach, 'Cockney Couplets: Keats and the Politics of Style', *Studies in Romanticism*, 25 (1986): 182–96.
7 'The Busy Time: Keats's Duties at Guy's Hospital from Autumn 1816 to March 1817', *Romanticism*, 13 (2007): 199–218.
8 'Dressing for Art', *Times Literary Supplement*, 27 May 2015: 13–15.
9 Philip Cox, 'Keats and the Performance of Gender', *Keats-Shelley Journal*, 44 (1995): 40–65; Adriana Craciun, *Fatal Women of Romanticism* (Cambridge: Cambridge University Press, 2003); Margaret Homans, 'Keats Reading Women, Women Reading Keats', *Studies in Romanticism*, 29 (1990): 341–70; Karen Swann, 'Harassing the Muse', in *Romanticism and Feminism*, ed. Anne K. Mellor (Bloomington, IN: Indiana University Press, 1988).
10 'Keats and Gender Criticism', in *The Persistence of Poetry: Bicentennial Essays on Keats,* ed. Robert M. Ryan and Ronald A. Sharp (Amherst: University of Massachusetts Press, 1998).
11 'Feminizing Keats', in *Critical Essays on John Keats, ed.* Hermione de Almeida (Boston: Hall, 1990), 317–56.
12 'Representing Time and Gender: Keats's Prose, Keats's Poetics', *E-rea*, 2 (2004), http://erea.revues.org/442 [Date of access: 23.10.2015].
13 'Beyond the Fragmented Word: Keats at the Limits of Patrilineal Language', in *Out of Bounds: Male Writers and Gender(ed) Criticism*, ed. Laura Claridge and Elizabeth Langland (Amherst: University of Massachusetts Press, 1990), pp. 110–31.
14 *Essay on the Origin of Human Knowledge*, pp. 91, 84.
15 *Marcian Colonna … and Other Poems* (1821), p. 205.
16 *The Life and Letters of Joseph Severn*, ed. William Sharp (1892), p. 32.
17 'Keats and Ekphrasis', in *The Cambridge Companion to Keats*, ed. Susan Wolfson (Cambridge: Cambridge University Press, 2001), pp. 172, 183.
18 'Keats's Realm of Flora', *Studies in Romanticism*, 31 (1992): 71–98, at 74–5.
19 'John Keats's "Green World": Politics, Nature and the Poems', in *The Challenge of Keats: Bicentenary Essays 1795–1995,* ed. Allan C. Christensen, Lilla Maria Crisafulli Jones, Giuseppe Galigani and Anthony L. Johnson et al. (Amsterdam: Rodopi, 2000), p. 64.
20 *The Song of the Earth* (London: Picador, 2000), p. ix.
21 'Keats and Language', in Wolfson, *Cambridge Companion*, pp. 138–40.
22 'Keats and the Impersonal Craft of Writing', in *Romanticism and the Object*, ed. Larry H. Peer (New York: Palgrave, 2010), p. 125.

Further Reading

1 Biographies and Film

MacGillivray, J. R. *Keats: A Bibliography and Reference Guide with an Essay on Keats' Reputation*. Toronto: University of Toronto Press, 1949.
Marquess, William Henry. *Lives of the Poet: The First Century of Keats Biography* University Park, PA: Pennsylvania State University Press, 1984.
Matthews, G. M. Ed. *John Keats: The Critical Heritage*. London: Routledge, 1971.
Stillinger, Jack. 'The "Story" of Keats'. *The Cambridge Companion to Keats*. Ed. Susan J. Wolfson. Cambridge: Cambridge University Press, 2001, pp. 246–60.
Wallace, Jennifer. Ed. *Lives of the Great Romantics II: Keats, Coleridge and Scott by Their Contemporaries*. Gen. Ed. John Mullan, 3 vols. London: Pickering & Chatto, 1997, vol. 1.

2 Formative Years and Medical Training

Barnard, John. ' "The Busy Time": Keats's Duties at Guy's Hospital from Autumn 1816 to March 1817'. *Romanticism* 13. 3 (2007): 199–218.
Gittings, Robert. *The Keats Inheritance*. London: Heinemann, 1964.
Pierpoint, William S. *John Keats, Henry Stephens and George Wilson Mackereth: The Unparallel Lives of Three Medical Students*. London: The Stephens Collection, 2010.
Roe, Nicholas. *John Keats: A New Life*. London and New Haven: Yale University Press, 2012.
White, R. S. *John Keats: A Literary Life*. Basingstoke: Palgrave Macmillan, 2010.

3 Surgery, Science, and Suffering

Barnard, John. ' "The Busy Time": Keats's Duties at Guy's Hospital from Autumn 1816 to March 1817'. *Romanticism* 13. 3 (2007): 199–218.
Burch, Druin. *Digging Up the Dead. Uncovering the Life and Times of an Extraordinary Surgeon*. London: Chatto & Windus, 2007.
Goellnicht, Donald C. *The Poet-Physician. Keats and Medical Science*. Pittsburgh: University of Pittsburgh Press, 1984.
Sperry, Stuart M. *Keats the Poet*. Princeton: Princeton University Press, 1973.

4 Fanny Brawne and Other Women

Brawne, Fanny. *Letters of Fanny Brawne to Fanny Keats*. Ed. Fred Edgcumbe. London: Oxford University Press, 1936.

Homans, Margaret. 'Keats Reading Women, Women Reading Keats'. *Studies in Romanticism* 29. 3 (1990): 341–70.

Kucich, Greg. 'Gender Crossings: Keats and Tighe'. *Keats-Shelley Journal* 44 (1995): 29–39.

Mellor, Anne K. 'Keats and the Complexities of Gender'. *The Cambridge Companion to Keats*. Ed. Susan J. Wolfson. Cambridge: Cambridge University Press, 2001, pp. 214–29.

Richardson, Joanne. *Fanny Brawne: A Biography*. London: Thames and Hudson, 1952.

5 Mortality

Bari, Shahidha. *Keats and Philosophy*. London: Routledge, 2012.

Bennett, Andrew. *Keats, Narrative and Audience*. Cambridge: Cambridge University Press, 1994.

Corcoran, Brendan. 'Keats's Death: Towards a Posthumous Poetics Author(s)'. *Studies in Romanticism* 48. 2 (2009): 321–48.

Gigante, Denise. *Life: Organic Form and Romanticism*. New Haven: Yale University Press, 2009.

Jones, John. *John Keats's Dream of Truth*. London: Chatto & Windus, 1969.

6 Travel

Jarvis, Robin. *Romantic Writing and Pedestrian Travel*. Basingstoke: Macmillan 1997.

Joris, Pierre. *A Nomad Poetics*. Middletown, CT: Wesleyan University Press, 2003.

Levinson, Marjorie. *Keats's Life of Allegory: The Origins of a Style*. Oxford: Blackwell, 1988.

Marggraf Turley, Richard, H. Thomas and J. E. Archer. 'Keats, "To Autumn" and the New Men of Winchester'. *Review of English Studies* n. s. 64 (2012): 797–817.

Morton, Timothy. *Ecology without Nature*. Cambridge, MA: Harvard University Press, 2007.

Robinson, Jeffrey C. *Reception and Poetics in Keats: 'My Ended Poet'*. Basingstoke: Macmillan, 1998.

Walker, Carol Kyros. *Walking North with Keats*. New Haven: Yale University Press, 1992.

7 Letters

Barnard, John. *John Keats*. Cambridge: Cambridge University Press, 1987.
Sperry, Stuart M. *Keats the Poet*. Princeton, NJ: Princeton University Press, 1973.
Thomson, Heidi. 'Keats's Letters: "A Wilful and Dramatic Exercise of Our Minds towards Each Other"'. *Keats-Shelley Review* 25.2 (2011): 160–74.
Trilling, Lionel. *The Opposing Self: Nine Essays in Criticism*. 1950; New York: Viking, 1968, pp. 3–49.
Webb, Timothy. '"Cutting Figures": Rhetorical Strategies in Keats's *Letters*'. *Keats: Bicentenary Readings*. Ed. Michael O'Neill. Edinburgh: Edinburgh University Press, 1997, pp. 144–69.
Wolfson, Susan J. 'Keats the Letter-Writer: Epistolary Poetics'. *Romanticism Past and Present* 6 (1982): 43–61.

8 Manuscripts and Publishing History

Gittings, Robert. *The Odes of John Keats*. London: Heinemann, 1970.
Harvard Keats Collection. http://hcl.harvard.edu/libraries/houghton/collections/modern/keats.cfm
Hebron, Stephen. *John Keats: A Poet and His Manuscripts*. London: British Library, 2009.
Lau, Beth. *Keats's 'Paradise Lost'*. Gainesville, FL: University Press of Florida, 1998.
Stillinger, Jack. 'Keats and His Helpers: The Multiple Authorship of *Isabella*'. *Multiple Authorship and the Myth of Solitary Genius*. New York: Oxford University Press, 1991, pp. 25–49.
The Texts of Keats's Poems. Cambridge, MA: Harvard University Press, 1974.

9 The Hunt Circle and the Cockney School

Cox, Jeffrey N. *Poetry and Politics in the Cockney School: Keats, Shelley, Hunt and their Circle*. Cambridge: Cambridge University Press, 1998.
Cronin, Richard. *The Politics of Romantic Poetry: In Search of the Pure Commonwealth*. Basingstoke: Macmillan, 2000, pp. 181–99.
Roe, Nicholas. *John Keats and the Culture of Dissent*. Oxford: Clarendon Press, 1997.
Roe, Nicholas. Ed. *Leigh Hunt: Life, Poetics and Politics*. London: Routledge, 2003.

10 London

Baron, Xavier. Ed. *London 1066–1914: Literary Sources and Documents*, 3 vols. Mountfield, East Sussex: Helm Information, 1997, especially vol. 2, part 5 ('Regency London: 1800–1837').
De Almeida, Hermione. *Romantic Medicine and John Keats*. Oxford: Oxford University Press, 1991.

Ford, Mark. Ed. *London: A History in Verse*. Cambridge, MA: Harvard University Press, 2012.

Gigante, Denise, *The Keats Brothers: The Life of John and George*. Cambridge, MA: Harvard University Press, 2011.

Gittings, Robert, *John Keats*. 1968; London: Penguin, 1985.

Peer, Larry H. Ed. *Romanticism and the City*. New York: Palgrave Macmillan, 2011.

11 Politics

Cox, Jeffrey N. *Poetry and Politics in the Cockney School: Keats, Shelley, Hunt and their Circle*. Cambridge: Cambridge University Press, 1998.

Kandl, John. 'The Politics of Keats's Early Poetry: "Delight" with "Liberty"', *The Cambridge Companion to Keats*. Ed. Susan J. Wolfson. Cambridge: Cambridge University Press, 2000, pp. 1–19.

McGann, Jerome. 'Keats and the Historical Method in Literary Criticism'. *The Beauty of Inflections: Literary Investigations in Historical Method and Theory*. Oxford: Clarendon Press, 1985, pp. 18–65.

Roe, Nicholas. Ed. *Keats and History*. Cambridge: Cambridge University Press, 1995.

Wolfson, Susan J. Ed. 'Keats and Politics: A Forum'. *Studies in Romanticism* 25.2 (1986): 171–229.

12 Sociability

Barnard, John. 'Keats's Letters: "Remembrancing and Enchaining"'. *The Cambridge Companion to Keats*. Ed. Susan J. Wolfson. Cambridge: Cambridge University Press, 2001, pp. 120–34.

Cox, Jeffrey N. *Poetry and Politics in the Cockney School: Keats, Shelley, Hunt and their Circle*. Cambridge: Cambridge University Press, 1998.

Ricks, Christopher. *Keats and Embarrassment*. Oxford: Oxford University Press, 1974.

Sharp, Ronald A. 'Keats and Friendship'. *The Persistence of Poetry: Bicentennial Essays on Keats*. Ed. Robert M. Ryan and Ronald A. Sharp. Amherst: University of Massachusetts Press, 1998, pp. 66–81.

Tomko, Michael. 'Leigh Hunt's Cockney Canon: Sociability and Subversion from Homer to *Hyperion*'. *A Companion to Romantic Poetry*. Ed. Charles Mahoney. Malden, MA: Wiley-Blackwell, 2011, pp. 285–301.

Wolfson, Susan J. 'Keats the Letter-Writer: Epistolary Poetics'. *Romanticism Past and Present* 6 (1982): 43–61.

13 The Visual and Plastic Arts

Ferris, David. *Silent Urns: Romanticism, Hellenism, Modernity*. Stanford: Stanford University Press, 2000.

Levinson, Marjorie. *Keats's Life of Allegory: The Origins of a Style*. Oxford: Blackwell, 1988.

Roe, Nicholas. *John Keats and the Culture of Dissent*. Oxford: Clarendon Press, 1997.
Rohrbach, Emily and Emily Sun. Eds. *Studies in Romanticism,* special issue: 'Reading Keats, Thinking Politics' 50.2 (Summer 2011).
Vendler, Helen. *The Odes of John Keats*. Cambridge: Belknap Press, of Harvard University Press, 1983.

14 Religion and Myth

Aske, Martin. *Keats and Hellenism: An Essay*. Cambridge: Cambridge University Press, 1985.
Evert, Walter H. *Aesthetic and Myth in the Poetry of Keats*. Princeton: Princeton University Press, 1965.
Kandl, John. 'The Politics of Keats's Early Poetry: "Delight" with "Liberty"'. *The Cambridge Companion to Keats*. Ed. Susan J. Wolfson. Cambridge: Cambridge University Press, 2001, pp. 1–19.
Newey, Vincent. '*Hyperion*, *The Fall of Hyperion*, and Keats's Epic Ambitions'. *The Cambridge Companion to Keats*. Ed. Susan J. Wolfson. Cambridge: Cambridge University Press, 2001, pp. 69–85.
Roe, Nicholas. *John Keats and the Culture of Dissent*. Oxford: Clarendon Press, 1997.
Ryan, Robert M. *Keats: The Religious Sense*. Princeton: Princeton University Press, 1976.

15 The Enlightenment and History

De Almeida, Hermione. *John Keats and Romantic Medicine*. New York: Oxford University Press, 1991.
Fermanis, Porscha. *John Keats and the Ideas of the Enlightenment*. Edinburgh: Edinburgh University Press, 2009.
McLane, Maureen. *Romanticism and the Human Species: Poetry, Population, and the Discourse of the Species*. Cambridge: Cambridge University Press, 2000.
Roe, Nicholas. Ed. *Keats and History*. Cambridge: Cambridge University Press, 1995.
Ryan, Robert M. *Keats: The Religious Sense*. Princeton: Princeton University Press, 1976.
Sperry, Stuart M. 'Keats's Skepticism and Voltaire'. *Keats-Shelley Journal* 12 (1965): 75–93.

16 Keats and Hazlitt

Bromwich, David. *Hazlitt: The Mind of a Critic*. New York: Oxford University Press, 1983.
Burley, Stephen. *Hazlitt the Dissenter: Religion, Philosophy, and Politics, 1766–1816*. Houndmills, Basingstoke: Palgrave Macmillan, 2014.
Jones Stanley. *Hazlitt: A Life*. Oxford: Oxford University Press, 1991.

Metaphysical Hazlitt: Bicentenary Essays. Ed. Uttara Natarajan, Tom Paulin, and Duncan Wu. Abingdon: Routledge, 2005.

Natarajan, Uttara. *Hazlitt and the Reach of Sense*. Oxford: Clarendon Press, 1998

Paulin, Tom. *The Day-Star of Liberty: William Hazlitt's Radical Style*. London: Faber, 1998.

17 Imagination, Beauty and Truth

Bate, Walter Jackson. 'Negative Capability'. *John Keats*. Cambridge, MA: Harvard University Press, 1963, pp. 233–63.

Bromwich, David. 'Keats'. *Hazlitt: The Mind of a Critic*. Oxford: Oxford University Press, 1983, pp. 362–401.

Engell, James. 'Goethe and Keats'. *The Creative Imagination*. Cambridge, MA: Harvard University Press, 1981, pp. 277–98.

Sheats, Paul D. 'Keats, the Greater Ode, and the Trial of Imagination'. *Coleridge, Keats, and the Imagination*. Columbia, MO: University of Missouri Press, 1990, pp. 174–200.

Vendler, Helen. *The Odes of John Keats*. Cambridge, MA: Harvard University Press, 1983.

Waldoff, Leon. *Keats and the Silent Work of Imagination*. Urbana, IL: University of Illinois Press, 1985.

18 The Poetical Character

Barnard, John. *John Keats*. Cambridge: Cambridge University Press, 1987.

Bayley, John. *The Uses of Division: Unity and Disharmony in Literature*. London: Chatto & Windus, 1976.

Everett, Barbara., *Poets in their Time*. 1986; Oxford: Oxford University Press, 1991.

Jones, John. *John Keats's Dream of Truth*. London: Chatto & Windus, 1969.

Ricks, Christopher. *Keats and Embarrassment*. Oxford: Clarendon Press, 1974.

Sperry, Stuart M. *Keats the Poet*. 1973; Princeton: Princeton University Press, 1994.

19 The Senses and Sensation

Bari, Shahidha. *Keats and Philosophy: The Life of Sensations*. London: Routledge, 2012.

Bayley, John. 'Keats and Reality', *Proceedings of the British Academy* 47 (1962): 91–126.

Jones, John. *John Keats's Dream of Truth*. London: Chatto & Windus, 1969.

Ricks, Christopher. *Keats and Embarrassment*. Oxford: Clarendon Press, 1974.

Sperry, Stuart M. *Keats the Poet*. Princeton: Princeton University Press, 1973.

Vendler, Helen. *The Odes of John Keats*. Cambridge, MA: Harvard University Press, 1983.

20 Prosody and Versification in the Odes

Bate, Walter Jackson. *The Stylistic Development of John Keats*. 1945; Abingdon: Routledge, 2014.

O'Rourke, James L. *Keats's Odes and Contemporary Criticism*. Gainesville, FL: University Press of Florida, 1998.

Wolfson, Susan J. *Reading John Keats*. Cambridge: Cambridge University Press, 2015.

21 Poetic Precursors (1): Dante and Shakespeare

Bate, Jonathan. *Shakespeare and the English Romantic Imagination*. Oxford: Oxford University Press, 1989.

Bindman, David, Stephen Hebron, and Michael O'Neill. *Dante Rediscovered: From Blake to Rodin*. Grasmere, Cumbria: Wordsworth Trust, 2007.

Havely, Nick. *Dante's British Public: Readers and Texts, from the Fourteenth Century to the Present*. Oxford: Oxford University Press, 2014.

Pite, Ralph. *The Circle of Our Vision: Dante's Presence in English Romantic Poetry*. Oxford: Oxford University Press, 1996.

Wasserman, Earl R. *The Finer Tone: Keats' Major Poems*. Baltimore: Johns Hopkins University Press, 1953.

White, R. S. *Keats as a Reader of Shakespeare*. Oklahoma: University of Oklahoma Press, 1987.

22 Poetic Precursors (2): Spenser, Milton, Dryden, Pope

Amarsinghe, Upali. *Dryden and Pope in the Early Nineteenth Century: A Study of Changing Literary Taste 1800–1830*. Cambridge: Cambridge University Press, 1962.

Cheatham, George. 'Byron's Dislike of Keats's Poetry'. *Keats-Shelley Journal* 32 (1983): 20–5.

Jones, Steven E. *Satire and Romanticism*. New York: St. Martin's, 2000.

Kucich, Greg. *Keats, Shelley, and Romantic Spenserianism*. University Park: Pennsylvania State University Press, 1991.

Lau, Beth. *Keats's 'Paradise Lost'*. Gainesville, FL: University Press of Florida, 1998.

Newlyn, Lucy. *'Paradise Lost' and the Romantic Reader*. Oxford: Clarendon Press, 1993.

Shears, Jonathan. *The Romantic Legacy of 'Paradise Lost'*. Farnham: Ashgate, 2009.

23 Contemporaries (1) (and Immediate Predecessors): Tighe, Radcliffe, Southey, Burns, Chatterton, Hunt, Wordsworth

Kucich, Greg. 'Keats and English Poetry'. *The Cambridge Companion to Keats*. Ed. Susan J. Wolfson. Cambridge: Cambridge University Press, 2001, pp. 186–202.

Lau, Beth. *Keats's Reading of the Romantic Poets*. Ann Arbor: University of Michigan Press, 1991.

Mellor, Anne K. *Romanticism and Gender*. New York: Routledge, 1993.

Sperry, Stuart M. *Keats the Poet*. 1973; Princeton: Princeton University Press, 1994.

24 Contemporaries (2): Coleridge, Byron, Shelley

Cox, Jeffrey N. *Romanticism in the Shadow of War: Literary Culture in the Napoleonic War Years*. Cambridge: Cambridge University Press, 2014.

Fulford, Tim. *The Late Poetry of the Lake-School Poets: Romanticism Revised*. Cambridge: Cambridge University Press, 2013.

Kucich, Greg. *Keats, Shelley and Romantic Spenserianism*. University Park: Pennsylvania State University Press, 1991.

Newlyn, Lucy. *'Paradise Lost' and the Romantic Reader*. Oxford: Clarendon Press, 1993.

O'Neill, Michael. *Romanticism and the Self-Conscious Poem*. Oxford: Clarendon Press, 1997.

Wolfson, Susan J. *Borderlines: The Shiftings of Gender in British Romanticism*. Stanford: Stanford University Press, 2006.

25 Ballad, Romance and Narrative

Cox, Jeffrey N. '*Lamia*, *Isabella*, and *The Eve of St. Agnes*: Eros and "Romance"'. *The Cambridge Companion to Keats*. Ed. Susan J. Wolfson. Cambridge: Cambridge University Press, 2001, pp. 53–68.

Kern, Robert. 'Keats and the Problem of Romance', *Philological Quarterly*, 58 (1979): 171–91.

Sperry, Stuart M. *Keats the Poet*. Princeton: Princeton University Press, 1973.

Stillinger, Jack. *The Hoodwinking of Madeline and Other Essays on Keats's Poems*. Urbana, IL: University of Illinois Press, 1971.

Swann, Karen. 'Harassing the Muse'. *Romanticism and Feminism*. Ed. Anne K. Mellor. Bloomington: Indiana University Press, 1988, pp. 81–92.

Wolfson, Susan. 'Keats's *Isabella* and the "Digressions" of "Romance"', *Criticism*, 27.3 (1985): 247–61.

26 Epic and Tragedy

Bewell, Alan. 'The Political Implication of Keats's Classicist Aesthetics'. *Studies in Romanticism* 25 (1986): 221–30.

Ende, Stuart. *Keats and the Sublime*. New Haven: Yale University Press, 1976.

Hartman, Geoffrey H. 'Spectral Symbolism and Authorial Self in Keats's *Hyperion*'. *The Fate of Reading*. Chicago: University of Chicago Press, 1975.

Lau, Beth. *Keats's 'Paradise Lost'*. Gainesville, FL: University Press of Florida, 1998.

Levinson, Marjorie. 'The Dependent Fragment: "Hyperion" and "The Fall of Hyperion"'. *The Romantic Fragment Poem*. Chapel Hill: University of North Carolina Press, 1986.

Newey, Vincent. '*Hyperion, The Fall of Hyperion, and Keats's Epic Ambitions. The Cambridge Companion to Keats*. Ed. Susan J. Wolfson. Cambridge: Cambridge University Press, 2001, pp. 69–85.

Sperry, Stuart M. *Keats the Poet*. Princeton: Princeton University Press, 1973.

Wolfson, Susan J. *Reading John Keats*. Cambridge: Cambridge University Press, 2015, chapters 5 and 9.

27 Lyrical Genres

Culler, Jonathan. *Theory of the Lyric*. Cambridge, MA: Harvard University Press, 2015.

Fry, Paul H. *The Poet's Calling in the English Ode*. New Haven: Yale University Press, 1980.

Smith, Charlotte. *The Poems of Charlotte Smith*. Ed. Stuart Curran. New York: Oxford University Press, 1993.

Vendler, Helen. *The Odes of John Keats*. Cambridge, MA: Harvard University Press, 1983.

Coming of Age as a Poet. Cambridge, MA: Harvard University Press, 2003.

Todd, Janet. *Sensibility: An Introduction*. London: Methuen, 1986.

28 Tennyson to Wilde

Bennett, Andrew. *Romantic Poets and the Culture of Posterity*. Cambridge: Cambridge University Press, 1999.

Ford, George H. *Keats and the Victorians: A Study of His Influence and Rise to Fame 1821–1895*. New Haven: Yale University Press, 1944.

Najarian, James. *Victorian Keats: Manliness, Sexuality, and Desire*. Houndmills: Macmillan, 2002.

Robinson, Jeffrey C. *Reception and Poetics in Keats: 'My Ended Poet'*. Houndmills: Macmillan, 1998.

Tontiplaphol, Betsy Winakur. *Poetics of Luxury in the Nineteenth Century: Keats, Tennyson, and Hopkins*. Farnham: Ashgate, 2011.

Wootton, Sarah. *Consuming Keats: Nineteenth-Century Representations in Art and Literature*. Houndmills: Macmillan, 2006.

29 Hardy, Edward Thomas, Stevens, Bishop, Heaney

Costello, Bonnie. *Elizabeth Bishop: Questions of Mastery*. Cambridge, MA: Harvard University Press, 1991.

O'Neill, Michael. *The All-Sustaining Air: Romantic Legacies and Renewals in British, Irish, and American Poetry after 1900*. Oxford: Oxford University Press, 2007.

Thomas, Edward, *Keats*. 1916; Cheltenham: Cyder, 1999.
Vendler, Helen. 'Wallace Stevens'. *Part of Nature, Part of Us: Modern American Poets*. Cambridge, MA: Harvard University Press, 1980.

30 American Writing

Baker, Carlos. *The Echoing Green: Romanticism, Modernism, and the Phenomena of Transference in Poetry*. Princeton: Princeton University Press, 1984.
Bornstein, George. *Transformations of Romanticism in Yeats, Eliot, and Stevens*. Chicago: University of Chicago Press, 1976.
Chavkin, Allan. Ed. *Romanticism and Modern Fiction*. New York: AMS, 1993.
Davies, Damian Walford and Richard Maggraff Turley. Eds. *The Monstrous Debt: Modalities of Romantic Influence in Twentieth-Century Literature*. Detroit: Delaware State University Press, 2006.
Sandy, Mark. Ed. *Romantic Presences in the Twentieth Century*. Farnham: Ashgate, 2012.
Tovey, Paige. *The Transatlantic Eco-Romanticism of Gary Snyder*. London: Palgrave Macmillan, 2013.

31 Contemporary Reviews

Everest, Kelvin. 'Shelley's *Adonais* and John Keats', *Essays in Criticism* 57 (2007): 237–63.
Schwartz, Lewis M. *Keats Reviewed by His Contemporaries*. Metuchen, NJ: Scarecrow Press, 1973.
Stillinger, Jack. 'John Keats'. *The English Romantic Poets: A Review of Research and Criticism*, 4th edn Ed. Frank Jordan. New York: Modern Language Association, 1985, pp. 665–718.
Wolfson, Susan J. 'Keats Enters History: Autopsy, *Adonais*, and the Fame of Keats'. *Keats and History*. Ed. Nicholas Roe. Cambridge: Cambridge University Press, 1995, pp. 17–45.

32 Critical Reception, 1821–1900

Barfoot, C. C. Ed. *Victorian Keats and Romantic Carlyle: The Fusions and Confusions of Literary Periods*. Atlanta: Rodopi, 1999.
Najarian, James. *Victorian Keats: Manliness, Sexuality, and Desire*. New York: Palgrave, 2003.
Wootton, Sarah. *Consuming Keats: Nineteenth-Century Representations in Art and Literature*. Basingstoke: Palgrave Macmillan, 2006.

33 Keats Criticism, 1900–1963

Bayley, John. 'Keats and Reality'. *Proceedings of the British Academy* 47 (1962): 91–126.

Brooks, Cleanth. 'Keats's Sylvan Historian: History without Footnotes'. *The Well Wrought Urn: Studies in the Structure of Poetry*. New York: Harcourt Brace, 1947, pp. 139–52.

Leavis, F. R. 'Revaluations IX: Keats'. *Scrutiny* (March 1936): 376–400.

Murry, John Middleton. *Keats and Shakespeare*. London: Oxford University Press, 1926.

Stillinger, Jack. 'The Hoodwinking of Madeline: Skepticism in "The Eve of St Agnes"'. *Studies in Philology* 58 (1961): 533–55.

Trilling, Lionel. 'The Poet as Hero: Keats in His Letters' (1951) rpt. in *The Moral Obligation to Be Intelligent: Selected Essays*. Evanston, IL: Northwestern University Press, 2008, pp. 224–58.

34 Keats Criticism, Post-1963

Levinson, Marjorie. *Keats's Life of Allegory: The Origins of a Style*. Oxford: Blackwell, 1988.

Najarian, James. *Victorian Keats: Manliness, Sexuality and Desire*. Basingstoke: Palgrave, 2002.

Ricks, Christopher. *Keats and Embarrassment*. Oxford: Oxford University Press, 1974.

Roe, Nicholas. *John Keats and the Culture of Dissent*. Oxford: Clarendon Press, 1997.

Index

For titles of Keats's poems and plays, please see the entry 'poems and plays of John Keats', which has further references to individual works. Titles to individual poems appear without quotation marks.

Abbey, Richard (Keats's trustee), 24, 27, 38
Adonais (Shelley), 54, 281, 331
  impact of Keats's literary reputation, 320–21
Aids to Reflection in the Formation of a Manly Character (Coleridge), 179
American poets and writers, Keats and
  Bellow and, 306–07
  Dickinson and, 304–05
  Emerson and, 300–01, 302
  Fitzgerald and, 305–06
  Frost and, 307
  Roth and, 307
  Thoreau and, 301–02
  Wallace Stevens and, 307–08
  Whitman and, 302–04
  William Carlos Williams and, 307
Annals of the Fine Arts, 128
Anxiety of Influence, The (Bloom), 341
Apollo, 136, 138, 141, 191, 258–61
Apollo Introducing the Greatest Poets to the Goddess Minerva (painting, Cammarano), 136
Arnold, Matthew, 285–87
  on Keats, 327
As Hermes once took to his feathers light. *See* On a Dream *under* poems and plays of John Keats
Aske, Martin, 53, 138, 346
At Lulworth Cove a Century Back (Hardy), 291–92
Augustan poets
  Keats's and Hunt's dislike of, 221–22

Bailey, Benjamin, 59, 66–68, 172–73, 209
Bailey, Paul, 105
ballads, 274
  interplay between genre and narrative rhetoric in, 248
  in Meg Merrilies and La Belle Dame sans Merci, 253–55
Bate, Walter Jackson, 9–10, 198, 231–32, 334, 336, 340–41
Bayley, John, 191, 331–32
Beattie, James, 195
beauty, 334
  Brooks on beauty and truth in Keats, 335–36
  imaginative truth and, 171–72, 173
  melancholic in Ode to a Nightingale, 174
  melancholic in On Visiting the Tomb of Burns, 174
  moral beauty, 227
  in Ode on a Grecian Urn, 172, 173
Bellow, Saul, 306–07
Biographia Literaria (Coleridge), 178, 239
biographies and films of Keats, 9, 332, 340–41
  by Bate, 9–10
  Bright Star (film, Campion), 10–13
  John Keats (Lowell) and, 14
  John Keats, A New Life (Roe) and, 15–16
  Keats (biography, Motion) and, 13–15
  60s as golden age of Keats scholarship, 9–10
  travel and, 56
Bishop, Elizabeth, 297–98
Blackwood's Edinburgh Magazine, 249, 313
Bloom, Harold, 341
Boccaccio, 112
botanical knowledge, of Keats, 347
Bradley, A.C., 241–42
  on Keats, 334

Brawne, Fanny, 14, 38, 39, 44–45, 64, 262
  death and desire in letters to, 52
  friendship of Keats with Brawne's mother, 40
  letters written to from Rome, 57
  love letters to from Keats, 69–70
  as only friend of Keats, 123
  publication of *Letters of John Keats to Fanny Brawne* (Buxton Forman) and, 324–26
Bright Star (film, Campion), 10–13, 16
British Critic, 317
Brooks, Cleanth, 335–36
Brown, Charles, 54, 214–16
  Keats's last letter to, 72–73
Browning, Elizabeth Barrett, 288
Burns, Robert, 272, 273
  influence on Keats, 230–31
Butler, Marilyn, 91
Buxton Forman, Harry, 324–26
  criticism of for publishing *Letters of John Keats*, 328–29
Byron, Lord, 245–46
  critical view of Keats of, 321
  Keats and, 242–43

Calendar of Nature (Hunt), 108
camelion Poet, 96, 212–13, 259, 267
Cammarano, Giuseppe, 136
Campion, Jane, 10–13, 16
Chatterton, Thomas
  influence on Keats, 231
Christabel (Coleridge), 181
Clarke's Academy. *See* Enfield School
classical literature
  Keats's familiarity with, 136–37
Cockney and Cockney poetry, 4, 92, 96, 99, 107, 109–10, 117, 118, 120, 131, 222
  Cockney Carnivalesque, 61
  Cockney sociability, 118, 121
  Croker on Cockney School, 90–91
  Lockhart on Cockney School, 89–91, 249, 343
  post-1963 critiques of Keats and, 343–44
  Thomas Hood as, 282
Coleridge, Samuel Taylor, 162, 171, 179, 181
  critical reviews of in *The Examiner*, 238
  Keats on, 239–40
  kissing in poems of, 243–44
  on poetic character, 178–79
Colvin, Sidney, 69
Conder, Josiah
  on bad influence of Hunt on Keats's poetics, 316–17
contemporary poets, Keats and. *See also* Byron, Lord; Coleridge, Samuel Taylor; Shelley, Percy Bysshe
  Keats's anxiety over, 238–39
contemporary reviews of Keats, 313
  Adonais (Shelley) and, 320–21
  Conder on Hunt's influence, 316–17
  by Croker, 314
  by George Felton Mathew, 315
  Hunt and, 313, 315, 316–17
  Patmore on *Endymion*, 317
  by Reynolds, 314–15
Cowden Clarke, Charles, 23, 24–25, 137, 138
Cox, Jeffrey, 117, 132
critical reception of Keats (1821-1900)
  essay on in *The Olio*, 323–24
  Hallam on Shelley *vs.* Keats, 327
  Hazlitt on Keats, 323
  Milnes biography of, 324
  publication of *Letters of John Keats to Fanny Brawne* (Buxton Forman) and, 324–26
  Swinburne on, 325–27
critiques of Keats (1900-1963)
  Bate on, 334
  Brooks on beauty and truth, 335–36
  centrality of Keats to English Romanticism and, 333
  of Henry James, 331
  idea of divided poetic consciousness and, 333
  of John Bayley, 331–32
  John Middleton Murry on Shakespeare and Keats, 333–34
  lack of single accepted orthodoxy on Keats, 333
  on letters of Keats, 334–35
  post-war critiques, 336–37
critiques of Keats post-1963
  biographies by Ward and Bate and, 340–41
  biographies emphasizing maturity and development of Keats, 340–41
  Cockney critiques, 343–44
  counternarratives on maturity of Keats and, 341–42
  eco-sensitivity of Keats and, 347–48
  gender identity and, 345–46
  historicist and cultural materialist critiques, 342
  Keats's use of language and, 348
  on medical and poetic ambitions of Keats, 344
  need for hybrid modes of critique, 348
  political analyses and, 342–43
  tensions between formalist and historicist critiques and, 344–45
Croker, John Wilson, 249, 314
  reviews of Cockney School of, 90–91
Cronin, Richard, 95

Dante Alighieri. *See also Divine Comedy* (Dante)
  influence of on Keats, 209

influence on La Belle Dame sans Merci, 211
influence on On a Dream, 212
influence on On Sitting Down to Read *King Lear* Once Again, 211–12
influence on To Autumn, 218
Keats's first intense readings of, 211
Keats's responses to, 213–14
newly acquired high status during Keats's lifetime, 209–10
Darkling Thrush, The (Hardy), 293
de Man, Paul, 341
death and mortality, Keats and
in Bright star, 52
death mask of Keats, 54
death of Keats's maternal grandmother and, 39
effect of death of mother and father of on Keats, 39, 47–48
in *Hyperion*, 49–50, 54
Keats's death in Rome, 47, 72–73
last letter of Keats to Charles Brown, 72–73
on nursing his brother Tom, 49, 259
in Ode on a Grecian Urn, 52–53
in Ode to a Nightingale, 47, 50–52
sexuality and, 52
Shelley's elegy to Keats, 54
in This Living Hand, 49
in When I Have Fears, 54
in Why did I laugh tonight? No voice will tell, 51
Death on a pale horse (painting, West, Benjamin (painter), 126–28
Dickinson, Emily, 304–05
Dickstein, Morris, 341
Divine Comedy (Dante), 144. *See also* Dante Alighieri
disapproval of in Britain, 213
Hunt on, 213
influence of on *Hyperion*, 216–18
influence on *Fall of Hyperion*, 209
influence on La Belle Dame sans Merci, 209
Don Juan (Byron), 245–46
Dryden, John
influence on Keats, 224–27
Dunciad, The (Pope), 220

Eclectic Review, 316
eco-sensitivity, of Keats, 60, 347–48
Edinburgh Review, 318
ekphrasis (category of figuration), 129, 131, 132, 347
Elgin marbles, 347
Keats's introduction to, 128
Keats's sonnets on, 52, 128, 272
Eliot, T.S., 53, 108
on Keats, 333, 335
Emerson, Ralph Waldo, 300–01, 302
Empson, William, 188, 333
Endymion, 21, 34, 111, 152, 233
classical mythology in, 138–40
critical attacks on, 249–50, 317
critical review of in *Blackwood's Edinburgh Magazine*, 313
dual expression of politics and poetries transcendence of politics, 112
Enlightenment thinking in, 150
Keats's criticism of, 250
non-epic nature of, 258
Peona as inspired by sister and sister-in-law, 40
poetic imagination in, 169
public affairs in, 108
sensory description in, 189–90, 192–93
Spenser's influence on, 222–23
writing of in Isle of Wight and Oxford, 57
Enfield School, 20, 23
Keats's study of classical literature at, 136–37
Enlightenment and history, Keats and, 156–57
Fall of Hyperion and, 153–54
historicist and cultural materialist critiques post-1963, 342
Hyperion and, 152–54
Keats's life of sensation and, 155–56
Keats's sceptism towards perfectibility models and historical progress, 156
Lamia and, 154–55
literary anthropology of Keats, 150
Mansion of Many Apartments letter and, 149–50
passive receptivity and poetical character and, 156
scepticism of Keats towards perfectibility theories, 152
The Eve of St. Agnes and, 155
Epithalamion (Spenser), 137
Essai sur les mœurs (Voltaire), 153
Essay Concerning Human Understanding (Locke), 156
Essay on the Principles of Human Action (Hazlitt), 161–62
European Magazine, 315
Eve of St. Agnes, The, 23, 24, 152, 155, 198
aged nurse as mediator for young people in, 39
distinction between painting and sculpture in, 131
generic ironisation of romantic form in, 255–57
influence of Shakespeare and Dante on, 218
influence of Spenser on, 223
sexuality in, 42–44, 113–14, 255–56, 336

Examiner, The, 25, 33, 108, 159
critical review of Keats in, 315
critical reviews of Coleridge in, 238
as first publisher of Keats, 93
on publication of Keats's letters to Brawne, 326
To Solitude in, 269
Excursion, The (Wordsworth), 233

Faerie Queene, The (Spenser), 222, 227
Fall of Hyperion, The, 20, 30, 152, 198. *See also* Hyperion; *Hyperion, A Fragment*
association of human and poetic development, 153–54
Enlightenment thinking in, 150
female suffering in, 41
influence of Dante and Shakespeare on, 209, 216–18
medical imagery in, 27, 35
mythology and, 144
as tragic epic, 264–67
Fate of Reading, The (Hartman), 341
Feast of the Poets, The (Hunt), 233
Fitzgerald, F. Scott, 305–06
Ford, Mark, 105
formative years of Keats
apothecary apprenticeship with Hammond, 24–25
birth date of, 19
childhood anecdotes of, 19
death of Thomas (father of Keats), 21
disappearance of mother in 1806, 22
at Enfield School, 20, 23, 136–37
finances after death of mother, 24
financial difficulties after death of father, 21–22
illness and death of mother, 23–24
life on Craven Street (London), 19
mother's remarriage to William Rawlings, 21
move to Moorfields in 1802, 19
parents and siblings of, 19
physique of, 19
reappearance of mother in 1808-9, 23
relationship with Charles Cowden Clarke, 23
summer of 1806 at Edmonton with grandmother, 22
voracious reading of after mother's return, 23
French Revolution, 151
Frost, Robert, 307

Garrod, H.W., 333
gender identity
criticism of masculinity of Keats, 327–28
in critiques of Keats post-1963, 345–46
cross-gendering in Keats, 229
Gittings, Robert, 9, 56
Goblin Market (Rossetti), 287
Gosse, Edmund, 326
Grafty, Mrs. (neighbor of Keats), 19
Greek mythology, 129

Hallam, Arthur Henry, 189
on Keats *vs.* Shelly, 327
Hamlet (Shakespeare), 50, 218
Hardy, Thomas
influence of Keats on, 291–94
Hartman, Geoffrey, 341
Harvest Bow, The (Heaney), 298
Haydon, Benjamin Robert, 128, 141
Hazlitt, William, 163–66
education of, 159
on Greek statuary, 173
influence of *An Essay on the Principles of Human Action* on Keats and, 161–62
influence of on Keats on imagination, 170
influence of on Keats's desire to distinguish himself from Wordsworth and, 160–61
influence of on Keats's views on literature, 162–63, 213
on Keats, 323
negative capability and, 159
On Poetry in General lecture, 30
On Posthumous Fame, 160, 165
on Shakespeare, 159–60, 179, 212–13
Heaney, Seamus, 298
history. *See* Enlightenment and history, Keats and
History of America (Robertson), 150, 153
History of the Reign of the Emperor Charles V (Robertson), 151
Hood, Thomas, 106–07, 282
Hoodwinking of Madeline and Other Essays, The (Stillinger), 341
Hopkins, Gerard Manley, 283–85
Hull, Jane (patient of Keats), 32–33, 34, 344
Hunt Circle, 4, 92–94
admiration of Greek mythology of, 94–95
classical poetry and, 138
Cockney Hellenism of, 97
Hunt, Leigh, 26, 30, 32, 33, 56
on Augustan poetry and Pope, 220–22
Cockney poetry and, 109–10
Conder on bad influence of on Keats's poetics, 316–17
critical review of Keats in *The Examiner*, 315
on Dante, 213
as Deist, 138
impact of on Keats's literary reputation, 313
influence of on Keats's poetry, 231–33
sociability of, 123
sonnet-writing contests of, 269, 270

Hutcheson, Francis, 155
Hyperion, 19, 34. *See also Fall of Hyperion, The*; *Hyperion, A Fragment*
as lyrical epic, 259
association of human and poetic development in, 152–54
D. G. James on, 333
death and mortality in, 49–50, 54
distinction between painting and sculpture in, 130–31
Enlightenment thinking in, 150
female beauty in, 41
illness and death of his brother Thomas and, 259
influence of Dante and Shakespeare on, 216–18
Keats's abandonment of, 291
Milton's influence on, 223
myth and, 141
Paradise Lost (Milton) and, 260–61

imagination, 176
agency and, 172
beauty and imaginative truth and, 171–72
imaginative mobility, 67, 73
influence of Hazlitt on Keats on imagination, 170
Keats on in letter to Reynolds, 176
Keats on sublime, reason and intellect in, 59–60
Keats's on in letter to Benjamin Bailey, 172–73
in Ode on a Grecian Urn, 172, 173
in Ode to a Nightingale, 175
in Ode to Psyche, 174, 175
Romantic imagination, 170, 333
sensual imagination of Keats, 115
in *Sleep and Poetry*, 169
sympathetic imagination, 170, 171, 179
tension between reality and illusion in Keatsian, 168
in To Fancy, 175
influence of Keats
on Edward Thomas, 294–96
on Elizabeth Bishop, 297–98
on Hardy, 291–94
on Seamus Heaney, 298
on Wallace Stevens, 296–97
influence of Keats on Victorian poets, 281–82
on D.G. Rossetti, 288–89
on Elizabeth Barrett Browning, 288
on Hopkins, Gerard Manley, 283–85
on Matthew Arnold, 285–87
on Tennyson, 285, 289–90
Inquiry into the Original of our Ideas of Beauty and Virtue (Hutcheson), 156
Irony and Authority in Romantic Poetry (Simpson), 341
Isabella, 24, 52, 112–13, 152, 256, 343
aged nurse as mediator for young people in, 39
medical imagery in, 29, 35
suffering in, 41
writing of in Teignmouth, 57

James, D.G., 333
James, Henry
on Keats, 331
Jarvis, Robin, 61
Jeffrey, Francis, 249, 318
Jennings, Alice (maternal grandmother of Keats)
death of, 39
Keats's elegy for after her death, 39
move to Edmonton of, 22
as principal woman in Keats's early life, 39
Jennings, Frances (mother of Keats). *See* Keats, Frances (mother of Keats)
Jennings, John (maternal grandfather of Keats), 21–22
John Keats (Bate), 336, 340–41
John Keats (Lowell), 14
John Keats, A New Life (Roe), 15–16
Jones, Isabella, 42–44
Jones, John, 51, 52, 181

Keach, William, 95, 100, 108, 111
Kean, Edmund, 214–16
King Stephen and, 216
Keates, Thomas (father of Keats), 19
death of, 21
Keates Livery Stables of, 19
Keats (Garrod), 333
Keats (Motion), 13–15
Keats and Embarrassment (Ricks), 341
Keats and Hellenism (Aske), 346
Keats and his Poetry (Dickstein), 341
Keats and Shakespeare (Murry), 333–34
Keats and the Historical Method (McGann), 342
Keats-Shelley Memorial House, 54
Keats the Poet (Sperry), 3, 341
Keats, Edward (brother of Keats), 19
Keats, Frances (mother of Keats), 19
battle over will of father, 21–22
disappearance of in 1806, 22, 38
illness and death in 1810, 23–24, 38
impact of death on Keats, 39
reappearance of in 1808-9, 23, 38
remarriage of to William Rawlings, 21, 38

Keats, Frances (sister of Keats), 19, 40, 181
Keats, George (brother of Keats), 19
Keats, John. *See also* American poets and writers, Keats and; biographies and films of Keats; contemporary reviews of Keats; critical reception of Keats (1821-1900); critiques of Keats (1900-1963); critiques of Keats post-1963; death and mortality, Keats and; Enlightenment and history, Keats and; formative years of Keats; influence of Keats; influence of Keats on Victorian poets; letters of Keats; London, Keats and; manuscripts and publishing of Keats; medical training of Keats; poems and plays of John Keats; politics, Keats and; senses and sense experience in Keats; sociability, Keats and; travels of Keats; visual and plastic arts, Keats and; women, Keats's relationships with
  as an apothecary, 9
  death of due to tuberculosis (1821), 38
  medical training of, 9
  self-consciousness about his short stature, 41
  visual portraits of, 56
  Yeats on, 114
Keats, Thomas (brother of Keats), 19, 49
  effect of illness and death of on Keats, 259
  letter to on waterfalls seen on Scottish Tour and, 59–60
Keats's Boyish Imagination (Marggraf Turley), 342
Keats's Life of Allegory (Levinson), 341, 345
Keats's 'Paradise Lost' (Lau), 347
King Lear (Shakespeare)
  influence on Keats's On the Sea and, 211
King Stephen (drama, Keats), 44, 57, 78, 151, 216
kissing, in Keats and his contemporary poets, 243–46
Kucich, Greg, 150

La Belle Dame sans Merci, 28, 39, 155
  Dante's influence on, 211
  death and sexuality in, 52
  influence of *Divine Comedy* on, 209
  as modernisation of ballad form, 251–53
Lake Isle of Innisfree, The (Yeats), 106
Lamia, 23, 24, 28, 152, 224–26
  Enlightenment thinking in, 150, 154–55
  medical imagery in, 30
Lessing, G.E., 127
Letter to William Gifford Esq. (Hazlitt), 162
Letters of John Keats to Fanny Brawne (Buxton Forman), 324–26
letters of Keats, 73
  allusions from Shakespeare and Dante in, 210
  anxiety over his contemporary poets in, 238–39
  to Benjamin Bailey, 59, 66–68, 172–73
  catalogue of London place-names in, 99–100, 102–03
  on country dancing school's performance, 68–69
  criticism of Buxton for publishing *Letters of John Keats*, 328–29
  critique and study of in 1900-63 period, 334–35
  to George and Georgiana Keats, 70–72
  to John Hamilton Reynolds, 35, 140, 149–50, 159, 160, 176
  to John Taylor, 214
  Keats's relationship with women in, 68
  language use and idiomatic expression in, 120–21
  last letter of to Charles Brown, 72–73
  letter to Tom Keats on waterfalls seen on Scottish Tour, 59–60
  love letters to Fanny Brawne, 69–70
  Mansion of Many Apartments letter to Reynolds, 149–50, 157, 214, 218, 269
  to Percy Bysshe Shelley, 213
  poetic imagination in, 66, 168, 170
  publication of *Letters of John Keats to Fanny Brawne* (Buxton Forman) and, 324–26
  to Richard Woodhouse, 159, 178, 179, 180
  vale of Soul-making letter, 71, 152, 214, 264
  women in letters of the Scottish Tour, 40
Levinson, Marjorie, 341, 345
Life, Letters, and Literary Remains, of John Keats (Milnes), 324
Lines Written a Few Miles above Tintern Abbey (Wordsworth), 34, 35, 173, 234
literary anthropology, 150
Locke, John, 155
Lockhart, John Gibson, 249, 313
  on Cockney School, 89–91, 111
London Magazine, 317, 318
London, A History in Verse (Ford), 105
London, Keats and
  Keats's interest in theatre and, 103–04
  place-names in letters of, 99–100, 102–03
  social life and, 101–02
  walks and excursions and, 100–01
Lowell, Amy, 14
Lutz, Deborah, 52

Making of John Keats, The (Ward), 340–41
Man is like a Magnet, A (letter, Keats), 122
Mansion of Many Apartments (Keats, letter), 149–50, 157, 214, 218, 269
manuscripts and publishing of Keats, 313
  1817-1821, 75–77
  1883 to 2015, 79–82

from 1821 to 1883, 77–79
John Taylor and, 75–77
manuscript facsimiles, 82–84
Richard Woodhouse and, 75–77
The Examiner as first publisher of Keats, 93
masculinity, criticism of Keats, 326, 327–28
Mathew, George Felton, 315
McFarland, Thomas, 54
McGann, Jerome J., 108, 115, 342
McLane, Maureen, 150
medical training of Keats, 25–26
apothecary apprenticeship with Hammond, 24–25
as assistant surgeon at Guy's Hospital, 28, 31–32
coursework of, 29
daily routine at Guy's Hospital, 29
ending of in favour of poetry, 26–27
Jane Hull and (patient of Keats), 32–33, 34
medical and scientific imagery in poetry and, 28–31, 33, 35
in post-1963 critiques of Keats, 344
transitions in medicine and, 28
Mellor, Anne K., 229, 345
Milnes, Richard Monckton, 324
Milton, John, 143, 178, 260–61
influence on Keats, 223, 227, 264, 270–71, 291, 347
misspellings, in Keats, 238
moon, in poems of Keats, 294, 340
Morning, on the Sea-Shore (Radcliffe), 229
Motion, Andrew, 9, 13–15
Murry, John Middleton, 333–34
myth and religion
critics' perception of as used up after Pope's death, 137
Endymion and, 138–40
Fall of Hyperion and, 144
Hunt Circle's admiration of Greek mythology and, 94–95
Hyperion, A Fragment and, 141
as imaginative response to nature, 137
Keats on future of religious belief, 143
Keats's reading of classical literature and mythology as student, 137
Keats's reading of New Testament and, 142
Keats's turn away from Enlightenment Deism and, 140
Ode on a Grecian Urn and Ode to a Nightingale and, 143
Ode to Psyche and, 142–43
in post-1963 critiques of Keats, 346
Spenser's influence on Keats and, 137
The Eve of St. Agnes and, 256
as vehicle for serious reflection on his own times, 141
Napoleon, 259
narrative poems
interplay between genre and narrative rhetoric and, 248
nature, 140
negative capability, 10, 15, 34, 58, 63, 96, 121, 122, 155, 181, 182
Coleridge and, 239
Dickinson and, 304
Hazlitt and, 159
Hazlitt's influence on Keats and, 170
Shakespeare as exemplifying, 170–71
truth and beauty and, 171

O Sorrow (Book 4 of *Endymion*), 41
O'Neill, Michael, 344
Ode on a Grecian Urn, 9, 113, 155, 205, 276–77
beauty, truth and imagination in, 172, 173
Brooks on beauty and truth in, 335–36
death and mortality in, 52–53
distinction between painting and sculpture in, 131–33
mythology and, 143
prosody and versification in, 199–200
Ode to a Nightingale, 28, 155, 275–76, 277
as city poem, 106
death in, 47, 50–52
imagination in, 175
influence on Hardy of, 293
lack of revisions in, 84
melancholic beauty in, 174
myth and, 143
spondees in, 201–03
Ode to Melancholy (Hood), 282
Ode to Psyche, 142–43, 155, 198, 275
imagination in, 174, 175
influence of Keats's contemporaries on, 229
prosody and versification in, 200–01
Ode, Autumn (Hood), 282
Ode, Intimations of Immortality (Wordsworth), 233
odes, 175, 273–77. *See also* by individual odes; poems and plays of John Keats; prosody and versification in odes
Odes of John Keats (Vendler), 344
Old Cumberland Beggar, The (Wordsworth), 163
Olio, The
essay on Keats in, 323–24
Olson, Charles, 62
On Poetry in General (lecture, Hazlitt), 30
On Posthumous Fame (Hazlitt), 160, 165
On the Morning of Christ's Nativity (Milton), 143
Othello (Shakespeare), 180

Otho the Great (play, Keats and Brown), 44, 57, 76, 78, 103, 151, 214–16, 217, 224
Oxford Book of London (Bailey), 105

Panthea (Wilde), 282
Paradise Lost (Milton), 127, 168, 171, 173, 223, 249, 264, 270, 347
  Hyperion and, 260–61
  Keats's reading of, 130
Patmore, P.G., 317
Penetralium, 34
Perry, Seamus, 332
Pleasure Thermometer, 214
poems and plays of John Keats. *See also* *Endymion*; *Eve of St. Agnes, The*; *Fall of Hyperion, The*; *Hyperion, A Fragment*; *Isabella*; La Belle Dame sans Merci; *Lamia*; Ode on a Grecian Urn; Ode to a Nightingale; Ode to Psyche; odes; *Poems* of 1817; prosody and versification in odes; *Sleep and Poetry*; sonnets; To Autumn
  A Song about Myself, 62
  Ben Nevis (sonnet), 62, 63
  Bright star (sonnet), 52, 346
  Epistle to Reynolds, 39, 57
  Fill for me a brimming bowl, 42
  Fragment of Castle-Builder, 105
  I stood tip-toe upon a little hill, 56, 58, 109, 110, 138, 194, 221, 232–33
  If by dull rhymes our English must be chain'd, 71, 198
  King Stephen (play), 44, 57, 78, 151, 216
  Lines on Seeing a Lock of Milton's Hair, 223, 274
  Many the wonders I this day have seen, 137
  Meg Merrilies, 39, 253–55
  Ode on Indolence, 44, 76, 142, 218, 275
  Ode on Melancholy, 39, 45, 114, 203–04, 277, 333
  Ode to Apollo, 136, 137
  On a Dream, 212
  On First Looking into Chapman's Homer, 20, 26, 31, 61, 106, 138, 152, 271, 297, 300
  On Hearing St Martin's Bells on My Way Home from a Sparring Match at the Fives-Court, 106
  On Receiving a Laurel Crown from Leigh Hunt, 272
  On Seeing the Elgin Marbles, 105
  On Sitting Down to Read *King Lear* Once Again, 211–12, 226, 258
  On the Grasshopper and the Cricket, 109, 270, 304
  On the Sea, 211, 286, 288, 303
  On Visiting the Tomb of Burns, 174, 230
  Otho the Great (play), 44, 57, 76, 78, 103, 151, 214–16, 217, 224
  Poems of 1820, 108, 112–15
  Poems, by John Keats, 26, 27, 28
  Sonnet to Vauxhall, 106
  The Eve of St. Mark, 43, 195–96
  The Jealousies, 28, 44, 105, 226–27
  There is a joy in footing slow across a silent plain, 62, 230
  This Living Hand, 49, 123
  This Mortal Body of a Thousand Days, 272
  This pleasant tale is like a little copse, 213
  To Charles Cowden Clarke, 24, 26, 92–93, 110, 193–94
  To Fancy, 42, 175
  To George Felton Mathew, 118, 137
  To Kosciusko, 109
  To Leigh Hunt, Esq., 93
  To My Brother George, 26, 110
  To one who has been long in city pent, 105, 106
  To Sleep, 274, 275
  To Solitude, 25, 33, 269, 271
  To the Nile, 270
  Upon my life, Sir Nevis, I am piqu'd, 40
  When I Have Fears, 42, 54, 271, 275, 289
  Why did I laugh tonight? No voice will tell, 51, 71
  Written in Disgust of Vulgar Superstition, 94, 143
Poems of 1817, 75, 111
  politics and, 115
  Reynold's review of, 315
poetical character, 34, 159, 171
  Adam Smith and, 180–81
  Coleridge on, 178–79
  influence of Enlightenment thought, 156
  Keats on in letter to Woodhouse, 178, 179, 180
  Troilus and Cressida (Shakespeare) and, 58
Poetical Works and Other Writings of John Keats: Now First Brought Together, Including Poems and Numerous Letters not before Published, 325
Politics and Poetics – The Desperate Situation of a Journalist Unhappily Smitten with the Love of Rhyme (Hunt), 94
politics, Keats and, 138
  Cockney poetry and, 109–10
  Cockney School of Politics and, 111
  in *Endymion*, 108, 112
  in *Isabella*, 112–13
  in *Poems* of 1817, 111, 112
  in *Poems* of 1820, 112–15
  in post-1963 critiques, 342–43
  sexual politics, 113–14
  in To Autumn, 108–09
Pope, Alexander, 220–22
  Hunt's and Keats's criticism of, 220–22

posthumous, as word in Keats, 53, 57
Prometheus Unbound (Shelley), 244–45
prosody and versification in odes, 198, 316
  Croker on Keat's versification, 222
  dismantling and reconstruction of the sonnet and, 198
  in Ode on a Grecian Urn, 199–200
  in Ode on Melancholy, 203–04
  in Ode to a Nightingale:, 201–03
  in Ode to Psyche, 200–01
  in To Autumn, 204–05
Prynne, Jeremy, 110
Psyche (goddess), 142–43
Psyche (Tighe), 143, 229
Purgatorio (Dante), 264, 267

Quarterly Review, 249, 313

Radcliffe, Ann, 229
Rape of the Lock, The (Pope), 220
Rape of the Sabine Women, The (painting, Poussin), 113
Rawlings, Frances (mother of Keats). *See* Keats, Frances (mother of Keats)
Rawlings, William (stepfather of Keats), 21
Renaissance Revival in Romantic period, 220
Reynolds, John Hamilton, 106, 159, 160, 176, 314–15
  Keats's letters to, 35, 140, 149–50
  review of *Poems* of 1817, 314–15
Ricks, Christopher, 118, 181, 341
  on kissing in Keats and his contemporary poets, 243–46
Robertson, William, 150, 151, 153, 156
Roe, Nicholas, 15–16, 56, 332
romance poems of Keats
  generic ironisation in, 248, 250–51
Romantic Ideology, The (McGann), 342
Romantic imagination, 170, 333
Romantic period
  Renaissance Revival in, 220
  view of Alexander Pope during, 220
Romanticism and Gender (Mellor), 345
Rome, 57, 63–64
  death of Keats in, 47
  Keats's viewing of painting depicting Apollo in, 136
Rossetti, Christina, 287
Rossetti, D.G., 288–89
Rossetti, William Michael
  on Keats, 328
Roth, Philip, 307
Round Table, The (Hazlitt and Hunt), 159
Royal Academy, establishment of, 128

Scott, Grant F., 128
senses and sense experience in Keats
  communication of in two related modes, 195
  influence of Enlightenment thought on Keats and, 155–56
  Keats on how words become palpable feeling, 194
  sensory description in *Endymion*, 189–90, 192–93
  sensory description in *The Eve of St. Mark*, 195–96
  sensory description in To Autumn, 196
  sensory descriptions in I stood tip-toe upon a little hill, 194
  sensory descriptions in *Sleep and Poetry*, 190–92
  sensory descriptions in To Charles Cowden Clarke, 193–94
  sensual imagination of Keats, 115
Severn, Joseph, 47, 56, 124, 136
sexuality
  Byron on sexual perversion in Keats's poetry, 321
  death in poems of Keats and, 52
  in Fill for me a brimming bowl, 42
  in *The Eve of St. Agnes*, 42–44, 255–56, 336
  kissing in Keats and his contemporary poets, 243–46
  male sexuality, 346
  sexual politics in *Poems* of 1820, 113–14
Shakespeare, William
  Hazlitt on, 159–60, 179, 212–13
  influence of on Keats, 209, 270–71, 275–77
  influence on *Hyperion*, 216–18
  influence on *King Stephen* (play, Keats), 214–16
  influence on Ode to a Nightingale, 50
  influence on On a Dream, 212
  influence on On Sitting Down to Read *King Lear* Once Again, 211–12
  influence on On the Sea, 211
  influence on *Otho the Great* (play, Keats and Brown), 214–16
  influence on To Autumn, 218
  Keats's first intense readings of, 211
  Keats's veneration for, 21, 209
  Murry's *Keats and Shakespeare*, 333–34
  negative capability and, 170–71
  newly acquired high status during Romantic period, 209–10
  Troilus and Cressida and, 58
Shelley, Percy Bysshe, 54, 213, 244–45, 281, 320–21, 331
  Hallam on *vs.* Keats, 327
  Keats on, 240–42
  view of Keats of, 321
Short Introduction to Moral Philosophy (Hutcheson), 156

Sibylline Leaves (Coleridge), 239
Simpson, David, 341
Sleep and Poetry, 33, 93, 95, 138
  denigration of Pope and Augustan writers in, 221–22
  poetic imagination in, 168, 169
  sensory descriptions in, 190–92
Smith, Adam, 150, 180–81
sociability, Keats and
  disillusionment with sociability of Keats, 121–24
  Fanny Brawne and, 123
  Joseph Severn and, 124
  Keats's social life in London and, 101–02
  language use and idiomatic expression in letters of, 120–21
  This Living Hand and, 123
sonnets. *See also* by individual sonnet; poems and plays of John Keats
  on Elgin Marbles, 128, 272
  Keat's artistic evolution and, 269
  Keats criticism of Petrarchan and Shakespearean sonnet form, 269
  Keats's elegy for his grandmother, 39
  Keats's participation in Hunt's sonnet-writing contests, 269, 270
  Keats's real-time sonnets, 272
  Milton's influence on, 270–71
  Shakespeare as model for, 270–71
Spenser, Edmund, 137, 227
  influence on Keats, 222–23, 227
Sperry, Stuart M., 49, 53, 152, 341
sprezzatura, 270
Spring (Hopkins), 283
Stabler, Jane, 229
Stevens, Wallace, 296–97, 307–08
Stillinger, Jack, 336, 341
Story of Rimini, The (Hunt), 109, 111, 213, 232–33
Structure of Complex Words, The (Empson), 188
Stylistic Development of Keats, The (Bate), 198
suffering, 33, 41–42, 142
Swinburne, Algernon Charles
  on Keats, 325–27

Taylor, John (publisher of Keats), 54, 75–77, 214
Tennyson, Lord Alfred, 285, 289–90
The Poet as Hero, Keats in his Letters (essay, Trilling), 335
theatre, Keats's interest in, 103–04
Theory of Moral Sentiments, The (Smith), 150
Thomas, Edward, 294–96
Thoreau, Henry David, 301–02
Tighe, Mary, 143, 229
time-switching, as Keatsian device, 292
To Autumn, 14, 57, 115, 143, 152, 198, 270, 277, 341
  ecological awareness of Keats and, 347, 348
  influence of Shakespeare and Dante on, 218
  politics in, 108–09
  post-1963 critiques of, 342
  prosody and versification in, 204–05
  sensory description in, 196
travels of Keats, 211
  A Song about Myself and, 62
  Ben Nevis sonnet and, 62, 63
  effect of on Keats's poetics, 63–64
  effect of Scottish tour on Keats's poetics, 60–63
  Jarvis on Scottish tour and, 61
  penchant for homes away from homes and, 58
  satirizing of middle class aesthetics on Socttish Tour and, 59
  to Rome, 57
Trilling, Lionel, 67
Troilus and Cressida (Shakespeare), 58

vale of Soul-making letter, 71, 152, 214, 264
Vendler, Helen, 9, 51, 108, 142, 205, 296, 344
visual and plastic arts, Keats and
  Benjamin Robert Haydon and, 128
  Britain's enthusiasm for the visual arts and, 128
  Death on a pale horse (painting, West) and, 126–28
  distinction between painting and sculpture in *Hyperion*, 130–31
  distinction between painting and sculpture in Ode to a Grecian Urn, 131–33
  distinction between painting and sculpture in *The Eve of St. Agnes*, 131
  ekphrasis as category of figuration and, 129, 131, 132, 347
  Elgin marbles and, 128
  Keats's viewing of painting of Apollo in Rome and, 136
  Keats's visits to art exhibits and, 128–29
  theatrical pantomines and light shows and, 129
  Victorian artists responses to Keats and, 133–34
visual portraits, of Keats, 56
Voltaire, 150, 151, 153, 155, 156

walks and excursions, of Keats in London, 100–01
Ward, Aileen, 9, 56, 337, 340–41
Webb, Timothy, 66
West, Benjamin (painter), 126–28
Whitman, Walt, 302–04
Wilde, Oscar, 282
Williams, William Carlos, 307
Wolfson, Susan J., 3, 95

women, Keats's relationships with, 38, 68, 114. *See also* Brawne, Fanny; Keats, Frances (mother of Keats); Jennings, Alice (maternal grandmother of Keats)
  female suffering in poetry and, 41–42
  friendships with Mrs. James Wylie and mother of Fanny Brawne, 40
  Isabella Jones and, 42–44
  mistrust of women as lovers, 41
  sexual tension in Fill for me a brimming bowl and, 42
  with sister Frances, 40
  with sister-in-law Georgiana Wylie, 40
  sympathetic characterizations of old women based on maternal grandmother, 39–40
Woodhouse, Richard, 75–77, 159, 178, 179, 180
  on lewdness in *The Eve of St. Agnes*, 256
Wordsworth, William, 137, 160–61, 163, 173
  influence on Keats, 229–30, 233–36
Wylie, Georgiana (sister-in-law of Keats), 40
Wylie, Mrs. James (mother-in-law of Keats's brother), 40
Yeats, William Butler, 106, 114

Lightning Source UK Ltd.
Milton Keynes UK
UKHW020201030620
364184UK00001B/5

9 781107 674370